Praise for *A Burning*

'Immaculately constructed, acidly observed and gripping
from start to finish, *A Burning* is a brilliant debut'
The Guardian

'Megha Majumdar's *A Burning* is an uncanny debut, a
fierce condemnation of modern India – the corruption,
racism, misogyny, the feverish obsession with
celebrity – this is the antithesis of shrill. The author,
although still in her early thirties, has the composure
of a mature artist, and has produced a political
novel that makes its wider points through the subtle,
intimate exploration of three characters' lives'
Sunday Times

'This is a short, sharp shock of a novel that shows us how
easy it is to rally a mob, to kill a Muslim woman and to
silence a whole community. These are things we all know
on paper, but the power of a great novelist – and Majumdar
has a Dickensian flair and scope – is to transform what
we simply know into something we can feel. What a
treat to start the year with a talent as fresh as this'
The Times

'A big hit in America last year, this buzzy debut
about the impact of a terrorist attack in a Kolkata
slum on three connected characters is full of hot-
button global topics, including violent nationalism'
Metro

A
BURNING

MEGHA MAJUMDAR

SCRIBNER

LONDON NEW YORK SYDNEY TORONTO NEW DELHI

First published in the United States by Alfred A. Knopf, a division
of Penguin Random House LLC, New York, 2020, and in Canada
by Penguin Random House Canada Limited, Toronto, 2020
First published in Great Britain by Scribner,
an imprint of Simon & Schuster UK Ltd, 2021
This paperback edition published in 2022

SCRIBNER and design are registered trademarks of The Gale Group, Inc.,
used under licence by Simon & Schuster Inc.

1 3 5 7 9 10 8 6 4 2

Simon & Schuster UK Ltd
1st Floor
222 Gray's Inn Road
London WC1X 8HB

www.simonandschuster.co.uk
www.simonandschuster.com.au
www.simonandschuster.co.in

Simon & Schuster Australia, Sydney
Simon & Schuster India, New Delhi

A CIP catalogue record for this book
is available from the British Library.

Paperback ISBN: 978-1-4711-9029-2
eBook ISBN: 978-1-4711-9028-5

Printed and bound by CPI Group (UK) Ltd, Croydon CR0 4YY

MIX
Paper from
responsible sources
FSC
www.fsc.org
FSC® C171272

For my mother and father,
who have made everything possible

A
BURNING

JIVAN

"You smell like smoke," my mother said to me.

So I rubbed an oval of soap in my hair and poured a whole bucket of water on myself before a neighbor complained that I was wasting the morning supply.

There was a curfew that day. On the main street, a police jeep would creep by every half hour. Daily-wage laborers, compelled to work, would come home with arms raised to show they had no weapons.

In bed, my wet hair spread on the pillow, I picked up my new phone—purchased with my own salary, screen guard still attached.

On Facebook, there was only one conversation.

These terrorists attacked the wrong neighborhood #KolabaganTrainAttack #Undefeated

Friends, if you have fifty rupees, skip your samosas today and donate to—

The more I scrolled, the more Facebook unrolled.

This news clip exclusively from 24 Hours shows how—

Candlelight vigil at—

The night before, I had been at the railway station, no

more than a fifteen-minute walk from my house. I ought to have seen the men who stole up to the open windows and threw flaming torches into the halted train. But all I saw were carriages, burning, their doors locked from the outside and dangerously hot. The fire spread to huts bordering the station, smoke filling the chests of those who lived there. More than a hundred people died. The government promised compensation to the families of the dead—eighty thousand rupees!—which, well, the government promises many things.

In a video, to the dozen microphones thrust at his chin, the chief minister was saying, "Let the authorities investigate." Somebody had spliced this comment with a video of policemen scratching their heads. It made me laugh.

I admired these strangers on Facebook who said anything they wanted to. They were not afraid of making jokes. Whether it was about the police or the ministers, they had their fun and wasn't that freedom? I hoped that, after a few more salary slips, after I rose to be a senior sales clerk of Pantaloons, I would be free in that way too.

Then, in a video clip further down the page, a woman came forward, her hair flying, her nose running a wet trail down to her lips, her eyes red. She was standing on the sloping platform of our small railway station. Into the microphone she screamed: "There was a jeep full of policemen right there. Ask them why they stood around and watched while my husband burned. He tried to open the door and save my daughter. He tried and tried."

I shared that video. I added a caption.

Policemen paid by the government watched and did nothing while this innocent woman lost everything, I wrote.

I laid the phone next to my head and dozed. The heat brought sleep to my eyes. When I checked my phone next, there were only two likes. A half hour later, still two likes.

Then a woman, I don't know who, commented on my post, *How do you know this person is not faking it? Maybe she wants attention!*

I sat up. Was I friends with this person? In her profile picture she was posing in a bathroom.

Did you even watch the video? I replied.

The words of the heartless woman drifted in my mind. I was irritated by her, but there was excitement too. This was not the frustration of no water in the municipal pump or a power cut on the hottest night. Wasn't this a kind of leisure dressed up as agitation?

For me, the day was a holiday, after all. My mother was cooking fish so small we would eat them bones and tail. My father was taking in the sun, his back pain eased.

Under my thumb, I watched post after post about the train attack earn fifty likes, a hundred likes, three hundred likes. Nobody liked my reply.

And then, in the small, glowing screen, I wrote a foolish thing. I wrote a dangerous thing, a thing nobody like me should ever think, let alone write.

Forgive me, Ma.

If the police didn't help ordinary people like you and me, if the police watched them die, doesn't that mean, I wrote on Facebook, *that the government is also a terrorist?*

Outside the door, a man slowly pedaled his rickshaw, the only passenger his child, the horn going *paw paw* for her glee.

LOVELY

Sunday morning! Time to go to acting class. With my hips swinging like this and like that, I am walking past the guava seller.

"Brother," I am calling, "what's the time?"

"Eight thirty," he is grumbling, because he is not wishing to share with me the fruits of his wristwatch. Leave him. I am abandoning my stylish walk and running like a horse to the local railway station. On the train, while I am touching my chest and forehead, saying a prayer for those poor people who were dying a few days ago at this very station—

"Who is pushing?" one aunty is shouting. "Stop it!"

"This hijra couldn't find a different compartment to hassle?" the peanut seller is hissing, as if I am not having ears.

Nothing is simple for a person like me, not even one hour on the train. My chest is a man's chest and my breasts are made of rags. So what? Find me another woman in this whole city as truly woman as me.

In the middle of this crowd a legless beggar is coming

down the corridor, sitting on a wheeled plank of wood, which he is rolling on everybody's feet.

"Give me one coin," he is whining.

People are yelling at him.

"Now you need to pass?"

"No eyes or what?"

"Where will I stand, on your head?"

Now he is also shouting back, "Let me cut off your legs, then you see how you manage!"

It is true to god making me laugh and laugh. This is why I am liking the local trains. You can be burning one train, but you cannot be stopping our will to go to work, to class, to family if we have them. Every local train is like a film. On the train, I am observing faces, body movements, voices, fights. This is how people like me are learning. When this train is swaying, picking up speed, wind whipping my hair, I am putting my fingertips on the ceiling, making my body straight and tall for Mr. Debnath's acting class.

———

At Mr. Debnath's house, he is resting in a chair, drinking tea from a saucer. That way the tea is cooling fast and he is not having to do *phoo phoo*.

I have heard of acting coaches who are taking advantage of strugglers. But Mr. Debnath is not like that. He is having morals. In his younger days, he was getting a chance to direct a film himself, but the opportunity was in

Bombay. So he was having to go to Bombay for six months, minimum. At that time, his old mother was in a hospital. What kind of monster would abandon his mother to chase his dreams? So he was sacrificing his own goals and staying with his mother. When he was telling us this sad story, it was the only time I was seeing him cry.

Next to his feet are sitting six other students. Brijesh, who is working as an electrician; Rumeli, who is selling magic ointment for rashes; Peonji, who is working as a clerk in the insurance office; Radha, who is studying how to be a nurse; and Joyita, who is doing bookkeeping in her father's pen refill business. Nobody is really sure what Kumar is doing because he is only laughing in answer to all questions.

We are all saving and saving and handing over fifty rupees each class.

Today, in this living room, which is our stage, we are pushing the dining table to one side and practicing a scene in which a man is being suspicious of his wife. After some, if it can be said, lackluster performances, it is my turn. I am placing my phone on the floor to record myself for study purposes, then going to the center of the room and rolling my neck, left to right, right to left. Mr. Debnath's deceased parents, please to pray for them, are looking at me with strict faces from photos on the wall. I am feeling hot, even though the fan is running on maximum speed.

Time for my artistic performance. This time my partner is Brijesh, the electrician. According to the script that Mr. Debnath is giving us, Brijesh, now the suspicious husband, is having to hold my shoulders forcefully, angrily. But he is holding my shoulders too lightly. I am being forced to leave my character.

"Not like that!" I am saying. "If you are holding me like a petal, how will I have the strong feeling? You have to give it to me, the anger, the frustration! Come on!"

Mr. Debnath is approving of this. If you are not feeling it, he is always saying, how will your audience be feeling it? So I am hitting Brijesh's shoulder a little, making him a bit angry, showing him that he can be a little more manly with me. He is mumbling something, so I am saying, "What? Say it loudly."

After a long time, Brijesh is finally saying, "Uff! Don't make me say it, Lovely. I can't do this marriage scene with a half man."

At this time, the clock is gonging eleven times, making us all silent. My cheeks are getting hot. Oh, I am used to this—on the road, on the train, at the shops. But in my acting class? With Brijesh?

So, I am just throwing away his insult. It is garbage.

"Listen, Brijesh," I am saying, "you are like my brother. So, if I can act romantic with you, then you can also act romantic with me!"

"That's right," Mr. Debnath is saying. "If you are serious about films, you have to be fully in your role—"

He is giving Brijesh a real lecture. When he is pausing, you can even hear the ticking of the big clock on the wall.

Finally Brijesh is joining his hands to beg forgiveness from me, per Mr. Debnath's suggestion, and I am having a few tears in my eyes also. Rumeli is blowing her nose into her dupatta. Mr. Debnath is clapping his hands and saying, "Channel this emotion into your scene!"

The moment is full of tension. The other students are putting their mobile phones away when I am roaring: "You have the audacity to hit a mother!"

This character's rage, I am feeling it in my chest. This living room, with chair and table pushed to the corner, with cabinet full of dusty teddies, is nothing less than a stage in Bombay. The tubelight is as bright as a spotlight shining on me. Outside, a pillow filler is walking by, twanging his cotton-sorting instrument like a harp. Only windows, with thin curtains, are separating me from the nobodies on the street.

Then, holding the emotion but lowering my voice, I am delivering the next line: "Have you not fallen from your mother's womb?"

Brijesh: "Mother, hah, as if you have that dignity! You think I don't know about *him*?"

Me: "I swear it's not what you are thinking. Let me explain. Oh, please give me one chance to explain."

Brijesh: (stone-faced, looking out of imaginary window)

Me: "I was never wanting to talk about my past, but you are forcing me. So now I have to tell you my secret. It is not me who has been with that man. It is my twin sister."

What dialogue! The scene ends.

My palms are chilled and sweating. But my heart is light like a kite. There is thundering silence in the room. Even the maid is watching from the doorway, both broom and dustpan in her hand. Her jaw is falling open. Seeing her, I am feeling like smiling. I am finally coming out of the scene and back into the room.

Mr. Debnath is looking a bit crazed.

"This is how you do it!" he is whispering. His eyes are big. He is trying to put on his sandals and stand up from the chair, but one sandal is sliding away every time he is putting his foot on it. Never mind, he is looking very serious.

"My students, see how she used her voice?" he is saying. "See how she was feeling it and that feeling was being transferred to you?" Spit is flying from his mouth, showering the heads of his students.

Radha, who is sitting below him, is tearing a corner of the newspaper on the floor. Then she is wiping her hair with it.

Almost one year ago, I was coming to Mr. Debnath's house for the first time. He was asking to take my interview in the street. Because—he was saying, this was his explanation—the house was being painted, so there was nowhere to sit.

Rubbish. Where were the painters, the rags, the buckets, the ladders?

I was knowing the truth. The truth was that Mrs. Debnath was not wanting a hijra in the house.

So I was standing in the street, making sure a passing rickshaw was not hitting my behind. Mr. Debnath was saying, "Why you are so bent on acting? It's too hard!"

My kohl was smearing and my lipstick was gone on

some cup of tea. My armpits were stinking, my black hair was absorbing all the heat of the day and giving me a headache. But this was the one question I was always able to answer.

"I have been performing all my life," I was saying to him. I was performing on trains, on roads. I was performing happiness and cheer. I was performing divine connection. "Now," I was telling him, "just let me practice for the camera."

Today I am standing up and joining my hands. I am bowing. What else to do when there is so much clapping? They are clapping and clapping, my fans. My bookkeeper fan, my ointment-seller fan, my insurance-clerk fan. Even when I am waving my hand, smiling too broadly, saying, "Stop it!" they are going on clapping.

JIVAN

A few nights later, there was a knocking. It was late, two or three a.m., when any sound brings your heart to your throat. My mother was shouting, "Wake up, wake up!"

A hand reached out of the dark and dragged me up in my nightie. I screamed and fought, believing it was a man come to do what men do. But it was a policewoman.

My father, on the floor, his throat dry and his painful back rigid, mewled. Nighttime turned him into a child.

Then I was in the back of the police van, watching through the wire mesh a view of roads glowing orange under streetlamps. I exhausted myself appealing to the policewoman and group of policemen sitting in front of me: "Sister, what is happening? I am a working girl. I work at Pantaloons. I have nothing to do with police!"

They said nothing. Now and then a crackle came from the radio on the dashboard, far in front. At some point, a car filled with boys sped by and I heard whooping and cheering. They were coming from a nightclub. The doddering police van meant nothing to those boys. They did not slow down. They were not afraid. Their fathers knew police commissioners and members of the legislature, figures who were capable of making all problems disappear. And me, how would I get out of this? Whom did I know?

LOVELY

At night, after the acting class, I am lying in bed with Azad, my husband, my businessman who is buying and reselling *Sansung* electronics and *Tony Hilfiger* wristwatches from Chinese ships docking in Diamond Harbor. I am showing him my practice video from the day's class and now he is saying, "I have been telling you for hundred years! You have star material in you!"

He is pinching my cheek and I am laughing even though it is hurting. I am feeling peaceful, like this thin mattress on the floor is our own luxury five-star hotel bed. In this room, I am having everything I am needing. A jar of drinking water, some dishes, a small kerosene stove, and a shelf for my clothes and jewelry. On the wall, giving me their blessings every day, are Priyanka Chopra and Shah Rukh Khan. When I am looking around, I am seeing their beautiful faces and some of their good fortune is sprinkling down on me.

———

"Azad," I am saying this night. My face is close to his face, like we are in a romantic scene in a blockbuster. "Promise you will not get angry if I am telling you something?"

I am taking a moment to look at his face, dark and gray. Some long hairs in his eyebrows trying to escape. I am having difficulty looking eye to eye for these hard words.

"Aren't you thinking," I am saying finally, "about family and all? We are not so young—"

Azad is starting to talk over me, like always. "Again?" he is saying. I am knowing that he is annoyed. "Was my brother coming here?"

"No!"

"Was my brother putting this rubbish in your head?"

"No, I am telling you!"

Why Azad is always accusing me of such things?

"Everyone knows it is the way of the world, Azad," I am telling him. "Yes, the world is backward and, yes, the world is stupid. But your family is wanting you to marry a proper woman, have children. And look at me—I can never give you a future like that."

Immediately, I am regretting. This is a great big mistake. I am wishing to be with Azad always, so why I am pushing him away?

———

Actually, Azad is right. His brother was coming one night. He was coming before dawn, ringing the bell, banging his fist on the door. He was making such a racket the street dogs were barking *gheu gheu*.

When I was finally leaping out of bed and unlatching the door, Azad's brother was immediately shouting at my face, "Whatever curse you have given him, let him go, witch!"

"Shhh!" I was saying. "Be quiet, it's the middle of the night!"

"Don't you tell me what to do, witch!" he was screaming, wagging a finger in the air. One man pissing in the gutter was looking at him, then at me, then at him, then at me. Otherwise all was quiet and dark, but surely everybody was hearing everything.

"You have trapped him!" this brother was screaming. "Now you have to free him! Let him get married like a normal person!"

I was only standing, holding the open door. "Calm yourself," I was saying quietly. "You will make yourself sick."

I was wearing my nightie. My ears were burning. The whole neighborhood was learning my business. Now this was making me angry. Who was giving this good-for-nothing brother the right to shout at me in front of the whole locality? All these people were hardworking rickshaw pullers, fruit sellers, cotton fillers, maidservants, guards in the malls. They were needing sleep. Now what respect was I having left in their eyes?

So finally I was shouting back some rude things. I don't like remembering them.

———

"Okay," I am admitting to Azad now. "Fine, your brother came. He was saying to me, 'Lovely, I know your love is true. My brother refuses to even eat if you are not there. But please, I am begging, talk to him about marriage and children, for our old parents' sake.'"

Azad is looking at me. "My brother? Said that?"

He is not believing his ears.

"Yes, your own brother," I am saying. "So I am thinking about it."

A spider with thin brown legs is crawling through the window. With all eight legs, it is exploring the wall. Both of us are watching it. When Azad is getting up and about to slap the spider with his shoe, I am saying, "Leave it."

Why to always ruin other creatures' lives?

"No!" Azad is saying. "I am not going to follow such stupid rules! I will marry *you*!"

JIVAN

The next morning, at the courthouse, a policewoman opens for me a path through a crowd moving like they are joyous, like they are celebrating at a cricket stadium. The sun blazes in my eyes. I look at the ground.

"Jivan! Jivan! Look here," shout reporters with cameras mounted on their shoulders or raised high above their heads. Some reporters reach forward to push recorders toward my mouth, though policemen beat them back. I am jostled and shoved, my feet stepped on, my elbows knocked into my ribs. These men shout questions.

"How did the terrorists make contact with you?"

"When did you start planning the attack?"

I find my voice and shout, a brief cry, which dies down like a rooster's: "I am innocent! I don't know anything about—"

I stand tall, though colors appear bright in my eyes, the greens of trees luminous as a mineral seam, the ground beneath my feet composed of distinct particles. My legs buckle and the policewoman catches me. A shout goes up among the crowd. The policewoman's grip on my arm is the kindest thing. Then indoors, where the noise recedes and I am allowed to slump in a chair.

A lawyer appointed to me appears. He is young, only a little older than me, though he has the potbelly of a wealthy man.

"Did you get food this morning?" is the first thing he says.

I look at my policewomen handlers and cannot remember. I nod.

"I am Gobind," he says. "Your court-appointed lawyer. Do you understand what 'lawyer' means? It means that—"

"Sir," I begin. "I understand what it means. I went to school. I am a sales clerk at Pantaloons, you know that shop? You tell me this, why am I arrested? Fine, I posted one stupid thing on Facebook, but I don't know anything about the train."

The lawyer looks not at me but at a folder in his hands. He licks a finger and turns the pages.

"Are you telling the truth?" he says. "They found your chat records talking to the terrorist recruiter on Facebook."

"Everybody keeps saying this to me, but this boy was just someone I chatted with online. We were online friends," I plead. "I didn't know who he was."

From my chair, I hear the wheeze of a ceiling fan above me and the chatter of visitors entering the courtroom behind. In front, all I see is an aunty sitting at a typewriter. Tendrils of hair slip loose from the coil at the base of her neck.

"On Facebook, I made many friends, including this friend in a foreign country. At least, that is what he told me," I explain to Gobind. "This friend asked me about my life and my feelings. I sent him emojis sometimes, to say hello. Now they tell me he was a known terrorist recruiter. Known to whom? I didn't know any of this."

Gobind looks at me. A woman like me is never believed.

"What about these cloths soaked in kerosene found at your house?" says Gobind after a while. "Very much like the kerosene-soaked torches that were tossed into the train. What about that?"

"Those were . . ." I think hard. "Probably my mother's cleaning cloths. Kerosene to get grease off. I don't know! I have never seen them."

They say I helped terrorists set fire to the train. Not only do they have Facebook chat records with a man I now know is a recruiter, there were witnesses at the railway station who saw me walking there with a package in my arms. Must have been kerosene, they say. Must have been rags or wood for torches. Other witnesses saw me running away from the train, with no package in my arms. Though they saw no men with me, they allege that I guided men, terrorists, enemies of the country, down the unnamed lanes of my slum, to the station where the cursed train would be waiting.

When I protest my innocence, they point to the seditious statements I posted on Facebook, calling my own government a "terrorist" and showing, so they say, a marked absence of loyalty to the state. Is it a crime to write some words on Facebook?

Gobind points to a document I signed while in police lockup. He tells me I confessed.

"Who believes that?" I charge. "They forced me to sign. They were beating me."

I turn to the courtroom, wishing for my mother and father to be here, for their soothing hand on my head, at the same time as I wish for them to never see me here. They would not be able to bear it.

Then the judge arrives and reads a list of charges.

"Crimes against the nation," he says. "Sedition."

I hear the words. I raise my hand and gesture no, no, no.

"I was taking a few books, my schoolbooks," I say. It is the truth, so why does it sound so meager? "That was my package. I was taking my schoolbooks to a person in the slum. Her name is Lovely. Ask her. She will tell you that I was teaching her English for some months."

From the back, a voice scoffs, "Keep your stories for the papers. A terrorist doing charity! What an A-plus story! The media will eat it up!"

The judge threatens to throw the voice out of the room.

"They made me sign the confession," I tell the judge later. I lift my tunic to reveal my bruised abdomen and hear people shift behind me.

This time the judge listens, his eyebrows raised.

Days later, in a newspaper, I will see an artist's drawing of me appearing in court that morning. The sketch shows a woman with her hair in a braid. Her hands are cuffed but raised as in prayer or plea. This is a mistake, I think. I was not in cuffs. Was I? The rest of her body is hastily penciled, decaying already.

JIVAN'S MOTHER AND FATHER

No more than an hour after Jivan was arrested, a reporter found the house in the slum and knocked. The door was a sheet of tin, unlatched. It fell open. Jivan's mother was sitting by Jivan's father on the raised bed, fanning him with a folded newspaper.

At the sight of the reporter, Jivan's mother rose and walked to the door. "Who are you?" she demanded. "Are you police?"

The newsman held a recorder at a respectful distance and said, "*Daily Beacon*. I am Purnendu Sarkar." He flipped open his wallet to show her ID, then tucked it into a back pocket. "Do you know why your daughter has been arrested?"

Jivan's mother said, "They will send a policeman with the information, that is what they told me. Where did they take Jivan?"

This mother was confused, the reporter saw. She did not know anything. He sighed. Then he turned off his recorder and told her what he knew.

"Mother," he said in the end, "did you understand what I said?"

"Why would I not understand?" said she. "I am her mother!"

And to her husband she turned. Jivan's father, stiff-backed on the bed, knew, had known, something terrible was happening.

"They are saying something about Jivan," she cried. "Come here and see, what are they saying?"

But her husband only lifted his head, sensing a frightening disturbance in the night. He moved his dry mouth to speak and stopped. His chin trembled and his arm, raised from the elbow, hailed somebody for help.

A figure peeled away from the carrom players outside. He was Kalu the neighbor, with his bulging neck tumor. By that time, more reporters had arrived and a curious crowd had formed outside the house. This crowd made way for him in fear and disgust. Kalu shut the door behind him and a shout of protest went up from the gathered reporters.

"Mother," he said, "have you eaten? Then let's go. These people are saying they know where Jivan is."

Then he took her, sitting on the back of his motorcycle, her legs dangling like a schoolgirl's, to the police station the reporters had named. By the time Jivan's mother stepped off the motorcycle, in her arms nothing but an envelope, much crushed—her daughter's birth certificate, school-leaving certificate, polio drop receipt, for documents were all she had—the sky was turning from black to blue.

Jivan's mother made her way to the entrance of the police station, where, she had been told, her daughter was held. There was a crowd of reporters here too. They had lights and cameras. One reporter applied lipstick, while another crushed a cigarette underfoot. At the gate stood two guards, rifles strapped to their backs. Periodically they shouted at the journalists to step back. Otherwise they leaned in the doorway, chatting.

They turned to look at the stooped woman who came right up to them, her feet in bathroom slippers.

"Stop, stop," one said. "Where are you going? Can't you see this is a police station?"

Jivan's mother told them she was there to see her child.

"Who is your son?" said the guard, irritated, while his friend wandered away.

"My daughter. Jivan, she is called."

The guard's mouth fell open. Here she was, the mother of the terrorist.

"Not now," he said finally. "No visiting in the lockup."

The guard, on order to let nobody meet with the terrorist, refused to let her mother in.

JIVAN

Early one morning, a man appears outside my cell, holding in his hands a foolscap sheet of paper. "Undertrials!" he barks.

A line of filthy men forms. The men wear slippers, rubbed thin at the heels, and vests pasted to their sweating chests. One shouts, "Is this the line for omelets?"

A few of the men laugh, no mirth in their voices.

Some say nothing, watching the specimen of me in my cell. I am to stay in prison until my trial a year later.

The man in charge unlocks the gate and pokes his head in.

"You, madam! You need a special invitation?"

So I scramble up from the floor. With a dozen others, I climb into a police van. When a man raises his handcuffed hands to touch my breasts, I slap them away.

"Keep your hands to yourself!" I shout.

The driver shouts at me to be quiet.

That is how I am transported from temporary lockup to this prison, where I now live.

PT SIR

The playground is a rectangle of concrete, surrounded first by a slim row of trees wilting in the sun, then by the five-storey building of the school. The physical-training teacher, in collared shirt and ironed pants, his mustache thick as a shoe-brush and his bald pate shiny, stands in the sun and shouts commands for the students to march in rhythm, arms raised in salute, feet landing sharply on the ground.

The girls, his students, are thirteen years old, their skirts down to their knees, bra straps falling off their shoulders, tired socks curling off their shins. Many have cleaned their white sports shoes with a rub of blackboard chalk. Now their backs slouch and their arms flop when they should be rigid as blades.

"Haven't you seen," PT Sir scolds as he walks down their rows, "the soldiers' procession on TV? You should look exactly like that!"

Republic Day, the national holiday celebrating the country's constitution, is coming up and this will not do. The students' parade, the most patriotic performance on this patriotic occasion, is PT Sir's responsibility. It is the one time in all the school year when he, this odd teacher who teaches not geography or mathematics or chemistry, not even home science, showcases his work. Well, he thinks meanly about himself, that is other than all the times he steps up during assembly to fix a malfunctioning microphone, the only man at this girls' school called on for handiwork.

"Quiet!" he scolds when murmurs arise from the girls. "Be serious!"

The class falls silent. Girls look at the ground, laughter suppressed in their mouths.

Off to the side, two girls sit in the shade of a tree and giggle. At the beginning of class, they had come up to him and each whispered in his ear, "Sir, I have got my period. Can I please be excused?"

PT Sir thinks, but is not sure, that they perhaps had their periods last week also. Frowning, he removes a handkerchief from his breast pocket and wipes the sweat off his head, his forehead, his nose. What else can he do?

———

A few nights later, on TV, a banner flashes *Breaking news! Breaking news!*

The host of the show walks down the corridors of a newsroom and, pen in hand, announces that a young woman has been arrested in connection with the train bombing. Her name is Jivan. Last name currently unknown.

PT Sir slams his after-dinner dish of sweets on the table

and lunges for the remote. At the sound, his wife emerges from the kitchen, asking, "What happened?"

He raises a finger to his lips and presses his thumb down on the volume button until sound fills the room. He leans so far forward his face is no more than a few inches from the screen. There, in a video clip being played and replayed, among the jostle of policemen and reporters, is that face, that poorly made plait, that scar on the chin, elements of a person he knows or knew. Now the girl keeps a hand on her back, like an elderly lady who aches. PT Sir's mustache nearly falls off his face. "Look at this," he whispers to his wife. "Just look."

"Do you know her?" says his wife. "How do you know her?"

"This young woman, all of twenty-two years old," yells a reporter standing in the middle of a lane, curious onlookers crowding into the frame, "was arrested from the slum where I am standing right now. It's the Kolabagan slum, that's right, the Kolabagan slum next to the Kolabagan railway station, where the train was brutally attacked six days ago, killing one hundred and twelve people. In that attack, as we know—"

PT Sir presses a button and the channel changes. Jivan appears once more, a camera zooming in on her face.

"This Muslim woman is charged with *assisting* terrorists who plotted this heinous attack—"

"She has been booked under a very serious crimes against the nation charge *and* a sedition charge, which is highly unusual—"

"She allegedly made contact with a known recruiter for a terrorist cell on Facebook—"

PT Sir presses a button and the channel flips again.

"Why did she bear so much hatred in her heart for her own country? Sociology professor Prakash Mehra is joining us to talk about the alienated youth and how the Internet—"

PT Sir watches until his eyes smart. He watches until he has seen every bit of footage and analysis available. Outside, the din of car horns.

———

It was not so long ago that Jivan was his student. When she started, one of the school's charity students, as they were bluntly called, she had never seen a basketball in her life. But the rules were intuitive and she played with energy, her legs uninhibited, her arms flung, her mouth open in laughter. Jivan scared the others. The aggressive game of kabaddi came to her naturally and she was perhaps his only student who was disappointed when he asked them to play mild dodgeball.

PT Sir understood, from the fervor with which she played and how she responded to compliments with a close-mouthed smile, that she needed this class in a way the other girls did not. So he pardoned her soiled skirt. He forgave her old shoes.

Once, when she fainted in the heat of the playground, he took it as his opening to offer her a banana. After

31

that, every now and then he gave her a sandwich from his own tiffin box or an apple. Once, a bag of chips. She didn't get enough to eat, he worried. He couldn't have his prize student falling sick. He already had her in mind for march-past at school functions, for training so she could play basketball, or even football, at the city level. She could grow up to be an athlete, like him. Not once had he come across a student of his who showed real promise in his field, until Jivan.

Then, after the class ten board exams, she left school. He never knew why. He understood it to be a matter of school fees. But she offered him no explanation, never acknowledged how he had gone out of his way to support her. A small thing, but he found it rude.

Well, was it a small thing?

When he thinks about it, an old anger flickers to life. He had begun to dream of her as a mentee, but she had not considered him a mentor. She had considered him perhaps no more than a source of occasional free food. She had fooled him.

The TV plays, indifferent to its tired viewer.

"What happened to make this ordinary young woman, Jivan is her name, a terrorist? What led her down the path of anti-national activity, bringing her into alliance with a terrorist group and conspiring to bring down the government? After the break—"

He cannot believe what she has gone on to do.

His nerves thrum. His life is just the same and yet this proximity to disaster electrifies PT Sir.

Now he knows, there *was* something wrong with Jivan the whole time. There *was* something wrong in her thinking. Or else she would never have left without telling him, a teacher who cared for her, farewell and thank you.

JIVAN

This morning, after Uma madam, the chief guard of the women's prison, wakes us up, I find Yashwi in the court-yard. Yashwi, in clean yellow salwar kameez, who has robbed ten or twelve houses. In one of them, she left a grandfather tied up so tight he suffocated. But she is a nice girl, always smiling.

She pumps the tube well for me, hopping up, then crouching down with her weight on the lever as water falls like stones into my cupped hands. With the cold water, pulled from reserves deep underground, a taste of minerals on my lips, I wash my face.

When my eyes feel fresh and new, we join the crowd on the other side of the courtyard for our hunks of bread. There is a fist's scoop of potato on top and a glass of tea ladled from a bucket. I eat, standing on the side, looking to see if anybody is getting more than me. It has happened. I am ready to fight if it happens again.

But the women are in the haze of sleep, the sky is just turning to morning and the green algae on the ground are damp under my feet. It is as peaceful as it gets in a cage.

After breakfast, we gather in the TV room. Beside me sits Nirmaladi, dupatta drawn over her head, a corner of cloth clenched in her teeth. She sucks the cloth like a baby at a nipple. She used to work as a cook in the outside world, until she accepted twenty thousand rupees for putting rat poison in a family's lunch. Behind me is one-eyed Kalkidi, half of her face burned, laughing hard when I turn to look, the gaps in her teeth showing. Her husband threw acid on her but, somehow, she is the one in jail. These things happen when you are a woman.

Rumors drift. Among us, some have killed a child in bed or slit the throat of an abusive husband. A few things I know, a few things I don't want to know.

On TV, our favorite drama plays: *Why Won't Mother-in-Law Love Me?*

My first day inside, there was an episode of this endless show playing. Here in this TV room, I asked questions: "Listen, sister, did you keep the court-appointed lawyer? Or did you find a better one? How did you pay for your own lawyer?"

I spoke, but it was as if I had said nothing.

All faces were turned to the TV.

What was this place? Before I knew it, I was saying, "I am innocent, I swear I didn't—"

Some women turned. Their faces, with jutting teeth, earlobes slit from years of wearing hoops—so human, yet each one a stranger to me—made me feel that I knew nobody in the world.

I cried. I was a child.

Everyone stopped watching TV then and turned to watch me. The woman with patches of light and dark skin, a kind of leader in the prison, I knew even then, got up from her position on the floor within licking distance of the TV and came waddling to me. I had heard she was the one who arranged an upgrade from a black-and-white to a color TV. Americandi, American sister, as she was called for her pink skin, took my chin in her hands. She was gentle as a mother. I felt a moment of relief, assurance that made me wipe my tears. Then she slapped me. Her hand, tough as hide, struck my ear and left it whining.

"Blind or what?" she said. "Can't you see we're watching TV?"

Now I watch TV, openmouthed like the others. More than the show, it is the world I watch. A traffic light, an umbrella, rain on a windowsill. The simple freedom of crossing a street.

———

Before I lived here, I was a working woman. I had a job at a big shop, where we sold clothes—Indian, Western—suitcases, perfumes, wristwatches, even a few books that customers flipped through and put back on the shelves. Day after day, I worked my long shifts, keeping stacks of clothes folded and tidy, bringing different sizes to ladies who yelled from the fitting room. I looked at them when they weren't looking at me—their shiny hair, pedicured feet. Their purses with little plastic cards, sources of end-less money. I wanted all that too.

They say the recruiter offered me money, plenty of money, to help them navigate the unmarked lanes of the slum, to bring supplies of kerosene to the train.

I live—I lived—in the Kolabagan slum, near the Kolabagan railway station, with my mother and father. Our house, one room with two brick walls and two walls of tin and tarp, was behind a garbage dump, a dump that was so big and occupied by so many crows screaming *kaw kaw* from dawn to night, it was famous. I would say, "I live in the house behind the dump," and everybody would know where I meant. You could say I lived in a landmark building.

A hijra called Lovely, who went around blessing chil-dren and newlyweds, lived in the Kolabagan slum too and some evenings I taught her English. It began as a compulsory school program where each student had to teach the alphabet to an illiterate person. But we continued long after the school graded me on it. Lovely believed she would have a better life someday and so did I. The path began with *a b c d*. Cat, bat, rat. English is the language of the modern world. Can you move up in life without it? We kept going.

And I was moving up. So what if I lived in only a half-brick house? From an eater of cabbage, I was becoming an eater of chicken. I had a smartphone with a big screen, bought with my own salary. It was a basic smartphone, bought on an installment plan, with a screen, which jumped and credit, which I filled when I could. But now I was connected to a world bigger than this neighborhood.

———

On my way to my job in the kitchen, I peep in the door of the pickle-making room, where six women prepare lime and onion pickles to sell outside. For years, the space was no more than an accidental warehouse of broken goods, until Americandi, our local entrepreneur, set up this operation from which the prison makes petty cash. Now the room is painted and lit, tables covered with jars, the air smelling of mustard. When she sees me, Monalisa takes off her glove to hand me a triangle of lime peel, dark and sour. A few days ago, I helped her daughter learn the Bengali alphabet: *paw phaw baw bhaw maw*. The fragrance of the pickled lime makes my tongue water. The salt and acid play on my tongue and I chew the sourness down.

PT SIR

At the end of a school day, when the bottoms of his trousers are soiled, PT Sir holds his bag in his armpit and exits the building. Outside, the narrow lane is crowded with schoolgirls who part for him. Now and then a student calls, "Good afternoon, sir!"

PT Sir nods. But these girls, to whom he taught physical training just hours before, have hiked up their skirts and coiled their hair into topknots. Their fingers are sticky with pickled fruit. They are talking about boys. He can no longer know them, if he ever did.

When the lane opens up onto the main road, PT Sir is startled by a caravan of trucks roaring past. Three and four and five rush by in a scream of wind. Young men sit in the open truck beds, their faces skinny and mustached, their hands waving the saffron flags of ardent nationalism. One young man tucks his fingers in his mouth and whistles.

———

At the train station, PT Sir stands at his everyday spot, anticipating roughly where a general compartment door will arrive. He is leaning to look down the tracks when an announcement comes over the speakers. The train will be thirty minutes late.

"Thirty minutes meaning one hour minimum!" complains a fellow passenger. This man sighs, turns around, and walks away. PT Sir takes out his cell phone, a large rectangle manufactured by a Chinese company, and calls his wife.

"Listen," he says, "the train is going to be late."

"What?" she shouts.

"Late!" he shouts back. "Train is late! Can you hear?"

After the terrorist attack on the train, just a few weeks ago, the word "train" frightens her. "What happened now?" she says. "Are things fine?"

"Yes, yes! All fine. They are saying 'technical difficulty.'"

PT Sir holds the phone at his ear and surveys the scene in front. Passengers arrive, running, then learn about the delay and filter away. To those who spread out the day's newspaper on the floor and relax on it, a girl sells salted and sliced cucumber. In his ear, PT Sir's wife says, "Fine then. Can you bring a half kilo of tomatoes? There is that market just outside your station."

A spouse always has ideas about how you should spend your time. Couldn't he have enjoyed thirty minutes to himself, to drink a cup of tea and sit on the platform?

PT Sir goes to look for tomatoes. Outside the station, on the road where taxis and buses usually honk and curse, nearly scraping one another's side mirrors, all traffic has halted. Motorcyclists use their feet to push forward. PT Sir learns, from a man who grinds tobacco in his palm, that there is a Jana Kalyan (Well-being for All) Party rally, in the field nearby. It is the biggest opposition party in the state. Film star Katie Banerjee is speaking at the rally.

Katie Banerjee! Now, PT Sir thinks, is it better to spend twenty minutes looking for tomatoes or catching a glimpse of the famous Katie? Tomatoes can be found anywhere. In fact, tomatoes can be bought ten minutes from his house at the local market—why doesn't his wife go there?

So he follows the street, which opens up onto a field trampled free of grass. The crowd, a thousand men or more, waves the familiar saffron flags. They whistle and clap. Some men cluster around an enterprising phuchka walla, a seller of spiced potato stuffed in crisp shells, who has set up his trade. The scent of cilantro and onion carries. On all the men's foreheads, even the phuchka walla's, PT Sir sees a smear of red paste, an index of worship—of god, of country. The men, marked by the divine, wear pants whose bottoms roll under their feet, and hop up now and then to see what is happening. The stage is far away.

"Brother," he says to a young man. He surprises himself with his friendly tone. "Brother, is it really Katie Banerjee up there?"

The young man looks at him, hands PT Sir a small party flag from a grocery store bag full of them, and calls a third man. "Over here, come here!" he yells. Soon that man rushes over, holding a dish of red paste. He dips his thumb in the paste and marks PT Sir's forehead, drawing a red smear from brow to hairline. All PT Sir can do is accept, a child being blessed by an elder.

Thus marked, party flag in his hand, PT Sir steps forward to hear better. Onstage, it is indeed movie star Katie Banerjee, dressed in a starched cotton sari. She too is marked by holy red paste on her forehead, PT Sir sees. Her speech drawing to a close, she raises both hands in a namaste. "You all have come from far districts of the state," she says. "For that, you have my thanks. Go home safely, carefully."

The microphone crackles. The crowd roars.

When the star leaves the stage, her place at the microphone is occupied by the second-in-command of the party. Bimala Pal, no more than five feet two, arrives in a plain white sari, her steel wristwatch flashing in the sun. The crowd quiets for her. PT Sir holds the flag above his head for shade, then tries his small leather bag, which works better.

In the microphone, Bimala Pal cries, her words echoing over the speakers: "We will seek justice . . . ice! For the lives lost in this cowardly . . . ardly attack . . . tack on the train . . . train! I promise you . . . you!"

After a minute of silence for the lost souls, she continues, pausing for the echoes to fade, "Where the current government is not able to feed our people! Jana Kalyan Party—your idle government's hardworking opposition!—has provided rice to fourteen districts for three rupees per kilo! We are inviting plastics and cars, factories that will bring at least fifteen thousand jobs—"

While PT Sir watches, a man wearing a white undershirt pulls himself up, or is pushed up by the crowd, onto the hood of a jeep far ahead. PT Sir had not noticed the jeep until now, but there it is, a vehicle in the middle of the field, still a distance from the stage. The man stands on the hood of the car, surveying the raised arms, the open mouths and stained teeth. Then he climbs onto the roof of the car, the car now rocking from the crowd shoving and slamming, their fury and laughter landing on the polished body of the vehicle.

"Fifteen thousand jobs!" they chant. "Fifteen thousand jobs!"

Whether they are excited or merely following instructions from party coordinators is hard to tell. A few TV cameras will pick this up, no doubt.

"We know that you are sacrificing every day!" Bimala Pal calls, shouting into the microphone. "And for what? Don't you deserve more opportunities? This party is standing with you to gain those jobs, every rupee of profit that you are owed, every day of school for your children!" Bimala Pal pumps a fist in the air.

PT Sir watches, electricity coursing through him despite himself. Here, in the flesh, are the people of the hinterland about whom he has only seen features on TV. He knows a few things about them: not only is there no work in their village, there is not even a paved road! Not only is the factory shut down, but the company guard is keeping them from selling the scrap metal!

"Remember that this nation belongs to *you*, not to the

rich few in their high-rises or the company bosses in their big cars, but *you!*" Bimala Pal wraps up. "Vande Mataram!"

Praise to the motherland!

The man at the top of the car repeats, screaming, "Vande Mataram!"

PT Sir might have thought that this man, along with hundreds of others, had been trucked here from a village, his empty belly lured by a free box of rice and chicken, his fervor purchased for one afternoon. He might have thought that, for these unemployed men, this rally is more or less a day's job. The party is feeding them when the market is not.

But the man's cries make the hairs on PT Sir's arm stand up and what is false about that?

The man on the car lifts his shirt and reveals, tucked in the waistband of his trousers, wrapped in a length of cloth, a dagger. He holds the handle and lifts it high in the air, where the blade catches the sun. Below him, surrounding the car, a man dances, then another and another, a graceless dance of feeling.

The dagger stays up in the air, itself a sun above the field, and PT Sir looks at it, frozen in alarm and excitement. How spirited this man is, with his climb atop a jeep like a movie hero, with his dagger and his dancing. How different from all the schoolteachers PT Sir knows. How free.

———

When the men begin to tire, a coordinator announces, "Brothers and sisters! There are buses! To take you home! Please do not rush! Do not stampede! Everyone will be taken home free of charge!"

PT Sir returns to the train station. He has missed the delayed train and, when the next one comes, he finds an aisle seat, tucking his behind, the fifth, into a seat meant for three. The soles of his feet itch, reminding him they have been bearing his weight for much of the day. Somebody shoves past, dragging a sack over his toes. The person is gone before PT Sir can say anything. A woman then stands beside him, her belly protruding at his ear and her purse threatening to strike him in the face at any moment. In this crowd, a muri walla, a puffed rice seller, makes his way. "Muri, muri!" he calls. The coach groans.

"Today out of all days!" comes the woman's loud voice above his head. "First the delay, now there is no place to stand, and you have to sell muri here?"

"Harassment, that's what this is," says a voice from somewhere behind PT Sir. "This commute is nothing less than daily harassment!"

"Here, here, muri walla," somebody objects. "Give me two."

"And one here!" someone else calls.

The muri walla mixes mustard oil, chopped tomato and cucumber, spiced lentil sticks, and puffed rice in a tin. He shakes a jar of spices upside down. Then he pours the muri into a bowl made of newsprint.

PT Sir's stomach growls. He lifts his buttocks to try to reach his wallet.

"And one muri this way!" he says. "How much?"

The muri walla makes him a big bowl, heaping at the top.

"Don't worry," he says, handing the bowl to PT Sir. "For you, no charge."

"No charge?" says PT Sir. He laughs, holding the bowl, unsure whether it is truly his to eat. Then he remembers: the red mark on his forehead, the party flag in his lap. PT Sir feels the other passengers staring at him. They must be thinking, who is this VIP?

———

At home, after dinner, PT Sir sits back in his chair, gravy-wet fingers resting atop his plate, and tells his wife, "Strange thing happened today. Are you listening?"

His wife is thin and short, her hair plaited such that it needs no rubber band at its taper. When she looks at him from her chair, it appears she has forgiven him for the forgotten tomatoes.

Something has happened at the school, she thinks. A man teaching physical training to a group of girls, all of whom are growing breasts, their bellies cramping during menstruation, their skirts stained now and then. A bad situation is bound to arise.

"What happened?" she says fearfully.

"There was a Jana Kalyan rally in the field behind the

station," he begins, "then one man climbed on a car—understand? *Climbed on top of a car*—and took out ... Tell me what he took out!"

"How will I know?" she says. When she bites into a milk sweet, white crumbs fall on her plate. "Gun or what?"

"Dagger!" he says, disappointed. The truth is always modest. He goes on, "But Katie Banerjee was there—"

"Katie Banerjee!"

"Then Bimala Pal also was there. Say what you like about her, she is a good orator. And she was saying some correct things, you know. Her speech was good."

His wife's face sours. She pushes back her chair and its legs scrape the floor. "Speech sheech," she says. "She is pandering to all these unemployed men. This is why our country is not going anywhere."

"They are feeding a lot of people with discounted rice," he says. "And they are going to connect two hundred villages, two hundred, to the electricity grid in two years—"

"You," says his wife, "believe everything."

PT Sir smiles at her. When she disappears into the kitchen, he gets up and washes his hands clean of turmeric sauce, then wipes them on a towel that was once white.

He understands how his wife feels. If you only watch the news on TV, it is easy to be skeptical. But what is so wrong about the common people caring about their jobs, their wages, their land? And what, after all, is so wrong about him doing something different from his schoolteacher's job? Today he did something patriotic, meaningful, bigger than the disciplining of cavalier schoolgirls—and it was, he knows as he lies in bed, no sleep in his humming mind, exciting.

JIVAN

In the days-old papers that make it to the prison, they write versions of my life. They report that I grew up in Sealdah, Salpur, Chhobigram. My father, they share, has polio, cancer, an amputated limb. He used to cook food in a hotel; no, he used to be a municipal clerk; no, in truth, he used to be a meter reader for the electricity supply company. They have not found out about my mother's breakfast business, because they write that she is a housewife, when they mention her at all.

"Look," I say to Americandi, who is my cellmate because, I learned, she demanded to be housed with the famous terrorist. "*Desher Potrika* says I used to work at a call center and they have pictures of somebody! Somebody else on the back of a motorcycle with a man. I have never even been on a motorcycle."

It is midday, after bath time, and my cellmate has hiked up her sari to her thighs and is giving herself a massage, running her fingers up and down calves. Her veins are crooked, like flooding rivers.

"Reporters write anything," she says. "Take my case, where I said—"

But I don't want to hear about her.

"They hear something in the street," I say. "Then they write it down."

"They work on deadlines," she says. "If they miss their deadlines, they are fired. Who has time to ask questions?"

"And it says here, listen," I continue, " 'An Internet cafe operator in the neighborhood said Jivan would often make calls to Pakistan numbers.' Why are they lying about me?"

Americandi looks at me. "You know, many people don't believe you. Myself, I heard everything. There was kerosene in your home. You were at the train station. You were friends with the recruiter. Did you do it?" She sighs. "But somehow, I don't see you as a bad person."

A sob rises thick in my throat.

"Listen," she says. "I am not supposed to tell you, but you know reporters are beating down the gates trying to get an interview with you?"

I wipe my eyes and blow my nose. "Which paper?" I say.

The Times of India! Hindustan Times! The Statesman! she says. "Name any paper. All are offering money, so much money, just for one interview with you. That's what I heard. But Uma madam is forced to say no to all of them. There is pressure from above."

"It is my right to talk to them!" I shout.

Americandi makes as if to slap me. "Keep your voice down!" she hisses. "This is why I shouldn't be nice to anyone in this rotten place."

She picks a sari from the stack of four that I have washed and folded for her. She winds the sari about herself. She tucks in the top of the pleats. "You have the *right*?" she says, kicking a leg under the fabric to order the pleats. Under a smile, she buries all else she meant to say.

"I want to talk to them," I say softly. "What is Gobind doing for me anyway? I have not seen him in days. Not once has he called me."

If only I could speak to a newspaper reporter, a TV camera, wouldn't they understand? Every day, I bear this dark corridor with its rustle of insects' wings, the drip of a leak that conveys news of the rains, the plaster on the ceiling swelling like a cloud. Days have turned into weeks and still I kneel by the gutter in the back, washing Americandi's nighties by hand, the smell of iron rising where we all wash our monthly cloths. I have been a fool to wait for Gobind's plan, I see. He may be my court-appointed lawyer, but he is no advocate of mine.

This is why, I think, we are all here. Take Americandi. She pushed a man who was trying to snatch her necklace on the street. The man fell and struck his head on the pavement. He went into a coma. The court charged Americandi and here she is, a decade or more into confinement that never ends. If she had received a chance to tell her story, how might her life have been?

———

The next morning, Americandi gathers her thin towel, rough as a pumice stone, and a bottle of perfumed liquid soap she guards with her life. She is off to take a bath.

"Listen," I say, while the day is new and Americandi's mood unspoiled, "will you do one thing for me?"

I hold up the newspaper I have been looking at.

"Will you send word to this reporter?" I unfold the newspaper, *Daily Beacon*, and look at the name Purnendu Sarkar. "Ask this Purnendu Sarkar to come? My mother said he visited her. He was helpful."

Americandi looks about for her shower slippers.

"Good plan!" she says, mocking. "Why should I be bothered?"

She waits and turns to me. I have one moment of her attention, no more.

"The money," I tell her. "What they offer for an interview. You just said, they are offering a lot? You can take it all. What can the courts do if the media does not—"

"You really love lecturing," says Americandi. "Did you say *all* the money?"

"Every rupee."

"When did you become such a rich person?" she says.

PT SIR

Nothing good comes of contacting the police. Everybody knows that. If you catch a thief, you are better off beating the man and, having struck fear in his heart, letting him go.

But this is no ordinary thief. This is a woman who attacked a train full of people. She killed, directly or indirectly, more than a hundred people. Now, the TV channels are reporting, she is silent in prison. She has granted no interviews. She has offered no details and, other than a confession, which she insists she was forced to sign, she has shared no information. She is protesting that she is innocent.

The police, desperate for progress, have asked Jivan's friends and associates to step forward. Nobody will be harassed, they have promised. They are only looking for insight into the character of the terrorist, some scrap of information that will crack the case open. The men involved in the case have long slipped across the border and fled. Jivan is the only hope.

So it is that one morning, encouraged by his wife, PT Sir, in fresh clothes, his sparse hair combed, his belly full of breakfast, picks up the phone and calls the local police station. When the superintendent on duty, a man who insists on speaking in English, urges him to come to the station right away, PT Sir does. So consumed is his mind that it is only halfway on his walk to the station that he realizes he is still wearing his house slippers.

JIVAN

When my mother came to visit for the first time, she cried to hand over a tiffin carrier, full of home-cooked food, to the guards. She did it again and again, hoping the meals would reach me. Then I told her, "Why are you cooking for the guards?"

I watched her cry then, my own eyes dry.

Today, upon my request, she hands me not cooked food, but a small pouch, knotted shut, filled with golden oil. It is ghee.

"What will you do with this?" she asks.

I tell her.

Then she is gone, all the mothers are gone, and the rest of the day stretches before us. In the courtyard, I see a fight among three women—teeth bared, hair coming unclipped. They scream about a missing milk sweet.

For the rest of the day, we fall and die from knowing, but never being able to say, especially to our mothers, that the inside of the prison is an unreachable place. So what if there is a courtyard and a garden and a TV room? The guards tell us over and over that we live well, we live better than the trapped souls in the men's prison. Still we feel we are living at the bottom of a well. We are frogs. All we can bear to tell our mothers is, "I am fine, I am fine."

We tell them, "I walk in the garden."

"I watch TV."

"Don't worry about me, I am fine."

The kitchen, where my work is to make ruti, holds a large grill, which allows me to make bread in batches of ten. One woman kneads the dough, one tears balls and flattens them into disks, several roll them flat and round, and I tend them as they're tossed on the grill. When they're done, I lift them with long tongs and flip them onto the stone surface next to the grill. There a couple of women dust the flour off and stack them.

After making a hundred and twenty pieces of ruti, I pour the ghee on the grill. The scent is the luxury that I imagine sleeping on a bed of feathers must be or bathing in a tub of milk like the old queens of our country. With my hand, I flip the dough in the pool of clarified butter and the edges crisp. The bread rises and its belly gains brown spots.

When I take a plate to Uma madam, she is sitting on a plastic chair in the courtyard, her arms draped on the sides, like the ruler of a meager kingdom. Surrounding her, in tidy rows, inmates eat. She accepts the plate and looks at me with a sly smile.

"Why this preparation?" she says. "What do you want now?"

She is not angry.

I step back and watch her eat the porota. I hear the shatter of the crisp dough or maybe I imagine it. She folds the porota around a smear of dal and lifts it to her mouth. I watch like a jackal. My stomach growls.

In the row of seated inmates and their children, a little girl cries. A boy whines for food, though he has just eaten. The children are each given a boiled egg and milk every other day. Other than that, there is no concession made to their growing bodies, their muscles stretching overnight. They eat the same stale curry as the rest of us. The mothers have agitated over this, but who will listen to them?

Uma madam twists around in the chair, spots me, and gives me a thumbs-up. She lifts the plate to show me. She has eaten every bite.

Kneeling at Uma madam's feet, I take the empty plate from her. I can feel the damp algae green my knees.

"So," she says, digging in her teeth with her tongue, "what was this about?"

"I have a brother," I say. "He wants to visit. Can you approve him for my visitors' list? His name is Purnendu Sarkar."

I try to smile. My lips manage it.

"Brother, hmm?" she says. "You never mentioned him. Was he living in a cave until today?"

"No, he was working outside the city—"

When Uma madam stands up, she puts her hands on

her waist and arches her spine. She squints at the sky. With a look of great boredom, she turns to me. "The fewer lies you tell, the better for you. God knows how many lies you tell every day."

Then she is gone and I am left holding the plate. There is a thin shard of porota sticking to the rim, an airy nothing made of flour. Not even a fly would be nourished by it. I pinch it with my fingers and put it in my mouth.

LOVELY

Even a future movie star is having to make money. One morning, my sisters and I are spraying rose water in our armpits, braiding our hair, putting bangles on our arms, and together we are going to bless a newborn. The general public is believing that we hijras are having a special telephone line to god. So, if we bless, it is like a blessing straight from god. At the door of the happy family, I am rattling the lock *thuck thuck thuck*.

"Give, mother," we are calling so that our voices can be heard deep within the big house. When nobody is coming, I am stepping back and looking up at a window. It is a big house and the window is covered by a lace curtain.

"Mother!" I am calling. "Let us see the baby, come."

Finally the door in front of us is opening and the mother, wearing a nightie that goes only to her calves, her oily hair sticking to her scalp, her eyes looking like she has seen battle, is holding the baby and coming out. Poor woman is yawning like a hippopotamus. I am feeling that maybe I can make the mother cheer up, along with the baby.

So I am taking the baby in my arms, inhaling the milk scent of his skin. My eyes are falling in love with those soft folds in his wrists, the plump inside of his elbows. The others are clapping above the baby, singing, "God give this child a long life, may he never suffer the bite of an ant! God give this child a happy life, may he never suffer a lack of grains!"

The baby is looking surprised, with those big eyes. Maybe he is never coming out on the street before, never feeling the smoke and dust. For sure, he is never seeing a group of hijras in our best clothes! He is screaming. His little mouth is opening to show pink gums and pink tongue and he is screaming in my arms. He is a little animal. We are laughing. He is going to be fine, I am thinking, because he is having no defects, unlike myself.

The mother is looking harassed and taking the baby inside. We are waiting for the sound of a drawer opening, some cash being counted by mother and father. But what is this, she is going inside a room, where a tap is running and water is falling. From here, over all the sounds of the street, I am hearing one sound clearly: she is washing her hands. She is washing her hands of us.

Meanwhile, the father is coming out in shorts and giving Arjuni Ma, our hijra house's guru, three thousand whole rupees. He is sliding his glasses down his nose and looking at us from the top. One of my sisters is flirting with him for an old microwave or old TV. He is looking unhappy and pleading, "Where am I having so much, sister? Look at me. New baby and all."

Me, I am only trying to see what the mother is doing behind him, in the dark corridor, her hands so, so clean.

———

It is not new, this insult. But it is not old. I am leaving the group and hurrying to the sweet shop down the street. Inside, there is running a long glass case holding trays full of sweets. The pyramids of sweets, some dry, some soaking in syrup, are tempting me. There is brown pantua, fried and syrupy; there is white chomchom, so sweet your tongue will be begging for salt; there are milky and dry kalakand; and there is my favorite, kheer kodom. I am smelling the whole case from where I am standing, believe me. I am feeling the flavor of the flies buzzing over the sweets and how some of the old sweets are beginning to sour in the hot day.

"How much is this?" I am saying. "And how much this one?"

The man behind the counter is grumbling. He is unhappy that he is having to serve me, I know. Finally I am getting one small roshogolla, ten rupees. The man is giving it to me in a small bowl woven with dried leaves. I am lifting the bowl to my forehead. I am giving thanks. It is no small thing to buy a sweet and that is enough today. That is how my life is going forward—some insult in my face, some sweet in my mouth.

Someday, when I am a movie star, that mother will be regretting that she washed me off her hands.

———

In the evening, when my sisters are coming to my house, wearing nice saris for their outing, mosquitoes the size of birds are flying in happily also. One of my sisters is saying, "Did the police ask you anything?"

It is true that Jivan was teaching me English, so for sure the police will be coming to interrogate me. How come they are not coming yet?

In the corner of the room, hanging from a nail, is a coil of cables. One of my sisters is pulling a line and plugging it into the boxy TV on the floor. After she is slapping the top of the TV, it is waking up. That classic movie *A Match Made by God* is starting.

While the songs are playing, Arjuni Ma is raising her notebook close to her old eyes and reading what we have earned this week. Five thousand for a marriage, three thousand for a baby blessing. A few hundred rupees from the train.

My mind is somewhere else. Who is liking the police? Nobody. But I am also hoping that they are coming and I am getting a chance to tell them that Jivan was teaching me English. Impossible that Jivan is a criminal. Cannot be. I am wanting to tell the police this.

"When they come," Arjuni Ma is telling me later, "be careful when you talk to them. Maybe it is better that you try to avoid them."

We are all knowing what is happening to hijras who

are displeasing police, like Laddoo, our young hijra sister who was going to the police to report harassment from a constable and was herself put in the lockup. There she is staying for days and days. Many years ago, I would have been asking why is this happening? But now I am knowing that there is no use asking these questions. In life, many things are happening for no reason at all. You might be begging on the train and getting acid thrown on your face. You might be hiding in the women's compartment for safety and getting kicked by the ladies.

I was almost being arrested one time also. A constable named Chatterjee was catching me when I was begging near the traffic light. He was saying to me, "Now you are trying to do this nonsense in my area?"

"What?" I was challenging him. "I can't stand on the road?" I was speaking like a heroine. I was new. I was not knowing.

Anything could have happened. But he was a reasonable man. He was letting me go after I was buying him a single cigarette and lighting it for him.

JIVAN

In prison, our main activity is waiting. I wait for Americandi to get confirmation from the journalist that he will come and to see if Uma madam will look the other way. In the complete black of night, I wonder if there are other ways. If my hands were spades, they would burrow from my cell to beyond the garden wall, where buses race, where beggars loiter, where women wearing sunglasses buy chop-cutlet for evening tea.

In the morning, I stand in line for breakfast. A rumor goes around: Sonali Khan, the famous film producer whose name every household is knowing, was spotted in the booking room. Everybody cheers. What did *she* do? we wonder. Did she hit somebody with her car? Did she hide some money in Switzerland?

"You all," says Americandi, ahead of me in line, "don't know anything. It's that rhino."

The film producer once shot, from the safety of a jeep, an endangered rhino. The ghost of this rhino has caught up with her. She is finally being punished for it. Now she will live with us and tell us all about the cinema.

Yashwi says, "Definitely we will get a new TV, then!"

"What's wrong with this TV?" snaps Americandi. "If you don't like it, see if you can arrange for a new TV for yourself."

"No, I mean ..." Yashwi looks at her feet. I know she dreams of a TV whose pictures will not jump, whose remote control will work.

Komla, who once robbed a family, striking with an iron rod a mother who was left paralyzed, begins to salivate thinking of the meals in store.

"Chicken curry," she calls, turning her head up and down the line for the benefit of all, "for sure we will get chicken curry. Regularly!"

She sticks a finger in her ear and shakes it vigorously to scratch an unreachable itch. "Maybe mutton also, who knows?"

I listen, believing myself far away.

When we have returned to our cells and Uma madam comes on her round, I catch her eye.

"Have you put my brother on the list?" I ask her.

She looks at me blankly and continues on her path, the ring of keys singing at her hips. But Americandi, greedy for the two hundred thousand rupees the *Daily Beacon* has promised for an interview with me, leaps up and stands at the gate.

"Uma," she calls. "Come here."

Down the corridor, the constant chatter and clang of our prison pauses.

There is a long silence while Uma madam saunters back.

"What did you say?" she says softly. "Am I your best friend? Talk to me with respect."

Somebody in a neighboring cell whistles.

"What is this, TV hour!" somebody else comments.

"Okay, Uma *madam*," my cellmate says. "This poor girl," she continues, pouting, in a voice loud enough to carry down the corridor, "got ghee from her mother to cook for you. And you won't let her see her own brother? Shame! How must her mother be feeling?"

"Let her see her boyfriend, for god's sake!" somebody says, laughing.

Uma madam stands still. I watch from behind Americandi.

"Don't interrupt my round again," Uma madam says quietly. Then she is gone.

———

The weeks pass and nothing changes. In the courtyard? No Sonali Khan. In the TV room? The same old TV. Every week, the women pin their hopes on a different day— surely she will be transferred here this Sunday or next Thursday. Then we hear that Sonali Khan is being kept under house arrest, which means that she lives, as before, in her own house. Even the meaning of "prison" is different for rich people. Can you blame me for wanting, so much, to be—not even rich—just middle class?

PT SIR

The second time PT Sir goes to a Jana Kalyan Party rally, he stands close to the stage.

"You can see with your own eyes," Bimala Pal continues, "what this party—"

The microphone screeches. Bimala Pal takes a step back. The crowd roars and waves tiny flags. PT Sir waves his flag, saved from the previous rally.

"What this party brings to districts across the state," Bimala Pal says. "The auto parts factory—"

The microphone screeches again and the crowd murmurs. Some cover their ears with their palms.

"The factory employing three! thousand!—"

Screech. This time Bimala madam looks about with a stern face for a technician. Behind her, a number of assistants dash about, looking for the sound guy, who has probably wandered off to smoke a cigarette. The crowd stirs in boredom.

In a mad and decisive moment, PT Sir marches forward, angling his body sideways and holding an arm out in front of him.

"Side," he calls, "side!" He climbs the steps to the stage two at a time, assuring Bimala Pal's bodyguards that he intends only to fix the microphone. He wiggles the cord and tests the jack, then moves the microphone farther away from the speaker. He steps up and says, "Testing, testing."

His voice rings out clean and sharp over the crowd.

PT Sir's drumming heart calms.

Bimala Pal resumes her speech and, from a plastic chair somebody offers him at the back of the stage, PT Sir looks out over the vast number of men who have gathered. It is many stadiums' worth of men, their heads like the bulbs of ants. These are not the spoiled and lazy students who occupy his days, nor the teacher aunties who proceed as a horde after school to watch Bengali detective films and eat Chinese noodles. When has he ever been among so many patriots, men who are invested in the development of the nation, who are here in a field listening to an intellectual lecture rather than at home, under a sheet, taking a nap?

After Bimala Pal closes her speech, she comes around to the back of the stage and thanks him. PT Sir jumps up and folds his hands in greeting.

"I am just a schoolteacher." PT Sir gestures down the road. "At the S. D. Ghosh Girls' School."

Bimala Pal leans in.

"*That* school?"

"Yes, that one," PT Sir says. The terrorist's school. "In my school functions, I set up the microphone, so . . ."

Both turn to look at the microphone. It is turned off and silent on its stand. Somebody has garlanded it.

"Well, teacher sir," says Bimala Pal, "it is our good fortune that you came."

Later PT Sir's wife will say, "*That* was a scolding for coming to the stage! Don't you know that politicians always say the opposite of what they mean? It is called diplomacy."

But PT Sir is glad. An esteemed public figure taking note of him! A gathering of assistants behind Bimala Pal nods and voices its agreement.

Bimala Pal draws the anchal of her sari around her shoulders and continues, "We need educated people like you to support our party. More educated people must care about what is happening in our state, in our country. So to see a teacher like you at our rally makes me glad."

PT Sir opens his mouth to say something. He must clarify that he teaches physical education. He is not the kind of teacher she imagines, he is only—

A boy appears with dishes of samosas and after that there is chicken biryani for all. The men in the fields have received, away from the glare of a TV camera and distributed from the rear of a discreet van, their dinner boxes of biryani too. They take their boxes quietly and disperse.

But there is a problem. There are more men in the field than boxes of biryani. A scuffle breaks out. The man handing out boxes of biryani immediately closes the back doors of the van. Bimala Pal and her lackeys turn to look and PT Sir looks too.

A man, not too far from the stage, points his finger at another. "This one is taking three boxes! He is hiding them in his bag!"

That man demands, "Who are you calling a thief?"

An open palm slaps a face, a leg kicks a leg.

Bimala Pal has slipped away, cupping a hand around her mouth on her phone, occupied by a more pressing matter. One of her assistants turns to PT Sir and jokes, "Well, sir, look at these rowdy children."

The other assistants, young men holding two mobile phones each, wait with hidden smiles to see what the teacher will do.

PT Sir feels the eyes on him. The pressure is subtle but great. He steps up to the edge of the stage, sits on the pads of his feet, and calls, "Brothers, brothers! There is food for all! Why are you fighting like children?"

The men in the crowd look up at him.

"Are you children," PT Sir continues, "that you are spoiling the gathering here with your fight? Do you want to disgrace the party, and our elders who have gathered here, in front of those reporters over there?"

"Who are you?" a man shouts at PT Sir. "Who are you, mister, to tell me what to do?"

But the fight has lost its air. The men separate with some curses. When PT Sir returns to his seat and picks up his box of biryani, one of the assistants stops him.

"Wait, please," he says, "the rice has grown cold by now, wait one minute."

He calls the tea boy—"Uttam!"—and asks him to bring

a "VIP box" right away. A fresh, hot box of biryani, with two pieces of mutton, arrives for PT Sir.

———

"Today I am not hungry," PT Sir announces at home. "Today I had biryani with, guess who? Bimala Pal!"

His wife looks up from her phone. In the background, softly, the news plays. PT Sir settles heavily on the sofa and picks up the remote. He turns up the volume. A reporter shouts: "This alleged terrorist used a very modern way of spreading her anti-national views, find out how she used *Facebook*—"

On another channel, a soft-spoken news host says: "On top of throwing torches at the train, dear viewers, let me tell you all, she was also sharing anti-government views on Facebook, and who knows where else, for *years*—"

"Beware," PT Sir tells his wife. "What all you do on Facebook. It's full of criminals."

"Your head," she says, "is filled with all this. I only look at cooking videos. It's a totally different part of Facebook. People abroad make such nice things, you don't know— like apple pie with ready-made whipped cream! I have never seen such things. The cream comes out of a can."

At bedtime, when they climb under the mosquito net, his wife marvels at the story he has told her. "Imagine that!" she says. "You saving the day at a JKP rally!"

A mosquito has followed them inside the net. It buzzes near their ears until she locates the mosquito resting on the sheet and smacks her hand down on it. A blot of blood appears, and she carries the corpse of the mosquito off the bed and flings it out of the window.

Then she stands by the window and pulls the glass closed. She draws the curtain. Only then does she say, "Can I tell you something?"

He waits.

"I don't know about these politicians," she says. "In our country, politics is for goons and robbers, you know that."

PT Sir sighs.

His wife continues, "When you do something for them, like you helped them when their technician was not there, they make you feel nice. On a stage, in front of so many people—who wouldn't feel like a VIP? But associating with such people—"

This irritates PT Sir. He lies with his head on his thin pillow and wonders why his wife cannot tolerate something exciting that is happening in his life. She is annoyed, he feels, because he didn't have much of an appetite for the yogurt fish she cooked. She is annoyed because he filled his belly with store-bought biryani. But he is a man! He is a man with bigger capacities than eating the dinner she cooks.

"Well," he says in as calm a voice as he can manage. It is easier in the dark. "Why are you getting worried? I just went to one rally."

She slides back into bed, her silence thick. "You went to two," she says finally. After a pause, she speaks again. "Please, I ask you," she says, "don't go to more rally shally."

PT Sir thinks about this for hours, until deep night has settled into the home, turning their furniture unfamiliar, amplifying a squeak here, a knock there. Somewhere a clock ticks. Far away, an ambulance siren sounds.

JIVAN

This visiting day, seated on a bench waiting for me, is not my mother but a man. He has a beard and a cloth bag in his lap. At his feet, a plastic sack, which he lifts and hands to me. His soft fingers against mine are a shock.

The bag is heavy. Inside, I see a bunch of bananas and a packet of cookies.

"You are . . ." I say.

"Purnendu," he says, with no hi or hello. He is gentle, gentler than any reporter I have encountered. "How is your health?" he asks me.

"Fine," I tell him. I look again inside the bag, at the perfectly yellow bananas, no bruises on them that I can see. I want to eat them all, right now.

"Sit," he suggests when I remain standing.

"You are not allowed to take notes," I say, pointing at the pen in his fingers. "Didn't they tell you that?"

"Oh," he says, looking down at the pen in his hand, as if he has just noticed it. He puts it on the bench between us. "Then this is useless," he says, smiling. There is a joke in his words that I don't catch. Is it a pen or . . .?

"Please don't do anything so that they will kick you out," I say. "I want to tell you everything, if you promise to print the truth. The other newspapers are printing rubbish, lies, they know nothing about my story—"

"That's what I do," he says. "Report the truth. That's why I'm here."

He glances at the clock on the wall. The guard on duty stands in a far corner and looks at us.

"Tell me your story," says Purnendu.

————

When I was a child, I lived—

Believe me when I say you must understand my childhood to know who I am and why this is happening to me.

"Tell me one thing first," says Purnendu. "Did you do it?"

I lick my lips. I try to look him in the eye. I shake my head.

————

In my village, the dust of coal settled in the nooks of our ears and, when we blew our noses, it came out black. There were no cows or crops. There were only blasted pits into which my mother descended with a shovel, rising with a basket of black rock on her head.

"Did you see her working?" Purnendu asks.

"I watched her once," I tell him. "Never again."

It frightened me to see her as a worker. At night, I held

her palm in my palm. The lines in her hands—lifelines, they call them—were the only skin not blackened.

———

Many days I went to school for the free midday meal of lentils and rice. There were rumors that we would get chicken in the festival season. Somebody said they saw a man ride in the direction of our school on a bicycle weighted with chickens, their legs bound, hanging upside down from the handlebars, all those white hens silent and blinking at the receding path. But that hoped-for bicycle never arrived.

I sat in this class or that class. It did not matter. When the language teacher reappeared after a long absence for her wedding, she chewed a paan stuffed with lime and betel nut and told us to write our names on the tests. One day, she reminded us, "Stick five rupees to the page if you can."

She would fill in the rest of the test if we did.

Soon, only goats were going to school, leaving pellets on the porch.

———

"Tell me," I say. "How does this sound to you? What kind of start did I get in life?"

Purnendu looks at me and smiles sadly. "Such is our country," he says.

———

Then the policemen came to evict us. The company wanted to mine the land on which we lived, rich with coal. Why should the company let some poor people sit and bathe and sleep on top of vast sums of money?

For a week, we had saved our shits in plastic bags, which we twirled closed, and our urine in soda bottles we capped tight, to make what my mother and father called bombs. The rickshaw Ba occasionally drove, ferrying mine workers, stood outside, its accordion roof folded, blue seat gleaming, and I prayed for mercy—where could he hide a rickshaw?

We waited in our huts, tarp snapping in the wind, our throats parched but nobody willing to leave their house to go to the municipal tap.

The policemen were late.

When they came, they came holding bamboo sticks, followed by the rumble of bulldozers, whose treads I watched, frightened. Mother slapped my head and said, "What are you looking at with your mouth open? Can't you hear I'm calling?"

Hit me again, Mother, I think now. I will bear it like a blessing.

I rubbed my head and unscrewed my soda bottle a little, so that the cap would fly off midair and spatter the policemen. I threw my urine bombs at them, traces of liquid on my fingers. I untwisted the plastic bags and

77

threw the hard and dry cakes of shit, the dust of our own waste making us sneeze.

The policemen laughed at our poor weaponry. Their bellies, hanging over their belts, quivered. They swung methodically with their bamboo rods, bringing down our asbestos and tarp roofs. They grunted and yelled with the exertion. One gentle policeman lined up the glinting sheets of asbestos against a naked wall, as if somebody would come to collect them.

Soon our houses were exposed to the sun, all lime walls and cracked corners. They looked like we had never lived in them at all.

The sight of our houses, so easily broken, startled me. I knew it would happen, but like this? Kitchens in which we had eaten before a flickering kerosene lamp, rooms in which we had combed each other's hair, all roofless, soon to be crushed into a heap of brick.

News of our bombs had reached the police station and new policemen arrived, this time wearing helmets and carrying shields of cane, which looked like the backs of chairs, meant to deflect knives and stones. They had heard "bombs," they were expecting bombs, and they were angry. But we had no real weapons. We had our bodies and our voices, our saved waste long gone.

When a policeman raised his bamboo stick to strike my mother, she screamed and threw herself at him, her voice strangled and soaring at once, her sari unfurling into the mud and shit at our feet, loose blouse slipping off her shoulders, her face black with rage.

"Leave our houses alone," she screamed. "Where will we live?"

Until then, I had naively believed another home would materialize, but in my mother's transformation I saw the truth: we had nowhere to go.

Another policeman held her legs and began dragging her and I watched in horror until I felt my arms rise and push him away, striking his face so that his spectacles fell and were trampled. My mother scrambled up and retreated, screaming curses until her voice snapped, the thread of it drifting down. In the meantime, somebody had smashed my father's rickshaw. I looked, uncomprehending, at the bent wheels and slashed seat, my father kneeling to reattach, futilely, the cycle chain to the ruined vehicle.

The houses fell. Walls and roofs of our shelter turned enemy, wreckage coming down on our heads, the rising dust making us cough, paint and brick in heaps on the ground. The policemen, finally calm, bamboo limp by their sides, looked frightened. Maybe the houses looked too much like their own. In the end, one policeman pleaded with us, "Orders came from above, sister, what will I do?"

———

"Time, time," calls a guard. She strides about the room, striking each bench with a stick. Our hour is over.

My brother, Purnendu, stands up and lifts the cloth bag on his shoulder.

"Next week," he says, "and the week after that and the week after that, for as long as it takes."

His words play in my ears with the sweetness of a flute. I watch him go, past a door, which magically opens for him, and I turn back. Inside, a woman beats her head on the wall. Once, I might have felt that way too, but now I don't. Now I float beside her, her scrape only hers, not mine. I am on my way out. As soon as the newspaper publishes my story, the door will begin to open for me. Where public feeling goes, the court follows. Freedom will result not from boxes of papers and fights over legality, but from a national outcry.

I walk past the woman striking her head. A guard appears and tells the woman, in a tone of boredom, to stop striking her head.

"What are you doing?" the guard drones. "Stop it right now."

The woman pauses, turns, and strikes the guard with her head.

"Ooh!" gasps the corridor.

The woman is taken away, screaming, for something they will call treatment.

INTERLUDE

A Policeman Fired for Excessive Violence
During Slum Demolition Has a New Gig

"Highway." You see, this is a fancy word. This road is just a road. It runs straight through the forest. It is paved and in the rains it is potholed. You see the mounds of red soil? Termite hills. There used to be deer, but we haven't seen any all year. So my friends and I, we come usually at night, yes, regularly at night. Ten o'clock, eleven o'clock. After our women and children have gone to sleep.

Me, personally, after I lost my job after that cursed slum demolition, more than a decade ago, I never got a job again. I do some of this, some of that. Some transportation business. Some import-export. Some middleman fees. That's how I manage.

These days, as I was saying, my friends and I come to this highway and we park in our cars by the side and wait. One time, a poor old villager, maybe the village guard, came tottering up to us saying, "What, son, did your car have a breakdown?"

We laughed. "Grandpa," we said. "Have you seen this car? It's from foreign! It doesn't break down!

"You go," we said to him, "go back to sleep. Go."

The old man understood and went away or else some of our younger brothers were just itching to use their cutlasses for something other than cutting weeds, you know what I am saying?

Gradually a truck came. It had one of the major signs of cow transportation—some liquid dripping from the back. Now it could be water, okay. But really? It could also be cow urine. It could mean there are cows on that truck, holy mother cows being taken to slaughter by some bastards. We made it our job to stop the slaughter. If we don't defend our nation, our way of life, our holy cow, who will? We waved our flashlights and the driver stopped.

When the truck stopped, our men went around to the sides and hit the truck, *bang bang bang*, so that any cows inside would move. That's how we would know if that truck was carrying cows. We heard nothing. Meanwhile, in front, the driver was yelling, "What are you all doing? This truck has only potatoes! I am taking potatoes to cold storage!"

"So what is the water?" challenged one of our men, holding his cutlass by his side.

"It rained!" shouted the driver. "It didn't rain here?"

Turned out, he was telling the truth. So we let that truck go.

We are moral men. We are principled men.

But let me tell you, there are persons who don't have

any respect for our nation. They don't have any respect for mother cow and they attack her for beef, for leather, all sorts of disgusting things. There is really no place for such persons in our society, don't you think so?

PT SIR

Early in the morning on Republic Day, a haze of pollution softens the skyline and children stand sleepy-eyed before the national flag, singing the anthem. Teachers watching the show hold handkerchiefs on their noses to ward off smog and chill.

When it is time for the students' parade, PT Sir walks down the line of schoolgirls, reminding them to swing their arms high, to beware of limp salutes. He inspects their uniforms: their white shoes are clean, their fingernails are clipped. He is almost done with his final check when there is a murmur of activity at the school gate. Somebody has arrived.

Leading a small group of people, the principal shows the way to somebody who follows. Then PT Sir sees a familiar saffron scarf hanging loosely about the neck of a woman in a white sari. Bimala Pal shushes his exclamations.

"I had work right next door, I will only stay for two minutes," she says.

A student promptly unfolds a chair in the front and a few more for the assistants and bodyguards who follow.

Another student is dispatched to buy tea and freshly cooked shingara, pastry filled with spiced potatoes and peas. The principal, too flustered to look for the petty cash box, hands the student money from her own purse.

Bimala Pal protests, "Please, nothing special for me. I have just come to visit, even though your sir did not invite me!"

At this, she looks at him, teasing.

PT Sir bites the tip of his tongue and shakes his head. "How would I invite you to such a humble event?" he says.

Rows of teachers and students gape at the VIP visitor, while her bodyguards stand as a wall behind her, sunglasses on their noses, declining the plastic chairs procured for them.

Now, with Bimala Pal seated and a dish of shingara in front of her, an earthen cup of milk tea at her feet, the principal offers, "PT Sir is one of our most valued teachers."

PT Sir looks at her, amazed.

"He is beloved by the students," the principal continues. "Really, it is his hard work that has made this ceremony come together."

PT Sir smiles graciously at the lies, then turns away to help the students begin the parade. The girls march in single file, their knees rising higher at the sight of Bimala Pal, their voices crisply calling out the beat, "One-two-one! One-two-one!"

PT Sir watches as the playground fills with his students. His back is straight as a rod, a pen smartly tucked into his shirt pocket, his chin held a little higher.

―――

At home, PT Sir's wife offers him a paneer kebab, cooked on the stovetop.

"Don't make that face," she says. "Paneer is good for you. With your cholesterol, you should be eating less meat."

So he eats the cubes. They are a bit dry.

"You can't make proper kebab without a tandoor," responds his wife, miffed. "Don't eat it then."

But he eats. While he eats, he tells her the story of Bimala Pal's visit. How the Jana Kalyan Party's second-in-command came to *his* school to see *his* ceremony.

"You are so easily flattered!" his wife says. "She was coming to see where the terrorist went to school. What else did you think?"

―――

Only a few weeks after PT Sir's ego is thus punctured, he comes home from school to find a letter in the mailbox. Inside, on the sofa, when he tears the edge open, he sees an invitation on Jana Kalyan Party letterhead. He jumps up and waves it before his wife, who is seated at the dining table, tucking cheese inside slit chicken breasts.

"Look what has come!" he says. "How did they find my address?"

His wife wipes her hand on her kameez and takes the letter in hand.

"They have their ways," she says with a smile.

To go to this special event, which will be held on a Monday, PT Sir requests a half day off from school.

On the given date, PT Sir rides a train, then a rickshaw, to the Kolabagan slum. He holds his small leather bag on his lap as the rickshaw descends from the main road into the lanes of the slum, jerking and bouncing over potholes, crossing buildings of brick, then half-brick, then tin and tarp. Jivan lived nearby, he knows, so he observes the surroundings all the more keenly. At a corner, before a municipal pump where water spills, men with checkered cloths wrapped around their waists rub their torsos with soap, their heads white with froth and their eyes closed to the street. The rickshaw moves on, the driver's legs pumping. On a rickety bench before a tea shop, customers sitting with ankle resting on knee and drinking from small glasses in their hands look at PT Sir as he passes by.

When the rickshaw deposits PT Sir at his destination, he finds a crowd gathered in front of a primary school. Damaged in the attack at the railway station nearby, the school building has been renovated over the past months and is being reopened with great ceremony by the Jana Kalyan Party. The school is no more than a five-room shed. Murals on the exterior walls show a lion, a zebra, and a giraffe strolling alongside a herd of rabbits. A sun with a mane like a lion's smiles at them all. A civic-minded artist has included, low to the ground, an instruction to passersby: *Do not urinate.*

There are children here. The students, presumably.

They hold stick brooms and sweep the grounds around the school building. Bent over like that, one hand on knee, the other on the handle of a broom, sweeping dust from dust—the children's posture is that of service. It moves PT Sir. This is what a school ought to teach, he thinks. How come his school doesn't instill such feeling in the students?

When a party assistant arrives, he recognizes PT Sir, thumping him on the back and asking how the school building looks. PT Sir says, "First class!"

"Have you seen inside?" the assistant asks. The two of them walk up to the door and peep in.

There is a vacant room. It looks incomplete, until PT Sir realizes there will be no benches here, no chairs. The children are used to sitting on the ground. Probably they will share one textbook, photocopied to death. After the first wave of donated supplies runs out, the children will write with pencil nubs chewed and sucked.

Still they will come to school.

"And look at my own students," PT Sir shares. "They are fed and clothed and schooled, given every convenience and comfort."

"My son," agrees the assistant, "goes to extra coaching for every subject. English, maths, chemistry, everything. I think, what are they teaching him at school? If they are not teaching him the subjects, are they teaching him manners, loyalty to the country, et cetera, et cetera? No!"

The two men pause when a box of sweets comes around.

"Take my students," says PT Sir. "Will they ever sweep the school grounds? Will they ever paint a beautiful mural like this? Never! Because they"—and here he pauses to chew his sweet—"are trying their level best to flee the country. They work so hard on applications to American universities that they ignore the school exams, failing and crying and pleading—they had SAT I! They had SAT II! What are these nonsense exams? Why will the school allow such brain drain?"

The party man listens intently. When he is done with his sweet, he claps crumbs off his hands, then clasps his hands behind his back like a diligent schoolboy. "The problem, you see," he joins in, "is we teach our children many things, but not national feeling! There is a scarcity of patriotic feeling, don't you think so? In our generation, we knew our schooling was to . . . was to . . ."

"Serve others," offers PT Sir. "Improve the nation."

"Exactly!"

The thought stays with him when he returns to his school. The girls run a simple relay race. They huff and puff, carrying a stick in their hands, and afterward lean on their knees to catch their breath. They high-five and laugh so loud a teacher from the third floor emerges to give them a stern look.

What is the meaning of such an education? PT Sir thinks as he walks down the lane at the end of the day. Around him, girls suck ice candies and call with orange mouths, "Good afternoon, sir!"

JIVAN

The next time Purnendu comes, I try to see everything the way he must see it. The guard's pacing and the stench of sweat which rises off her. The benches around us where visitors and inmates sit, a third person's worth of space between them. The instructions painted on the wall:

Please hand all home-cooked food to prison personnel
Please no body contact
Be respectful and talk at low volume
Any cell phone or camera will be confiscated

"Have you printed the first part of my story?" I demand.

Once more, he has placed that useless pen on the bench between us. The guard has seen it, but, whatever it is, she does not want to deal with it.

Purnendu smiles. "We have hardly begun! Once we have the full story, my editor will help me—"

"Why do you need some editor?" I charge. Then I try to be polite. "I need this story printed. I am telling it to you in order, arranged nicely, exactly how things happened. Just print it. You have to do it quickly, don't you understand?"

Purnendu looks at me and pats my hand, on the bench.

How soft his fingertips. I wish he would keep them there, on the bony back of my hand, where my knuckles sprout hairs.

"It doesn't work like that. We want the public to see the full story, beginning to end, rather than leaking a piece here, a piece there. Do you trust me?"

———

The morning after the eviction, when we woke up in a displeased aunt's house in the neighboring village, my father complained of "a little pain." His neck was held stiff, his whole body turning when he looked this way and that. This new village bordered a site at which garbage was burned. The rot and smoke made us all feel sick. But my father, I could see, was injured, perhaps from a policeman's blow.

My mother, her own bones sore, lay quietly in bed, saying nothing. I took charge, suddenly my parents' parent, and took my father to a doctor who, the aunt told us, was part of a clinic at a district government hospital. There the doctor saw the poor and the illiterate for no more than a flat fee of twenty rupees.

The hospital compound looked like a village in itself. Under the trees, on the porch, every spot of shade was taken by a family. Each family surrounded a patient who lay, moaning or blank-faced, on unfolded leaves of newspaper. My father walked straight past them, looking ahead and nowhere else. Into the hospital building we went and I filled out a form and paid twenty rupees. Then we sat in a room, under a ceiling fan whose blades were so weighted with cottony dust that they barely moved. My father held a gentle hand to his shoulder, not rubbing it, but seeking to soothe it in some way that was beyond him. Finally the doctor called us, "Patient party? Where is the patient?"

"He," I began, calling my father by the respectful pronoun, "he has a lot of pain in his shoulder." We scrambled into the tiny chamber and sat in two chairs, both with woven seats on the verge of tearing from the weight of hundreds of patients over the years. On the wall fluttered a calendar with pictures of pink-cheeked babies. "Please see what happened to his shoulder," I said.

My father looked at the doctor, his eyes glistening with tears he would not release.

"Fell or what?" said the doctor, looking at us over his spectacles.

"No, they hit him," I said.

Immediately, as the doctor asked, "Who hit him?" my father spoke up.

"Somebody on the road," my father said, with a small smile. "Who knows? It doesn't matter. I am only here for some medicine. I couldn't sleep last night because of the—"

My father cried in pain. The doctor had reached over and was laying cold fingertips on my father's upper back, pressing at various points. My father, whose calves had carried three people at once up slopes in his rickshaw. My father, whose back leaned forward in strength as he pedaled, up and down, up and down, for twenty-five rupees per ride. A tense silence descended on the room.

I grew angry—why wasn't my father telling the doctor the police did it? Catch the police! Put them in jail for hurting him like that! How would he drive the rickshaw again with such pain?

Now I understand his silence. Now I know his reluctance.

The doctor stopped his examination and spoke in an irritated tone. "You could have gone to a general physician and had an X-ray first, why didn't you do that? I can't give you anything except this painkiller when you have come like this, with no test. Maybe the bone here is broken, but maybe not. How can I tell? You are not letting me touch the place, saying, 'Oo aa, I am in pain.' Go get the X-ray first—"

"Yes, yes, sir," my father said, timid. "Can you write it down, please, the X-ray place where I should go—"

"Do you know how to read?" the doctor demanded.

"My daughter knows," said my father. Even in his pain, he looked at me and smiled with pride.

———

When I return to my cell, it smells like flowers. Americandi is surrounded by five or six others, including Yashwi, who is spraying something from a bottle.

I sneeze.

"Not in your armpit!" Americandi scolds her. "You

don't even know *how* to put perfume. Like this," she says, "watch me."

Americandi turns her chin up and tilts the bottle at her neck. Striated with lines, a column wobbly with fat, her neck newly glistens with a patch of scent.

"Like this," she says once more, now holding a delicate wrist upturned. "You have to put it on the places where your blood is beating."

"Then why aren't you putting it on your chest?" someone challenges her.

"I wish we had a party!" Kalkidi moans. "Don't we smell so nice?"

"Smell it," Americandi demands when she sees me. She hands me the bottle. "Pure rose and . . . and . . . !" She thinks for a moment. "Some other things. Doesn't it smell costly? Even Twinkle Khanna wears this perfume."

I wipe my nose with the back of my hand and sniff the air around me. It smells like roses and chemicals. It smells like a disguise. Beneath it, there is sewage and damp and washed clothes hung to dry. There is indigestion and belching and the odor of feet.

For a moment, I wonder how Americandi has the means to buy expensive perfume. Then, of course, I know.

On the floor, I see a thick new mattress. On top, folded, are a soft blanket and clean sheets. Now I hear the crinkle of paper behind me and turn to see Kalkidi holding a bar of Cadbury chocolate. Americandi holds up a dozen more bars.

"For the children!" she says and a mother looks like she will cry.

Her purchases agitate me. I could have bought a few things for myself. Oils and soaps, some cream biscuits to eat. A better mattress, a sheet with polka dots. I could have given most of it to Ma and Ba. Ba's medicines are not cheap. What have I done?

Late into the night I think about this, regret raising its head like a snake in the bushes. Is one story in a newspaper going to persuade anyone?

LOVELY

One morning, on the way to a blessing ceremony in a nearby village, the boys in front of the tailor's shop are staring, so I am teasing: "You want to visit my bed, just tell me!"

They are ashamed and giggling at the floor, holding scissors in their hands.

In this life, everybody is knowing how to give me shame. So I am learning how to reflect shame back on them also.

At this pre-marriage party, where we are coming to bless and earn money that way, we are climbing up to a roof where, under one old towel drying on a string, there is an old woman, the bride's grandma. With her knees folded on the ground, she is pumping air into an old harmonium and playing the keys, which are the color of elephant tusks. The thin gold bangles on her arms are clinking softly as she is pumping and playing, pumping and playing. In the gentle winter sun, in the breeze, I am seeing her as a young woman, learning to play harmonium. The morning is softening for me.

Then Arjuni Ma is singing and I am stepping in the center and loosening my shoulders, pinching a bit of sari in my left hand, to lift the hem away from the ground, and with my right hand making stars and suns in the air. Arjuni Ma is singing an old romantic classic. I am turning this way and that way and with my turns my sari is flowing like a stream, catching the light. I am using my eyes to match the expressions in the song, I am really "emoting," as Mr. Debnath would say. Now my eyes are loving, now they are seducing, now they are looking shyly at the ground, as if Azad is sitting right here too among the women. Since I was telling him to marry a woman, he is not coming to see me even one time. What a mistake! I was thinking I would be feeling noble, but no, I am only feeling sad.

Though this is a private ceremony, some donkey villagers are standing in the doorway, spilling down the stairs, laughing and pointing, taking pictures of me with their mobile phones. What can I be doing? This is my job, to perform.

The bride-to-be is shyly sitting on the ground, looking at the dancing. She is wrapped in a starched yellow sari and eating peeled cucumber dipped in pink salt.

When I am getting tired of dancing and sweat is starting to pour down my back, I am bending and taking the bride's chin in my hands, saying, "God keep this beautiful girl in rice and gold."

Finally the mother of the bride, who is standing in the doorway, is seeing me admiring the girl's looks and she is complaining, "This girl is getting so dark! You tell her, please. She is always riding her bicycle in the hot sun, no umbrella, no nothing."

So I am giving the bride a sideways look and saying, "Why, child? Now you put some yogurt and lemon on that face! Look at me, dark and ugly, do you think anybody wants to marry me?"

"Yes!" the girl's mother is saying. "Are you listening? Listen to her. She is telling you these things from experience. It is for your own good."

So this is how my job is. You can be making fun of me, but, tell me, can you be doing this job?

PT SIR

"More anti-national statements have been uncovered," shouts a reporter standing at the Kolabagan railway station, "after the *Your News, Your Views* team studied Jivan's Facebook page. She posted seditious statements, no doubt testing whether—"

PT Sir's wife picks up the remote and lowers the volume.

"This student of yours!" she complains. "This case will go on for ever. You went to the police, you did your part. When did we last do something fun?"

So, after dinner, PT Sir and his wife leave the house and walk to the local video rental shop, a one-room operation called Dinesh Electronics. Inside, before shelves of lightbulbs and wires, the owner sits viewing his own stock, surreptitiously stored on tiny USB sticks, no bigger than half a thumb. These recordings of the newest movies he rents out.

"Try this one, sister," he suggests to PT Sir's wife. *"Something Happens in My Heart When I See Her*! In demand this week, I just got it back from a customer. New actress in it, Rani Sarawagi. And filmed fully in Switzerland!"

PT Sir's wife accepts the USB stick and tucks it in her purse. Outside, the air smells of fried food. A vendor dips lentil balls in a dark wok filled with oil and sells paper bowls full, alongside a cilantro and green chili chutney. Next to him, a shoe repairman works under the thin light of a bulb, gluing a separated sole.

The sidewalk is cracked and uneven, so PT Sir and his wife keep to the edge of the road, near the dry gutter, as they walk. Headlights of cars approach and swerve by. Often there is no space to walk side by side.

———

When the end credits roll across the TV screen, PT Sir shares his big news of the day.

"Oh, I almost forgot!" he feigns.

His wife looks at him, smiling from the romantic closing of the film, where the hero and the heroine found their way to each other and embraced on an Alpine meadow.

"I got a lunch invitation," PT Sir says. "Bimala Pal invited me to her house."

He speaks calmly. But he is aware that his heart is beating a little fast. The sleep has fled his eyes.

"Bimala Pal?" says his wife, surprised. "Lunch at her *house*? Why, what does she want?"

PT Sir braces himself. His wife will, no doubt, caution him against going. So far, she has said nothing about the school inauguration, for which he took a half day off work, but—

She laughs. "Look at you," she says. "First she comes to your school, now this. Maybe she really likes you!"

PT Sir smiles, relieved.

"Remember to take a box of nice sweets," she tells him, "not those cheap sweets you eat."

JIVAN

In the middle of TV hour, when the room is louder with our commentary than television, Uma madam appears, showily eating a pear.

"You." She points at me with the bitten pear. "Somebody to see you."

I jump up. My back seizes, a shock traveling up and down my spine. Clutching a hand to it, I make my way to the visiting room, where the lawyer Gobind waits.

"Where did you go?" I demand. "Every time I try to call you, I stand in line for half an hour, pay so much money to call, and then your assistant picks up—"

He holds both hands up. "I have seventy-four cases on my desk," he says. "I can't sit around waiting for your call. Anyway, I am doing the work, aren't I? I contacted the leader of your Lovely's hijra group. Her name is Arjuni. Do you know her?"

I shake my head.

"She told me that Lovely left," he says.

"What?"

"She said that Lovely went to her native village—"

"Where is that?"

"In the north. She doesn't know exactly."

I look at him for a long while. He coughs into a fist and says, "Want to tell me anything?"

"You think I'm lying?" I say. "That leader is lying. *You* are lying, for all I know! Did you even look for Lovely or do you think she is an imaginary character I have made up?"

I lower my voice. "I will tell my mother to go find Lovely. I am sure she is here. She never mentioned any village to me. She will come testify if I ask her. She will tell them that I was teaching her, that the parcel I was carrying was books for her."

"Try," sighs Gobind.

INTERLUDE

Gobind Visits a Spiritual Guru

By Friday at lunchtime, my office irritates me. There is no painless way to arrange my belly before my desk. The termite tracks on the wall seem to grow every time I look away. My assistant treats his hoarse cough by smoking cigarettes with greater devotion. When the phone rings, it is my daughter's school saying my daughter has been suspended for breaking a fellow student's spectacles. I call her mother. Her mother will pick her up. I have too much work.

Days like this, only one thing helps. I visit my guru. My guru, my spiritual leader, is in her seventies and lives on the ground floor of a house where the door is always open. Her living room has idols of gods on all surfaces. It smells of morning flowers. She does not eat meat, does not leave her house, does not watch TV. Once, I saw an iPad on her lap, but she put it away. She meditates. Her only bad habit is she feeds stray dogs.

"I thought you would come today, child," she says,

looking up from petting a tan stray. The dog barks. I hold my arms up as the dog jumps on my knees. I don't like dogs. My guru calls the dog away and instantly it settles at her feet and looks at me.

"I saw some clouds in your life," my guru says. "But clouds pass."

A glass of water appears in front of me and I tell her everything. I even tell her what I was not planning to reveal. My wife is upset with me. She thinks I spend too much money on my guru's recommendations—an onyx ring one day, a smoky quartz another day. But a garnet worn on the left pinky helped me win my first case. I am sure of it. A white coral, which is in fact red, helped me avoid a deadly accident on my regular route home, when a tree fell on top of a taxi in front of me. I have worn a green tourmaline close to my chest, I have worn a moonstone. The day I began wearing a golden citrine, a frightening medical test came back benign. Don't tell me there's nothing here. The world is made up of negativity, problems, hassles—trust me, a lawyer knows—and gemstones bring good energy.

I have sixty to eighty cases at any time. A big case like Jivan's means nothing but more misery— a dozen press people hounding me at all hours, pressure from all political parties, daily communication with police chiefs trying to hide their inept investigations. No matter the result, there will be plenty of people upset with me. It is trouble. The sooner it ends, the better for me.

"Will it end soon?" I ask. "It's too much."

My guru tells me yes, it will, but—she pauses.

"Your role," she says with a gentle smile, "will be bigger than you can see at the moment."

"In a good way?" I ask.

"In a good way," she says. "When paths show themselves, don't be afraid to follow them."

And I feel lifted on a wave and placed on a shore. I get up. I should call my wife, I think. Check how my daughter is handling her suspension. I need to get back to my office before the assistant turns it into an ashtray. On the road, I will eat an egg roll.

"Your wife may not support my suggestion," my guru says, "but I am getting a strong feeling that one thing will be especially valuable for you during this time. For your right index finger"—and here she holds up the finger she means—"an amethyst."

JIVAN

Purnendu has brought me a string of shampoo sachets, clothesline clips, and elastic hair bands. I hold the gifts in my lap. They are currency.

"Thanks," I say to him in English, so that he knows, even while he gives me products with which I will clean myself and groom myself, that I can be his equal.

———

We resettled in government housing in a town, fifty kilometers away from our village, with nothing in it but buildings whose walls were plump with damp, whose sewage flowed in open gutters, whose taps coughed rusty water. But it was my first and only time living in an apartment building and I was proud of my residence.

I heard the neighbor boy, fellow evicted, stomp down the stairs every evening. I watched, from the window, as he emerged into the lane, where a cohort gathered to play cricket. A plank of plywood served as a bat and the fielders chased a hollow plastic ball. They were my age. My limbs itched to play with them, to scream and run and skid on the small pebbles of the street, now that my known fields were gone. My mother said no.

I was a girl. I stayed home to watch my father, while my mother left at dawn and returned in the evening, seeking daily labor. A few days she was employed on construction projects, but, after that, the jobs ran out.

Then my mother cooked, hidden in the kitchen. An atmosphere of smoke and chili about her deterred conversation.

One night, I heard her and my father.

"Where is the work?" my mother said. "Everybody here is resettled like us. Who will hire me?"

"Wait a few days," said my father. "I will take a loan to buy a new rickshaw."

"Another rickshaw," my mother mocked. "Who will ride your rickshaw in this cursed town?"

I was ashamed to hear everything. I was ashamed to see my mother sinking into this gray mood.

I crept up on her one day as she was cooking.

"Bhow!" I said behind her. She jumped and smacked at my legs, but I escaped. From the doorway I said, in a monster's deep voice, "Ow mow khow! I smell some human chow!"

I crept closer, allowing my mother to take another swipe at my legs, to trap me this time, but she did not try.

———

So that is how I grew up, you see, Purnendu. When Ba's turn in the X-ray came, I took him. We took a bus, which sped down the highway, horn blasting, and brought us to an air-conditioned clinic. I gave a look to a woman until she moved her bag, so that Ba could take the chair. The woman's arms were white and plump. Diamonds sparkled on her fingers. Her feet were wrapped in the crisscrossing strings of a leather sandal and her toenails were painted pink. They looked like lozenges. She looked at us. I slid one cracked and soiled foot behind the other.

In a dark room, a technician positioned Ba against a cold glass plate, then disappeared. Ba flinched.

"Stand still!" scolded the technician, from a chamber we could not see. "Stand straight!"

But the X-ray man could not make the picture. He came out, irritated.

"What's the matter?" he said.

Ba rubbed his bare skin, chilled. Still he smiled as a way of asking forgiveness. "It's cold—"

"The plate is *supposed* to be cold!" said the X-ray man. "You have to stand firm, touching it, that's what I *told* you. I can't do my work with these unschooled people—"

Afterward I held the large envelope in my hand, within it a ghostly image of Ba's back and shoulders. I carried it home, like a parent carrying their child's schoolbag, the weight too heavy for the young one to bear.

At home, I began to show Ma the scan, but she shouted, "Put it back, put it back! You can't look at these things without a special light or it will be ruined. Fool child."

Was that right? I did what she said.

"X-ray today, then something else tomorrow," said my mother. "Wait and see, that doctor will keep you running around. That's what doctors do. They get paid to make you do tests and buy medicines, don't you know that? Where will we get the money?"

My father sat on the bed and, keeping his neck stiff, swung his legs up. He listened to my mother.

But I knew something was wrong. If I did nothing, Ba would suffer. At least, we had to show the X-ray plates to the doctor.

A rickshaw-driver friend of Ba's gave us his service one morning, rolling gently over the potholes that led out of the block of apartment buildings and on to the main road. Ba's eyes filled with water. He arrived at the hospital, defeated by the ride.

"Hmm," said the doctor, after we had waited for three hours and Ba had nearly fallen and broken one more bone while going to the slippery toilet. "The bone *is* broken, do you see here?"

He pointed a pen at the ghostly image.

"But there is a more serious problem," he continued. "This disk has been affected and that is serious. He needs absolute bed rest, otherwise there will be a chance of paralysis. And I see he is in pain, so he needs stronger medicines. Take this twice a day, with food."

"I *said* he was in pain," I complained, leaning forward in my chair. "He has been in pain since we first came to see you."

"Listen, why are you being so agitated?" The doctor put down his pen and glared at me. "For some people, an ant's bite is also serious pain."

Then he continued writing in his prescription book. In a penholder, a pen printed with the name of a pharmaceutical company shined.

"And what about the rickshaw, Doctor Shaheb?" my father asked. "I have to go back to work soon."

"Work?" said the doctor. "Be patient, mister. It's enough that you walked in here on your own. You can't drive a rickshaw any time soon."

———

After weeks of running to a municipal tube well early every morning and carrying water up five flights of stairs, Ma and I began going to the water board office, complaining about the rust-colored water spat out by the taps.

At the water office, a man with a ring of hair surrounding a bald head waved us away—he had begun to recognize us—as soon as we approached.

"Later, come later," he said. "I told you I can't do anything about the water in two–three days."

"Sir, we came seven–ten days ago."

"Is that so?" he said. "Now you know my schedule better than me?"

"We still don't have clean water, sir," said my mother, "and they said that by July—"

"Who said?" charged the man, pausing in the chewing

of gum. *"Who* said such things? July, August, am I in charge of carrying the water from here to your house?"

Ma said nothing and I felt like a small child next to her, though I was as much a grown-up as anybody in that office.

It was too much. "Sir, actually," I said, "you told us last time that the water supply would be fixed soon. My father is sick. He can't climb down five flights of stairs to the municipal tap for his baths." My cheeks were hot. My voice was hoarse. "Please do something, sir."

The man stared at me, eyes bulging, before picking up a phone.

"Yes, good morning," he said softly into the phone, a polite professional. "What happened to the work order for the water pipes . . ." He went on in this way, while we stood and looked at him. I was delighted, though the only expression I could wear was one of pleading.

Three days later, when the taps in our building deposited clean water into our buckets, my mother told everyone it was all my doing.

"Jivan spoke to the water supply man," she recounted to the neighbors. "Oh, you should have seen her!"

Later, in the quiet of the kitchen after we had eaten, she said to me, "The system doesn't always work for us. But you see that now and then you can make good things happen for yourself."

And I thought, only *now and then*? I thought I would have a better life than that.

PT SIR

A politician's house is marked by an atmosphere like a fair at all times. Feet from the door, reporters wait idly, smoking cigarettes and tossing them in the gutter. Clerks and lackeys keep an eye on those coming and going, occasionally stopping to chat with this or that person. Citizens with grievances arrive, holding folders. Less frequently arrive packages, sometimes a bouquet or a gift basket of dried fruit. Down the road, policemen assigned to the politician wait inside a vehicle. They sit, rifles strapped to their backs, the doors open for air.

On the porch, where PT Sir takes off his shoes, grateful for his clean socks, an assistant asks him: "You have an appointment?"

"No, I mean," says PT Sir, "I got a lunch invitation, so—"

"Oh," says the assistant, opening the door. "You are the teacher."

The house is ordinary. Apart from a few framed photographs of parents and grandparents, garlanded by fragrant white flowers, the walls are bare. Two sofas, with rather regal upholstery, face each other and beyond them stands a dining table with six chairs. The floor is laid with flecked tiles, as in any middle-class home. Some of the tiles are cracked.

PT Sir stands on this cold floor in socked feet, unsure of himself, until Bimala Pal emerges from an inner office. She invites him to sit at the dining table, whose plywood surface is covered by a plastic cloth, which mimics lace. Dishes appear from the kitchen. The food is humble—rice, dal, and fried eggplant, followed by rui fish curry. When, PT Sir wonders, will Bimala Pal tell him why he has been invited? She seems unconcerned.

"Just yesterday I was in Bankura district," says Bimala Pal, "and you know what is happening there? The midday meal funds for schools are disappearing into the pockets of school administrators. Those children are getting rice full of stones, lentils cooked in a tiny bit of oil. I said . . ." The story ends with a student's grandmother crying with gratitude in Bimala Pal's embrace.

It is when their plates are almost clean that Bimala Pal says, "You must be thinking why I have asked to see you today."

PT Sir looks at her and her plate, where she has made a pile of fish bones, curved like miniature swords.

"You see, I have a small hassle on my hands," she says. "I was thinking maybe an educated man like yourself can help us with it."

PT Sir sees, through the open door, a dark figure in the sun, holding a baby. A clerk comes by and says, "Madam, the society of mothers who—"

"Coming, coming," says Bimala Pal.

"The engineers are also waiting—"

Bimala Pal nods and the clerk retreats.

There isn't much time.

"I will be honored to help you in any way," PT Sir finds himself saying. "Tell me, what can I do?"

——

So it is that, a few weeks later, PT Sir finds himself at the courthouse. The grand British-era building has received a new coat of brick-red paint. Surrounding the building is a large garden planted with rows of hibiscus and marigold. Even at the early morning hour, the grounds have an air of harried activity. Lawyers in black robes cross the yard. PT Sir lets himself be passed. Under a row of oak trees, typists sit before typewriters, beside them stacks of legal paper. Next to them, tea-samosa sellers, resting kettles and cups on the ground, engage in a brisk trade.

No one pays any attention to PT Sir, so nobody notices that he is sweating excessively, armpit patches spreading under the blazer he has worn. His left thumb twitches, a tremor that he has never had before. He hides the hand in his pocket.

Up he goes into the old courthouse, then down a long balcony, off which he can see, through doors left ajar, a library with ceiling fans turning at the top. He walks by warrens of lawyers' offices, stuffed with leaning towers of folders. PT Sir retrieves a handkerchief from his trousers' pocket and mops his damp forehead. Before courtroom A6, he taps a guard at a door, clears his throat, and says, "I am a witness."

Then he sits on a hard wooden bench, watching in anxiety as three other cases are swiftly brought before the judge and resolved.

Half an hour later, when PT Sir is called to the front of the courtroom, his throat is parched and, while his left thumb has stopped twitching, his right eyelid has taken up the tendency. He walks slowly, trying to project calm. He stands in a witness box and a clerk warns him not to lean on the railing. It wobbles.

Before him appears a lawyer wearing a wrinkled robe and summer sandals with chapped edges. PT Sir looks at those feet, then at the room of dozing men awaiting their own hearings.

Now Bimala Pal seems very far away, her influence no more than a gentle memory.

PT Sir wonders in a panic if he can get out of this.

Is there a way? Maybe he can fake a heart attack.

The lawyer asks him: *"Habyusinthisparson?"*

"Hmm?" says PT Sir. He coughs and clears his throat.

He has spoken. Can he fake a heart attack now?

The lawyer says it again and this time PT Sir understands what he is saying: "Have you seen this person?"

The lawyer indicates a man seated at a table in front. The man wears an oversize blue shirt with short sleeves that fall to his blackened elbows. Through his half-open mouth, PT Sir can see that his teeth are stained red.

PT Sir knows none of these men, not the man with the stained teeth, nor the lawyer, but his job, per Bimala Pal's assistant's instructions, is to say yes, he has come across that man. He saw that man fleeing after a hardware store near his school was robbed.

PT Sir has never seen this man before, of course, but he knows—he has been told—that this is a man who has robbed and stolen for a living, but never been caught. There has never been evidence, though his neighbors and friends all know the truth. It is true that he also belongs to the wrong religion, the minority religion that encourages the eating of beef, but that is a peripheral matter, according to Bimala Pal's assistant. The main issue is a robber has to be stopped. What decent man would object to participating in the execution of justice?

Now PT Sir has to speak or else faint. He must speak or else surrender all hope of moving up in life by Bimala Pal's grace.

So, with his cool, teacher's diction, his nicely combed hair, his button-down shirt and black blazer, never mind the damp armpits, he stands before that filthy-faced, rotten-toothed criminal and says, "Him, yes, that man, I saw him there. He was running in a direction away from the hardware store."

Then, with an exchange between the lawyer and the judge that PT Sir does not follow, the matter is over. The criminal is taken away by a policeman to pay a hefty fine or else go to jail. It is clear that he does not have the means to pay a fine. When he walks past PT Sir, the man looks at him closely, squinting as if he is missing his spectacles. PT Sir turns away. The clerk calls the case number for the next case; the lawyer vanishes; a different set of people approach the bench.

PT Sir strolls casually out of the courtroom, unbuttoning his blazer. His neck prickles as he anticipates how the lawyer will reappear and challenge him. He waits for the judge to call him into chambers and demand to know who he really is. As he passes by guards patrolling the courthouse grounds, he expects an arm to shoot out and bar his way.

But, in a moment, he is on the street, where nothing more distressing happens than this: a pigeon pecking at the ground takes flight and flaps away from him, its wings nearly brushing his face.

———

In the months following, when Bimala Pal's assistant calls PT Sir and gives him a case, he prepares by purchasing a tube of antiperspirant and applying the white gel in his armpits. He carries a bottle of water and sips from it. He goes to sleep early the night before. Perhaps it is these measures, but PT Sir finds, by his fourth time at the courthouse, that there is little that agitates him.

At the doors to the courtroom, the guard greets PT Sir familiarly.

"All well?" he says.

"All well," says PT Sir. "Has my case started yet?"

"Going a bit late today," the guard says. "Not to worry. You go sit in the canteen, I'll send someone to call you."

For the first time, as he wanders down the familiar corridor, past the law library and to the canteen, PT Sir wonders if the guard is paid by the party too. For that matter, how about the courtroom clerks and the judges and the lawyers? Not one of them has ever said: "This man is really something! Everywhere there is a robbery, a domestic problem, a fight between neighbors, this man happens to be walking by! Is he Batman or what?"

But now is not the time to think about such things.

An hour and a chicken cutlet later, PT Sir takes the stand, opposite a man in a check-patterned lungi, knotted below a thin, hard belly.

PT Sir says, "This is the man I saw on the road. He was eve-teasing a lady. Making some disgusting gestures. Don't ask me to repeat them." He puts his teeth on his tongue in a gesture of shame and shakes his head. "God knows what would have happened to the lady if I wasn't going that way."

The accused looks bewildered. He opens his mouth to speak and is reminded by the judge to be quiet.

———

This is how Bimala Pal explained it to him and this is how he explains it to his wife. All these cases are instances in which the police are one hundred and ten percent sure that the accused is guilty. They don't have that much evidence, is all. But the accused are known in their neighborhoods. They have reputations. Should these dangerous men return to the streets on a technicality? Much better to fill the gap with a witness and make sure the guilty party lands in jail.

PT Sir cannot disagree. It is true that there is a lot about life that the law misses. And it doesn't hurt that each assignment comes with a "gift," delivered to him every month by an assistant, perhaps the assistant's assistant, who drives to the house on a noisy motorcycle and offers a pristine white envelope.

LOVELY

Today, when Mr. Debnath is giving us a scene where we are having to express tears, many of us are looking concerned.

"I have heard," Rumeli is saying, "that on real sets they are using some burning eye drops—"

"Burning eye drops!" Mr. Debnath's voice is booming. He is seeing red.

"If you want to be a C-level actor you can use all those cheap things!" he is saying. "Real actors cry from the heart. Real actors are reaching into their own selves and not imagining a false sad moment, but returning to a true sad moment in their own life. That is how you are crying real tears in a made-up scene."

We are all nodding seriously then. Mr. Debnath is saying such deep things.

———

Until I was thirteen–fourteen years old, I was living with my parents, who were both working in the local post office, and my grandparents, two uncles, their wives and children, all of us stuffed in a four-room apartment with a small balcony where we were sprinkling puffed rice for sparrows to eat. We were neither rich, neither poor. Once a month, we were going to the movie theater after eating rice and egg at home. The popcorn counter was not existing for people like us.

In the outside world, I was wearing boy's shorts and a boy's haircut and playing cricket. But secretly, at home, I was trying lipstick. I was wearing my mother's saris once, twice, thrice. The fourth time, my uncles were persuading my father to kick me out of the house. "What dignity will we have with this unnatural boy in the household?" they were shouting. "Our children are normal, think about them!"

My cousins were hiding in a bedroom, peeping out at me with big eyes.

My mother was fighting to keep me at home. She was saying I could be going to a special school! I could be seeing a doctor! But how long can a mother be fighting against the laws of society? So I was leaving.

In my heart I am knowing that my grieving mother must have been looking for me for years. Maybe she is still searching for me. I am not thinking about her any more.

When I was first finding my way to the hijra house, I was learning singing and dancing, the art of charming strangers and persuading them. In classes run by an NGO, I was continuing my studies of Bengali and arithmetic, until their funding ended. So I was never learning a lot from books. When I was a child, I was being taught that school was the most important thing in the world—my exams and my marks would make me successful! These days, I am seeing that's not true. Was Gandhiji spending his time sitting on top of a book? Was Rakhee, the greatest film star in history, spending her time saying no, please, cannot make films due to I am having to study a book? No. Me, I am learning from life.

———

Lovely is my hijra name, which I was selecting at my eighteenth birthday ceremony. That was the ceremony where I was becoming a real woman. Arjuni Ma was taking me into her own bedroom and standing me in front of a tall mirror. She was giving me a golden blouse and a black petticoat to wear and then she was wrapping a red sari around my hips. Her old knuckles and wrinkled skin were touching me with so much love. I was looking at myself in the mirror, making myself to be thinking of some jokes so that I was not crying. Finally I was knowing what it was feeling like, to be all the women I was seeing every day—on the train, holding children's hands, cooking with ginger-garlic. They were all doing this one thing before going out of the house, putting nine yards of fabric on their bodies. When Arjuni Ma was kneeling in front of me, separating the pleats, I was true to god giving up and sobbing.

That whole night I was dancing with my sisters. The Bollywood classics on the stereo were making me feel like a star, like my body was silk and gold. Everybody's eyes were watching me, full of admiration. Many of the sisters were having, how to say, eighty percent energy, twenty percent talent. But, for me, it was different. I was turning round and round and seeing the pink balloons and golden streamers like a film-set decoration. Even the dim tubelight of the room was looking to me like a spotlight.

Only one thing was making me sad. I am still not liking to think about it, but Mr. Debnath has given this assignment, so. I was knowing that even the sisters who were smiling sweetly were secretly complaining to each other: "Can you imagine, Lovely has not even had the cutting-cutting operation! But Arjuni Ma is giving her the ceremony anyway, what luck!"

———

A long time ago, before my ceremony, my closest sister in the hijra house was Ragini. When Ragini was turning eighteen, she was going with Arjuni Ma to a dentist's chamber for her operation. She was asking me to come also and I was saying yes, of course, so that after the operation we could be having ice candy!

The dentist's chamber was having a sign saying *Closed*, but when Arjuni Ma was knocking, a man who was talking on his Nokia phone was opening the door. Inside, the room was partitioned by a curtain, which was only going halfway to the floor. Behind it was a small space with stacks of medicine samples on the floor and a few calendars, which were also never put up. On the topmost calendar, there was a photo of a foreign baby with such deep dimples. I was almost smiling to see that baby, but the smell of the room, like a damp towel, was bringing me back. Above us, I was seeing black patches of mold on the ceiling and a narrow bed, which was covered with canvas sheeting, like a raincoat. When Arjuni Ma was giving her permission, Ragini was taking off her pants and lying down on this bed.

Arjuni Ma was telling me to stand above Ragini's head and be holding her hands. Ragini was so brave. In my eyes that day, Ragini was a heroine. When the doctor was entering the room, his face was already covered with a mask, so I was never knowing if this was the man on the phone or a different man. Arjuni Ma was telling Ragini to begin her chanting and Ragini was repeating the name of the goddess over and over. Chanting the name was supposed to make the ceremony blessed by god and also keep the pain away.

At this point, I was feeling a bit scared. I was holding Ragini's hand tighter and I was whispering: "From tomorrow all the Romeos will be falling for you."

Ragini was smiling with her dark gums.

The dentist was saying, mumbling mumbling, that he was having no anesthetic that day. How, I don't know, but I was having a gut feeling that he was lying. My gut was telling me that he was feeling nervous about using anesthetics, even when he was having them in stock. But, without anesthetics, Ragini was facing an impossible amount of pain. I was asking the doctor, "Why don't you give her a little bit of anesthetic, sir, or some numbing medicine?"

At that, he was getting irritated. "You are doing the operation or me?"

I was having nothing to say then.

Ragini was interrupting, "No problem, what is some pain? Some painkiller I will take after the operation." She was looking at me like *don't make the doctor angry*. She was eager to do the operation. So I was keeping my mouth shut.

I was keeping my eyes shut too. Just the sight of the blade was too much, leave alone the blood. With eyes closed, I was hearing the sounds—Arjuni Ma breathing sharply, some liquid squirting, something metal hitting the side of the table. When I was opening my eyes, so much bright red blood was in between Ragini's legs, I was thinking that Ragini was now a full woman. She was even getting a period.

Then I was thinking Ragini was dead.

Then Ragini was not dead. She was a ghost. She was not screaming, not crying. Her head was lolling from right to left, like her skull was loose on her neck, and she was shivering like she was having 104 degrees fever. Her hands in my hands were blocks of ice. I was letting them go and crying, "Arjuni Ma, see what Ragini is doing! She is acting strange!"

Arjuni Ma was watching the doctor like an eagle.

At last, with the help of many rags and one no-question-asking taxi driver, we were cleaning up Ragini's wound and

A BURNING

transporting her back to the house. For three–four days, she was having high fever and we were piling more sheets on her to sweat out the temperature. Finally, one day, Ragini was sitting up, accepting the sugar water I was bringing her. She was taking one sip and smiling. I was giving all my thanks to the goddess that day. I was believing in miracles. When Ragini was starting to spend the evenings sitting with us in front of the TV, dancing with her hands when her favorite songs were playing, I was smiling and smiling. I was holding her hand and never letting her go.

Then, one morning, she was not waking up.

"Ragini!" we were calling, "Ragini, wake up!"

I was splashing water on her face. I was pinching her toes. Somebody was putting an old shoe in front of her nose, in case the smell of leather was helping.

But Arjuni Ma was seeing, and I was seeing also, that Ragini was gone very far from us. Her eyes were still, her lips were cracking, her skin was bloodless. Ragini was dead.

From what was she dead? Nobody was knowing, because all of us, and even Arjuni Ma, were afraid of going to real doctors. But I was knowing, oh, I was knowing for sure, one hundred percent, it was the dentist. Maybe his blade was having rust on it or maybe his hands were not clean. Maybe, without anesthetic, the pain was storing and storing in Ragini's body until she was not being able to take it. Like that, Ragini's life was ending.

So I was sure I was never wanting the operation. I was wanting to stay a half-half my whole life.

———

That is the pain I am recalling in my acting class today and that is the pain I am carrying with me when I am going home and seeing a woman squatting outside my door. Her head is down and her hair is silver. Hearing my footsteps, she is standing up and immediately I am seeing the resemblance: it is Jivan's mother.

Inside, she is sitting on my mattress, because there is nowhere else to sit. With her legs folded, her glistening eyes, her small hands, she is looking like a child. Then she is asking me a question that no mother should be having to ask.

"Mother," I am saying to her afterward, "I am knowing what it is like to lose a loved one. And poor Jivan is also lost, at this moment. But the good thing is that she will be coming back."

Jivan's mother is holding her tea glass in her hand and looking at me, waiting for my lecture to get to the point. So I am saying it clearly.

"I will testify," I am saying. "Don't worry one bit. I will go to the court, I will tell them the truth, that Jivan is one kindhearted child teaching the poors, like myself! She was just a soul doing good for the uglies, like myself! I was having in mind that I would be saying all this when the police were coming, but they were not coming only. And I was not having the courage, mother, to walk into a police station myself."

Now Jivan's mother is crying and a tear is falling down my own cheek. I am closing my eyes and Ragini is beside me. This time Ragini is the one holding my hand through the pain. I am opening my eyes and seeing that it is in fact Jivan's mother who is holding my hand, her tears falling on my palms.

"Jivan was telling me once that you are good at blessing babies and brides," she is saying. "Today you have given this mother the biggest blessing."

True to god, I am crying even more.

JIVAN

Americandi unwraps a package of costume jewelry. I listen to the tinkle on her wrist of two glass bangles. When speaking with me, she gestures excessively to watch the fall and slide of the new bangles. Their movement delights her.

I soothe myself with daydreams of Lovely in the courtroom. Imagine when she comes to my trial and says, in that bold voice of hers, that the package all these fools keep talking about was a package full of old books. My dry lips smile to think of it. Even if they don't believe me, how can anybody refuse to believe Lovely?

———

When Purnendu comes, I tell him nothing about Lovely. I don't want to jinx it. But I am happy, so I tell him about an Eid festival, when the lane before our apartment building lit up green with bulbs strung in the trees. I wore a new dress and matching bangles borrowed from my mother and looked out the window with nowhere, really, to go. A wealthy man, a landlord who was making lots of money from this government resettlement program, had ordered a whole goat slaughtered and it was cooked into biryani. The scent rose up to our window. Late at night, due to the goodness of his heart, we ate. We ate with the whole neighborhood, off Styrofoam plates, which we tried to wash and keep.

After dinner, I eyed the vendors who had arrived, anticipating a festive marketplace, with trays of sweets and toys. A few boys bought the cheapest toy—tops—and spun them on the road. Other boys boldly asked for samples of cotton candy and then ran away, until the vendor stopped giving out any.

———

That was our last month in that town. When a house became available in the big city, my mother moved us, hauling sacks on the train, where a few people shoved us and grumbled about our belongings. Ba stood beside us, holding himself up by his grip on the seat backs, insisting he could.

———

How big was the big city! I had never seen a place like this, a tide of people rushing and receding at the railway station, announcements and bell tones over the speakers, and, in the middle of it all, a man selling newspapers. Somebody stepped on my foot or his suitcase did.

"Standing in the middle of the road," a voice grumbled and I jumped to the side.

Men were pushing wheeled carts bearing cold bins of fish, trailing a scent of ice. Other men were hauling sacks of cauliflower on their backs.

"Chai gorom!" cried a vendor. "Hot chai!" He carried a tower of washed glasses and a kettle of tea. I wanted tea and a bakery biscuit. My stomach gurgled.

I followed my mother and father closely and eventually the noise of the station opened up onto the impossible scene of a paved road, wide as a river, on which crawled cars of all colors. They beeped and honked. Their drivers leaned out of windows and shouted.

We climbed into a bus that was starting its route, a mini-bus painted maroon and yellow, with *Howrah to Jadavpur* written in beautiful letters on the side. I read it slowly. When Ba pulled himself up the high steps, straining with his arms, the conductor shouted, "What is this, why have you brought a patient on my bus? If he falls, then who will take the responsibility?"

Ba seated himself in silence, his back stiff, his neck turned to the window.

The conductor thumped the side of the bus and off it flew, lurching and jolting. Ba refused to make a sound, though I knew he was in pain. The conductor, braced in the doorway, cast a suspicious eye on me.

But I was excited. I was thrilled. I walked down the aisle, uneven planks of wood under my bare feet, and watched the men seated by the window, breeze cooling their bald heads, tubes of newspaper rolled up in their laps. Their shirts were clean and pressed, as if they had never been worn before. I didn't know I was staring until one man said, "What is your name?"

He thought I was a child.

"First time in the city?" he said.

My mother, turning around to look at who he was, said yes and I said nothing. His city accent intimidated me. In the time that it took me to comprehend his words, he said something new.

"I came here from Bolpur," he continued—a town two hundred kilometers away—"three–four years ago. You're coming from somewhere like that, aren't you? I can't imagine going back to a small place. You will like it here."

I couldn't stop thinking that I wanted to be like him. Clean shirt, shined shoes, a smart way of speaking. I hoped the city would make me rich, like him. He wasn't rich, of course. Later I learned that what he was was called middle class.

———

I realized how far we were from being middle class when I saw our house. It was deep in the Kolabagan slum and, though Ma had heard through her networks that it was a house made of brick, that turned out to be half-true.

Ma shouted, "This is the house? *This house?*" as we stood in front of its tarp and tin. "Let me call that fool broker right away," she fumed.

Ba smiled helplessly at the neighbors who were peeping or else boldly standing in doorways with hands on their hips.

"I'm going to lie down," he said in the end, when he couldn't bear something—the shouting, his broken back—any more.

———

Over the months, it became Ma's practice to go to the cheap, and illegal, market, which sprang up by the railway lines in the middle of the night. There she bought loaves of bread, beets, potatoes, and tiny fish, with which she cooked breakfast. These meals she sold in front of our house at dawn. Through heavy sleep, I heard the swish of her sandals and the clink of ladle against pot. If I opened my eyes, I saw customers standing illuminated in the battery-powered flashlight, which stood upright on the ground. The customers, our new neighbors, paid ten rupees for some bread and curry, with which they could fill their bellies and begin their day's work.

But my mother had to stop when the rains came, beating on roofs, muddy water rising from the wheels of passing rickshaws churning waves that soaked the stove and licked at our high mattress. I took a bucket, its handle cracked so that I had to hold it by the bottom, and tipped the water out on the street, where it joined a stream in which seedpods and the brown shells of cockroaches floated.

By then, Ba's condition was worse. He lay in bed, his

shape barely human. There the head. A foot slipped outside the sheet. An arm raised to show his pleasure at seeing me. While he slept, Ma cooked and cleaned, refusing to speak her worry. But I knew what it was. His medicines cost money and the monsoon wouldn't let her run her breakfast business. What would we do?

PT SIR

On the last morning of the summer holiday, PT Sir feels the mattress shift under him as his wife wakes. Up she sits, swinging her legs to the ground, yawning noisily, a whiff of her morning breath reaching him. He does not mind. He does not even think about it. He falls back into the delicious sleep of ten more minutes. Dozing, he hears her slippers on the tile floor, the clink of her bangles rolling to her wrist, the tumble of pots and pans as she pulls one from the drying stack. She is going to boil water for oats.

At this thought, he gets up. The sun shines directly in his eyes. Many times he has told her he wants a double-egg omelet and butter-cooked potatoes for breakfast, but she continues to make oats, like she did every morning for her elderly father. But that man is old. What is he, PT Sir? A young man. A man of vigor and power.

Well, today, he is going to buy himself the breakfast he deserves. It will be even better than omelet-potatoes. Off he goes to the marketplace, where a sweet shop makes kochuri with chholar dal for breakfast. Fried dough, stuffed with green peas, and a lentil curry. A breakfast of decadence. Let his wife eat her oats!

On the street, a stray dog ambles after him and he shoos it away.

"Go, hut!"

But the dog follows him, its ribs outlined in its skin, a patch of fur missing, its tongue hanging out of its pink mouth.

PT Sir dares to pick up a stick from the road and swat it at that dog. Only when he throws the stick does the dog retreat, trotting away in the other direction.

PT Sir has sent a dozen men to jail, does anybody know that? So this street dog better beware of him or he can have it locked up in a snap of his fingers, ha-ha!

———

One morning, daylight fails. The sky turns so dark that lights are flipped on throughout the neighborhood, lending the dawning of day a mood of dusk. With a storm that thunders and blazes, and whose rain strikes rooftops across the city, the monsoon arrives. PT Sir's wife draws the windows closed before the slanting rain and PT Sir emerges from the house with his trousers folded up to his calves, his feet in rubber slippers. His work shoes he carries in a plastic bag.

From his doorstep, PT Sir surveys the terrain. Brown water sloshes this way and that, the street turned into a stream, as office-goers wade. PT Sir spots a rickshaw churning water as it makes its way slowly down the lane. It has high wheels and a high blue seat sheltered under an accordion roof. When he raises an arm and calls, "Rickshaw!" the driver pedals toward him and comes to a lazy stop. With his shirt unbuttoned and calves muscled, his head dry under an umbrella held upright by the handlebars, the man looks blankly ahead and quotes a fare that is triple what it should be. PT Sir, with some pride, casually agrees to it.

"Fine," he says, "fine, let's go."

———

For years, the school has tried to get the drainage in the access lane fixed so that it doesn't flood. Every monsoon, it floods. So it has today too. Students, in school uniform and Hawaii slippers, hover by the dry mouth of the lane, on high ground. Rainwater has flooded the underground dens of cockroaches and now the insects emerge from cracks in the pavement. On land they dash, alarming girls who yell and stomp them dead. When a school bus arrives or a classmate's car pauses, girls pile into the vehicle to be carried to the gate of the school.

Classes proceed as usual, but whose mind can be on Mongol invasions and trigonometry when the city is flooded? All day, rain drips and drops and, when it pauses for a breath, it is replaced by the false rain of fat water from ledges and leaves.

In his class, PT Sir has them do yoga indoors, four

students at a time, because it turns out that's how many yoga mats there are. The others "meditate"—eyes half-open, a giggle spreading now and then. PT Sir says, "Quiet!" but he knows this too: the rules are different on a rainy day.

———

At lunchtime, the principal, in a show of solidarity, leaves her air-conditioned office and sits with the teachers. She too has arrived with feet soaked, the bottom of her sari darkened by water.

"Undignified," comments an English teacher. "All of us teachers lifting up our saris like that to walk to school. Imagine how it looks to the students!"

"It gives a poor impression to the parents," agrees the maths teacher.

The principal, before a tiffin box of sandwiches, teases, "PT Sir, we have all seen that you know powerful people."

PT Sir looks up from his lunch of noodles. He smiles and makes no protest.

"Any chance," the principal says, "something can be done for our lane?"

———

So it is that the following Monday, two laborers appear, wearing city corporation badges, and present themselves to the principal. "Your work order," they say, offering her a sheet of much-folded paper. "Work has been done. Sign and give back, please."

The principal cannot believe her eyes. "I noticed," she says, "that the lane looked dug up."

And here it is, indeed, a document detailing what has been done. Over the weekend, men dispatched by the municipal corporation ripped up the asphalt, pumped the old drainage pipes clean of muck and plastic, then sealed the road above.

The next time it rains, students and teachers walk down the school lane, clean and dry, while districts of the city drown.

LOVELY

At the end of a class, Mr. Debnath is sitting in his chair with a puddle of tea on a saucer and he is blowing *phoo phoo*. I am analyzing my performance that I was recording on my phone. On the wall, some brown flowers are hanging around the faces of his late parents. High time for Mr. Debnath to buy fresh flowers.

"Lovely, today I am realizing," he is saying, after the others have left, "that you are growing far beyond this class."

"Don't say such things, please," I am protesting, even though I am secretly thinking that maybe he is right. My performances are always outshining. In fact, I am having the same thought myself. But I am always being humble. "I have to learn a lot more from you," I am saying to him.

"I have been writing a script, Lovely," he is saying. "Remember how I was getting a chance to go to Bombay, twenty years back? From that time till now, I have been writing this script. And it is getting to the point where I am thinking about casting and so on and so forth."

"Wow!" I am saying with my neck coming out like a goose. "You are directing a film?"

"Writing," he is saying, "and directing, naturally. Now I have one question for you."

And just like that, with his tea breath on my face, he is asking me to be the heroine. The question is coming as such a shock I am taking one minute to understand fully what he is asking.

"Do you accept?" he is saying.

I am just looking at him like a fool. I am meaning *Yes! Yes! Yes!*

Mr. Debnath is telling me, "You must be wondering who is playing the lead opposite you? The hero, well, I am really writing that role for someone like Shah Rukh Khan."

"Shah Rukh Khan!" I am finally saying. My voice is catching in my throat. "Was I ever telling you that I am sleeping every night under a poster of Shah Rukh Khan?"

It is really too much emotion. I am feeling like I am on top of a high Himalayan peak of happiness. If I am having to be putting words to this feeling, that is truly how I am feeling.

"Someone *like* Shah Rukh Khan," Mr. Debnath is saying, "more or less."

But I am not even hearing.

"Accept?" I am saying. "Mr. Debnath, this is the greatest day of my life!"

JIVAN

In the beginning, the hot air of the kitchen made my head swoon. Once, I paused my work of flipping ruti and, recalling what I learned in PT class, lowered my head between my knees. Soon after, a guard, a man, noticed the slowed production line and said, in my ear, "Want to rest? I can take you to the clinic if you want."

Everybody knew what happened in the on-site clinic to women who were sedated and weak, unable to do more than lift a hand or briefly open their eyes.

No longer am I that light-headed woman. Every morning and every evening, I make more than a hundred pieces of ruti. My movements have become economical—slap and turn, pinch and lift. My head is down, my bony fingers swift. Looking at me, you might think I have become a servant, but that is true only of my hands. In my mind, I have resisted being imprisoned. In my mind, every morning I dress smartly, clip on my badge, and take the bus to my job at Pantaloons. That morning will come again. The clock, though reluctant, moves forward.

———

I have always believed in work. Only once, I promise Purnendu, only once did I think about committing a crime.

In the big city, one of the first things I noticed was how everybody had big cell phones like handheld televisions. One of those cell phones could pay for a few months of my father's medicines.

"So you stole a phone?" Purnendu says. He sits cross-legged on top of the bench, wearing office pants which smell like ironing. "From who?"

"No, wait," I say. "Listen first."

One day, on the main street, I saw a woman whose purse was unzipped. A wallet peeked out. The woman was holding a receipt and looking hopefully at the roll shop. My heart pounded in my ears as I reached forward and touched that wallet. I touched it gently at first, then nearly lifted it from the purse. Even while I was holding the wallet, indecision screamed at me: should I really do this? Was I a thief? In any case, the wallet had caught on something deep in the purse. I tugged once, then let it go.

No, I wasn't a thief.

No, I was never a thief, but the woman turned around, surprised, and gripped my wrist. With my bony wrist in her strong hand, she shouted, "What are you doing?"

Everybody at the roll shop looked at me. The man who was cracking eggs on the black pan paused. The boy who was chopping onions held his rag-wrapped knife still in the air.

I looked at the ground, my wrist still in the hand of the woman. How soft her hand was. I readied for a beating.

But the woman with the soft hands bent toward me and asked me a question, her voice suddenly different.

"How old are you, child?" she said. "Are you hungry?"

The kindness of her voice made me harden with suspicion. Why was she being nice? I refused to speak, turning my eyes to the road, where yellow Ambassador taxis rumbled along, honking their horns.

"Why didn't you ask me for something to eat?" she said.

She took her roll from the shop, bought me one, and took me back to her office, me agreeing to her soft hand on my back, her warm fingers touching my skin through the zipper fallen open, in my mouth delicious chicken, nothing more. Her office was up an elevator. The box moved and I kept a hand on the wall.

"Never been in a lift?" said the lady. She smiled. "Don't be afraid."

In the office, other ladies came forward and asked me many questions. After I devoured the chicken roll, one gave me two biscuits, which I crammed in my mouth, buttery crumbs sticking to my chin.

They were an education NGO and they provided scholarships for underprivileged children to attend one of the best schools in the area, S. D. Ghosh Girls' School.

——

On the path from our slum to my new school, there was a butcher shop. Every day, I walked past skinned goats hanging from hooks, their bodies all muscle and fat except for the tails, which twitched. The goat must have had a life, much like me. At the end of its life, maybe it had been led by a rope to the slaughterhouse and maybe, from the smell of blood, which emerged from that room, the goat knew where it was being taken.

Before I began going to the good school, I used to feel that way. In this prison, sometimes, I feel it again.

But at that time, with my clean school uniform, a bag full of photocopied books strapped to my shoulders, even a new pencil in my pocket, I did not feel like that goat any more.

———

That does not mean school was easy. I kept my distance, or others kept their distance from me, and, from their faces, I knew they found something physically unappealing about me: my hair, often knotted and chalky with dust, or my smell, like metal. But it did not keep me from laughing at what they said, accepting a glance thrown my way as a kind of friendship.

I learned English, the language of progress. I couldn't get anywhere if I didn't speak English, even I knew that. But I dreaded being asked to stand up and read from the textbook.

I read like this: "Gopal li-li-livaid—*lived* on a mou-mou-moonten, and he—"

The other girls, from middle-class homes where they read English newspapers and watched Hollywood films, disdained me. But, in the slum, I was the only one with an English textbook, and who cared whether I was good or not? It was a place where most could not read a word—Bengali or English—and what I had was a great skill.

PT SIR

In autumn, during the Durga Pujo festival, young lovers roam the streets, holding hands, till dawn. Ceremonial smoke wafts where priests worship and drummers keep their beat going until the next day arrives. The streets, closed to cars, fill with vendors of fried snacks and cotton candy. Some neighborhoods install Ferris wheels and swinging pirate boats where traffic might have been.

On such a night, while the city celebrates, the Jana Kalyan Party leader, whom PT Sir has only briefly met, a man with three mobile phones in his palms at all times, dies. It is late, well after dinner, when PT Sir gets the phone call. His wife, woken by the ring of the phone and worried by the tone of voice she hears, rises from bed and asks, "What happened?"

She tells him where he might be able to buy a grief wreath, of white evening flowers, at this hour.

PT Sir takes a rickshaw, then a taxi, then abandons the car and runs when the traffic stalls. Crowds stream past him in the opposite direction. Now and then a child, no taller than his hip, blows a pipe whose neck unfurls and reveals a feather.

The party leader's house is in the old part of the city, where lanes accommodate one Ambassador car at a time. Two police jeeps try to regulate the crowd, a mass of men holding hot earthen cups of tea by the cool rim. On balconies along the lane, neighbors watch the gathering like it is a festival of its own.

"Have they brought the body from the hospital?" PT Sir asks a stranger beside him, a man carrying a cloth bag like a scholar.

"Few minutes ago," he replies.

PT Sir sees no familiar faces, so he stands some distance from the house, holding a tall bunch of white flowers, the only flowers he could find at that hour. Murmurs spread that the chief minister is coming to pay his respects and the railway minister too. A car is allowed through, bearing a famous actor, who steps out in sunglasses. To the crowd, he joins his hands and bows his head. Then he disappears inside the house. The crowd roars and moves as one and, for a moment, PT Sir fears a stampede.

"Please keep order," shouts a man from the front. "His wife is inside, his elderly mother is inside, have respect for them!"

PT Sir feels ashamed of himself, a participant in this strangely excited crowd of the supposedly grieving. He feels the way he did at the first Jana Kalyan Party rally he attended, when he was a diffident man.

Should he go home? Should he, at a calmer moment,

phone the bereaved? But he has brought these flowers. Wouldn't he like to show Bimala Pal that he has come? There, inside the house, all the senior ministers are gathered. Wouldn't it be good to be acquainted with one or two of them?

At that moment, he hears a voice.

"You have come," says the assistant, the same one who delivers PT Sir's courthouse bonuses by motorcycle. PT Sir follows him gratefully. The man leads him through the crowd—"Side, side," he commands—and PT Sir feels eyes on him. He can feel the crowd thinking, reminding him of that long-ago moment on the train when he received free muri, who is this VIP?

LOVELY

When there are no babies or newlyweds to bless, the sisters of my hijra house are giving blessings for money on the local trains. It is our tradition and we are doing it more during Durga Pujo days, when the goddess is not in the sky but here in our city.

"Come now, sisters," Arjuni Ma is saying to everyone in the compartment, clapping her palms together, "don't you want your day to be blessed?"

The passengers hiding by the windows are trying to look outside and ignore, but they cannot. Arjuni Ma is specifically calling to them. "Listen, mother, give us a few rupees from the goodness of your heart."

Every face that is turning to me, I am hoping it is not somebody from Mr. Debnath's acting class. Please god, I am thinking. Now I am on my way to being a star, why to ruin that reputation? Those classmates are maybe the only people in my life who have not seen me in this trade. They have not seen how this trade is making me a little disgusting in the eyes of others. But if I am not having this trade, how am I saving money for acting classes?

I am always learning from the train. Here is a mother sitting cross-legged with her baby sleeping in her lap. Her head is tilting on her shoulder and she is sleeping also, dead to the world. She is not hearing any of our words. Next time when I am having a role as a tired mother, I will be thinking about her.

A lot of people are looking outside, to the fields of their country, the soothing green outside the window. The fields of paddy and coconut trees, the endless green of the rural parts. Oh, fantasy! They are actually looking at the ugly suburbs. Banners are hanging above a lane, advertising cold cream. The cloth of the banners is poked with holes for letting the wind through. In quiet towns, two-storey houses painted such colors like you may never see in the city—bright blue and yellow! Pink and green!—are jutting up from dust, some with flags of the local political party and one with a stray man on the roof, sent up to fix the satellite dish, scratching his head at the sky.

All this I am seeing through the windows of the train, like they are a kind of television.

———

The invitation card is arriving one morning, passed from hand to hand because there is no address on it except *Lovely Hijra, near Kolabagan Railway Station.* I am opening the card as if it is a flap of my heart. I am reading the words so many times I am knowing them like a song. Opening and closing the card, opening and closing the card—I am ready for my heart to be tearing at the fold.

On the given day, I am shampooing in the cold water of the municipal tap, oiling my elbows, putting some rose water on my face, putting a garland around the thick bun high on my head, and then I am setting out for the event hall where Azad is going to marry a woman. A real woman, with whom he is someday having children, just like I was pushing him to do. His days of being with a he-she like me are over. In my armpit, I am holding a nicely wrapped box with a small European-looking statue inside.

The hall is having a flower-and-leaf gate spelling out in front: *Azad weds Shabnam.* A lady standing over there is giving every guest a cup of cool rose-flavored Rooh Afza.

I am slurping it down, so thirsty I am suddenly feeling. Still my tongue is feeling thick, my throat is feeling dry. Inside, Azad and his bride are sitting on matching thrones. Behind the thrones is a heap of big wrapped boxes—must be they are toasters, blankets, dinner plates. Azad is smiling with all thirty-two teeth and shaking some old uncle's hand. Then he is seeing me and we are going on looking at each other. We are having no words.

I was the one who was telling Azad to move forward and marry a woman, am I not remembering? But now Azad is looking handsome. His hair is nicely combed and he is wearing an ivory dhoti kurta. His bride's face is powdered white like a ghost and her lips are red like a tomato. On her neck, she is wearing at least five–six gold necklaces. I am not caring about gold, but I am caring, with my empty Rooh Afza cup in my hand, that Azad was buying these for her with love. Wasn't Azad once telling me that he could not live without me? So why was he not marrying some ugly one-eyed person?

Anyway, I am having to be noble now. I am going up to the bride and groom with my gift.

"Lovely," Azad is saying uncomfortably, "good that you came."

I am feeling like I will cry. While my heart is bouncing like a Ping-Pong ball inside my chest, I am saying to them, "Long married life to both of you." The girl is bending low, wanting to be blessed, and I, Lovely, am feeling like a kind of goddess, a kind of saint, believing when you love him let him go.

In the dinner line, one eye on the biryani and one eye on the Chinese chili chicken, I am not knowing whether to laugh or cry. Look at me, waiting for the feast at my husband's marriage. With my plate and napkin in one hand, chomping chomping, I am looking around at the hall, decorated with plastic flowers, a small fountain in one corner. Isn't this life strange?

My love for Azad, I am telling myself, is existing in some other world, where there is no society, no god. In this life, we were never getting to know that other world, but I am sure it is existing. There our love story is being written.

At the end of the night, when I am walking down the lane, all the shops are shuttered other than a welder's shop where a masked man is working. From the machine, bright sparks are falling on the road. In the hands of this tired man, it is like Diwali.

———

Mr. Debnath is telling me to have a demo video prepared so I can be showing my reel to his movie's producers and starting to get small, small projects on my own also. At one demo office, the front desk man's mouth is hanging open and he is poking inside his mouth with a toothpick. This is the cheapest place I could be finding, so I am having to make my demo video here, no question.

"Which level?" the man is saying dully.

"What?"

"Which level demo video you are wanting? Basic level six hundred rupees, better variety a thousand rupees, deluxe package twenty-five hundred rupees."

I am gulping to hear the prices. Then I am choosing basic level. When he is filling out a form on a clipboard, he is asking, "What is your name?"

"Lovely," I am saying.

At this, he is snorting like a horse.

When I am looking at the form, I am seeing that he is writing next to my name: *B*.

"Why you are marking me *B* already?" I am demanding. "I didn't even perform."

"Calm down, madam," the man is complaining. "Why are you looking at what I am writing? It's just lingo, nothing personal about you."

But he is not telling me what it is meaning. I am learning later, on my own. B-class. An actor who is not having the pretty face or light skin color for A-class roles. B-class actor is someone who is only playing a servant, a rickshaw puller, a thief. The audience is wanting to see B-class actors punched and slapped and defeated by the hero.

I am going to a room and standing nervously in front of not a theoretical camera, but a real camera. It is balanced on top of a tripod and there is a blinking red light on it. The man with sleepy eyes is standing behind it and, even though I am not liking him and he is not liking me, I am feeling like a real actress. I am looking at the lens and knowing—through this lens, someday I am reaching a thousand people, a million people. So what if there is only one grumpy man here and he is receptionist and clerk and cameraperson also? It may be a boutique company, as they say.

The man is telling me that he will give me a fifteen-minute reel with different characters and looks. That is what I am getting for six hundred, he is reminding me.

"Now, if you are taking the deluxe package—"

"No need!" I am saying. "Basic package is okay for me."

I am tying up my hair and doing some voice exercises. In this empty room, my voice is sounding hollow.

Now he is saying, "Can you do an angry housewife?"

Then: "Now you try a person waiting for the bus and it is just not coming. Subtle expressions, see?"

Then: "You are a baby throwing a tantrum." To which I am saying, "A baby?"

But maybe these are tests for being an actress. You have to slide into the character, no hesitation.

I am lying down on a dirty mattress laid on the floor anyhow. A small worm is running along the edge of the mattress, trying to find an opening where it can be hiding. I am lying on my back with my hands and feet up, more like a dying cockroach than a baby. I am wailing *waan waan*.

The whole time, I am feeling like the man is secretly filming me for a bad website. How is it that this cashier is having full control of the camera? It is giving me an uneasy feeling in my chest.

When the man is taking six hundred and forty rupees from me—"tax," he is explaining—and giving me the CD, I am feeling somehow cheated.

———

When I am coming back home, there is one man waiting in front of my door. He is suited-booted and everybody is looking at him because his clothes are looking too clean. On his fingers he is wearing one green stone, one red stone, one blue stone, some copper rings.

"Is your name Lovely?" he is saying, as I am taking my key out of my purse.

"What is it to you?" I am saying. Men are always wanting things.

"Jivan said," he is gulping, like a nervous fish, "Jivan said you are willing to come to the court, her mother came and saw you—"

"Who are you, mister?" I am asking him.

Then he is saying, "I am Jivan's lawyer. I just need to confirm that you will come to the court."

He is giving me a form.

"I am not knowing how to read English," I am telling him.

"But she was teaching you?" he is asking.

"She was teaching me," I am sighing. "How is Jivan? Is she getting proper food?"

Instead of answering my question, this man is liking to ask more questions. Now he is saying, "Can I sit and talk with you? I can help you fill this out. Maybe at the tea shop over there?"

PT SIR

Two months after Bimala Pal becomes, quietly and without ceremony, Jana Kalyan Party's new leader, she sends PT Sir on a mission that, if PT Sir is being honest, he finds a little bewildering.

A winter chill is in the air when a party jeep takes PT Sir to a village called Chalnai, eighty kilometers away. On the highway, large trucks transporting the season's vegetables—cauliflower, potatoes—blow musical horns. Pedestrians, visible as triangles of wool shawls on two legs, run across the highway now and then, fearing nothing.

Nearing the village, the jeep slows as its wheels crush grain placed on the road by villagers. A girl sits on the pads of her feet, supervising the use of passing cars as millstones. Behind her, fields of stubble roll from the edge of the paved road to a horizon where woods blur.

In Chalnai, the government school is a doorless structure next to a dust field. Inside, a dozen men and women—teachers, PT Sir understands—sit cross-legged on the floor. When PT Sir enters, the teachers say nothing. They have about them an air of waiting to be instructed what to do, how to behave, whether to speak or smile. PT Sir joins his hands in greeting.

PT Sir's task is to impress upon the teachers that students must have a half hour of physical activity every day. They must be let loose from their books to eat the air, play a sport, or run races. If the school lacks large grounds, the students must be allowed to jump rope. After twenty minutes of lecturing, during which PT Sir feels slightly absurd, he distributes among the teachers pamphlets from the party, with illustrations showing overworked students choosing to hang themselves or jump from the roof. It has happened. It is a serious problem. But here, with the blank-faced teachers nodding at everything he says, PT Sir feels himself sent on a silly mission. This, after all, is a village, with abundant fields and woods where children run wild.

At night, at home with his wife, he takes off a shirt and undershirt going red from the soil of the region. When he washes his face, the red dust is in the crooks of his ears.

"So why did they *really* send you to this place?" demands his wife.

PT Sir thinks about this. He feels that this field trip was some kind of test, but, whether he has passed or not, he does not yet know.

JIVAN

Behind the main prison building there is a long gutter, green with growth. Running above it is a crooked water pipe with a dozen faucets. Here I kneel every other morning and wash clothes for Americandi.

One morning, I am kneeling and scrubbing, I am beating the kameez and salwar against the ground, watching a circle of foam spread, when I feel somebody behind me. It is a guard, who says, "Your lawyer is here. Leave that and come."

Is it so easy? Don't I know that Americandi will punish me for leaving her clothes unwashed?

Rapidly I rinse and wring, putting my weight into my arms, the wrung clothes releasing ropes of water. I flap the clothes in the air, a gentle rain falling back toward me, and hang them up to dry on a clothesline inside my cell. When I walk, finally, to the visiting room, with each step my back aches like its hinges need oiling.

———

I have never seen Gobind smile so wide.

"Lovely is here," he says, standing up when he sees me, "you are right. The message has been delivered."

"I know," I tell him. "My mother found her when you couldn't!"

"She has promised she will testify," he says, as if he can't hear me. "A win for us!"

A few days later, in the papers, I see stories, which claim Gobind did extensive on-the-ground investigation, endless nights of detective work, to track down the elusive hijra, Lovely.

———

When I speak about PT Sir, Purnendu raises his eyebrows.

"What?" I say. "Do you know him?"

"Is this the man who has been seen with Bimala Pal?" Purnendu says. "The new member of Jana Kalyan Party?"

"No, no," I tell him. "He was just my PT teacher at S. D. Ghosh School."

———

One day, after a class during which the sun made me feel faint, PT Sir called me. What was wrong now? I wondered. My hem fraying, my shoelaces soiled? But he said, in a scolding tone so as not to embarrass me, "Are you eating properly?"

I tried to smile, as if it was a silly concern. "It was too hot, sir, that's why I felt weak."

He looked at me for a while and I waited to be punished. When teachers called me, that was usually what happened.

But PT Sir took me up to the staff room and handed me a tiffin box from his bag. Inside, there were several pieces of ruti, folded in triangles, and vegetables.

"Sit and eat it," he said. I did, all those pipes in me clamoring for food, their need louder than my embarrassment. My mother always cooked food for us, but, that month, my father needed an injection, which cost us our grocery money. I had only eaten some rice and salt for breakfast.

After that, PT Sir kept an eye on me. He slipped me some bread and jam or a banana. I, in turn, participated enthusiastically in his class. I jogged in place—"High knee! Low!"—and bounced a basketball with vigor. I jumped toward the new hoops. I raced with my elbows slicing the air and my thighs pumping. I thought of all the times I had stayed home to look after my father and now my sweat shined on my limbs.

PT Sir, with his balding head ringed by a patch of combed hair, stood in the sun class after class, a whistle ready at his lips. He smiled at me and told me, "Well done!"

Once, he asked me if I was interested in going to a cricket camp.

I wondered sometimes if he paid attention to me because he felt like an outsider too. He was a father, I imagined, and all the other teachers were mothers. When the principal spoke about morals at the morning assembly and the microphone began to screech, the ladies looked around for PT Sir. Such was his place in the school, a little apart from everybody else.

———

Then two things happened.

One, I went to a classmate's birthday party. Priya's mother took us home in a bus and paid for my bus fare. I stood on the uneven wooden planks, this time in shoes, reaching high for the bar that ran along the ceiling. A lady was eating chocolate wafers and had a full bag in her lap. I looked at the chocolates, sitting ignored, nobody wanting them.

In Priya's room, she had a desk for working and a special lamp just for the desk, which curved downward to put light on the book but not in her eyes. I had never seen a lamp like it. I still covet it.

In the kitchen, Priya crushed biscuits and chocolate sauce to make a sweet dish that her mother scolded her for making, as it would spoil our appetite for the dinner. But I ate spoonfuls of it and then ate my fill at dinner. I had never seen such a spread. There was luchi, dal, chicken, but also Chinese noodles from the cart at the bus stop, in case we did not find the home-cooked food delicious. When I left, Priya's mother gave me a tiffin box full of food for my mother and father. Was Priya a millionaire? No, she was only middle class.

It made me proud. Look at me, Ma, with my middle-class friend. That's what I thought. One day I would be middle class too.

———

The second event happened one night, when I was woken by my mother shouting. It was dark and I rose in a panic.

"Look how they scratched me, those savages," my mother was saying, holding out a bare forearm. And they had, whoever they were. I climbed off the bed, my breath catching, and held her arm tenderly, as if my touch could soothe. A small circle of potential customers stood around, bereft of breakfast, agitated by the event they had stumbled upon.

At the nighttime market, two or three men had shoved my mother, grabbed her grocery-shopping money from her fist, and shouted at her to "go back to Bangladesh."

Later, when the audience had dispersed, Ma sat in the house with her head in her hands. When she looked up, after long minutes, she said, "They were touching me *here*, touching me *here*. Oh, my girl, my gold, don't make me tell you."

I saw my mother then as a woman. I felt her humiliation. And, where I had always felt shame, I now felt white-hot anger. Anger crept into my jaws and I had to gnash my teeth to be calm.

Why was this our life? What kind of life was it, where my mother was forced to buy cheap vegetables in the middle of the night and got robbed and attacked for it? What kind of life did we have, where my father's pain was not taken seriously by a doctor until it was too late?

So I made a decision. Whether it was a good decision or a bad decision, I no longer know.

INTERLUDE

Brijesh, Aspiring Actor, Visits a New Mall

A new mall opened where the sewing machine factory used to be. My jaw dropped when I saw it. It looked like an airport. Sharp and spiky. Glass here, glass there. Lights everywhere, like it was festival time.

On Sunday, after the acting class, I put on my new jeans and buttoned up my shirt with a horseman stitched on the chest pocket—Playboy shop in Allen Lane, go there sometime—then took out my phone and called my friend Raju, who does house-painting work. Together we went. Outside the mall, there were the snack boys and syrup-ice boys and a few of them I knew so I nodded to them and they said, "Go inside, go inside, see how it is!"

So Raju and I went. Raju had some paint on his arms. My hair was washed and combed. My shoes were a bit dirty, but I had put polish on top of the dirt and covered it up, almost. Then we stood in the line for the metal detector and I looked up at the big posters of ladies wearing golden watches. Then we walked through the metal detector and, at this point, I could smell the AC air coming from inside, with a smell of perfumes and leather bags also. Oh, that cool air on my face. I felt good. I felt excited. The cool, cool breeze coming, when suddenly the guard caught my arm.

"Fifty rupees," the guard said.

"What?" I said. "Go away, old man." Can't believe how anybody just asks for money, no excuse needed! I should also stand outside a mall and shout out amounts of money. See what I can get.

"Fifty rupees admission," said the guard, neither annoyed nor interested, his eyes looking somewhere else.

"Admission to go to where? We're just going to the shops," said Raju, taking out his big new smartphone and holding it casually, just to show that he is a moneyed man.

But the old guard was not fooled. "See, brother," he began, "fifty rupees and you can go in. Otherwise you enjoy the air outside.

"Like me," he added, but I did not have a mood to feel friendship with him.

"But you didn't take admission from that aunty!" argued Raju. The woman ahead of us, her soft white belly spilling over the waist of her pink sari, her elbows disappearing in folds of fat, a woman who surely eats mutton every day, she had already disappeared in the mall.

"Do I make the rules, brother?" said the guard. "I am just telling you what is what. Now you want to quarrel with me and say, this person, that person! So what will I do? I am just telling you what is the rule. Now you decide—"

So Raju and I stepped away from the entrance. We

looked at each other. Neither of us wanted to say it. So Raju clapped my back and I smacked his shoulder and we went to the syrup-ice stall and had some orange syrup-ice. Then we went back to work. Him to his house painting, that paint-smelling turban on his head again. Me to my electrician's shop. It was giving me pain in my wrist, pain in my thumb. At least the syrup-ice was delicious.

PT SIR

In court for what will be his last case, PT Sir faces a counterfeiter, a man who sells fake Nikees and Adidavs to the local malls. His name, PT Sir reminds himself from a chit of paper before taking the stand, is Azad.

The man looks suspect, that's what PT Sir thinks. There is something too new about his clothes. His hair is smoothed back with gel. Is he wearing eyeliner? Could be. PT Sir has been told he is a counterfeit goods trader, an immoral man who is harming the national economy and deserves to be jailed. That is the charge with which they have brought him to court today.

"Where do you get your supply?" says the judge.

"Judge sir," says Azad. "Believe me, this is all made up. I can't even—"

"Where?" repeats the judge. "You want to go to jail for this?"

"I don't know what you are saying, judge sir," protests Azad. "I am only transporting what the boss man tells me, I don't know real weal, fake shake—"

"Who has brought the charge?" says the judge,

exasperated. The lawyer points out PT Sir. He takes the stand. He tells his story: he bought shoes for eight hundred rupees, then after one walk found that the sole was ungluing from the shoe.

"Who are you, mister?" interrupts Azad. He is listening, wide-eyed. "Who is this man? I have never seen him in my life. What is your issue with me?"

The judge warns Azad to be quiet. In the end, the judge orders Azad to pay a fine of five thousand rupees.

PT Sir looks at the man and is shocked to see his eyes are wet. Azad is crying. In a panic, he wails, "Judge sir, I am just a transport man, where will I find five thousand rupees? I just got married, I have a wife to support now—"

The judge, irritated, announces that a trade in fake goods will not be tolerated, not while he has a courtroom to preside over. "If you cannot pay the fine, you can serve a jail term," he declares. "Is that what you choose?"

LOVELY

Now that I am owning a demo video, on Mr. Debnath's recommendation I am visiting a casting director, Mr. Jhunjhunwala.

Morning of the appointment, I am putting baby powder on my oily spots—forehead, nose, chin. Just in case he is asking me to film something right there!

Once again, I am going to the film district, but this time I am going in the opposite direction from Mr. Debnath's house. I am passing by a big studio, built a hundred years ago, which is now blocking part of the road. Since big-big stars are filming in that studio, the municipal corporation is letting the studio stay.

The casting director's office is not far. I am walking down a lane where there is an open gutter thick with mosquitoes and soon I am seeing a door that is saying *Jhunjhunwala*.

The door is thin and one plank of wood is splintered at the bottom. Along the stairway, I am feeling surprised to see red splashes of spit, which are soiling the walls. To be truthful, this office is looking quite dirty, but who am I to know where fame and success are coming from?

I am knocking on door 3C, hearing the loud voice of a man on the phone inside. The man is calling, "Come, come." Inside, the man's head is bent to the phone and he is waving me forward, showing me the two chairs on the other side of his table. I am sitting, touching the edge of my blouse on my shoulder to make sure the bra strap is tucked inside. Mr. Debnath has prepared me to always sit straight and tall. The pose is making me feel confident when I am actually feeling nervous. Then I am waiting, trying to look a bit humble and a bit royal.

The phone conversation is finally ending and Mr. Jhunjhunwala is standing up, coming around to my side, and taking my hand in both of his hands. He is shaking my hand like I am the prime minister.

"Forgive me for keeping you waiting," he is saying. When he is speaking, a scent of paan is coming from his mouth. I can see his teeth are red from betel stains, so maybe he is the one spitting in the stairs every day. "Some producers, they depend a lot on me and want to discuss every small detail . . ." He is shaking his head. What to do with these needy producers!

"Chai? Pepsi?" he is offering and a small boy is poking his head in through the door to take the order. How he is knowing that he is needed, I don't know. But this is a professional film office, so this is how things are run in an office. I am saying water only, thank you, but Mr. Jhunjhunwala is saying, "Only water?" And then he is telling the boy, "Bring a cold Pepsi, straight from the fridge."

So I am drinking Pepsi from a glass bottle, keeping the

thin straw in one corner of my mouth like film stars do. I am not wanting to spoil my lipstick. In front of me, there is a table topped with a glass slab and under that glass slab are autographed postcards by big movie stars. Some of the names I am recognizing. Are they prints or originals? I am thinking. And then I am scolding myself—look at me, so cynical! Of course they are originals. This is the society in which I move about now.

Then Mr. Jhunjhunwala is sitting down, with his chai in front, and he is looking at me with a strict expression. "Now your acting teacher, Mr. Debnath, is someone I respect very much. So I take it very seriously—very, very seriously!—when he says look, here's a student I think you should meet. Immediately I said it will be my honor, just tell her to come quickly."

I am smiling, sipping. The fizzy and sweet drink is making me feel good.

Mr. Jhunjhunwala is saying, "Now. Kamz, I mean, Kamal Banerjee, you have heard of him?"

Who has not heard of the great director Kamal Banerjee?

"So Kamz is casting for a film just now. Let me tell you the story. It will be a love story with a twist, set during a harvest season in which a whole village is suffering because too little rain, too few crops, you see, like that. It will be a blockbuster, mark my words. Now there is a scene in which a hijra, a bad luck hijra, comes to the village, saying, 'Give me money now, mother, please, my child is starving,' et cetera, okay? And our hero, who is suffering himself from his fields dying, mind you, in his suffering he comes out and chases away the hijra with a broom."

I am sucking my Pepsi too fast now. The main part is coming, surely.

"You," says Mr. Jhunjhunwala, "will be perfect for the hijra part. Do you have your demo CD with you?"

I am wanting to be a heroine on-screen. At least the heroine's sister or girlfriend. And here is the great casting director telling me about a minor role, where the character would be chased off-screen with a broom! I am putting the straw away from my lips. My heart is sinking and, all of a sudden, this room is making me unhappy. I am seeing the mousehole in the corner. I am feeling the wobble in this old chair. I am saying in a tiny voice, "Yes, sir." I am handing him the CD in its case.

Mr. Jhunjhunwala is feeling the disappointment in my voice. He is taking the CD and leaning back in his chair. "You know," he is saying, looking at the ceiling, "many people come to me and think I can put them in a movie instantly. But it doesn't work like that. If you are serious about your career, if you don't want to remain on an amateur level, then you have to start at the entry level."

"Yes, of course, sir," I am saying. "I did not mean—oh, I'm just learning how the business works! Forgive me for not knowing."

"No, there is nothing to forgive in not knowing," he is saying, feeling a bit friendly again. "Let me look at this CD and then I will call you, fine? Please pay the hundred rupees fee on your way out."

"Fee!" I am saying in a feeble voice. "There is a fee?"

"Am I looking like a nonprofit agency to you, Lovely?" Mr. Jhunjhunwala is saying, smiling. "Yes, the fee is for keeping you in my roster, looking for roles for you."

When I am climbing down the stairs, belly full of Pepsi sloshing inside, I am feeling scammed. One, he was taking my hundred rupees, and two, I will never be getting a good role from him. Are all these men playing a joke on me?

Outside, the sun is too bright. I am holding a hand above my eyes. I was hearing once that Reshma Goyal, who is now such a big star, was plucked by a casting director at a Café Coffee Day. One cup of coffee there costs one hundred rupees. This thought is making me sigh. If I was rich, I could be chasing my dreams in that way also.

For a few minutes, I am feeling so disheartened, all I am doing is walking down the street and scrolling through WhatsApp.

My sisters are forwarding me helpful advices.

Warning from All India Dieticians Professional Group: do not eat orange and chocolate in the same day, otherwise—

Don't answer phone calls coming from number +123456; it is a way of using your SIM to call internationally—

One sister is sending me a joke.

Why is Santa Singh keeping a full glass and an empty glass beside his bed at night? Because he may or may not drink water!

I am looking up and seeing a boy at a corner shop. He is refilling someone's cell phone credit, scratching a card with his fingernail to get the code, but his eyes are straight on my breasts.

"Want to come drink my milk?" I am shouting.

Now I am close to the train station, but, instead of taking the train, I am walking, walking, walking. My feet are turning left, right, left on their own, until I am standing in front of a house I am knowing very well. It is a two-storey house, painted yellow. Azad's house. So what if he is married? He was the one telling me that our bond cannot be broken by man-made rules. But now it has been many days, he has not come to me only. I am wishing for his embrace now. I am wishing that he is coming to me again and we are sitting on the floor eating chocolate ice cream. I can be telling him all about Mr. Jhunjhunwala. I know he will even be making me laugh about it.

He has been irritated by our marriage talk, that much I know. But he will come. I am looking at the balcony, eager to see a shirt or pant, which is holding the shape of him. But the clothes strings are empty. There are only Azad's shoes drying against the balcony railing. Azad wore those shoes so much, I can recognize them from this distance also. It is this Nike brand, but it is better because, instead of one tick, it has two. Azad was always knowing the latest style. My heart is thinking of all those times he was opening those shoes inside my house, my room, and embracing me—

Suddenly a man is saying, "O ma, please to let the customers come." I am turning around. There is a vehicle repair garage behind me, smelling of diesel. The man who is talking to me is a Sikh uncle. He must be owning the repair garage. He is wearing a gray uniform and a red turban.

"Why?" I am demanding. "Am I an elephant that I am blocking the whole path? Your customers can't walk here if they want?"

But immediately I am having one frightening thought: I am not wanting Azad to accidentally see me like this. So I am sashaying away.

"Okay, uncle," I am saying. "You asked nicely, so I am gone."

JIVAN

Uma madam taps her steel-tipped stick against the bars of our cells. Down the corridor she goes, *clang clang clang.*

"Up, up," she calls. "Time to get up!"

I hear the sound coming closer. In front of my cell it stops. I look up from the mattress, where I have been, not asleep, but unwilling to begin the day. It is six in the morning and the sun's heat has already warmed the walls and cooked the air. My skin sticks. When I raise my head, Uma madam points her stick through the bars. "Especially you!" she says. "Because of you, we are having to take all this trouble. Why are you still sleeping?"

My case has brought scrutiny upon the women's prison. TV channels and filmmakers want to show how we live, what we do. I imagine them crawling inside, observing us like we are monkeys in a zoo: "Now the inmates have one hour to watch TV. Then they will cook the food." The more requests the administration denies, the more suspicious they look. The men and women of the administration protest that it is a matter of security and safety. But what does our prison have to hide? How bad are the conditions?

The public wants to know. It is looking likely, we hear, that some TV requests will be granted. Before the camera crews appear, the prison must be "beautified."

"Beautification!" Uma madam scoffs as she walks away.

This morning, I receive the task of scrubbing decades of grease and black soot from the kitchen walls. Others mop and wipe the floors, replace lightbulbs, and plant saplings in the garden. A favored few do the gentle work of painting murals on the walls. Americandi, leader of all, sticks a melting square of Cadbury in her mouth and supervises.

——

The work causes old aches to flare. Throughout the week, women complain about the long hours on their feet. The steel wool and kerosene with which I scrub grease make my palm burn, but who knows if this hand, at this task, in this prison, is mine? In my mind, my hand grips the table in front of me in the courtroom, watching as my supporters—Kalu, with his neck tumor; Lovely, of course; some regular customers of my mother's breakfast business who have been asking her to reopen her morning shop— appear in the courtroom to tell all gathered that they have seen me taking books to Lovely. They know I teach her English. Lovely's neighbors know too. Isn't this, the knowledge of a dozen people, a kind of evidence?

——

The next time Purnendu comes, I tell him about the day I told my mother I was quitting school.

"Ma," I said to her one day, "I will tell you something, but you can't be angry."

Purnendu leans forward, as if he is my mother.

She turned around from the stove, a flour-dusted ruti on her upturned palm, and looked at me.

"After class ten," I said, "I will leave school. I will work and support you and Ba."

My ears were hot. My mouth was dry.

"Who taught you these stupid things?" Ma said, looking up at me. "You want to leave school? Look at this smart girl! And do what?"

"Work, Ma, work!" I said. "Ba has not worked in so long, because his back is not healing. That nighttime market is not safe for you. Did you forget how you got attacked? How are we making money?"

"That's nothing for you to worry about," she snapped. "When did you become such a grandma? Just go to school, study hard, that is your job."

But I could not give up. If I let her talk me out of it, I would never attempt it again.

"Class ten graduates," I said, "can get well-paying jobs. I can finish class ten, sit for the board exams, then look for a job."

After days of back and forth, Ma gave up. One night, as we were finishing our meal, she threw up her hands.

"Now this job ghost is sitting on your shoulder, what can I do?" she said. "So fine! Ruin your life, what do I care? Grow up and live in a slum, that will be good!"

MEGHA MAJUMDAR

Maybe that was a poor decision. But whom did I have
to teach me how to build a better life?

———

In the month leading up to the board exams, I studied
hard. Late nights I sat on top of the high bed, a flashlight
in one hand aimed at the page, my body swaying back and
forth as I murmured paragraphs. As night grew deeper, in
the silence around me, sometimes I heard a man pissing in
the gutter right outside the house. Sometimes I heard footsteps, soft like a ghost's. I don't know how much I learned,
but I did memorize whole textbooks by heart.

In March, the board exams began. I went to my assigned
school building—we were given seats in different schools,
away from our own, so that we could not scratch answers
into our desks beforehand. A few girls were pacing in the
lane, textbooks open in their arms, their lips moving. Some
distance away, a girl was bent over and vomiting while her
mother patted her back.

Inside, in a classroom, it was strange to take my chair,
a sloping desk before it that belonged to somebody else.
The desk was scratched with hearts which said *S+K*.
Sheets of answer paper were passed out by a teacher and
I waited with my sheets, gripping my new ball pen, until
the question paper was distributed. Outside the window,
a tree held still.

Three hours later, when the bell rang, I handed
over my sheets, bound with an elastic string, to the

invigilator. My middle finger was swollen with the pressure of the pen.

In the corridor, girls stood in clusters, hands smudged with ink, some rubbing their aching hands. I left, over-hearing pieces of conversations.

"What did you write for the summer crops question?"

"Sorghum!"

"I *knew* this diagram would come."

———

On the day of results, my heart leaped to see I had passed, with fifty-two percent. It was the poorest score in my class and my classmates looked at me with concern. They expected me to cry or collapse in despair. A few girls were standing in the corner, sniffling into handkerchiefs because they had received seventy percent. But, unlike them, I was not planning to go to college. All I needed was to pass and I had.

At home, I was feted as a graduate. How proud were my mother and father. In celebration, my mother pressed a milk sweet in my mouth and distributed a packet of sweets to the neighbors.

"My daughter," she announced proudly, "is now class ten pass!"

It was as if she had forgotten my plan. I had not.

The week after, with a copy of my exam certificate in hand, I walked into the New World Mall and got a job in the jeans section of Pantaloons.

———

And there, at Pantaloons, I picked up a bad habit. Everyone around me had bad habits. We were earning our own money, why should we not indulge? I started smoking cigarettes. Costly cigarettes, branded singles, which I bought with pride and lit from a slow-burning rope dangling from a corner of the shop. I held each cigarette between my fingers like a film star.

———

The night the train would burn, I walked to a place where my mother would not come upon me. The Kolabagan train station. There was a cigarette shop open there until late hours. I bought a single. I lit it. On the platform I stood like an independent woman, flicking ash. Next to me, I rested a package of my textbooks, which I was long past needing. I would give them to Lovely.

A few of the passengers inside the halted train looked at me, all alone at night, smoking a cigarette. They were thinking, I thought, that I was a risky girl.

This is what city girls do, I thought. I enjoyed troubling them.

Then I heard two slaps of thunder. Quick as lightning, a crackle of fire spread through the train. I saw two shapes slipping away into the overgrown public garden next to the railway lines, the slum's toilet. One minute, two

A BURNING

coaches were smoking, a trembling fire within them, and the next, the fire was roaring out of the windows, jumping from coach to coach. Other than the fire, I heard nothing, though I could see faces trapped and screaming. I stood, frozen, a tiny fire glowing in my hand. The air began to smell like burning hair.

Directly in front of me, locked in the train, a man was beating his wrist against the iron bars of a window. The man was looking at me. A grown man, he was looking at me and crying. He was speaking to me. Between his lips stretched saliva. I could not hear his words, but I could guess them. He was begging for help. He was holding up a little girl. She was struggling, squirming, crying.

He was pleading with me to come up and, somehow, grab his little girl, pull her through the window bars if I could.

I turned and ran. In a gutter somewhere, I dropped my cigarette. Then I ran and ran and did not stop until I arrived home.

———

All I am guilty of, Purnendu, listen—all I am guilty of is being a coward.

PT SIR

One morning, at the school assembly, while the principal speaks, the microphone shrieks.

Students cover their ears. Teachers keep sober faces.

Instead of hurrying forward to fix the problem, PT Sir stands with the other teachers, calmly sipping a cup of tea.

The principal calls, "Where is Suresh?"

Suresh is a peon in the administrative office. When he is fetched, he goes up to the microphone and jiggles the cables. He unplugs it and plugs it in once more. He taps the head of the microphone.

PT Sir looks on, not moving a finger.

JIVAN

Then Purnendu is gone. I wake with my heart clamoring in its cage. I force stale bread and dry potatoes down my throat—no tea today. The sun, unseen, makes itself felt in clothes sticking to our bellies and salt water dripping down our necks. Kneeling, I perform today's beautification task, which is to clean a bathroom. I scrub the toilet and pour boric acid down a pipe. The acid, diluted in water, stings where my hand holds old cuts. But it will kill the moving, pulsing soil smeared in the sewage lines—dozens of cockroaches.

All the while, in a clean office far from here, Purnendu writes my story and his editor makes it better.

"Your editor made the story better?" I laughed when Purnendu told me. "My story would be better if . . ."

I count on my hands. "If we had not been evicted, do you see? If my father had not broken his back, if my mother had not been attacked for trying to run a small business. If I could have afforded to finish school."

"Not better like that," said Purnendu.

"Then like what?"

He had no answer.

———

Two days later, I am standing in line for my morning meal, when Uma madam arrives in the courtyard, waving a newspaper in the air.

"You," she says, looking at me. Her mouth twists, hiding a smile. Then she hands me the newspaper. "Nice job."

The headline, in large text, reads, *"I THREW BOMBS AT THE POLICE": A TERRORIST TELLS HER LIFE STORY.*

The story begins: *Over several interviews conducted at the women's prison, this reporter heard a story of poverty and misfortune, as well as a lifelong anger at the government. It began when Jivan was a child and was, along with her family, evicted from their settlement near Kurla mines. At that time, she freely confessed to this reporter, she and her family prepared homemade bombs with which they attacked the police.*

I move out of the line and sit on the ground. I read the lines again. Did I forget to clarify to him that those bombs, as we called them, were nothing more than urine and shit? They were the pathetic defense of an insect.

I check the byline. *Purnendu Sarkar,* it reads. That was his name, wasn't it?

I read some more. *Her anger at the government is not recent and has roots in a lifetime of neglect. From mistreatment of her father at a government hospital, leaving him with chronic debilitating pain as the result of a back injury, to her time living in government housing where an unreliable water supply made daily life difficult, close analysis of her story reveals animosity toward the government—*

I finish reading the article and begin again. I finish it once more and return to the top of the column, over and over until the words become no more than balls of earth rolled by termites. I close my eyes and the ground tilts, taking me with it.

Uma madam takes the newspaper from me. I let her take it. From where I sit, I see only her feet, wrinkled skin in Bata slippers, and a sari reduced to rag in the humid air. "Feels good?" she taunts above my head. "This is what happens when you do secret interviews without permission! Do another! Do ten more! See how much they help!"

My head feels drawn to the earth, incapable of raising itself. So that is who he was, Purnendu. I listen to Uma madam's scolding in this posture of shame, until the posture is all I am.

———

Ma comes, holding a newspaper in her hand.

"Don't show that to me," I say, anger flaring at her.

She opens the leaves, turning the cottony pages one by one.

"Wait, wait," she says. "Kalu read this to me. He said it is good." She shows me a column inside, marked by pencil.

Beware of trial by media, says the article. This is a different paper. *Where is concrete proof that this young woman had involvement in the attack? Everything the police tells us is circumstantial evidence. The woman is being sacrificed because of her Muslim identity.*

"See?" says my mother. "Kalu told me this newspaper is speaking up in your defense. People are listening. Nothing is decided yet. Don't give up hope."

I don't know what this means, this matter of hope. Moment by moment, it is difficult to know whether I have it or not, or how I might tell.

"This just means you are being hopeless," my mother teases. Then she smiles and touches my cheek while the guard has her back turned to us.

There is nothing funny, but my mother's smile, those familiar folds of her mouth, that crooked tooth, the wisps of hair at her temples, soothes me.

At the end of the hour, when she gets up to leave, she reminds me, "Many people from Kolabagan are going to come speak about you in the court, you'll see. What a good girl you are, a good student, the only girl in our locality who speaks English. They will learn that you are nothing like what this one newspaper is saying."

I nod, willing no tears to spill from my eyes.

Then the guard calls, "Time, time!" and, after her hand rests for a gentle moment on my head, my mother is gone. I turn back inside. I brace for a collapse, a removal of light during which I will lie, my bones against the floor.

But I am surprised to find that it is bearable. I cook ruti, I clean the new exhaust pipes, which malfunction. Americandi's eyes follow me from task to task, waiting for my breakdown. But it doesn't come. From my mother's immense strength, I have borrowed a little.

JIVAN'S MOTHER AND FATHER

In the darkness of the house, Jivan's mother and father sit before meals of rice and yogurt, tears falling on their plates.

"It took everything I have," says Jivan's mother, "to smile before her."

"I know," says Jivan's father, a hand on his wife's shoulder. "I know. Eat."

JIVAN

On the first day of the trial, Uma madam brings me a sari to wear. I recognize it. It is the sari I purchased for my mother from Pantaloons, with my employee discount. It is light blue, the color of a winter day, with simple threadwork along the border. I wear it and feel my mother close by.

At the courthouse, there is a garden. There is new soil under my feet, the bigness of trees in the yard, light so bright it hits my eyes like broken glass, a stampede of reporters who scream questions and fight to take a picture of my face. Policemen surround me as soon as I exit the van and I walk as if inside a shell.

Still the reporters shout, "Here! Look here!"

They shout, "What will you say to the families of the dead?"

"What are you eating in the prison?"

"Are they beating you?"

"Has anyone from the terrorist group contacted you?"

"Have they coached you on what to say?"

Inside the courtroom, I sit in relief. The room is large, with ceilings so high they could have fit another floor inside. Long rods drop from the ceiling, holding ceiling fans that turn. Before me, a witness box covered by a white curtain, so that I cannot influence the witnesses.

My lawyer, Gobind, asks me again and again whether I want to eat.

"Want a banana?" he says. "You should eat before it starts."

I have no appetite.

The lawyer for the government begins. He spins a story in which I, unruly local youth, school dropout, angry at the government, cultivate a relationship with a known terrorist recruiter over Facebook. As proof, the lawyer points to the Facebook conversations I have had with my friend, my foreign friend. In this story, when the recruiter asks for my help, either through coded text messages or by calling me on the phone, I agree. The terrorists need a local contact, the lawyer insists, a helper who can guide them down the unnumbered, crooked lanes of the slum, all the way to the station and all the way out. In his story, not only do I lead them to the station, I also hurl a torch of my own at the train. I have, he reminds the gathered, hurled bombs at authorities before—

I cannot bear it. I stand up and say, "Those weren't *bombs,* my god, they were just our—"

Gobind hisses at me to sit. The judge, calmly, tells me to sit. Silence thunders in my ears. I lower myself into the wooden chair.

"And," the lawyer concludes, "let me remind the court that all of this is not some, what shall I say, *theory*

I have made up. This is all in the confession that the accused signed."

He points at me dramatically.

"Everything I have said," he continues, "is in the confession and, what's more, all of it is corroborated, like I have shown you. The accused herself has repeated many of these statements, as you all saw in her interview in the *Daily Beacon* done by esteemed journalist Purnendu Sarkar."

The judge frowns. He calls both lawyers to his seat, grand like a throne. In my chair, I wait, my limbs growing cold. What is the judge discussing in secret? I feel like a straw doll, dressed up for play, at the mercy of callous children who decide my fate.

Then, mercy. The judge throws out my "confession." He pronounces it inadmissible, as I was forced to sign it—this, he believes.

Gobind gives me an encouraging smile.

I am glad for this small triumph. I have done nothing, I have done nothing, but nobody in this courtroom believes that. Only my mother. My mother is sitting somewhere behind me, but I have no courage to turn around and face all the other eyes.

———

For four days, I go through the routine of coming to court. On the fourth day, a reporter, or maybe just a passerby, spits on my face outside the courthouse. My lawyer finds a canteen napkin with which I wipe my face, but there is no time to find a bathroom and wash. I sit with that stranger's hatred on my face all day.

By this time, the prosecution has called forty witnesses, including old neighbors from the slum eviction, the doctor who treated my father, the NGO lady who sponsored my education. They testify behind the white curtain, for fear that I—*I*—may intimidate them by making eye contact. I listen to their ghost voices. Some saw me smoking— several people mention this, as if lighting a cigarette is the same as lighting the tip of a torch.

Is smoking a cigarette as a young woman a crime?

Then, on the fifth day, a man arrives in the witness box. He speaks and his voice revives me. I know this voice.

I am back in the school courtyard, playing basketball. It is my old PT teacher. I wait for him to tell everyone that I was an ordinary student, that I used to love to play.

He says, "She was poor, always separate from the other girls. But she didn't behave badly in my class. She played very well, in fact. I had high hopes that she would be an athlete."

Listen to my teacher, I think. Listen to him. He knows. I want to catch his eyes to thank him, but it is not possible.

"Yes, my understanding was that she had a difficult life," he says. "Sometimes I gave her food for lunch. I never knew if she had enough to eat. She seemed grateful for the food."

I was, I remember. I was grateful. Perhaps in my child's arrogance I failed to thank him adequately. I will do it as soon as they let me speak to him. I will thank him for speaking up on my behalf. Nobody else has been willing to do it. Not a person from the NGO, not a person from my school, nobody yet from my locality.

Then he says, "But she disappeared. I tried to help her, by being encouraging, by giving her food, but one day she stopped coming to school. This was after the class ten exams. She didn't do so well, if I remember. But so what? You can make up with better marks in class twelve. But no. She just left. Vanished. Never saw her again, until I saw her on TV. Maybe she got involved with criminal elements after leaving school. It happens."

I feel a weight in my chest, the earth's pull within my ribs. I try to hear further, but there are wasps in my ears.

———

For the sixth, seventh, and eighth days, my lawyer presents our defense. When I try to persuade him to let me speak, he lifts a finger to his lips.

"Ninety-nine-point-nine percent of the time," he tells me during a break in the proceedings, "it does not help to have the defendant speak. It is a proven fact."

Is it? There is nothing I can do but trust him.

Though I have been in touch with a terrorist recruiter over Facebook, he concedes, all we spoke about was my job, my coworkers, my feelings. Not a word about an attack. I, Jivan, thought he was a friendly boy in a foreign country—what girl wouldn't chat with such a boy?

Gobind points out all the errors in Purnendu Sarkar's article. He corrects the notion that I threw real bombs at the police before. He asserts that my writings on Facebook were nothing more than a young girl expressing her feelings. He paints me as stupid and gullible. And how glad I am for it.

Then he says: "That package that you keep hearing about? That package? Was *not* an explosive of any kind. It was a package of books! She was going to deliver books to a hijra in the slum! That's right, my client was doing public service, she was teaching English to a hijra in her locality. We can hear about it from the hijra herself."

I hear Lovely called to the witness box. My heart lifts, the thread of a kite unspooled, fed into the sky by the hands of a hopeful child.

Lovely has come. The microphone catches her settling into the witness box and I hear her say, "You are only making these boxes for thin people or what?"

For the first time during the trial, a smile springs to my mouth. Lovely has come, with her voice, her unafraid manner, and the truth of my story.

"What is shocking me," she says in Bengali, "is how you all are making up such lies."

"Please," Gobind tells her, "stick to the facts."

"Fine!" she says. "Jivan was teaching me English. I was not knowing English and *in fact* I am still not knowing English."

The courtroom laughs.

The judge asks for order.

Lovely continues. "But it's not Jivan's fault. Every two–three days, she was coming to my house with some old textbooks. I was learning *a b c d,* then simple words like 'cat.' Like that. I was learning it all so that I was being able to audition better. I am"—she coughs bashfully—"an actress."

The courtroom laughs again.

Lovely continues seriously, as if she has not heard. "I am an actress, so I need to be reading scripts and having fluent English, you understand? So that is how I am knowing Jivan, sweet girl. She was spending her time on teaching the poors. How many of you are doing that in your own life?" she demands. "Who are you all to judge her?"

———

On the ninth day, when my one sari is wrinkled, its luster gone, the judge speaks. He clears his throat and speaks in English. First, he reads out the charges.

Waging of war against the government. Murder and criminal conspiracy. Knowingly facilitating acts preparatory to a terrorist act. Voluntarily harboring terrorists.

"We have given both sides a fair hearing," the judge reads from his prepared notes, his spectacles at the tip of his nose. "The defendant was at the train station, carrying a package. The defendant had an ongoing relationship, on this website called Facebook, with a known terrorist recruiter. The defendant's own former teacher has told us that she left school, discontinued her education, under suspicious circumstances. And, on the other hand, we have the word of a hijra, an individual who begs on the streets for money, saying the defendant taught her English. Be that as it may"—the judge takes a deep breath and I feel the air in my own lungs—"it is clear that the defendant has long been disloyal to the values of this nation. The defendant has spoken clearly against the government, against the police, on the Internet, on Facebook dot-com. This lack of loyalty is not something to be taken lightly. It is its own strong piece of evidence. There is a case to be made, as well, for soothing the conscience of the city, of the country. The people demand justice."

He goes on.

They have been unable to trace the terrorists and the railway station had no CCTV. Possibly the terrorists crossed the border. They have truly disappeared into the night. Only I, fool that I am, am here.

Then the judge pauses and turns the page. The sound, in the silent room, is like the crack of a whip. Then the judge sentences the accused to death.

I don't know whom he is speaking about.

Have we moved to a different case?

Somewhere behind me, an animal cries in pain, as if a bolt has been driven into its brain. It is my mother. I turn around. My mother, there in the third row, sari wrapped around her shoulders, stands up, then collapses. I hear the whole courtroom catch their breath. My mother falls and I stand. Two guards jump up from the back and shout for a stretcher. A huddle of policemen positioned at the exit nearest me watch me like hawks.

When a canvas stretcher appears, the two guards together load her on it—

I shout after them, "Where are you taking her?"

My lawyer tells me to sit down.

"Wait a moment," I shout. "She will get better."

"Please be quiet," calls the judge.

LOVELY

In the morning, at the municipal tap, I am hearing the news. When I am hearing the chatter about the "murderer," my heart is agitating inside my rib cage.

I was going, just a few days ago, to the court. Even though Arjuni Ma was telling me not to get involved in this court business, I was going. Everybody was thinking that I was being hauled in for something, so proudly I was telling everyone around me, from a Xerox shop lady to a lawyer who was chewing his lips and looking at his phone, that I was there to *give evidence*. That is how Gobind was explaining it to me. The whole time I was wishing for one moment to see Jivan, to be giving her one kind look, but they were putting up white cloths so we were not being able to see each other. One strange detail, which they are never showing in movies.

Truly I am not believing this verdict. Surely Gobind will be filing something, appealing something, saving Jivan somehow. Isn't that his job?

I am going to a small crossing by myself and half-heartedly begging for coins. I am knocking at this car and that car. I am seeing a cinema of faces in the windows. In a back seat, a child is squirming. Two men are sitting and drinking Mango Frooti. Even a dog, which is looking like a wolf is enjoying the ride in AC comfort. All of them are ignoring me.

The public is wanting blood.

The media is wanting death.

All around me, that is what people are saying. The public is killing her.

When an office worker is walking by, in his clean leather shoes and ironed pants, I am feeling like shouting at him, "People like you killed her! You put your own two hands on her neck!"

Instead I am finding my voice and saying, "Brother, give."

Out of nowhere, two child beggars are arriving. They are giving me dirty looks because I am in their territory. They are shouting, "Who made this your crossing?"

I am sticking my tongue out at them and walking away. Behind me, I am hearing the two children laughing, shrieking, feeling cursed themselves or maybe just making fun of me.

———

My feet are taking me to Jivan's house. There are fifty or a hundred reporters there. Their cars and trucks, with satellite dishes on top, are blocking all the lanes. Their cameras and lights and wires are everywhere.

Father of Jivan is leaning on his walking stick and

coming out blinking in the daylight. I am watching from the back of the crowd.

"Look," he is saying, "look at me, I am a lame man, a limp man, and I am not being able to save my daughter."

He is putting his neck forward, like a rooster. "What else are you wanting to know about me?

"Ask," he is saying. "Ask!"

He is looking mad. His arms are trembling. Kalu the neighbor is standing at his side, holding two fingers at the top of his nose, like his eyes are hurting.

"Why you are not asking me anything?" father of Jivan is saying.

The reporters are standing there quietly, for one minute.

Then they are shouting questions. "How do you feel about the ruling?"

"Does your daughter plan to appeal?"

"How is Jivan's mother's health?"

To get his attention they are saying, "Sir! Sir!"

"This way!" they are shouting for a picture.

——

Then the reporters are going, leaving behind a trail of crushed cigarettes. At night, I am going out with a broom and sweeping the butts into a corner. The dust is rising at my feet like a little storm.

INTERLUDE

Bimala Pal's Assistant Has a Side Hustle

Who does not have a side job? Bimala Pal is good to me, but even so, I am just an assistant. I have a family. Wife, school-going children. Have you seen how much school fees are these days? Besides, when they come home, tired, they don't want rice and egg every day. They don't want a tiny TV. We all want something nice. So I am a middleman, you can say.

Imagine you are a Muslim. One day, what happens? Your neighbors, good people, suddenly form a mob over some rumor and break your door, threaten your wife, frighten your crippled mother. They set fire to your house. Thankfully, they do it while you are all out. That is their kindness. You run. You leave your damaged house, your property, and you run. Life becomes so precious, so precious! For a few months, okay, there is refugee camp, some donated rice, some tin house.

But one day the government announces: no more this ugly refugee camp! You all get five lakh rupees, now go somewhere else and live. Shoo.

Immediately, who comes? Vultures.

You have your broker, your landlord, your town council, your water man, your electricity man, even your school man— what will your small children do, sit at home and grow up illiterate like you? So they all come and say, "Sir, there is a good plot here, you buy and build your own home. Most important you have your own piece of land in your name. There will be a water connection and electricity cables are already laid, you come and see just." So you look at the plot. The land looks fine. You give most of your compensation money to buy this plot.

Then one day everyone disappears—your broker who called you five times a day? Vanished. The electricity man, the water supply man? Vanished.

Then you go to the address given on your deed and feel confused when you arrive somewhere different from where you went the first time. You have never seen this plot! All the neighborhood boys nod and chew their twigs and nod and then they laugh. When they laugh, you realize—you have bought a patch of this swamp.

So this is the riot economy. In this economy, I am a broker, nothing more.

LOVELY

In the morning, my heart restless, I am calling the casting director, Mr. Jhunjhunwala. The phone is still charging, so I am bending my head close to the plug.

"Hello?" he is saying.

"Hello, me Lovely," I am saying, "good morning to you!"

Mr. Jhunjhunwala is quiet, only breathing, and I am feeling his irritation on the line. Now I am realizing, maybe he is always getting such calls from aspiring actors. Maybe they are not missing any opportunity to wish him good morning, happy Holi, good night, blessed Diwali.

So he is sighing and saying, "Yes, Lovely."

"Are you seeing," I am saying, "my demo CD yet? What are you thinking? Are you having a role for me?"

"Lovely," he is saying, "please do not call me like this. I am in a meeting, so I will call you later, okay?"

"Okay, Mr. Jhunjhunwala, but it has been some weeks and you keep saying—"

"I am in a meeting, Lovely," Mr. Jhunjhunwala is saying and cutting the line.

———

After class one Sunday, I am asking Mr. Debnath, with some nervousness in my throat, "Are you still keeping me for that role? I was making a demo video, like you were saying—"

He is sitting in his usual chair. He is sighing. I am seeing his belly rise and fall. He is putting his saucer of tea on a side table and crossing his fingers over his chest. The whole time I am standing before him with my hands crossed behind my back. Mother and father of Mr. Debnath are looking at me from their portraits on the wall. This time their portraits are having some red rose flowers in the garland, as if they are starring in a romance.

"Lovely," he is starting, "do you know how long it can take to make an epic movie like I am making? It can take one and a half years just to cast a film like that. You know, in one fight scene I need seventy-two extras? Just one scene. Seventy-two extras. Imagine. Do you think this happens quickly?"

I am hanging my head low like a scolded child.

"On top of that," Mr. Debnath is mumbling, "you have gone and said all these things in court."

"Mr. Debnath," I am saying straightaway, "are you upset with my testimony for Jivan?"

He is staying quiet.

"Don't be silly," he is saying after a while. "Politics

is not entering my mind. I am just feeling that, maybe, after the court case, you are already feeling like a big star. Two minutes on TV and, boom, you are thinking you are a legend. You are having so little patience." His thick brows are coming together like worms in the soil. "And the things you said, well, in the papers they are saying you are an unpatriotic ... I don't want to repeat those things."

"What things?" I am demanding.

I am always thinking that Mr. Debnath is believing in me, but this time, with my eyes on his hairy toes, I am feeling that he is a man I am not truly knowing and I am a person he is not truly knowing. How long can I keep trusting his words and waiting for his film? My chance to be a young star is reducing. Nobody is wanting to see a star with gray hair and saggy arms.

On the road outside, a blade sharpener is walking by with his tools. He is calling, "Sharpen your knife! Sharpen your knife!"

———

Just when we are thinking that the electricity supply is really improved, no load shedding in our locality any more, it is happening. Suddenly one night the tubelight is going dark. *Kabhi Khushi Kabhie Gham, Sometimes Happiness Sometimes Sorrow,* on the TV is shutting off, leaving some colors playing on the TV screen. It is feeling like something is going wrong with your eyes. But no. It is only load shedding. A few mosquitoes are immediately finding my arms and ears to nibble. Without the noise of fridges and TVs, voices are traveling far in the air.

For once, I am leaving my phone alone, because the battery is finished.

In the dark, with not even a candle in my house, I am sitting in the doorway and looking outside. One hour is passing, then two.

A few people are walking by. I am calling one neighbor lady by name, but it is not her. She is looking at me, a dark face like a silhouette.

Now the sky is holding more light than the ground. There is a half-moon, with gray spots on it that I was never noticing before. Like the moon is having pimples also. Clouds like cotton pulled from a roll are moving under the moon, sometimes hiding it, sometimes revealing it. I am feeling that the world is so big, so full of our dreams and our love stories and our grief too.

I am blowing my nose and getting up to go inside.

Alone inside, my tears are coming like a fountain. Poor Jivan. My testimony was proving as useful as a shoe is to a snake.

And Azad has not come to see me even once. I am wiping my tears on my dupatta. I was forced to, my heart, is he not knowing that? It was not me who was throwing him out. It was this society. This same society that is now screaming for the blood of innocent Jivan, only because she is a poor Muslim woman.

Like a heartbeat, the light is turning on and the fan

is starting to whir and I am hearing a cheer spreading throughout the neighborhood. Electric current is back.

I am wiping my tears. I am flinging my snot outside the window.

When I am thinking about it, I am truly feeling that Jivan and I are both no more than insects. We are no more than grasshoppers whose wings are being plucked. We are no more than lizards whose tails are being pulled. Is anybody believing that she was innocent? Is anybody believing that I can be having some talent?

If I am wanting to be a film star, no casting man or acting coach will be making it happen for me. So I, myself, Lovely with my belly and no-English and dramatic success only in Mr. Debnath's living room—I am having to do it myself. Even if I am only a smashed insect under your shoes, I am struggling to live. I am still living.

When my phone is a little bit charged, I am taking some of my practice videos from acting class, including my super-hit session with Brijesh, and sending them to my sisters on WhatsApp. *Please,* I am writing, *please to be sharing my videos with your friends and their friends. I am looking for acting roles. Tell me if you are hearing about opportunities!*

———

The next day, back to my normal life, where I am having to earn money. I am going to the number one tourist spot in the whole city, the white marble British palace Victoria Memorial. It is a place where donkey villagers are coming, especially on cool, cloudy days like these. Their mouths are always open when they are touring the city. They are looking at everything like it was made personally by god. Malls, zebra crossings, women who are wearing pants.

They are also wanting as many blessings as possible, so they are always wearing five holy threads on their wrist and seven holy threads on their upper arm and who knows what else. These poor people are afraid of many things and top of the list is bad luck from god. This I can understand, however, because me, I am the most cursed person.

Anyhow, I am entering the Victoria gardens and seeing the crowd. There is a straight white path going to the big palace and, on both sides, green lawns and trees. In the cool weather, the lawns are full of children who are playing badminton with their parents, and some lovers who are sitting too close together under trees and eating ice-cream cones. They are all taking off their shoes and I am seeing a parade of cracked soles when I am walking down the center. I am clapping my hands, saying, "Mother goddess sent me to bless you all today."

I am blessing one young girl. Then I am blessing a baby. Then a guard is tapping me with a stick.

"What?" I am saying to the guard. "I am having a ticket, look!"

And the guard is not knowing what to say to that, because that is true. So he is saying, "No walking on the grass!"

Then he is taking a close look at my face. "Aren't

you—didn't you testify at the big trial? Sorry, sorry," he is saying to me, I am not understanding why.

When a man is bringing his baby to me, I am dipping an old flower into my small jar of holy water—water from the municipal pump—and I am circling the baby's head with the flower, dropping dew on the baby, until the baby is looking like he is about to start wailing.

Suddenly a person is saying from behind me, "Lovely, is it you?"

Turning around, I am seeing Mr. Jhunjhunwala. He is wearing jeans and sunglasses, which he is pushing on top of his head.

"It *is* you! Ha-ha!" he is saying, like it is such a surprise that I can be roaming in a tourist spot.

I am saying hello, how is your family, and such things.

"Are you free for one minute?" he is saying after a while. "I wanted to—"

I am giving the baby back to the villager, but not wanting to take money for my non-acting trade in front of the casting director. I am saying, "Free blessing for your golden baby!"

Mr. Jhunjhunwala is now face-to-face with me. He is saying, "Look, Lovely, I finally heard about your testimony at the big trial. So I looked at your reel. Your reel is—!" And he is bringing all his fingers together and kissing them.

"My what?" I am saying.

He is continuing, "Then I saw your WhatsApp video. One hundred percent authentic!"

"WhatsApp—"

"The video from your acting classes—"

"My practice videos? From Mr. Debnath's class? How you are seeing it?" I am demanding. "Only my sisters are seeing it." For one moment, the mad thought is running in my head—is he coming to laugh in my face? Is he coming to personally tell me that my acting is B-class?

"Are you joking, Lovely?" he is saying. "I think your sisters must be sharing it, because it is all over WhatsApp. My friends forwarded it to me. So many of them forwarded it to me that in the end I was replying to them, 'Okay, okay, I saw it already!' Anyway, now directors are calling me up and saying, 'Is it the same person who gave the most passionate testimony at that trial? Can you book her?' So I think you can be perfect for this music video. Are you available tomorrow?"

———

The studio is full of stadium-strength lights and silver sheets that people are holding for bouncing the light correctly. I am watching from the side while the two main actors are embracing in front of a green screen.

"Turn, turn, turn," the director is calling. The couple is turning round and round. "Now kiss him on the cheek!"

The actress is looking like she will prefer to kiss an elephant's behind. But she is doing it.

"Cut it," the director is saying.

Then, after some minutes of setup, where they are

moving the lights and marking my place on the ground with chalk, it is time for my scene.

My scene is only one. But it is repeating and repeating.

Now the couple is getting married and I am looking up from blessing the bride and winking at the camera.

I am looking up from blessing the bride and winking at the camera.

I am looking up from blessing the bride and winking at the camera.

I am looking up from blessing the bride and, again, winking at the camera. My eye is twitching. The director is coming up to me in the end and saying, "Lovely, it is not mattering to me whether your words at that trial are true, false, or in between! All I care about is you have that star material. The nation wants to watch you. You will make this song a hit, I am feeling it!"

———

When a break is called, I am going searching for some food and seeing a table full of sponge cakes and fruits. In the heap, I am looking for a picture of a brown cake. I am wanting chocolate flavor. Why not fully enjoy? Finally I am spotting one, at the bottom of the heap, when an assistant is appearing. He is tapping my shoulder with his notepad and saying, "Your break area is over there, outside! This is A-category actors only."

I am still not really understanding this A-category B-category business.

"Okay," I am saying and turning away.

But the assistant is saying, "Please! You cannot be taking cake from here."

So I am putting it back. I am wishing to ask the assistant if he is not knowing who I am! Is he not seeing my video? But everywhere people are expecting that a person like me will make a scene, so it is my dear wish that I am not making any scene in this professional environment. I am going to join my B-category people, no problem.

Outside the studio, in the field, the light is bright in my eyes. My head is feeling woozy. So long I have been in that studio, where everything outside the circle of lights is black.

There is a crowd of extras around something on a table. A water filter.

A woman is shouting, "How can the water finish? Bring more water!"

I am walking closer and another man is saying, "Let someone faint, then they will learn the lesson."

Other than an empty water filter, there are some blackened bananas on the table. From looking at the bananas I am feeling them in my mouth—squishing on my tongue, smelling a bit fermented, rotting in the heat. So I am swallowing my saliva and waiting for the new water jar to come.

There is another dressed-up woman next to me, so I am tapping her arm and saying, "Sister, which way for toilet?"

The woman is looking me up and down. "What kind

of queen are you? Look around, it's all fields and bushes. Go there."

From the woman's voice I am knowing that she is working in the film line for a long time. Her voice is heavy with experience. But how to go to toilet like this, in the bushes, with everybody around? What if the director is coming and I am missing my chance to impress? Worse, what if he is seeing me standing in the field and pissing like a man from under my dress?

I am sighing in frustration and opening WhatsApp to tell my sisters what a mess this shoot is. As soon as I am opening WhatsApp, I am seeing there are forty messages. My phone was on silent all this time.

You superstar! one sister is saying to me.

Good job! World is your stage, another sister is saying.

They are all seeing how my video is spreading!

Good theater Lovely. What is this? Even Arjuni Ma has written me a WhatsApp message! Must be she has forgiven me for testifying.

Now I am seeing WhatsApps from people I am not knowing only.

Great acting! they are saying. *Where is this class? So cool!*

———

Back home, I am slapping the TV to come on and there I am, on a local news channel, my video with Brijesh playing on a big screen while some men are sitting in front of it and discussing.

"What is so refreshing about this, Aditya, is seeing these dreamers from all walks of life, gathering to pursue their dream in this authentic way."

I am changing the channel. And there I am again!

"This amateur video of an acting class," one bearded man is saying, "has become a viral sensation in the city. Given the brutal news of the recent days, is it any surprise that the public is hungry for a feel-good take, for a reminder that dreams and dreamers do exist in this city?"

I am pressing the button and—

"While some people are calling the star of the show, Lovely, a 'terrorist sympathizer,' there are many who insist she is simply standing up for a person she sees as her good-hearted neighbor."

"No doubt," another man is saying, "many are questioning the fairness of Jivan's trial and Lovely's courtroom performance has a lot to do with it. She is not a legal expert or an investigator, of course, so it is her *passion* that is getting attention. Stay with us as we will be joined by—"

"What avenues does the ordinary person have to chase their dreams? Tell me, if you don't go to an elite film-making academy and hobnob with—"

All these men are lecturing on me! They are having different opinions on whether I am right or foolish, whether Jivan is innocent or evil, but at least they are all discussing me on what they are calling prime-time news!

While I am looking at the screen, somebody is knocking on my door, then peeking in the window and saying, "It's me."

"Arjuni Ma?" I am saying. Immediately I am opening the door, clearing my clothes from the bed, slapping my palms around some over-smart mosquitoes. Inside, she is not sitting. Instead, she is putting her two hands on my cheeks, as if I am a child, and looking at the TV, which is still on.

"I am older than you," she is saying to the TV, "isn't it true, Lovely?"

I am looking at her.

"In life," she is saying, "I have learned that we cannot be having everything. For example. To be putting fish on the plate, we are having to sacrifice dignity on the streets. We are having to beg. Why? Because we would be liking to eat. To be left alone by the police, we are having to—well, I don't have to tell you. So this is a moment of sacrifice for you, Lovely. You are on TV. Your video is popular. Don't let that criminal, that terrorist—"

I am opening my mouth to protest, but Arjuni Ma is raising a hand.

"Let her go from your life. You may be fond of that girl, but you must choose: Are you wanting to rise in the film world? Or are you wanting the public to see you as a person who is defending a terrorist? Don't let that case drag you down, Lovely. That is my only advice for you."

"But some people are saying," I am telling Arjuni Ma, "that her trial is not fair—"

"Is that your fight to fight?" Arjuni Ma is saying. "The trial brought you closer to your dream, so aren't you going to reach for what you really want? You want to be a star or you want to be that girl's defender for ever?"

Then she is going and leaving me alone with the TV. I am muting the volume, which is seeming too high for this small room. On the screen is my practice video. I am watching it silently, feeling something heavy in my stomach, which is keeping me sitting on the mattress, keeping my feet stuck to the floor, even though I am wanting to look away. I was never thinking of the question like how Arjuni Ma was putting it, but now I am finding that I am not being able to think of it any other way.

When I am lying down in bed and closing my eyes, I am feeling my heart teaching me its own lesson. My heart is saying: this is who you are, Lovely. You are growing from a family that was betraying you, so this is nothing new. Jivan can be going forward without you also. In fact, this heart is reminding in my chest, you are not even her family. Leave her, this cold box is saying. Weren't you dreaming of being a movie star? Weren't you dreaming of being so close to fame?

This night, I am sleeping in shame and I am waking in shame and still shame is weaker than the other thing.

———

Sunday morning! Time to go to acting class. Fast fast, I am walking down the lane with my hips going like this and like that, past the small bank where the manager was demanding my birth certificate for opening an account. "I was telling him, 'Keep your account,'" I am saying to the camera that is following me. "I was telling him, 'Birth certificate! Am I a princess?'"

The interviewer who is walking beside me is laughing. She is brushing her glossy hair out of her eyes and saying, "Tell me, how did you start going to this acting class?"

"Well," I am starting. "It was happening like this—"

This time we are together walking past the guava seller in his corner. Usually he is acting like I am invisible, but today he is looking at me with big eyes.

"Here, TV!" he is calling, flapping his hand. "Come take a guava. For free!"

"Brother," I am saying to him, "please to have some dignity. Every other day you are ignoring me and today you are my best friend?"

The interviewer is laughing again. Many things I am doing are making her laugh. That is fine. Why not to laugh? This TV channel is paying me eighty thousand rupees just for letting them follow me to the acting class. Other TV channels were calling me and offering me money also, but I was choosing this channel because this channel is the most popular. My turn to laugh.

On the train, I am presenting my good profile to the camera.

"A train," I am saying thoughtfully, like a university professor, "is like a film. You see, on the train we can be observing behaviors, arguments, voices. How people are looking happy or upset. How they are speaking with their mother and with their fellow passengers and with a pen seller."

The interviewer is looking at me like I am a National Film Award winner. What wisdom is coming out of my mouth! She is nodding and nodding, her eyes shining with the thought of the hundred thousand viewers who will be watching this tonight.

———

In acting class, Mr. Debnath is feeling flustered. Now he is looking like somebody who is never even seeing a camera.

"What is that red light?" he is asking, pointing with a shaking finger at the main camera. "You want me to be looking there?"

"Please just relax, Mr. Debnath," the interviewer is telling him. "You have been teaching this class for years and years. You are the expert. Pretend that we are not even here!"

But that is impossible. Outside the windows of the living room, a crowd is gathering to watch what is going on. "*That* acting class is taking place here!" someone on the street is shouting. One smart fellow is even putting his hand in and moving the curtains so they can all be seeing better.

Inside, the maid is looking suspiciously dressed up, in a shiny sari, with a hibiscus flower in her hair. To the interviewer, she is saying, "Madam, I am watching your show always! And I have been the local cleaner for this class for, oh, don't ask me, *years*. I have seen some things. I am available for any show."

While the interviewer is managing her, smiling politely and saying, okay, thank you, Brijesh is coming up to me and mumbling, "Lovely, I am getting"—here he is giggling, hee-hee—"I am getting an offer to do an ad! Detergent ad. They saw me in your video!"

—

The TV people are bringing their own overhead lights, making this small living room a land of a thousand suns. Every pimple and scar on my face, you can see, except a professional makeup man put high-quality foundation and concealer. Mr. Debnath's deceased mother and father on the wall, please to pray for them, are looking like their eyes are popping out. Never were they seeing this much glamour in their living days.

For so long, I am dreaming of delivering dialogue in front of a real camera and now I am in front of three! For hours, the TV crew are filming us doing practice scenes. In front of them, we are turning up the drama. We are dying patients, supermodels on a runway, mothers cooking food for our husbands. In different scenes, we are having everything from indigestion to love affairs.

In the end, the interviewer is asking me some of my thoughts.

"Society is telling me that I cannot be dreaming this dream," I am telling her. "Society is having no room for people like me"—and inside I am thinking, forgive me, Jivan, I must be leaving you out of this—"because we are poor and we may not be speaking perfect English. But is that meaning we are not having dreams?"

Now I am confessing, on this show, that many times I was walking in front of the Film and Television Institute, just to see how it was. Just to be a little close to the success of the rich acting students. They were getting casting directors, not just casting agents and coordinators, coming to their classes. They were getting special classes from directors, actors, stuntmen, producers, choreographers.

One crazy day I was even thinking, what if I am giving up this rented room? What if I am just sleeping in the train station and spending my rent money on the big acting school?

I am laughing after I am saying that.

"Ha-ha-ha!" I am laughing. "Can you believe?"

But the interviewer, she is having tears in her eyes. She is putting a hand on my cold hand, like we are newly discovering that we are sisters.

———

Fifteen minutes after that TV segment is playing on cable, this very same night, my WhatsApp is going *prrng!*

I am sitting with my sisters in my room, munching some fried pumpkin snacks, discussing everyone's performance in front of the real cameras. Was Kumar keeping his nervous giggling to a manageable level? Was Peonji impressing with his life story of working in insurance and feeding his three children?

Dear Miss Lovely, my phone screen is saying.

When I am opening the WhatsApp from a number I am

not knowing, it is continuing, *I am from Sonali Khan's film production company. Can we talk on the phone?*

I am reading the words again and again. I am showing it, with big, big eyes, to all my sisters. Arjuni Ma, who is acting like she was never giving me any advices, is saying, "Is that—is that—*Sonali Khan*?"

Yes, that Sonali Khan, who is producing one blockbuster after another. Who in this entire country is not knowing the love story, filmed in foreign mountains, in *I Am Yours Forever*, or the fight sequences in the patriotic film *Cricket Mania*?

Suddenly, while we are all sitting there with mouths open, looking at the phone like it is a magic stone, it is ringing. When I am picking up, a woman is saying, "Lovely, did you get my WhatsApp message just now? We are thinking of you for a role in Sonali Khan's next production. It's a good role, a big role. Do you have time to come for an audition next week?"

My sisters are getting excited. They are leaning close to the phone and trying to hear. Everybody is pausing their eating of the pumpkin fritters so that their mouths are not doing *crunch crunch*.

While I am listening on the phone, I am looking with my eyes at my water filter, half-full, my mattress, flattened by our weight, my window, outside of which there is a woman carrying a tub full of soiled dishes for washing.

With all my dignity and all my calm, I, Lovely, am hearing this lady on the phone offering me my dream opportunity. "Yes," I am telling her. "Yes."

PT SIR

It takes two weeks to get an appointment with Bimala Pal and the appointment is no more than the chance to be in a car with her as she is driven from one place to another. The road they travel, in the center of the city, is thick with sedans and buses. A bicycle pushes forward in the wrong direction. Along the edge, tarps are strung between tree trunks for makeshift shops selling calendars, candy, cell phone covers. In the rearview mirror, PT Sir can see two white cars follow.

"Don't ask," says Bimala Pal when PT Sir asks how her work is going. The price of onions is soaring and this is a problem for the government. She, in the opposition, is getting plenty of mileage from it, at least.

"The public is unsatisfied," she says. "The government is failing to control the price. In the news, if you have seen the reports from local markets, every single person is complaining about the price of vegetables. It is hurting the common person."

Turning to him, she asks if the lane before the school has held up over the months. No more waterlogging?

"None," says PT Sir.

"And this has increased my prestige, in fact," he reveals in a moment of friendly feeling.

At this, Bimala Pal laughs.

PT Sir summons all his courage and says what he has wanted to say. "Madam, I want to do more for the party. I am ready for a bigger role. You have so many projects, maybe I can give my service—"

Bimala madam puts a hand on the headrest to brace against a bumpy stretch of road. Through the tinted windows, PT Sir sees street-side vendors toss noodles, ladle biryani from giant containers, and scoop the white batter of dosa onto hot griddles. Through the windshield, he sees now and then, without warning, a pedestrian who holds an arm up and dashes across the street. Horns blare, drivers pressing angry palms against the wheel.

After a minute or two of silence, Bimala Pal speaks. "Actually," she says, "good that you bring this up."

PT Sir imagines an office with a leather chair. A computer of his own. An air-conditioned room where he can sit in the evenings, a part-time position to begin with.

But Bimala Pal has something else in mind. He was so good with the teachers in the village of Chalnai, she says, that she would like him to headline a rally at a village where he can present the party's plans for the local school. They need a knowledgeable man like him in the field. And he will get a taste of a politician's life.

"What do you say?"

The balloon pops. Quickly the vision of a cool and comfortable office evaporates. This will be no different from standing out in the field all day, the blood circulation slowing below his knees. Of course, he accepts.

———

Winter is retreating, the sun regaining its strength, when PT Sir finds himself in a village called Kokilhat. In the shade of a mango tree with roots like knuckles grasping the earth, PT Sir holds a microphone while two lanky men, sitting on the branches above, support megaphones above his head.

A politician's persona slips easily over his clean white shirt and khakis, the garland of flowers around his neck. PT Sir speaks, recalling notes he studied the day before: "We know that your local school has been closed for over two years! I heard all about the absent teachers, the leaks during the monsoons, the textbooks that were not available. That is why we will renovate the building completely and hire teachers for every subject. We will make sure discounted textbooks are available before the first day of school for every child. What's more, there will be free midday meals for your children!"

His voice booms from the megaphones. Ducks in a weedy pond nearby flee to the far side.

"Think of this not just as education for your children, but jobs for your family! We will need construction workers, cooks—"

PT Sir feels himself to be a kind of Bimala Pal. He is pleasantly surprised by his confident voice, the feeling of uplift as he stands before a crowd that has grown to a hundred or more. They are mostly men. It is true that many of them are here for the free bags of wheat flour. Still, they are here. PT Sir sees them craning to get a better view of him. He sees them listening to his words. Is this how powerful people feel?

Then a man in the crowd shouts, "Will there be Muslims teaching their religion at this school? Then we will not send our children!"

PT Sir clears his throat. "Well," he begins. "I respect your religion. I respect your sentiment. Public schools are for all, but we will keep in mind your community—"

In the back, where the crowd consists of curious stragglers, some men laugh. A joke drifts through the margins that PT Sir cannot catch.

PT Sir calls, "The important thing is your religion will be respected, your morals will be taught, at this school. I assure you! Vote for Jana Kalyan Party in the upcoming elections!"

PT Sir thumbs off the microphone and hands it to a boy who begins bundling up the cables. The men holding the megaphones throw the metal mouths to a partner waiting below, then leap to the ground, their feet sending up clouds of dust. They clap their palms free of splinters.

It is then that a young man in the middle of the crowd shouts, "A holy mother cow was *killed*. Yes," he continues, as there is a stunned silence, "killed in our own village!"

People wandering away stop and turn toward him. A small circle opens up around this man, who continues, "What will we do? Will we stand here and listen to a speech about a school? Are we not *men*?"

PT Sir raises his arms. "Be calm, brother," he calls. "Better that you don't spread rumors."

But the crowd begins to agitate. Men shout, "Who was it? Who was it?"

"Who killed the cow?"

"Whose cow?"

From where he stands, PT Sir shouts, "Please be calm, your village chief will investigate—"

Nobody is listening to him. PT Sir hears names floating, names of the only ones who eat beef.

PT Sir shouts again, "Rain is coming, please be calm and—"

But the crowd bellows and lumbers, like a many-limbed animal discovering its ferocity. As one, they direct their feet to the area where the Muslim villagers live.

PT Sir follows the crowd. Only a few minutes ago, he was in full control of these men, inspiring them with words about school. Now they speed down narrow and narrower lanes, passing by children who look up from bathing, their eyes peering out from soaped faces. Mothers and fathers appear and snatch up the children, drawing them inside despite their cries.

"Stop," PT Sir cries. "Listen here! The party will not be happy with you all. Don't you want the school—"

Unbelieving, his heart beating too fast, beside him

the impassive face of the driver who drove him here, PT Sir watches the crowd find the house. He watches them rattle the chain on the doors, then break the flimsy panels open.

INTERLUDE

The Villagers Visit the Beef-Eater

Kill him because he ate beef, that Muslim.

Come prepared with daggers and homemade pistols and we will go as a force of the good god to that man's house. His door surprises us—two rotting planks of wood held together by a chain, which, when we grip it, leaves our fingers smelling of iron.

But no, it is not that which surprises us, but the fact that we remember gripping this chain to rattle, innocent. "Brother, borrow your ladder?" we asked him before.

You see, he is our neighbor. A decent man, sure. His beard descends as a cloud to his chest and our sons fear him for how he tests their mathematics whenever he sees them. "Eight times five?" he says to them. "Square root of forty-nine?"

They say he used to be a schoolteacher, but of what use is that? We all used to be something else.

Now, behind the door we know well, the stillness of the house strikes us as false. It makes us angry. The heat of the day, our empty stomachs—we are not happy. How could we be happy when our sacred mother cow is being senselessly slaughtered? Do not forget! The cow who has given us milk (oh, yes) and has drawn the plow through our great-grandparents' fields (yes) and has borne our goddess to her heavenly home (oh, yes), that very cow has been killed like a common pest by this Muslim. What can we do? What must we do?

In the room behind the door, three daughters, too young to be of any use. We cut them like their father cut our holy mother cow. Our people, the true people of this nation, are a flood of cleansing water, our arms and legs full of muscles, which grab and swing, our grip never more certain than when it closes around the resistant throat of the man's wife. Never more certain than when it stretches open her legs.

—Too ugly! We think at first.

—Aha, not too ugly after all, we know later.

We shatter the fading photographs on the wall, we shake the cupboard until a few gold bangles fall out, and we fall upon the gold like it is a drop of water in a desert.

Rolled up in the corner, a carpet for praying on, so we piss on it and laugh. A terrified man is dragged down from the roof, the Muslim we are after. He moves his mouth, but he has taken out his dentures and his sunken cheeks beg and beg before his voice finds itself. He joins his hands in prayer and we say, "Now you have learned to pray properly?"

He watches his wife's legs opened by the true men

of this country and he appears to die before we can kill him.

Anyway, we stomp on his skull so that the cream of his brain splatters on the floor. Teach him to have ideas about killing our holy mother cow, whom we love and respect.

Later my man says, opening the small icebox and hauling out a chicken, "But where is the beef?"

PT SIR

PT Sir lies in bed that night, an arm flung over his head, his wife snoring by his side. He looks at the shadows cast on the ceiling by passing headlights and, in a kind of daze, he knows this much: his career in politics is over. Never before has he thought of it in such grand terms—"career in politics"—but now, on the verge of losing it, he knows how close he has come to having it.

What did he witness today? With each turn of the ceiling fan's blades, he knows and he refuses to know. He pulls a blanket up to his chin and covers his ears in the warm cloth. He knows what he watched and, in watching and not lifting a finger, condoned. He is no less than a murderer. He turns from side to side, seeking a position of comfort, until his wife drowsily scolds him. Then he lies on his back, still as a corpse.

In the morning, eyes gritty with sleep, he cannot stand to shave his face. He cannot bear to look at his face in the mirror. What face is this? Does it belong to him? He prepares to tell Bimala Pal what happened and to offer his resignation from the party roll. Perhaps her benevolence will keep him out of jail, perhaps it will not. The massacre happened in his presence, perhaps even started from his comments about religion.

The sun rises higher in the sky and, somehow, absent from his body, PT Sir finds that he has bathed himself and eaten a simple breakfast of oats. He has worn his shirt and tied his shoelaces and now he stands at the door, ready to go.

———

When PT Sir appears at her door, Bimala Pal is pacing in the living room, a phone held at her ear. She wears a beige shawl whose frilly edge flaps as she walks. She gestures at him to sit and disappears into the office.

PT Sir sits at the edge of the sofa. He feels faint and lowers his head between his knees. A concerned assistant offers him cold water and he gulps down one glass, then another.

When Bimala Pal emerges, she asks, "How was your rally?"

Then, looking at his sweating face, she says, "Are you feeling all right? Do you need water?"

PT Sir shakes his head.

"I had water," he replies, the words catching in his dry mouth. A high-pitched keening lingers in his ears. Following her to her office, he feels that his legs have disappeared.

"Actually," he begins, once they are in the closed office. "The rally yesterday . . ."

"You don't look well," observes Bimala Pal. "I'll tell Raju to call a taxi for you—"

"No," he interrupts. He cannot leave now. "One thing happened at the village."

PT Sir tells Bimala Pal everything. His tongue forms its own words and he barely hears them over the drumbeat of his pulse. When he finishes, the two of them sit in silence. A crow alights outside the window and harshly caws. Through the closed glass of the window, PT Sir can see its outline.

For a while, Bimala Pal looks silently at the crow too.

PT Sir waits for her to tell him to leave, to never contact the party again. He will return to his schoolteacher's life. It was what he had, before. It was not unbearable.

Then she looks up and gives him a smile. "Have a biscuit," she says, pushing an open packet toward him. "You know, it is sad that a man died, very sad about the children too. I can see you are disturbed. I understand. But did you lay a finger on them? Did you personally hurt them in any way?"

When PT Sir realizes that she is waiting for his reply, he shakes his head.

"Then why," Bimala Pal says, "are you taking the weight of it on your own shoulders?"

PT Sir comprehends each word a moment after she speaks it. Could she be forgiving him?

"There is nothing to forgive," says Bimala Pal. "In politics, you will see, sometimes it feels that you are in charge of everything and everyone. But we can only guide them, inspire them. At the end of the day, are they our puppets? No. So what can we do if they raise their hand, if they decide to beat someone, if they feel angry?"

PT Sir dislikes this justification. At the same time, he reaches desperately for the only relief he has felt since the massacre. Bimala Pal does not seem angry. She does not even seem surprised.

Looking at Bimala Pal's good-natured face, her hands joined on the table in front, her kind eyes wrinkled at their corners, PT Sir feels that she has saved him. From what, he no longer wants to imagine. Yes, she has saved him.

When Bimala Pal speaks next, he understands that she has known what happened all along.

If anybody asks, she tells him, PT Sir is to say that the unstable brick house in which the man was living collapsed. It spontaneously collapsed. And how does PT Sir know? He was doing a rally nearby. It is true that the house did collapse—when the party wrecked it with hammer and ax. It is true that the house did fall upon a man who died.

All of that is true, Bimala Pal reminds him, a gentle smile on her face.

Afterward, PT Sir walks down the road, feeling the protective wing of the party sheltering him. He opens his mouth and gulps air until a beggar looks at him strangely. The Muslim man's family perished, nobody is denying that, but he himself will be all right. Maybe that is all that can be salvaged.

At home, when he parks himself in front of the TV—he

has taken a sick day from school—his mind wanders while his eyes remain captive. When late afternoon comes, with its hint of darkening, he surrenders to heavy sleep, which anchors him to his bed till he is running late for school the next morning.

For days, the matter eats away at him. His wife asks, meanly, "Have you fallen in love with a teacher at your school or what? Your head is somewhere else these days."

How he wants to tell her. One night, he climbs into bed beside her and smooths the rolled cotton inside the blanket cover for something to do with his hands. After a long while he says, "Are you listening?"

His wife, watching a recipe video on her phone, jumps and laughs. "I was so absorbed in this pasta, four different kinds of cheese, look, I forgot you were—"

PT Sir makes such an effort to put together a smile. He does. But he cannot knit one together.

"Who died?" she teases. "That teacher you are always dreaming of?"

PT Sir looks down into his lap then. If he looks her in the eye, he may cry. A grown man.

"Something has happened," he says. "It's bad."

This gets his wife's full attention. She casts her phone to the side of the pillow.

When she holds his hands in her own, he begins to speak. He tells her everything.

JIVAN

After the court's ruling, the prison newly encloses me, the walls more solid than they used to be. Americandi watches me return to my mat. She watches me take off the blue sari, my mother's sari, memory of its gifting removed from it. She watches me lie down, a storm in my mind so dark it pulls all light from my eyes. She chews popcorn with her mouth open and spits unpopped kernels in the corner, which I will later clean.

Then a skinny young woman appears and begins giving Americandi a foot massage, wrapping her soft arms around the smelly soles, calling her aunty. I have not seen this woman before. She is new. I watch from my mat, the weave of straw pressing itself into my knees and palms. My mind screams and quiets itself, screams and quiets itself.

Americandi leans back on her mattress, resting her neck on the wall. She asks no questions. She knows already or she does not care.

She closes her eyes and says, "Ah, yes," and the new prisoner sways with her whole body in the task.

———

"You come with me now," Uma madam says one day, after breakfast. She has come prepared. A male guard comes forward and grabs my arm.

"Where?" I say, wrenching free. He lets go. "Stop it! I need to talk to Gobind about the appeals."

"You walk or he will drag you," says Uma madam in reply.

Back in my cell, I gather my sleeping mat, my other salwar kameez, slip my feet into the rubber slippers, then look around for anything else that is mine. Nothing is.

Uma madam pulls my dupatta off my neck. When I grab at it, she clicks her tongue.

"What use is modesty for you any more?" she says.

We walk down the corridor, the three of us, and a few women look up from inside their cells. The corridor is so dim they are no more than movement, shapes, smells, a belch. Perhaps sensing my fear, Uma madam finds it in her heart to explain. "You can't have a dupatta in this place where you are going. Not allowed. What if you decide to hang yourself, what then? It has happened before." After a pause, she says, "Nobody's coming to see you, don't worry about looking nice."

Uma madam unlocks a door at the far end of the corridor, which opens onto a staircase I have never seen. Though the day is dry and sunny, there is a puddle of water on the top step.

"Go down," she says.

When I don't move, she insists, "Go! Don't look so afraid, we don't keep tigers down there."

I climb down, my slippers slapping the steps. When I touch the wall, it is cold and damp. On the floor below, there is another corridor, a shadow of the one above. This corridor looks like nobody has set foot in it for months. A bat flaps around, panicked, near the ceiling. It doesn't know how to get out of this place.

Uma madam looks upward, her eyes too slow for the winged rat. "This is the problem," she says to the male guard, who follows us, "do you see? I told them keep her upstairs, otherwise I have to go up and down, up and down. Can my knees take it, at this age?"

The guard looks at his feet and gives a dry laugh. I can tell he is laughing not at her knees, but at something else.

Then Uma madam unlocks a barred room. The guard, who has hovered behind my shoulder all this while, steps back.

Here it is, a special cell for the soon to be dead. A room under the ground for the ones who will be soil.

———

But they cannot kill me before they kill me.

Since my ruling was handed down by the highest court, I have only a mercy petition left. For this too, I need Gobind's help. There is no time for me to study the law books myself.

Some days, however, it feels like time is all I have. It is

cool here, where the sun never comes, even on the hottest days. I crouch on my mat, arms naked and cold like a plucked chicken. In one corner, a low wall separates the room from the toilet, which is a hole in the ground from which dark cockroaches emerge, their whiskers feeling. The first time I see one, I whack it with my slipper.

Now I flick one and another away with my fingers. It is a game of carrom. More fun when the carrom disks, tossed into the drain, come back for another round.

Night begins early and has no end. When I am certain the sun will never show its face again, I lie down on the mat and will myself to dream of a tunnel, scraped with nothing more than my fingernails, a tunnel, which sets me loose in a village far from here.

PT SIR

Weeks later, in an electronics shop, an employee with a lanyard around his collar sets a large box on the ground. PT Sir and his wife look expectantly at the box. Around them, a wall of televisions plays a football game. In the next section, customers stand thoughtfully before rows of refrigerators. PT Sir's wife has marveled at the fridges with two doors, the fridges which can create and deposit ice cubes, the fridges which have sensors which tell you when the door is left open.

"Technology," PT Sir has told her, "keeps moving forward."

"Demand for tandoor is a bit low," explains the salesman now. "It is such a specialized oven, for serious chefs. So we stock only one brand, the top brand."

PT Sir's wife looks at the box and smiles, her teeth bright on her face, her hands playing with the thin end of her oiled plait, like a child.

"It has an aluminum tray and toughened front glass window," continues the employee, a young man, removing the foam and plastic from the box. "Fully modern look.

Right now there is a special offer where you get kebab skewers free with this! And, best of all, efficient electricity consumption, sir, your bill won't increase at all!"

With the packaging removed, what sits on the ground is a low black cube.

"Madam," the salesman continues, holding the lanyard to his chest with one hand, "I will tell you the best advantage of this brand is—it cooks fast! If you try to make a chicken kebab in the oven, it may take almost an hour. But here it is done in fifteen–twenty minutes. And completely authentic clay-oven taste!"

"Hmm," says PT Sir's wife. "What about pizza?"

"Pizza like foreign, madam, you will think you are in London—"

"That is all okay," interrupts PT Sir, "but tell us the real information. How much is it?"

The employee laughs. "Sir, once you eat the five-star food from this tandoor, you will see it's *saving* you money. Your favorite restaurant is at home!"

PT Sir waits. His wife waits. Somewhere, in a section they can't see, a salesperson demonstrates the capacity of a speaker and a deep bass booms in their ribs.

"Okay," the employee begins, pulling out a calculator, "let's see. This model comes to five thousand seven hundred rupees."

"Why that much?" says PT Sir. "We were looking at other models on the online shops, maximum four thousand."

"Online shops," says the employee, "will ship you a bad

part or a defective secondhand machine. The stories we hear from customers, you don't want to know. Here you have a three-year warranty. My name is Anant, sir, call me any time, I work here six days a week."

PT Sir's wife turns to him. "This is a good brand," she whispers. "Top of the line. They use it on TV also. Don't be stingy."

The employee stands respectfully at a distance and looks at his phone.

"If we're buying," says PT Sir's wife, "we should buy the best. Especially now you are earning *double* income ..." She smiles.

"Not *double*," protests PT Sir.

"Almost double. Isn't the party giving you—"

"Shh!" says PT Sir. A flake of anger catches on his tongue. He swallows. His mouth is too dry and then—he can feel saliva filling his mouth, as it did while he watched the beef-eater murdered. Not a person knows—other than his wife and Bimala Pal and a few trusted party men.

"Be calm," his wife says. "So much tension is not good for your health. Anyway, you're a true party man now. Isn't this what you wanted? Aren't you proud?"

He notes in her words both reward and punishment. But she touches his arm gently and her presence soothes him. They buy the tandoor. Paying for the tandoor in a sheaf of cash, he feels rich. He feels powerful in how casually he decides that he will buy it, that he will pay the full amount right away. Monthly installments are for the common man. He? He has ascended.

245

———

Rewarded for his loyalty, now with a salary from the party, PT Sir spends evenings and weekends traveling to districts across the state, doing events for teachers, students, and parents. In Shojarugram, he sees banners with his face on it and, in Bengali, *Welcome to the headmaster of our village!*

"I got a promotion," he jokes with the driver.

The driver gives him a smile in the rearview mirror. "To the rural people, your visit is the biggest event of this month, maybe!"

At each school, students sweep the soil courtyard with brooms. Saplings, newly planted, grow within the protection of twig fences. PT Sir is jostled as he joins his hands in greeting before pushing through the crowd to enter the school building. Everywhere he goes, the scene is the same. About fifty teachers and parents are crammed into the building and dozens more wait outside. They are usually silent. This is how the events start, he knows now. They will find their voice by the end, when he has become less of a deity and more of a man, sometimes with a cough caused by the dust of the villages.

"Jana Kalyan Party is starting," he says into a loudspeaker, which echoes, "scholarship programs for girl children. In the coming election, remember to cast your vote for Bimala Pal and Jana Kalyan Party."

At one school, when the electricity cuts out, a loud generator powers a portable light. Winged insects buzz and knock. A tiny toad comes hopping into the school building and a schoolboy is made to pick up the creature and set it loose outside.

After the speech, the gathered share grievances with PT Sir. A group of gap-toothed mothers and frowning fathers complain: teachers don't bother to come to school. Of what use is a scholarship, and of what use a school building, if there are no teachers?

The teachers, in turn, tobacco tucked in their mouths, protest that they are not paid their salaries on time. Their monthly salary comes two months later, sometimes three. How are they supposed to feed their families?

The younger teachers argue: what about progress or raises for them? They find it a dead-end job.

"It is your work to build the nation's future!" says PT Sir. "Isn't that noble?"

When the moment of departure is near, no matter how fervently they had been complaining and protesting, the teachers clap for him, a cheerful din that PT Sir absorbs with a smile. What are they clapping for? He doesn't know, but he is used to it. The people clamoring to see him, to hear his words, the grandmothers holding his hands, the garlands and praise, the prayers, all directed to him, as if he is a god. Who wouldn't find something electric in it?

———

The next evening, there is an important meeting at Bimala Pal's house. As PT Sir sets off, his wife admires his traditional clothing, his shined shoes. "You are starting to look like a politician!" she says.

"Is that so?" he says.

This pleases PT Sir, though it is a meager reward. For what has he spent his days falsifying the truth in court? For what has he taken on the ghost of the beef-eater, that man who begs for mercy in the moments before sleep? That ghost who weeps in his mind when he is alone, who pleads with him when he waits for the schoolgirls to come to the field?

———

As the state elections approach, the party steps up its campaign to recapture the state legislative house. So long they have been the opposition. Here is their opportunity to form the next government.

At this meeting, Bimala Pal wishes to hear what their platform on education might be. From the past months of engaging with the teachers and parents among their constituents, what have they learned?

PT Sir clears his throat. Suddenly, he is thankful for all the field visits. "Bring another tea," whispers someone at the far end to the tea boy, who is hovering. Who knows what the boy makes of all this? Who knows if he goes to school?

In the silence of the party's gaze upon him, PT Sir recognizes all those teachers' complaints for the treasure chest they are. He has laid his ear to the ground and heard the unmediated voice of the public. There is no greater currency in this room at the moment. PT Sir tells the room, with casual gravity, what he has heard. Then he proposes, "The greatest issue in education around the state does not have to do with syllabi or supplies. It has to do with personnel. It is the personnel who are voting, not the books."

At this, some of the older men at the table chuckle. Historically, education strategy has focused on syllabi— altering syllabi to tell the histories that serve the ruling party.

"Forget syllabi," PT Sir continues. "First of all, teachers' salaries need to be paid within the first three days of the month, without fail. This is the single biggest complaint I have heard. Teachers don't want to do their jobs because they're not getting paid on time. So they don't show up to school. Then the students stop going. This is one change, a concrete change, we can make and talk about. I think it will bring the teachers' votes to us."

Bimala Pal listens. She has on her mind not only schools, but floods in the north of the state, ruined crops, and stranded villagers. She has on her mind new trains connecting the state to the capital, safety in the mines, quotas for different castes and tribes. She has on her mind beautification of the city, planting of flowers by the roads, and regular watering of trees in public parks. The city voters cannot be neglected. There will be a function the next day where she awards laptop computers to high-achieving students of the city.

"That may work," an older man says, now looking at

PT Sir. "Madan is eating everyone's head about the sylla-bus. So this is a fresh approach."

Madan Choudhury, the current education minister, is behind the state's push to include more patriotic texts in school syllabi.

"To be honest, I see his point of view," interrupts another man. "Who is this Hemingway? Who is Steinbeck? Madan is pushing to have more original Bengali literature and we have to continue that push."

PT Sir feels that he is vibrating with energy. Let the old-timers try to challenge him. Just let them. Hasn't he been a teacher? Doesn't he know what life in the school is really like? He knows, more than these career bureaucrats who have not seen the inside of a school since 1962!

He continues, "With all respect, we have to take care of the people before taking care of the ideology. Through people is how we will spread ideology, not by neglecting them."

Some raise their eyebrows in appreciation. Bimala Pal looks at PT Sir with a hint of a smile.

"You turned out," she says, "to be quite a persuasive orator!"

"He's a teacher after all," says someone else. "How can he *not* have a commanding side?"

On the train, PT Sir holds his head high. Near his house, he gives a five-rupee coin to a beggar child who sits on the pavement, looking up with blank eyes.

How did it happen? His colleagues at the school, those teachers, those ladies, with their cinema gossip and recipe trades, their husbands and children to return to—their lives continue as they always have, above the watermark of political tides. But, in the villages, those other teachers look at him with hope and desperation. They look at him as somebody who can do something. So, he thinks, perhaps he can.

———

It is summer, roadside trees dry and dusty, when PT Sir hands his resignation letter to the principal. She tears it open, glances at it, and jokes, "Now you are a powerful man, what use do you have for our humble school?"

PT Sir presses his teeth on his tongue in a show of humility.

Then, his three-week notice dismissed by the principal, having declined the offers of a farewell party, pleading to be excused for the busy electoral campaign, PT Sir is free. PT Sir is no longer a PT Sir. At this thought, he feels mournful. The defiant and silly girls were children, after all. Walking down the lane, he looks back at the building one more time. In the barred windows, ponytailed heads appear. He feels a tug of nostalgia for his old life and then, in a moment, it is gone.

———

The following day, when PT Sir visits Bimala Pal's house, the living room is a tangle of cables and chargers, young men and women on every available seat, their faces lit in the blue glow of screens. PT Sir notes, impressed, that this is the campaign's social media team.

At an office elsewhere in the city, a video production company releases short films on YouTube every week, highlighting the lives of ordinary people positively affected by the initiatives of the party. These films are played on LED billboards at intersections and on mobile screens carried by small trucks through villages. On Facebook, the films gather tens of thousands of views.

PT Sir's work is on the ground. Every day, he is driven in a party Sumo car to towns and villages across the state. When he covers all of the nineteen districts, he starts over again. His car speeds past vegetable markets under tarp, past green hills and rocky outcrops, past streams that run dry, their sandy bottoms exposed. He smiles at curious men, who tap on the car's tinted windows, and steps out and greets village elders, who sit on porches, their faces wrinkled from decades in the sun. He wags his finger and delivers speeches under welcome banners strung between the limbs of trees.

He meets with teachers and teachers' unions. He drinks endless cups of tea. He smiles until his cheeks ache.

"Until I gave up my job to represent you all," he begins every speech, "I was a teacher, like you!"

Now and then PT Sir looks, from the stage, for a glint of a knife or a weapon held high in the air.

———

From the young men and women working on social media, phones attached to their palms at all times, Bimala Pal learns about the angry Twitter and Facebook messages. They arrive, blips and bloops on laptops and phones, bubbles and boxes of typo-riddled, emoji-filled complaint.

Y is Jivan getting a shot at a mercy petition? Mercy 4 wut?? Justice now!!! Dont forget the 100+ innocents who died!!!

This case will drag on for a decade and use up our tax money, nothing else will happen.

Why r we payin 4 that terrorist 2 sleep and eat and relax in prison while some mercy petition goes thru the system? If u become the govt how will u handle?

It doesn't end.

———

On election day, a statewide holiday, PT Sir wakes up at four in the morning. A peculiar exhaustion slows his body, the exhaustion of getting up in darkness and turning artificial lights on. His limbs are slow. While the sky lightens, he bathes, a stream of cold water falling down his back to the bathroom floor.

Soon a car arrives to take PT Sir to cast his vote. His polling station, which is Bimala Pal's too, is a local school, closed for the day. Where on other days children fill water from coolers, where they linger and play and drop crumbs of lunch, there are now a dozen TV cameras and trucks carrying generators. Reporters drink paper cups of Nescafé purchased from a vendor who makes rounds with a kettle. Above them, barred windows conceal silent classrooms, their desks scratched in teenage love and impatience.

Already there is a long line of voters. A housewife with sequined slippers, a maid with a thin shawl thrown over her sari, a man with alcohol-red eyes. A woman feeds a stray dog a biscuit and the people behind her idly watch.

As soon as Bimala Pal and PT Sir emerge from their sober white Ambassador car, the reporters rush to them, jostling to position a microphone or a small recorder before them. Beside Bimala Pal, PT Sir joins his hands in greeting and bows his head. In the great humility of this gesture he feels a shiver of electricity run through him. How close to power he is. He will be on every television screen in the state and that is the least of it.

Inside the school building, in an assembly hall, Bimala Pal, like every other voter, casts her vote at a machine situated on a curtained desk. When she emerges, she receives an indelible ink dab on her index finger, at the border of fingernail and skin.

———

The next day, nearing the hour when election results will be declared, Bimala Pal's house bursts with people—politicians, clerks, assistants, union leaders, even a stray celebrity or two. A TV plays on high volume in the corner and shouted conversations are carried on over it.

Somebody comes through the door carrying a sack of kochuri, fried bread, and a tub of alur dom, potato curry.

Then a phone call comes and the room falls silent. Bimala Pal disappears into the office, the phone held at her ear.

"Where's the remote?" someone yells. "Turn this TV down."

PT Sir paces, smiling tightly at the others gathered. In his mind, a racetrack of worries: what if the party doesn't win? What if he gave up his job prematurely? An older man calls to him, "Be calm. Don't take so much tension, not good for your young heart."

He continues, "It hasn't been six months that I've had a pacemaker." He points to a spot below his left collarbone.

"I'm not worrying," lies PT Sir. "Why don't you sit, sir, let me find a chair ..."

When Bimala Pal emerges from her office, she holds the receiver at her side, a sly smile on her face. Men in front break into shouts and a whoop of triumph lifts the room. Bimala Pal laughs as men around her, her assistants, playfully raise her arms in theirs, like she is a boxing champion.

"Did we win?" PT Sir asks, unbelieving. "Did they call it?"

Jana Kalyan Party has won the majority of seats in the legislative assembly. Bimala Pal, as the leader of the party, is now chief minister of the state.

"Get ready," says the man with the pacemaker, "for the real work to begin."

PT Sir nods gravely, as if he understands what is to come.

Boxes of sweets promptly appear and are passed from hand to hand. Somebody sends sweets out to the reporters swarming the lane and a din rises from the gathered men and women of the media. Soon they make way for visitors arriving to congratulate the party. A rival party chief graciously brings an enormous bouquet and the scent of roses fills the room. A renowned football player arrives and a cricket player too. Musicians arrive and film stars in sunglasses. A garland is draped about Bimala Pal's neck, then another and another, petals drifting down to the floor, pausing now and then in the folds of her sari.

PT Sir watches the hoopla and eats a sweet, grinning from ear to ear. He shakes hands when hands are offered and claps backs when he is embraced. The vitality of the moment dazes him. Never has he been in a place that felt so much like the center of the world.

When he looks for an empty surface on which he can sit, he notes how the room has filled up with bouquets and garlands, dewy petals duly misted by an assistant who carries a water bottle with him, looking harassed. Through the windows, he sees the crowd outside grow bigger and noisier, a collection not only of cameramen, but of well-known reporters, bigger television crews, neighborhood fans, even one comedian. They chant and cheer. Snacks that are brought to Bimala Pal are frequently distributed among those waiting outside. PT Sir watches them, those common people who will always be on the outside.

———

Late in the afternoon, the chief minister-in-waiting beckons PT Sir to join her in her small office. She closes the door behind them.

Inside, banners rolled into tubes lean in the corners and old desktop computers sit on the floor. Though Bimala Pal's seat is a luxurious leather chair, a towel draped on it for protection and cleanliness, the new chief minister does not sit. She stands before the dark wood desk.

"What do you think," she says, "about a senior secretary post? In the education ministry, of course. It will be good for you."

PT Sir forces himself not to grin. He must look like a serious man. In this room, with the tubelight casting a sad glow on the large table, the idols of gods arrayed in a nook in the wall, the scent of incense curling upward from sticks, his life is transformed. It is the kind of room that, at night, attracts the attention of flying insects and house lizards.

"The teachers," PT Sir says instead, "they delivered, didn't they? Our work with them was good."

This much he has learned: a successful person is a magnet for resentment. Deflecting the light of success away from him is a better practice. But Bimala Pal will not accept it.

"*Your* work with them," she says. "Don't be humble. You can't be humble in politics."

PT Sir smiles.

"How does it feel?" she asks.

"I am ready to serve," he replies. "I will gladly accept that post you are thinking about."

He turns to leave, his body buoyant with relief. Outside, he will glide past the men drunk on syrup from sweets, their heads big with knowledge of their new importance. He will glide past the assistants and interns, the social media youths, no longer required to remember their names. At home, no doubt over a celebratory meal, he will tell his wife. He relishes it. He is about to turn the doorknob when Bimala Pal speaks.

"One thing," she says. "Jivan, that terrorist. She has been polling high on voters' priorities."

"Oh," says PT Sir, taken aback by the turn in the conversation. He should have known.

"This issue is not going away." Bimala Pal touches her forehead in a gesture of worry. "Something will have to be done. The public is unhappy that she is appealing for mercy and whatnot."

"I testified—"

"That is why I am telling you," Bimala Pal interrupts.

"And the mercy petition is her legal right, so I don't know—"

"Legal right? You have much to learn about politics," says Bimala Pal, smiling.

Then her smile fades and she looks at him, unblinking, until PT Sir feels his relief vanish.

It is clear what he has to do. He draws a breath to speak,

keen to crack the tension in the room. "Isn't it always the quiet ones who turn out to have dangerous thoughts in their head?"

"That may be so," says Bimala Pal. "Listen, this is a result we can deliver as soon as we take power. It will be a big victory for us."

PT Sir knows that if the terrorist is—well, if the matter of the terrorist is *resolved* during their tenure, this government's approval from the public will know no limits. They will have bought themselves time to implement other campaign promises.

"The mercy petition is all that stands in the way," says Bimala Pal. "See what you can do about it? The court gave its verdict. The people want justice. Anyway"—she smiles—"you will know best. Your student, after all."

LOVELY

Day of the audition! On the road, my slippers are going *flap flap* and I am praying, please slippers please not to tear today. I have tied my petticoat too low and my belly is jiggling, but no time to fix that. The guava seller is there again. For fun, I am asking him the time.

"Were you showing my guava on your TV interview?" he is grumbling. "Why I am telling you the time, then?"

I am laughing and waving my hand. I am knowing what the time is, because I am planning my whole morning so I can be taking the eight fifteen local train to Tollygunge.

"This is a ladies' compartment," one aunty is yelling, "can't see or what?"

"Move, madam," I am replying respectfully. "I am just going to the other compartment."

"Oh!" she is saying after she is seeing my face. "Aren't you—I saw you on—"

I am squeezing past her.

In Tollygunge, I am walking under a row of trees. Under one tree, a man is ironing clothes with a coal-loaded frame. Under another tree, a sweeper is sweeping plastic from the gutter. Then I am seeing a villa, surrounded by a clean white wall over which pink flowers are spilling.

Outside the gate, sitting on a plastic chair, there is a man. He is thin like a grasshopper and his freshly cut hair is standing straight up on his head. He is looking at me coming closer and closer and he is saying, "Please, ma, not today, there is an audition going on—"

"Very strange you are!" I am telling him right away. "I am coming for the audition only!"

To this, the man is not knowing what to say. He is looking like his boss is going to fire him, but he is not knowing how to stop me. I am looking that good. I am feeling that confident. So what if some man is trying to put a barrier in front of me?

Inside, there is a big white building, surrounded by a tidy garden. So many flower beds and so many nice benches. They are all empty because people are preferring the cool weather of AC.

So I am pushing open the big wooden door and feeling the air on my skin. Inside, there is a big room with colorful sofas, on which people with stylish hair are sitting. Their perfumes are mingling and my nose is enjoying. Behind glass partitions are other people working. Some framed film posters are on the walls. The reception is a big desk, with a vase of flowers on top, and the lady behind it is wearing Western clothes and talking on the landline.

"One minute, please," she is telling me softly. She is even smiling at me.

Then, in a room with floors so shiny I am feeling that

I will slip and fall on my behind, Sonali Khan herself is coming to take my hand.

"Lovely," she is saying, "I am so pleased you could come. Your video was touching me right here." And she is putting a palm to her heart. "I see audition videos all the time, but yours? It was something special.

"For you," she is explaining, "we are thinking about this role in my movie *What Do You Know About Mother's Love?* It will be about a single parent, a hijra, stigmatized by society, who is smashing—I mean *smashing*—all of society's rules by adopting a child on her own. A parent who is fierce and ferocious and full of love. A parent who lives life on her own terms. Blockbuster drama, mark my words. And we need a fresh face, authentic talent."

Her words are feeling to me like Azad's embrace when we were falling in love, like a tub full of syrupy roshogolla whose sugar is flowing in my veins, like Mr. Debnath accepting me to his acting class. It is feeling like Ragini's hands in mine, our laughter during the national activity of watching TV together in the evening.

"But listen," she is saying, putting her head close to mine, "one concern that my team has is we want to avoid bad publicity. Your testimony for the terrorist—"

I am looking at the floor, showing shame. "Don't worry," I am saying. "She was my neighbor, but I am understanding now that maybe I was never really knowing who she was." The shame is burning in my cheeks.

"Good," Sonali Khan is saying. Then, in a normal voice, she continues, "Your video in which you were playing a mother, oof! Such feeling! Such emotion! Such drama in your eyes and voice! I said, 'This is a star being born right here. We must call her in.' "

After that, can you guess how my audition is going?

———

On the first day of the shoot, in front of the studio doors, the whole unit is coming together, from driver to caterer to cameraman to director, and we are doing a prayer, then cracking a coconut for god's blessings. For all my life, everybody is believing that I am having a direct line to god, but I am knowing the truth. Whenever I am calling god, her line is busy. So today I am bowing my head deep. Please to let me act well today. Please to not let me get kicked off this film!

In my purse, I am bringing my own lipstick, just in case, but after the prayer, when I am going into the makeup van, my eyes are growing big like pumpkins. This van is having a big mirror, lit up with rows of bright bulbs. On the counter, there are open boxes of pastes and powders and colors, wigs and little cotton sheets and glues and clips. Then the makeup artist, Hema, who is smiling and calling me madam, is using one of those soft cotton sheets to clean my face. I am smelling mint, like a chewing gum. The hair artist, Deepti, is pulling and tying, pinning this and gelling that. When I am saying, "Aaoo!" she is saying, "Oh, sorry, madam."

"Close your eyes, madam," Hema is gently saying, but

how am I closing my eyes when they are making me look like a superstar in the mirror?

Inside the studio, which is a big warehouse with nothing stored inside it, I am walking carefully, looking at the ground for the cables that are running everywhere.

"Madam!" Someone is giving me a thumbs-up, a boy carrying silver umbrellas. "I saw your video!"

I am giving him a smile.

On the other end of the large studio is a set like the living room of my dreams—a big sofa, many plants, paintings on the walls, a cup of tea on a table. The cinematographer and director are making me sit here and sit there, stand at this angle or that angle. I am feeling afraid that my makeup will be melting.

Then the studio is becoming so quiet I am hearing somebody sniffle.

"Silence!" someone is calling.

"Rolling!" someone is calling.

"Action!" someone else is calling.

And me, from the depth of my heart, I am becoming the mother I am needing to be, even though the child actor will be coming tomorrow and I am only imagining her today. Every wish of motherhood that I am having, for all my life, I am pouring into the lines they are giving me. I am dreaming this child into being before my eyes and I am holding this beloved little person. How real is she, my child.

This child is having the face of Jivan, daughter of those poor parents, donor of pencils and textbooks. How is she living, alone in some dark cell? Even if she is not feeling the knife at her neck, I am feeling myself holding it. Now my face thick with makeup, my hair stiff with gels, I am knowing what Arjuni Ma was truly telling me: in this world, only one of us can be truly free. Jivan or me. Every day, I am making my choice and I am making it today also.

"Daughter," I am telling this child, looking directly at the lens, "never let anyone tell you those lies. You are coming from the most precious place. Not from my womb, no, but from the deepest dreams of my heart."

"Cut it," the director is calling. When I am stepping behind the camera, looking at the small TV where my shot is playing, I am saying, "Excuse, excuse," to get through the dozen people crowding.

They are all wiping their eyes.

———

At the end of the day, when we are wrapping, Sonali Khan is personally coming to me. She is holding my arms and saying, "Lovely, you are going to be the country's next big star, you just wait!"

Then she is handing me an envelope and telling me to open it at home.

On the train, I am eating jhalmuri to celebrate, crunchy puffed rice and chopped cucumber in my mouth. I am walking past the guava seller and turning around. To him, for the first time, I am saying, "You give me three good ones!"

He is looking up and having a heart attack to see his new customer.

"Yes, it's me!" I am saying. "I am making a film now, so I am having to be fit! I am going to be eating fruits!"

In my room, I am eating a washed guava and opening the envelope that Sonali Khan was giving me. Inside, there is a big glossy photo of me in scene.

I am finding some Sellotape and tearing it with my teeth. Then, beside my posters of Shah Rukh Khan and Priyanka Chopra, I am putting up this photo. Me, Lovely, in full hair and makeup, delivering a line to the camera in a Sonali Khan film.

The country is not knowing her yet, this new superstar. But me, I am knowing her.

PT SIR

One morning begins with a red sun, light that slips around the curtain and finds his eyes, and it is the same as all other mornings, except it is wholly different. It is PT Sir's first day as an education secretary in the government.

PT Sir lingers for as long as he can bear it at home, then dashes to his new office. The city is wide awake. Flocks of schoolgirls, some holding hands, cross the street before his car. Their ironed and pleated skirts, their big laughs, tug at who he used to be. A boy scrubs dishes with ash in the gutter before a street-side booth hawking noodles. A stray dog trots along, no longer able to bother the man in his car.

Before the metal-detector gates of the state government building, turbaned guards salute PT Sir. He wonders whether they know who he is or whether they salute anybody who arrives in a government-issue white Ambassador. One of the guards shows him to an elevator designated for use by VIPs only. In the rising compartment, heart drumming, PT Sir inspects his face in the shined metal doors. He may run into all sorts of VIPs in this building. From lobbyists to industrialists to movie stars, all have been known to discreetly visit this building.

On the seventh-floor corridor, PT Sir walks by a cleaning lady sitting on the pads of her feet, pushing a wet rag in wide arcs. She does not even glance up as he passes by.

PT Sir unlocks the door to his new office with a brand-new key. Inside, a tiny room, windowless. PT Sir closes the door behind him and sits in a chair with a high leather back. The chair tilts pleasingly under his weight. It rolls too, on wheels that don't get stuck. PT Sir sits like that for a few minutes, now and then tapping his fingers on the expanse of polished wood before him. Aside from a desktop computer and, puzzlingly, a packet of pencils, there is nothing else on the desk. The newness of it pleases him.

———

PT Sir knows what he has to do. He has to get his hands on Jivan's mercy petition and add to it his recommendation, as a member of the new government, that the petition be denied. This is a criminal who deserves no mercy. The court's decision, the death penalty, ought to be carried out swiftly and with minimal burden to the taxpayer.

There is only one hitch: the mercy petition is with the girl's lawyer.

PT Sir picks up the phone and dials.

———

"Sir!" says Gobind into his phone, sitting up on one elbow in bed. His voice is thick with sleep. On the other end of the line is PT Sir, calling at an absurdly early hour. He asks after Gobind's wife, his parents, whether he has followed the cricket on TV lately.

"TV, sir," groans Gobind. "What are you saying, I have not sat down on my sofa for one minute. This case is taking everything, everything. You saw the disastrous ruling for my client."

And PT Sir begins his work.

"Bimala Pal was telling me," he begins smoothly, "well, you know what she was telling me? She was saying, 'That Gobind is a hardworking man.' She sees it. I see it. We all see your work. So I am just calling to convey that. You are a man of justice and you are defending the girl, of course, that is your job."

Gobind says, "Kind of you to call about it, sir."

"But we all know," PT Sir continues, "what happened, I think."

Gobind is silent on the phone. Then he says, "Do we, sir?"

PT Sir laughs. He looks at his closed door, at the vents in the ceiling, which gently pump cool air for his comfort. From somewhere, even he is not sure where, he has acquired a politician's persona. This big laugh was never his. "A man of principle," he says. "I like it.

"Gobind, listen," he continues, taking a deep breath, the laughter leaving his voice. "Justice in this case must be served. You think that. I think that. The public thinks that. So the long trial, the petitions, all of that I admire, believe me. But the court has shown this girl is guilty. Nobody"—his voice softens—"nobody feels more sad about that than me. She was my student. I saw her potential."

Gobind breathes noisily into the phone. He remains in his awkward position on the bed, afraid of the rustle of sheets, afraid of his footfall, afraid of missing any of what is being said.

"What I am saying is it would be a shame if, after all this, the mercy petition hangs, going nowhere, for months and months. Don't you think so?"

PT Sir leans back in his chair. The chair, subservient, tilts. From Bimala Pal, he has learned to withhold words in favor of long seconds of silence. They tick. He feels the man on the other end evaluating his words. Cautiously, Gobind says, "It's true, these petitions can take time."

"So," PT Sir declares, "why don't you hand the mercy petition to me. I will try to expedite it. Now I am in a position where I can expedite it, add my voice to it. We want swift justice, that is all I'm saying. Whatever outcome will be is not in my hands, but it is not good to keep the public waiting. It makes our new government look—"

He throws up a hand, a gesture of not knowing, though Gobind cannot see him.

"Let me send a messenger for it," PT Sir continues. "He will pick up the papers from you. And, for your trouble, we will of course send you a small gift, just a token of thanks for your hard work on this case. You don't have to tell me, but I know how this work becomes a sacrifice—of family time, of time with children. Don't you have a daughter,

Gobind? Doesn't she want more time with her papa, maybe a holiday next year?"

"Okay, sir," Gobind agrees. He is unsure if he chooses this.

JIVAN

Uma madam says, "Look who has come."

Who? I wipe sleep from my eyes and smooth the tangles of hair at the back of my head. A smell of cigarettes enters the room. The flash of gemstones up and down fingers. I stand. My skull, lifted so far from the ground, feels uncertain of itself.

My lawyer, Gobind, looks at me sorrowfully. Then he takes a deep breath, which I can hear.

"What can I say? This case has become politicized. It is not even about you. I am sorry about the mercy petition. I truly did not think they would reject it."

"You told me they would let me go," I say. "Remember? You told me I am young and I promised in my letter to be a teacher, serve anywhere in the country, dedicate myself to the country. I wrote all that in my letter. Then what happened?"

"Tell me," he says, after a pause, "are you getting enough to eat here? Do you want phone calls every day? I can try to bring you some magazines, something to read. What about a blanket? Is it cold here at night?"

"I ..." I say after a while, my voice a croak. I have not had a drink of water all night, if this is morning. All day, if this is evening.

Then I find my voice.

"Am I cold?" I say.

"Enough food?" I spit.

"A magazine?" I scream.

"Stop it!" shouts Uma madam.

Gobind looks at my face, my bony body in the yellow salwar kameez, a reminder of sun. Soon the color will fade.

The lawyer looks at Uma madam, who is standing just outside the door, fiddling with the lock and key in her hand. She frowns at me.

"There is really nothing to do after the mercy petition is rejected," he says.

"Don't treat me like I am stupid," I shout. I don't know why I am shouting. I have a voice, I remind myself. This is my voice. It booms. It startles. "The country needs someone to punish," I tell him. "And I am that person."

"That blanket looks thin," Gobind says, his voice withdrawn. "What do you need to be comfortable? Better blanket, maybe."

"Blanket?" I say. "Blanket?"

I want to take off my slipper and whack him over the head with it. He is no better than a toilet cockroach.

"If you are not going to help me, then fine. I will write a hundred letters. I have time," I am shouting again. "I have time."

A coterie of flies rises from a heap of—is that my shit? The sewage lines are blocked again. This late at night, someone walks up, sending the soft sound of bare feet on floor to my alert ears. "Uma madam!" I say. I am happy she has come. "It is you!"

But she does not respond.

Maybe it is only a rat.

Twice a day, a guard, a different guard, opens the gate and shoves in a plate of ruti and lentils, a watery soup specked with cumin or dirt, impossible to tell.

"Who is making ruti now?" I ask, but she doesn't answer. "It was my job. I was the one making ruti."

Roars of disgust rise from someone—me?—but in the end I eat, my back and my elbows working.

It takes long for me to get a notepad and a pen. The ink in the pen has dried, so I lick the nib to get the blue flowing.

In school, I learned how to write letters. I put the notepad on the ground, kneel before it in a posture of praying, and begin.

Dear Hon'ble Chief Minister Madam Bimala Pal,
*   This is in regards to my curative petition (BL9083-*
A). Respectfully I am writing to see if your office may

please forward my petition one more time to the Council
of Ministers in Delhi. As you know the evidence against
me is circumstance-based. I am innocent. I lived in the
Kolabagan slum, but I did not have anything to do with
the train. If I am pardoned, I am willing to serve the
nation for the rest of my life. My goal is to be a teacher
and teach English to the children living in poverty.
Without me, my poor mother and father will have
nothing left in their life. I am their only child.

      Respectfully yours, your loyal citizen.

———

Waiting for some reply in the mail, I travel along with the letter in its hopeful van.

I travel along with the letter on a train, paddy fields outside.

I travel along with the letter in the air, on a plane where rich men eat chocolates.

But the letter lands on an indifferent desk.

Days pass. Weeks too. Maybe the minister's assistant glances at it, no more. Maybe they are overwhelmed by letters from prison.

Who am I except one of many?

My pen grows feeble.

What can words do? Not very much.

———

My mother doesn't come this week. I wait alone, licking puffed rice from my palm, waiting for Uma madam to fetch me. I listen to the roar from the building above me grow and subside—a hundred conversations in one hour.

After the roar of the visitors is gone, I hear some repair work outside. It seems to me that a shovel scrapes on the other side of a wall. And then, a glorious thing. A hole, the size of a cigarette, opens up on a high wall. I see sun. In delight, I slam my palms on the wall.

But my palms make no sound. The wall, high above my head, is cold and feathery with algae. The scraping stops, eventually, and the repairmen go away, leaving me this present.

The light alerts me when morning comes. Now that I know it is morning, I practice the yoga I learned long ago, on rainy days in school. But my body is reluctant. It adheres, like a block of concrete, to the floor. There is nothing supple in my arms. They are twigs, waiting to snap. When I look down, my legs are dry and scaly, white with skin that is neither alive nor willing to shed.

———

It is early when Uma madam comes for me. She tells me to bathe.

"Has my mother come?" I say.

When I rise slowly on knees that creak, I wait for her to snap at me, but she doesn't. Softly she tells me to go to the bathroom, to use the toilet and take a bath.

Oh, a bath. I follow her to the bathroom, a spacious room whose walls and floor are brown with the filth of bodies, accumulated over the years. There stands a bucket of water, with a plastic mug floating in it.

Now Uma madam stands in the doorway, waiting for me to undress. She will stand there the whole time, her back turned to me if she is feeling kind.

"Do you have," I say, "any letters . . .?"

Before she has said, "No! No letter! How many times do I have to tell you?"

Today she silently shakes her head.

I drop my clothes on the floor just outside the doorway, so they will not get wet. Inside, I crouch on the floor by the bucket. I can smell myself. I lift a mug of water and tip it over my head and it drips over my oily hair, barely wetting it. The water is cold. Goose bumps rise on my skin. I feel a breeze that I did not know was there.

Another mug of water and another.

I remember bathing as a child in the village, in the pond ringed by tal trees. My mother would press my head so I dipped in the green water, soap frothing about me. The bar of soap we used then was thin from her body. This bar is too. It is a sliver that I hold tight or else it will fall and spin across the floor.

After I am dry and clothed, Uma madam waits for me to come out of the room, on my own. Nobody grabs me. The door is open. I step out. Then she locks the door and there we are, standing in the corridor.

———

I could have been an ordinary person in the world. Ma, I could have gone to college, the city college where girls my age sit under trees, studying from their books, arguing, joking with boys. This is what I have seen in the movies.

Then I too would have given scraps of my meal to the stray dogs. I too would have had nostalgic corners of campus, corridor romances. I might have studied literature and I might have spoken English so well that, if you had met me on the street, Ma, you would not have known me! Ma, you would have thought I was a rich girl.

THE PAST TENSE OF
HANG IS HUNG

Unless what is being hung is a person, in which case the word is "hanged." One morning, after the president of the country rejected her mercy petition and before the journalists loitering outside the prison walls had a chance to crush their cigarettes underfoot and ask what was happening, Jivan was taken from her cell to the courtyard. As soon as she saw the platform, the length of rope thick enough to tether a boat to land, she fell. An attendant caught her. He was waiting for this purpose. In his arms, her body was a sack.

When she recovered, in the startling bright of the courtyard, she was given a minute to speak her last words. She licked her lips. Swallowed. Rubbed a cold palm on her kameez. "Where is my mother?" she asked. "Where is my father?"

She looked wildly about.

"You are making such a mistake," she said, voice cracking. "Minister madam, Bimala madam, see my letter. Please, have you got my letter?"

They were not there. Nobody was there, other than a few prison officials.

When Jivan was hanged, her neck snapped. The hair that had grown unruly during her time in prison fell over her face and drooped to her belly. The executioner, patches of sweat creeping up his armpits, shook his arms loose of the tension. A doctor, standing by with what looked like a receipt book, noted the time of death. Then a clerk went inside and dispatched a letter by speed post to inform Jivan's next of kin—a mother, in the Kolabagan slum—that her daughter had been killed by the state.

JIVAN

Mother, do you grieve?

Know that I will return to you. I will be a flutter in the leaves above where you sit, cooking ruti on the stove. I will be the stray cloud that shields you from days of sun. I will be the thunder that wakes you before rain floods the room.

When you walk to market, I will return to you as footprint on the soil. At night, when you close your eyes, I will appear as impress on the bed.

PT SIR

The new apartment comes with lights built into the ceilings. There is a balcony that an assistant has filled with potted plants. PT Sir accepts a window AC in the bedroom, though he declines ACs for the living room and the guest bedroom. He cannot hide the pleasure of no longer waking up sweating like a peasant.

He is now, he realizes, a cup of hot tea resting on the railing, a man who lives here, in a top-floor apartment in Ballygunge, a nice, upper-middle-class neighborhood of the city.

The party has seen fit to improve his salary. On top of that, it is true that, very occasionally, educational institutions send him a little token in return for having their licenses and permits renewed in a timely manner.

Sometimes they go overboard. One private university offered him and his wife a week at a bungalow in Singapore, all expenses paid. He thought about it more than he would have liked to. Then he declined.

Nobody can say that PT Sir is not an ethical man.

In the field close to the railway station, where PT Sir, then an ordinary teacher, first saw Katie Banerjee and Bimala Pal, a thousand men wait once more. They fill the field, its boundaries marked by lights which make day of the arriving dusk. Under the lights, unruly rows of ice-cream carts wander, no doubt announcing orange ices and cups of vanilla. PT Sir is too far away to hear. He is also too far to see the distant protesters, though he has been informed that they are there, university students who hold banners that say *Justice for Jivan.*

PT Sir stands high above the crowd, on the stage, before a microphone. He joins his hands and continues with his speech. "Soon after the people called for the terrorist to be brought to court," he says, "for the case to be swiftly resolved, look at how your ruling party handled it! Have you ever seen a government so attentive to the will of the people? Have you ever seen a government which demands that the courts move with speed?"

On he goes.

Among the frowning men in the crowd, some looking his way, others distracted by a pen of TV cameras off to the side, a woman stands, looking at PT Sir. She pays no attention to the man with the basket of chips who makes his way through the people. She pays no attention to a man with arms folded who digs his elbow in her side. When a breeze picks up, it fails to cause a ripple in her dupatta, the one she was not allowed to keep for modesty.

PT Sir knows who she is. Isn't she the ghost who begs him for mercy? Isn't she the ghost who searches the gaze of her teacher, hoping that he might offer rescue? Maybe that is why they had the white curtain up at the court—not so that Jivan could not influence his testimony, but so that he would not have to face her.

PT Sir's mouth speaks, while his eyes remain locked on hers.

"The vanquishing of good over evil is a signal! It is a signal of a party that listens to the public. It is a signal of a party that does what it promises!"

The crowd roars. They whistle and laugh. They wave flags raised high. One man is lifted onto another's shoulders and a few TV cameras turn to capture this.

PT Sir surveys the crowd, his lips pulled into a smile and, when he looks for her once more, he cannot find her. The dust of the field tickles his throat and PT Sir makes a fist before his mouth, takes a step back from the microphone, and coughs. From a bottle on the floor, he takes a sip of cold water. The irritation is gone.

When he speaks once more, his voice finds courage and he finds courage too. Look at the rapt crowd. Look at the public, gathered before him, drinking in his words while he stands where Bimala Pal stood not so long ago.

By the end of the speech, he feels barely anchored to the stage by his hands on the microphone, his whole self charged as if by the wind in the field and the electricity in the wires. When the crowd disperses, they fill buses where they hang from open doorways and return to homes where the pride of the year is a new refrigerator. They will bend in fields, earning two rupees for crops that will sell in the city for forty, and stand by roadsides hawking stacks of dinnerware that will chip at first wash. They will watch, wide-eyed, the one movie that plays in the theater on their half day off from carpentry or construction or cleaning bathrooms, while PT Sir, in the government office's special elevator, moves upward.

ACKNOWLEDGMENTS

This book would not be in your hands without the tireless work and faith of Eric Simonoff and Jordan Pavlin. It has been a dream and an honor to have their creativity, their brilliance, and their generous hearts touch and transform this book. Immense gratitude also to magnificent Gabrielle Brooks, who took on this book and championed it in a way that has left me marveling.

My warmest thanks and admiration to the intimi-datingly on-top-of-everything, smart people who have assisted them and given time and thought to this book: Jessica Spitz, Taylor Rondestvedt, Nicholas Thomson, and Demetris Papadimitropoulos.

I hope Sonny Mehta knew what it meant to me to receive his blessings. I treasure his memory.

I'm in awe of icons Ruth Liebmann, Paul Bogaards, Nicholas Latimer, and Emily Murphy for their advocacy and endless behind-the-scenes work, and for bringing such care to this book. A thousand thanks wouldn't be enough.

Gratitude to Kim Shannon for guiding me expertly and good-naturedly through my first galley signing.

I know that a book comes into being because of the astute reads, creativity, and hard work of many, many people. My gratitude to the teams at WME, especially Fiona Baird, Laura Bonner, and Lauren Rogoff, and at Knopf, especially Ellen Feldman and Lara Phan. Thank you.

Warmest gratitude to my colleagues and mentors at Catapult, especially visionaries Andy Hunter, Pat Strachan, Jonathan Lee, and Nicole Chung, who have created a workplace full of trust and creativity, a workplace that cheers on writers, poets, and artists. Thank you for your extraordinary support.

Gratitude to guiding lights Katie Raissian, Mark Krotov, Alane Mason, James Meader, and Peter Joseph for including me in the literary community and lifting me—and many others—up.

Countless thanks to my teachers, especially Amy Hempel, Lynn Steger Strong, Colum McCann, Peter Carey, Nathan Englander, Veena Das, and Anand Pandian in the United States, and to all at Ashok Hall in Kolkata, especially Jharna Ganguli, Chaitali Sen, Mamta Chopra, and Sangeeta Banerjee.

My love and gratitude to Caroline Bleeke for her incomparable kindness, wisdom, and steadfast friendship. Her faith has buoyed me through the years. Much of this book was written in the quiet of Caroline's living room. I will not forget it.

My love and gratitude to Laura Preston, whose groundbreaking writing inspires me to reach for greater complexity in my work. Our two-person workshops provided what I needed. It is in the light of Laura's generosity that this book has grown.

Immense gratitude to Julia Firestone and Jenny Shen for their early reads, insightful comments, and great enthusiasm. Many thanks to Mark Chiusano for offering encouragement and advice.

Love and gratitude to my friends Emma McGlennen, Alex Primiani, Sharon Wang, Maria Xia, Katie Vane, Mahum Shabir, Shreya Biswas, Rishika De, and Annesha Pramanik.

Love and gratitude to Beatrix Labikova, Ludovit Labik, Bea Labikova, Raphael Roter, and Halina Labikova. I got very lucky.

With this writing, I seek to remember and hold close my beloved grandparents, who taught me to be curious, to be kind, and to revere books.

All my love to my mother and father, Sucharita and Partha Majumdar, who taught me to work hard, to live with discipline, and to dream. All my love to my sister, Roshni Majumdar, whose humor, drive, and ability to form communities wherever she goes I deeply admire.

All my love to Michal Labik, my husband, for his brilliant criticism of early drafts, for being a true partner in all things difficult and ordinary and joyous, and for his great friendship. Time with Michal is the best thing in the world. I am grateful.

A NOTE ABOUT THE AUTHOR

Megha Majumdar was born and raised in Kolkata, India. She moved to the United States to attend college at Harvard University, followed by graduate school in social anthropology at Johns Hopkins University. She works as an editor at Catapult and lives in New York City. *A Burning* is her first book. Follow her on Twitter @MeghaMaj and Instagram @megha.maj.

TAIPEI EAST

TAIPEI SOUTH

OLD WALLED CITY
AND ZHONGZHENG

OLD TAIPEI: DATONG

INSIGHT ⊙ GUIDES

TAIPEI

CITY GUIDE

PLAN & BOOK
YOUR TAILOR-MADE TRIP

BRAZIL **CHILE** **ECUADOR**

TAILOR-MADE TRIPS & UNIQUE EXPERIENCES CREATED BY LOCAL TRAVEL EXPERTS AT INSIGHTGUIDES.COM/HOLIDAYS

Insight Guides has been inspiring travellers with high-quality travel content for over 45 years. As well as our popular guidebooks, we now offer the opportunity to book tailor-made private trips completely personalised to your needs and interests. By connecting with one of our local experts, you will directly benefit from their expertise and local know-how, helping you create memories that will last a lifetime.

HOW INSIGHTGUIDES.COM/HOLIDAYS WORKS

STEP 1

Pick your dream destination and submit an enquiry, or modify an existing itinerary if you prefer.

STEP 2

Fill in a short form, sharing details of your travel plans and preferences with a local expert.

STEP 3

Your local expert will create your personalised itinerary, which you can amend until you are completely satisfied.

STEP 4

Book securely online. Pack your bags and enjoy your holiday! Your local expert will be available to answer questions during your trip.

BENEFITS OF PLANNING & BOOKING AT INSIGHTGUIDES.COM/HOLIDAYS

PLANNED BY LOCAL EXPERTS

The Insight Guides local experts are hand-picked, based on their experience in the travel industry and their impeccable standards of customer service.

SAVE TIME & MONEY

When a local expert plans your trip, you save time and money when you book, even during high season. You won't be charged for using a credit card either.

TAILOR-MADE TRIPS

Book with Insight Guides, and you will be in complete control of the planning process, from the initial selections to amending your final itinerary.

BOOK & TRAVEL STRESS-FREE

Enjoy stress-free travel when you use the Insight Guides secure online booking platform. All bookings come with a money-back guarantee.

WHAT OTHER TRAVELLERS THINK ABOUT TRIPS BOOKED AT INSIGHTGUIDES.COM/HOLIDAYS

Trip to Portugal

Every step of the planning process and the trip itself was effortless and exceptional. Our special interests, preferences and requests were accommodated resulting in a trip that exceeded our expectations.

Corinne, USA   ★★★★★

Trip to Vietnam

The organization was superb, the drivers professional, and accommodation quite comfortable. I was well taken care of! My thanks to your colleagues who helped make my trip to Vietnam such a great experience. My only regret is that I couldn't spend more time in the country.

Heather   ★★★★★

Contents

THE BEST OF TAIPEI: TOP ATTRACTIONS

At a glance, the Taipei attractions you won't want to miss, from sky-scraping architecture and colorful temples to hot springs and buzzing nightmarkets.

◁ **Taipei 101.** Until 2010 the world's tallest building, standing at 508 meters (1,667ft), this iconic tower is a wonder of design and engineering. Be sure to inspect the giant Tuned Mass Damper. See page 150.

▽ **Longshan Temple.** In the heart of the old Wanhua District and filled day and night by those seeking divine aid. Check out the icon of the main goddess Guanyin, which miraculously survived direct bombing hits in World War II. See page 102.

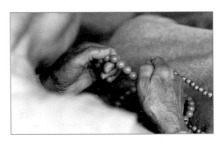

▽ **Beitou Hot-Springs Area.** A lovely valley carved by a bubbling hot-springs stream dotted with new and old resorts, public baths, and large sulfur pits and pools. See page 175.

▽ **Raohe Nightmarket.** This is Taipei's most atmospheric night market, with the ostentatious Ciyou Temple at its entrance. Also, the food on offer is a smorgasbord of savory and sweet delights. See page 153.

△ **Danshui.** It's not just ice creams and boats at this riverside-seaside town. Up on the hill you'll find old consular residences, missionary houses, and two fabulous forts. See page 195.

▷ **National Palace Museum.** With well over half a million rare documents and artifacts, this museum is home to the world's greatest vault of Chinese treasures. See page 184.

▷ **Dihua Street.** The old merchant's quarter is now a fantastic network of restored heritage buildings housing museums, cafés, restaurants, and stores. See page 113.

◁ **Muzha Tea Plantations.** In a steep hill valley in Taipei's southeast corner, scores of plantations with highly personalized teahouses dot the slopes, serving up "tea cuisine," and dreamy faraway views. See page 162.

▷ **Liberty Square.** This complex was built to an imperial scale and rivals Beijing's Forbidden City for awe-inspiring grandeur. The roof of the National Theater was modeled after Beijing's Hall of Supreme Harmony. See page 124.

▽ **Yangmingshan National Park.** The world's largest national park within a city's limits is perched on a mountain and offers hiking, hot-springs soaking, picnicking, flower gardens, giant fumaroles, historic sites, and much more. See page 188.

THE BEST OF TAIPEI: EDITOR'S CHOICE

Setting priorities, saving money, unique attractions... here, at a glance, are our recommendations, plus some tips and tricks even locals don't always know.

BEST WALKS

Erziping trail . A popular walk on Yangmingshan, a beautiful mountain park filled with trails and hot springs, plus hundreds of butterfly and bird species. See page 192.
Qingtiangang. Also found high on Yangmingshan, this plateau with ocean views features fumaroles and idyllic pastures grazed by water buffalo. See page 193.
Tianmu Steps. An easy pathway up the side of

Taipei life on Ximending's pedestrian streets.

Yangmingshan from the Tianmu expat enclave. Popular with families. See page 175.
Taipei Botanical Garden. Take a leisurely stroll past exotic flora and linger by a huge lotus pond. See page 130.
Guandu Nature Park. This boardwalked marsh brings one close to birds and other species that can only be found here. See page 181.
Dadaocheng and Wanhua. Let an historical walk through two of Taipei's oldest districts – lined with old shophouses and heritage sites – transport you back in time to the heyday of immigrant settlements and river trade. See pages 99 and 113.
Ximending. A walk down pedestrianized Wuchang and Emei streets provides some retail therapy, and insight into the latest youth crazes and fashions. See page 106.

Taipei offers good family activities.

BEST FOR FAMILIES

Taipei Water Park. A perfect place for kids to frolic in water-based amusements. See page 163.
Science Education Center. Here, science is taught through interactive displays and 3D movies. Next door, the Astronomical Museum has iWERKS and IMAX theaters. See page 171.
Taipei Zoo. With a Children's Zoo, an ever-popular koala sanctuary, live-in pandas, and a butterfly conservation area. See page 166.
Miramar Entertainment Park. The giant rooftop Ferris wheel, also known as the Taipei Eye, is best ridden at night. See page 183.
Mango shaved ice. This incredible and enormous dessert is a Taiwan classic and will take some time to finish, so you may have to help!
Su Ho Paper Memorial Museum. Paper-making workshops make this magic for young ones. See page 142.
Riverside Bike Paths. The city is encircled by easy-grade bike paths meandering through parks, with cheap bike-rental kiosks.

PLACES OF WORSHIP

Taipei Confucius Temple. One of Taipei's grandest, the temple comes alive on Teachers' Day, when age-old rites are performed at dawn. See page 121.

Ciyou Temple. The annual birthday celebrations for Mazu, patron saint of seafarers, are most elaborate here. See page 154.

Taipei Grand Mosque. The country's main mosque, built with Saudi Arabian funding, is open to guided public visits for Muslims and non-Muslims alike. See page 159.

Xiahai City God Temple. This becomes a sea of raucous activity during the City God's birthday procession. See page 115.

Xingtian Temple. Dedicated to Guan Gong, patron saint of businessmen, this is one of Taiwan's richest temples, famous for the efficacy of its *shoujing*. See page 140.

Zhinan Temple. In the hills of Muzha, always thronging with devotees of Lü Dongbin, one of the Eight Immortals. See page 166.

Tianbula.

Baosheng Festival warrior.

ONLY IN TAIPEI

Shung Ye Museum of Formosan Aborigines. One of the best places in the world to learn about the indigenous tribes of Taiwan. See page 173.

EcoArk. Located at the Taipei Expo Park, the EcoArk is the world's first giant building made from 1.52 million recycled PET bottles. See page 139.

Nightmarkets. These are the places to get your nightly grease fix, cheap clothing, and an authentic taste of local street life. See page 86.

Temple festivals. Birthday celebrations for deities such as Mazu are conducted in the streets of Taipei, with processions, firecrackers, and huge effigies. See page 52.

Changing of the Guard. Members of the armed forces in snappy uniforms, polished boots, white gloves, and mirrored helmets perform a rigid slow-motion march as they swap sentry duty. See them at Sun Yet Sen Memorial Hall, Chiang Kai-Shek Memorial Hall, or Martyr's Shrine, once every hour. See page 135.

FAMOUS FOOD

Tianbula. A Taiwanese version of tempura, this snack features fried tubes of fish paste, dried beancurd, and pig's blood cakes, dunked in a sweet and spicy sauce.

Stinky tofu. You either love or you hate this fermented beancurd snack, often called "Chinese cheese." Found at nightmarkets.

Soy braised foods. Called *luwei*, from tofu to tongue, all manner of meats are stewed for long hours in sauce and spices for a deep, rich, salty flavor.

Pearl milk tea. This cold beverage (very occasionally hot), also called bubble tea, comes in myriad flavors with a dollop of chewy "pearls" made from tapioca flour.

Pineapple cakes. Cubed pastries with pineapple paste filling, invented in central Taiwan. A delicious gift.

See page 68.

Aiyu. Chilled *aiyu* is a "cooling," jelly-like dessert made from the eponymous fruit. Exclusive to Taiwan. See page 172.

Shaved ice. A generous heaping of crushed or shaved ice, topped with red beans, yam, or fresh fruits, then drizzled with condensed milk.

Three Cup Chicken. Perhaps Taiwan's most representative dish, meats and other tasties slowly pot-simmered in a cup of soy sauce, rice wine, and sesame oil. See page 64.

At the Shung Ye Museum of Formosan Aborigines.

BEST BARS AND PUBS

Blue Note. Taipei's homey home for jazz-lovers. Brings in talent, has a house band, and features regular jam sessions. Tel: 02-2362 2333.
Carnegie's. A big venue open to the street, one of the city's few nightlife spots with alfresco seating. Wide bartops, made for dancing, are well used. www.carnegies.net.
EZ5. Taipei's best-known dinner club, renowned for hosting the top homegrown club singers from Taiwan and around, who like to sing their favourite English tunes here. www.ez5.com.tw.
23 Public Craft Beer. Cashing in on the craft-beer craze, this funky corner bar has 12 different draught brews. Get here early as it is popular even on weeknights. www.facebook.com/23Public.

Carnegie's is a hugely popular bar, known for its lively atmosphere and wide selection of shooters.

BEST VIEWS

Four Beasts Mountain. From the westernmost peak of this mountain on Taipei's east side, the whole city sits before you like a giant scale model. See page 151.
Muzha Tourist Tea Plantations. The city sparkles at night from the teahouses on the highest slopes here. See page 167.
Mt Qixing. From here, Yangmingshan's tallest peak, the ocean and Taipei Basin is laid out before you. See page 193.

Taipei 101 Observation Decks. Catch stunning views from the main 89th-floor Observatory and 91st-floor outdoor deck. See page 150.
Jiufen. This small town, on the slopes of Mt Jilong, provides panoramic views of the mountains and sea from teahouse decks. See page 215.
Wulai Cable Car. Soars high over a hot-springs valley, brushing past a waterfall that bursts from the bluff-top you fly to. See page 227.

A detail at the Baoan Temple.

BEST ARCHITECTURE

Longshan Temple Dragons. In the graceful, ornate southern Chinese style, the temple is famed for its dragon carvings, notably the writhing pillars. See page 102.
Baoan Temple. It's not easy to beat Longshan Temple for color and decorative intricacy, but this Unesco-recognized temple does; the *koji*-pottery roof work is magical. See page 120.
Presidential Office Building. A red-brick neo-Renaissance edifice built by the Japanese on a scale worthy of any head of state. Its tower was the tallest structure during the colonial era. See page 126.
Shihsanhang Museum of Archaeology. Located outside of the city, in the tiny town of Bali, is this distinctively angular building that garnered the Far East Architecture Award in 2003. See page 203.
Taipei 101 Fengshui. A wonderful example of traditional *fengshui* symbolism in action, the bamboo stalk shape symbolizing people's fortitude, ancient coin symbols inviting wealth. See page 150.

An amazing view of the Taipei 101 tower and city skyline from Four Beasts Mountain.

TOP SHOPPING

Eslite Bookstore, Dunhua Branch. Open 24 hours daily, this is a nice alternative nightlife option, with thousands of English-language titles and a foodcourt downstairs. See page 146.

Guang Hua Digital Plaza. One of the best places in the city to buy or just window-shop for state-of-the art electronic goods. See page 142.

Weekend Jade Market. This jade-lovers' mecca is one of the Asia's largest markets to buy this precious stone along with other jewelry and prayer beads. See page 142.

Nanmen Market. Taipei's renowned and biggest day market. The city's number one spot to shop for traditional sausages, snacks and cookies. See page 130.

MONEY-SAVING TIPS

Cheap food and drink. Though the food at Taipei's nightmarkets may be slightly too greasy for sensitive stomachs, it is mostly clean, tasty, and very cheap. Visitors can feast on all sorts of traditional Taiwanese snack foods and drinks and still come away with change from a NT$500 bill.

Biandang are Taiwan's answer to the lunchbox. During lunch hour, locals move out in droves to the ubiquitous *biandang* outlets, where for merely NT$80–120 you're given a bed of rice in a disposable, sealable box, and allowed a choice of three or four toppings from a buffet selection of 15–20 dishes. Cheap and tasty.

Drinking in Taipei is not cheap, but luckily many bars in the city have a daily happy hour early in the evening that lasts a couple of hours or so. The cheapest drink is usually bottled Taiwan Beer, priced at around NT$100. Another option is to buy your brew from one of the ubiquitous convenience stores, such as 7-11, and drink it in one of the many beautiful parks.

Many bars and clubs also have a weekly Ladies' night, generally on Wednesdays. The usual deal is one free drink and a waiver of the cover charge at venues where there is canned or live music.

Free views. Rather than pay for entry into the observatories at the city's two tallest man-made structures, head for one of two hillside stairways that lead to views just as uplifting. Both start from easily accessible trailheads, and are calm and pleasant 20-minute hikes. The first is up Elephant Mountain, just south of the Taipei 101 skyscraper. It has its own MRT station, one stop east of Taipei 101 at Xiangshan. The other is up Yuanshan behind the Grand Hotel, just 5 minutes from Jiantan MRT station.

Refunds. Foreign travelers who make purchases of at least NT$2,000 on the same day, and from the same Tax Refund Shopping (TRS)-posted store, are eligible for a refund of the 5 percent VAT paid (see page 70).

Tourist Information. Pick up free maps, money-off vouchers, and a wealth of travel information booklets and brochures from one of the many helpful Tourist Service Centers around the city. The most central are inside Ximen and Taipei 101 MRT stations and in the main hall at Taipei Main Station.

Museums and attractions. Many museums and attractions in Taipei do not charge admission, including the Discovery Center of Taipei, Beitou Hot Springs Museum, and the Ketagalan Culture Center, the Chiang Kai-shek Memorial Hall, Lin An Tai Historical House and Museum, Sun Yat-sen Historic Events Memorial Hall, and the National Revolutionary Martyrs' Shrine.

Parks and Gardens. The city's many public parks, such as Daan Forest Park, 228 Memorial Peace Park, Sishoushan Community Forest, Dajia Riverside Park, Yangmingshan National Park's hiking trails, and the Botanical Garden, do not charge admission fees.

Temples. Three is an open invitation to the city's scores of Taoist, Buddhist, and Confucian places of worship, large and small.

Festivals. Plangent pageants of color and ceremony, all of Taipei's temple festivals are free, as is the Taipei Lantern Festival and other secular celebrations throughout the year.

Concerts. Check the local newspapers for free concerts at Daan Forest Park's amphitheater, or Taiwanese celebrity appearances in *Ximending*.

Taipei has many peaceful parks.

Aerial view of Zhongxiao West Road.

Making music at Sun Yat-sen Memorial Hall.

NEW TAIPEI

In many ways, Taipei is a tale of two cities. The old city was crowded, polluted, and chaotic. But the modern city is very different. It has evolved over the years, and is now staking a claim as one of the best in Asia. Call it the New Taipei.

When Chiang Kai-shek's government set up camp on the island in the late 1940s, the idea was that it was temporary and its members would go back to mother China shortly. Little thought was put into beautifying their capital, defined by row after row of unsightly cement-block residential buildings hastily put up to accommodate the new arrivals.

Raohe Night Market

Since the lifting of martial law in the late 1980s, and the burgeoning of disposable incomes as a result of the economic miracle of the 1960s and 1970s, the improvement of the city has been a key goal. Taiwan is the fourth-richest country in East Asia in terms of per capita income and enhancing quality of life has become one of the primary pursuits. Indeed, the pace of change has been startling. Metro lines have opened, and new freeways move traffic briskly, while tough pollution laws have throttled the two-stroke scooters that once belched the city's signature pollution. Two large squatter villages were razed, and are now leafy parks filled with in-line skaters and tai chi practitioners.

The Taiwanese love sophisticated technology – Apple had to wait but it now has several stores including in and near Taipei 101 – and the new Taipei (not to be confused with New Taipei city, the name given to the city's newer suburbs) is a hyper-modern city, thanks to the billions of dollars the government has poured in. Almost the entire city is WiFi accessible.

The city's important heritage sites are no longer being torn down in the headlong pursuit of maximum lucre; many are being restored and given a second lease of life. A key government program is to uphold a "necklace of cultural pearls" through the city – a long line of irreplaceable historical sites.

The new Taipei is big (it rivals any capital city), but not too big (you can cross town in 20 minutes by Metro). It's exotic, but not too exotic. It's crowded enough to be *renao* (literally "hot and noisy"), buzzing with restaurants, nightclubs, and boutiques, but not chronically gridlocked like, say, Bangkok or Beijing.

But best of all are the friendly residents who cheerfully direct visitors to the Metro station and write down Chinese characters for the taxi driver. They are the *Xin Taiwanren*, or New Taiwanese, and the heart and soul of the city.

Girls hit the town in trendy Ximending.

PEOPLE

The educated and well-traveled residents of Taipei have higher incomes and greater fashion consciousness than their countryside kin, but at heart they still embody the Taiwanese spirit of *renqingwei*, or "human feeling."

Since late imperial times, Taipei has been the center of political and economic power on the island. It has long been the norm for people of ambition and talent to move here from their hometowns in the central, southern, and eastern regions. On top of this demographic imbalance, a common complaint is that for too long the Kuomintang (KMT) government poured an unfair share of financial resources into the capital city's development, leaving the other regions to fend for themselves.

There is some truth to these accusations. When Chiang Kai-shek's Nationalists landed on the island in the late 1940s, most of the 2 million or more mainlanders who came settled in and around Taipei. Though it was still somewhat under-developed by international standards then, it was Taiwan's leading city. The Kuomintang government saw Taipei as its base, and other areas as populated by outsiders and Japanese sympathizers. It hoarded resources for itself and the city.

Since the end of martial law in 1987, things have been changing. Political leadership is moving towards greater ethnic and geographical representation, and resources are in turn being spread out more evenly.

It is also recognized that given its limited land area, Taipei is far too heavily populated; since 1968 and the era of Taiwan's "economic miracle," the population has grown dramatically and continues to rise. More recent initiatives such as the creation of satellite cities and what are called "new towns" have aimed to encourage Taipei residents to move to outlying areas – or

Crowds of scooter-riders stuck in traffic hint at the city's population density.

at least to deflect the influx of citizens from other areas.

Population size and density

At the end of 2018, Taiwan's overall population was 23.6 million; Taipei City (excluding the suburban areas of New Taipei City) itself was home to 2.69 million people (that's over a million households). With about two-thirds of the island mountainous, Taiwan trails only Bangladesh in population density among states with a population over 10 million. The problem is exacerbated in Taipei, ringed as it is by mountains and plunked down in the small Taipei Basin. With approximately 9,900 people per square kilometer, this is one of the world's most crowded cities. Heavily residential Daan District is the most crowded, with 27,384 people per square kilometer.

In the 1980s, almost all of the city's green areas had been built over. Since then the city administration has been working hard to increase public green spaces, and the city has been growing upward instead of outward. Stand-alone single homes are almost non-existent except on Yangmingshan, where the richest live. Most citizens live in residential high-rises, packed side by side in solid rows, in units akin to what Westerners would call a condominium. Whereas in the 1980s most such high-rises were only 3–5 stories tall, today they are 8–10 stories, and even higher downtown. Elevators are common only in the newer (and thus taller) residential buildings.

The tradition of the extended family, with parents living in the house of the eldest male offspring (or vice versa), is breaking down in Taipei. A major reason is that sons and daughters have left their parents behind in central and southern Taiwan in order to take advantage of

Longshan Temple, one of Taipei's most important.

A modern Taipeier.

Taipei's better work prospects, especially for those with tertiary qualifications.

Stereotypes

Taipeiers tend to see themselves as more sophisticated than the residents of the island's other areas. The schools tend to be better, and the salaries and disposable incomes are higher. The average monthly earnings per capita for March 2019 was NT$41,674. Taipei citizens also travel overseas more, and doggedly pursue international trends in fashion, with a noted preference for conspicuously displayed brand names. There is also greater sophistication with regards to animal welfare, eco-friendly living, and other issues.

The Taiwanese in general tend to see people from the erstwhile motherland of China as backward and dishonest, and those with enough disposable income to travel to Taiwan as somewhat loud and gauche. The Taiwanese will also mention racism seen in the West, and maintain that Taiwan suffers no such discrimination. However, what is not recognized is that the Han Chinese homogeneity of local society is extant in large part because of a lack of acceptance of outsiders other than those of white skin from rich Western nations. Overseas guest workers from Southeast Asia, in particular, are often looked down on, and accounts of exploitation are regularly reported in the papers. The same is true of the increasing number of foreign spouses, mostly women from China and Vietnam, who only in recent years have been granted the right to work and are now slowly organizing and fighting for their rights. In 2016, Lin Li-chan, who was born in Cambodia, became the first immigrant in Taiwan to be elected to the Legislative Yuan.

Population breakdown

Taiwan's population profile is approximately 97.71 percent ethnic Han Chinese and 2.29 percent indigenous; according to statistics, the indigenous population has increased by over 30 percent since 2001. Among the Han Chinese, about 70 percent are Fujianese, 14 percent are Hakka, and 14 percent mainlander. In local parlance, a "mainlander" is someone who came to Taiwan from China with the KMT in the late 1940s and early 1950s, or a descendant of such an individual. A member of the Hakka community is one whose ancestors came to Taiwan during imperial times from the mountainous areas of Guangdong Province in China. The ancestors of the Fujianese came almost exclusively from the southern part of Fujian Province, or "south of the Min River," and their language is still referred to as *Minnanyu* (Southern Min) today, though some variation now differentiates the mainland China and Taiwanese dialects.

POPULATION MOVEMENTS

The imbalance in Taiwan's population is most evident in the run-up to the Chinese New Year holidays each year. Normally bustling Taipei becomes eerily quiet as people vacate en masse for parents' hometowns in the island's center and south. A drive south to Kaohsiung that might normally take 5 hours may take as long as 15; buses, trains, and planes are booked months ahead.

This phenomenon is now evolving, as the elderly parents of Taipei residents are now passing away, and the Taipeiers who moved to the city in the 1960s and 1970s have become parents and grandparents, shifting the center of familial gravity to the city.

A 2017 interview poll run by the National Chengchi University revealed that over 56 percent of the country's inhabitants identified themselves as Taiwanese only, up from merely 13.6 percent in 1991.

Taipei's demographics do not match the island's overall ethnic breakdown. Though there has been much intermarrying between mainlanders and Taiwanese – comparatively few women came over in the great exodus of the 1940s – identity remains strong through patrilineal descent, and today about half the city's population identify themselves as mainlanders. As a result, the two main parties that seek eventual reunification with China, the Kuomintang and the People First Party, have unusually strong political bases here.

The Hakka population in Taipei is close to 8 percent. They are a tightly knit community that has traditionally frowned on intermarriage. Even during the "economic miracle," comparatively few moved from traditional

Enjoying quality time in the Dajia Riverside Park.

Commuters line up at an MRT station.

farming villages in the foothills to the cities. This isolation is now breaking down, and the growth of the middle class among the Hakka is growing.

The city's indigenous community is small, with just 16,713 individuals as of the end of

IDENTITY

Ask four citizens of Taipei who they are and you'll likely get four different answers. Much of the population now sees China as politically distinct, so do not like the term *Zhongguoren*, literally "people of China." Many of those whose ancestors arrived during imperial times now simply refer to themselves as *Taiwanren*, "Taiwanese." Some mainlanders who arrived after World War II, however, do not use this term. Many Taiwanese themselves wish to identify with the shared Chinese cultural legacy, so *Huaren* is often used, a term derived from the more literary designation for China. The term *Hanren* is used to emphasize Chinese ethnicity, meaning "Han people," referring to China's Han Dynasty.

2018 (about 0.6 percent of the total population). There is no concentration in any district. The Ketagalans of the Taipei Basin have long been absorbed into the Chinese community, or have moved into the hills to the south and been absorbed by the native peoples there. Like other native populations around the globe, the indigenous community is in crisis. Its members are failing in the school system, and the school system is failing them. They remain uncompetitive in the job market because of lack of necessary skills, limited ability in the major languages, alcoholism, and discrimination.

The majority of indigenous residents are blue-collar laborers who work on large-scale construction projects, moving back and forth between Taipei and their home villages, especially when the projects end and work temporarily dries up. Members of the island's tribes constitute Taipei's poorest communities, subsisting at or below the poverty line, and living in close proximity to each other. The majority of Taipei families own their own homes, but few indigenous families do.

National psyche

The Taiwanese people are well known for putting in long hours at work. Among the Chinese, a long history of economic instability has given rise to a belief in hard work and saving up to weather the inevitable hard times. Traditionally, trust was only placed in family and a small circle of friends.

This is now changing, with the younger generation not having known poverty and, in the eyes of more senior generations, assuming that money grows on trees. Young workers are often called "strawberries," meaning they go all squishy when given even the slightest pressure. The "strawberries" are considered too demanding, wanting extra pay first before they are willing to take on job pressures, rather than proving themselves first in order to receive the award of a higher salary.

A national identity is also slowly emerging. In imperial times, the Chinese moved to Taiwan to escape oppressive Chinese officialdom. Here they developed an independent streak, akin to that of the American pioneer. In fact Taiwan was once something of a "Wild,

The Taipeier understands the concept of going Dutch, but sometimes someone will qingke or play host. Counting one's individual due, down to the penny, is seen as demeaning.

Wild East." During the Japanese colonial era, the rulers tried to "Japanize" the population. Later, during the martial-law period, the KMT tried to remake the population as citizens of China – no local languages in schools, no TV, radio, or movies in Taiwanese. In spite of this, a "Taiwan first" attitude is now shared by many locals, whether they support unification with China, formal independence, or the status quo.

Social etiquette and behavior

The norm of the family unit is shifting, with the extended family being replaced by the nuclear family, and younger people becoming increasingly individualistic. But traditional values still predominate in social life. Where this

Shopping in Ximending.

Traditions at temples are kept alive among both young and old.

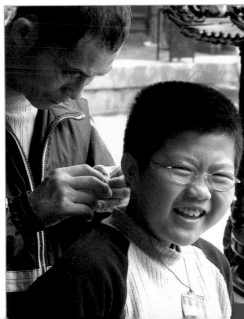

> You won't see much touching between the sexes here, save for the youth. It is more polite to keep overt displays of affection private; many a Western male has been secretly labeled a *selang*, or "color wolf."

is most obvious to the overseas traveler is in the spirit of *renqingwei*, which loosely translates as "human feeling." The city's people, as do all Taiwanese, see themselves as *reqing*, which roughly means "warmhearted."

Once a personal connection is made with a local, the importance of being *haoke*, or a "good host," comes to the fore. The visitor will be taken out and any small favor asked will be quickly handled. Be wary of idly commenting how much you like a person's jewelry, clothing, painting, and so on, because they may well turn around and give it to you. If you are taken out, be sure to invite the person out yourself before leaving the island. Not to do so may be seen as being manipulative, or at the least ill-mannered. If unsure of where to host a

Taipei's working professionals.

Young Taipeiers making the most of a day out in Danshui.

gathering, simply explain the situation to your guest, who will be glad to help. The Taiwanese embrace with open arms the foreigner who tries to understand the local culture, and will forgive almost any faux pas.

Locals are aware that the tradition of being *haoke* goes all the way back to the time of Confucius, who taught "Do not do unto others what you would not have them do unto you." Ergo, you should be a good host at all times, for would you not want to be treated the same way if you yourself were traveling?

The Taiwanese are well known for their politeness and readiness to help visitors. Just stand looking clueless in front of one of the maps in the MRT for a moment and someone will likely tap you on your shoulder and ask if they can help you, even going out of their way to walk you to your destination if it's not too far. And that also goes for friendly bus drivers and the many elderly volunteers who are stationed in hospitals to help non-Chinese speakers navigate the system.

Taipei residents, while considered less friendly than their fellow citizens in small towns and the countryside, are still more courteous and helpful than many other societies. Simply ask any foreigner who has lived in mainland China or Hong Kong before how Taiwan compares. Taiwan almost always comes out top.

While Taipei still lacks recognition as a major capital city, things are changing quickly in light of Taiwan's high level of education, increasingly trusted official enforcement of the individual's legal rights, and government campaigns, especially prior to international events for which the city is serving as host. While the city may not sparkle like Shanghai, it has been given a huge facelift in terms of both greenery and cleanliness. The newer areas of the city, such as Xinyi District with its gleaming office towers, were the first to herald a change. The introduction of a rigorous mandatory recycling system with the pay-as-you-throw scheme has created an infinitely cleaner and tidier city. Taipei is now a capital highly committed to green living and ecology.

As prosperity has increased, the Taiwanese have embraced their leisure time.

An indigenous artisan at work.

Freddy Lim, politician, musician, and independence activist.

DECISIVE DATES

From prehistory to the Qing dynasty

5000 BC to 2000 BC
Neolithic Tapenkeng people inhabit the Taipei area.

4000 BC
The island is settled by peoples of Austronesian ethno-linguistic stock, the ancestors of today's indigenous people.

AD 200–1500
The Taipei area is inhabited by the Shihsanhang people, a non-Chinese race possibly related to the Austronesians.

1544
Portuguese sailors passing Taiwan call it Ilha Formosa, "Beautiful Island."

1622
Dutch traders establish a base on Penghu in the Taiwan Strait.

1628
Spanish troops build Fort San Domingo in Danshui, with the intention of further territorial expansion.

1642
The Spanish are driven from Taiwan and the Dutch take over.

1662
Koxinga, or Zheng Chenggong, a Ming dynasty loyalist, drives the Dutch from Taiwan, and Taipei falls under Chinese control.

1737
Immigrants, mostly from China's southern Fujian Province, continue to settle in the Taipei area, which soon hosts a number of prosperous trading centers.

A woodblock print depicting the Japanese takeover in 1895.

Leaders including Chiang Kai-shek, Franklin Delano Roosevelt and Winston Churchill at the Cairo Conference in 1943, which addressed the Allied position toward Japan during World War II.

1858
The Treaty of Tianjin, resulting from the Second Opium War, opens several ports, including Danshui, to foreign trade. Taipei prospers.

1885
Liu Mingchuan becomes the first Qing dynasty governor of Taiwan. He moves the capital from Tainan to Taipei, and launches a series of modernizing reforms.

Japanese presence
1895
China loses the First Sino-Japanese War, and cedes Taiwan to Japan under the Treaty of Shimonoseki.

1930
The Wushe Uprising, the last major indigenous rebellion against the Japanese, is forcibly suppressed.

1935
An Exposition to commemorate Japan's administration of the island is held, showcasing the great improvements made to the colony's infrastructure and economy.

1937
The Second Sino-Japanese War begins.

1943
Franklin Roosevelt, Winston Churchill, and Nationalist leader Chiang Kai-shek meet in Cairo, and declare that when World War II ends, Taiwan will be returned to China.

1945
World War II ends. The Japanese surrender. Taipei returns to Chinese control.

The Republic of China
1947
The 2-28 Incident sparks off protests in Taipei and across the island. Nationalist troops kill up to 28,000 civilians in response. The event launches the White Terror,

an era of harsh political repression.

1949
The communist People's Republic of China (PRC) is proclaimed under Mao Zedong. Chiang Kai-shek and the defeated Kuomintang (KMT) flee to Taiwan, where the Republic of China (ROC) is established, with Taipci named as its temporary capital.

1950s
The US Seventh Fleet deters an all-out war across the Taiwan Strait, despite the ferocious 1954–55 and 1958 bombardments of Quemoy (Kinmen Island).

1960s
Taiwan starts to become an exporting powerhouse, launching four decades of spectacular economic growth.

1965
The National Palace Museum opens on the outskirts of Taipei.

1971
The UN admits the PRC as the legitimate representative of China, and expels the ROC.

1975
Chiang Kai-shek passes away, paving the way for political reform.

1978
Chiang Kai-shek's son Chiang Ching-kuo becomes president of Taiwan.

A Taipei pro-independence rally.

1979
The US switches recognition to the PRC, and ends formal diplomatic relations with Taiwan. The US Congress then passes the Taiwan Relations Act, which implies that the US will defend Taiwan in the event of an attack by mainland China. The Kaohsiung Incident galvanizes opposition to martial law.

1980
The Hsinchu Science Park is established near Taipei, and becomes a driving force in Taiwan's high-tech economy.

1986
The opposition Democratic Progressive Party (DPP) is founded.

1987
Martial law is lifted. Taiwanese are allowed to travel to China.

Taipei continues to have a thriving technological industry, as here at Hsinchu Science Park.

1988
Lee Teng-hui becomes the first Taiwan-born president of Taiwan. Opposition parties are legalized.

1992
Taiwan and China loosely agree that there is "One China," but disagree on what that means, exactly.

1995–96
China launches missile tests near the coast of Taiwan, and some of the missiles land in the ocean near Taipei. US warships move closer to Taiwan.

1996
Lee Teng-hui wins a landslide victory in Taiwan's first presidential elections. The first Taipei Metro line opens.

1997
The opposition DPP wins 12 out of 23 mayoral and county seats, and for the first time receives more votes than the KMT.

1999
President Lee Teng-hui abandons the fuzzy "One China" principle, and declares "special state-to-state" relations. China again threatens to retake Taiwan by force. A devastating earthquake, measuring 7.6 on the Richter scale, kills over 2,300 people and injures over 8,000.

Modern politics
2000
Chen Shui-bian is elected president, temporarily

ending 50 years of KMT rule. Taiwan becomes a member of the WTO.

2001
The Dalai Lama arrives for a spiritual visit. Tropical storm Nari causes widespread flooding and kills at least 66 people.

2002
President Chen Shui-bian declares that Taiwan is "not someone else's province." This sparks an uproar in China and at home, prompting him to back away from his rhetoric. China surpasses the US as Taiwan's top trading partner.

2003
Taipei is gripped by the SARS epidemic, and the economy suffers. After three months of drama, the WHO declares the infection contained.

2004
The Taipei 101 tower, then the world's tallest building, is completed, a status maintained until 2010, when it is surpassed by Dubai's Burj Khalifa. Chen Shui-bian and Annette Lu are shot and wounded in a bizarre assassination attempt a day before the presidential election. Chen narrowly wins re-election, but the results are disputed, and half a million people swarm into Taipei to protest. Chen is eventually affirmed as the winner.

The Taipei 101 tower, which held the record for being the world's tallest building for five years.

2005
KMT politician Lien Chan pays a landmark visit to China, and is received by president Hu Jintao.

2008
The DPP loses national elections after weakened support because of spreading scandals. The KMT's Ma Ying-jeou is elected president, and immediately moves to bring Taiwan closer to China.

2009
Typhoon Morakot lashes Taiwan, bringing a deluge of rain and causing over 600 deaths, largely in the south. The Dalai Lama makes his second visit to the island to pray for victims. Former President Chen Shui-bian is given life in prison after a corruption trial.

2010
Taiwan and China sign a free trade pact, regarded as the most important

bilateral agreement in 60 years of separation.

2012
Ma Ying-jeou of the KMT is re-elected President of Taiwan.

2014
A new services-trade pact with China raises concerns that it will hurt Taiwan's industry, and provokes enormous opposition protests.

2016
Tsai Ing-wen of the pro-independence DPP is elected Taiwan's first female president. China responds by cutting off official communications and poaching Taiwan's diplomatic allies.

2019
Taiwan illustrates its progressive credentials by becoming the first country in Asia to legalise same-sex unions.

Tsai Ing-wen.

A 1930s poster advertising the Taiwan Expo.

A MODERN MIRACLE

With its turbulent past and location at the crossroads of East Asia, Taipei has, at one time or another, been seized and shaken by history's major forces and trends. Today it is experiencing a period of political ambiguity but great prosperity.

The Taipei area has undergone successive cycles of colonization – by the Spanish, Dutch, Chinese, and Japanese – and has suffered the virtual extinction of its indigenous peoples. It has gone through lawless periods, when warlords, pirates, and clan families fought over the area's spoils.

Natural disasters have been frequent, such as the devastating quake of September 21, 1999 and the 2009 typhoon-induced deluge that killed 600 people. Nor has Taipei been spared the ravages of war. During World War II, Allied bombs pounded the city before the Japanese surrendered the island. This was followed by a period of bitter oppression under the tyrannical rule of Generalissimo Chiang Kai-shek.

But the city has enjoyed good times as well, and in the past few decades, riding the crest of Taiwan's transition from rural backwater to economic powerhouse, Taipei has blossomed. It now boasts a fully democratic government and an excellent infrastructure. It nurtures a rich flowering of culture, and its educated populace enjoys a higher quality of life than at any other time in history.

Indigenous inhabitants

The history of human inhabitation in what is present-day Taipei began perhaps 7,000 years ago, when it was settled by the Tapenkeng people. These Neolithic people, like later settlers, were attracted to the lush Taipei Basin, a fertile land that enjoyed steady and predictable rainfall, was good for growing crops, and was rich in clams, fish, deer, and other food sources. The Tapenkeng were succeeded by the Ketagalan.

Detail from a 15th-century Chinese map depicting Taiwanese indigenous people hunting deer.

When ethnic Chinese immigrants first arrived four to five centuries ago, they encountered these and other Austronesian ancestors of today's indigenous groups. The 19 tribes on the island lived in large communities and practiced agriculture, but those in and around Taipei were eventually almost entirely assimilated or extinguished by successive waves of newcomers.

Western traders

In 1544, Portuguese sailors passing the island dubbed it *Ilha Formosa*, meaning "beautiful island," a name that belied the terrifying

Busy Dadaocheng port in the 19th century.

The battle between Koxinga and the Dutch.

reputation the island soon acquired. Sailors shipwrecked on its coasts were seized and robbed of everything, lucky to escape with their lives. More often than not, they were speedily killed by head-hunting indigenous people.

In the early 1600s, the Dutch East India Company arrived in the Taiwan Strait. They were followed soon after by the Spanish, whose troops built Fort San Domingo in Danshui in 1628. Over the following decades, the Dutch and Spanish vied for control of the Taipei area. Under Dutch rule, rebellious indigenous groups were forcibly suppressed, converted to Christianity, and schools were set up. It was also this period that saw the overhunting and extinction of Taiwan's native species of deer to fuel Dutch trade. Eventually, in 1662, the Dutch were driven from Danshui by the Ming dynasty loyalist Koxinga, or Zheng Chenggong. Zheng had hoped to retake China from its new Qing dynasty rulers using Taiwan as his base, but that did not happen.

Danshui River communities

After Taiwan came under Chinese control, settlers poured into Taipei, most of them from Fujian Province, just across the strait from Taiwan.

In those days, the Danshui River was still deep enough for river transport, and settlements sprang up along its banks. Wanhua, in the southwest corner of today's Taipei (the site of Longshan Temple today), prospered as a trading center, as did adjoining areas. Expansion was steady, and by the mid-1700s Taipei had become a collection of prosperous farming and trading neighborhoods. The fertile basin produced staples like rice and vegetables, while the rich seas off Danshui provided abundant fish. Business was brisk, with tea and camphor from the hills above Taipei creating a lively market for overseas trade after the 1858 Treaty of Tianjin.

A tough environment

Like the rest of Taiwan then, Taipei was only loosely governed by the Qing administration. During the 1700s and 1800s, it was not a city as such, but a series of small fiefdoms carved out by local warlords, trading companies, and large clan families. Forced to contend with invasions from rival gangs of immigrants and

A Taipei street scene during Japanese rule.

from indigenous groups in outlying areas, each neighborhood in Taipei built narrow stone gates to seal itself off, a hallmark of those lawless times.

But Taipei was also a city of great opportunity. Far from the regulations of imperial China, Taiwan was a sort of untamed frontier, where immigrants who had vision and energy could prosper. Farmers with landholdings amassed fortunes, as did moneylenders and traders in tea, camphor, and opium. In their wake came craftsmen, laborers, and fortune-seekers from China.

Chinese control

Life took a turn for the better in the late 1800s. In 1875, Taipei was named a prefectural city, and in 1885 Taiwan became an official province of China. A city wall was built from 1882 to 1884. In 1885, an ambitious governor named Liu Mingchuan moved the provincial capital from Tainan to Taipei, and launched reforms. He brought electricity to the city – the first in China to have it – and laid a railway from

Taipei to the port of Keelung, about 30km (20 miles) away.

Alas, the period of reform was short-lived. In 1894–5, far to the north, the Japanese pounded the ill-equipped Chinese troops in the First Sino-Japanese War. One of the spoils of Japan's easy victory over the crumbling Qing dynasty was Taiwan, ceded under the 1895 Treaty of Shimonoseki.

Qing supporters among Taiwan's ruling class tried to prevent Japanese occupation of the island by declaring a Republic of Formosa, but the plan fell through when troops from China began rampaging. Japanese soldiers soon restored order, and sporadic indigenous resistance over the years was eventually quelled.

> *Owen Rutter writes of mid-1800s Taiwan in Through Formosa: An Account of Japan's Island Colony: "The government was corrupt… the country was ravaged by bands of brigands… sanitary conditions were filthy…"*

Propaganda during the Chinese Civil War.

Japanese rule

The Japanese were harsh rulers, forcing the Taiwanese to learn Japanese, and strip-mining the island's resources for imperial Japan. Still, some historians argue that the Japanese occupation was the dawn of modern Taiwan, and that stern discipline was necessary to bring the

COLONIAL TAIPEI

Eager to make a success of their first colony, the Japanese built majestic theaters, lively restaurants and bathhouses, and tree-lined boulevards. They carved out a prime piece of riverfront property – today's Ximending – and declared it a pleasure zone. Many of the classic buildings in Taipei date from this era, including the Presidential Office Building, the Red House theater, and others. Owen Rutter, who visited in 1923, describes the city as such: "Taihoku [Taipei] is undoubtedly laid out on a finer scale than any other city in the Japanese empire, with wide streets, spacious parks, and public buildings that would not disgrace any capital in the world."

fractured Chinese together under one government. The Japanese rigorously enforced their laws – then a new concept to the people of Taipei – and ended the ceaseless plundering, gang violence, and bandit/indigenous raids that had plagued the city.

The Japanese tore down the old city walls, a traffic-stopping anachronism, and also built roads, harbors, railroads, and crucially, power plants, giving birth to the city's first light industry. They also established banks and standardized the monetary system. They built schools islandwide, and many Taiwanese received a formal education for the first time. The unpleasant open sewers and outhouses that typified Taipei life were replaced by modern underground pipes.

Civil war in China

But the era of Japanese rule did not last. When World War II ended in 1945, Taiwan was formally returned to Chinese rule under terms previously agreed upon in Cairo between Allied leaders Winston Churchill, Franklin Roosevelt, and Chiang Kai-shek, who was then

> *The arriving Nationalists treated Taipei citizens with contempt, seeing them as Japanese sympathizers and citizens of a defeated nation. Indeed, many men had fought China beside the Japanese.*

nominal leader of China's government. Events on the mainland would once again determine the island's fate.

In the years leading up to World War II, even as Taiwan enjoyed peace and stability, China had entered a period of chaos. The Qing dynasty collapsed in 1911, and the Republic of China was established the following year, under the leadership of revered revolutionary Sun Yat-sen. However, Sun was unable to maintain his hold on power, and for the next three decades, various warlords and factions fought for control of China.

Eventually, the struggle was dominated by two groups: the Nationalists, or Kuomintang (KMT), under Chiang Kai-shek, and the Chinese Communist Party, under Mao Zedong. The two sides briefly ceased open hostilities under an uneasy truce during World War II, but in 1946, as the world watched, China was once again plunged into a civil war between the American-backed Nationalists and the Russian-backed Communists.

The February 28 Incident

On October 21, 1946, Chiang Kai-shek visited Taiwan on a groundswell of goodwill and hope. The crowds were happy to welcome Chinese rulers after 50 years of Japanese occupation. However, their smiles turned to shock and dismay when they saw the ragged soldiers who accompanied Chiang, many of whom were rude, dirty, uneducated, and penniless. The Taipei people, accustomed to rule by the clean and orderly Japanese, were aghast.

Preoccupied by the ongoing civil war with the Communists, Chiang returned to China and appointed the corrupt Chen Yi to govern Taiwan. Trouble was not long in coming.

On February 27, 1947, officers from the Monopoly Bureau in Taipei tried to stop an elderly widow from selling black-market cigarettes, and she was wounded. A crowd gathered, a scuffle broke out, and the officers

opened fire, killing a man. The next day, on February 28 (which later became known as the 2-28 Incident), crowds gathered to protest, and were met with resistance. This ignited a violent uprising that spread throughout the island. Governor Chen Yi sent for reinforcements, and a massacre began. Thousands of unarmed Taiwanese were shot and killed, and thousands more were dragged from their homes and later disappeared. The brutal suppression took between 18,000 and 28,000 lives, according to a government report released in 1992.

Nationalist exodus

Meanwhile, after a protracted struggle on the mainland, the Communists seized control of China, establishing the People's Republic of China (PRC) in 1949 under Mao Zedong. Chiang Kai-shek fled to Taiwan in the same year with the defeated Nationalists – more

Chinese Nationalist soldiers head for Taiwan, bearing the Republic of China's flag.

> The immigrants from China in 1949 were mostly male, giving Taipei a high ratio of men to women. The city's sex gap widened further after abortion became legal in 1985.

than 2 million ragged immigrants from mainland China. Most of them settled in Taipei – which became the base for Chiang Kai-shek's Republic of China (ROC) – filling the spacious Japanese parks with squalid shanty towns.

Since taking over the island the KMT had treated the city as its own, illegally annexing property owned by the Taiwanese. Because officers and other well-connected immigrants had no land and no jobs, they were given all the top government positions; the regular troops were largely left to fend for themselves, especially after demobilization was commenced. The people of Taipei had no role in government

Woodcut depicting events of the 2-28 Incident.

and no voice in political affairs, though many were educated and wealthy. Resentment grew over the nepotism of the new government. Given Chiang's propensity for ruthless and autocratic rule, well established in mainland China, it soon became clear that he would continue the period of oppression known as the White Terror, not end it.

The White Terror

The 2-28 Incident set the tone for the White Terror that followed, a frightening era that was typified by executions without trial, midnight knocks on the door, long prison terms for political dissidents, and strict suppression of everything Taiwanese, including the indigenous languages. Chiang Kai-shek's secret police were unpredictable and arbitrary, and his victims had no legal recourse. Chiang himself is said to have signed at least one execution order every day, and sometimes up to 10, for almost a decade. In this way, many of Taipei's best and brightest – students down to high-school level, professors, doctors, and scholars – were imprisoned or killed.

The White Terror repression was sweeping. A few of the victims were avowed communists, seduced by the same spell that had captivated mainland China. More were critics who spoke out against the inefficiency and corruption of the Chiang dictatorship. Others were innocent students who shared the same campuses with the communists and critics.

Chiang and his Nationalist government were, during the first 15 years of their rule, obsessed with retaking mainland China. They saw Taipei as merely a temporary capital and a launchpad. Thus, they paid little attention to the utilities, transportation, housing, parks, and other amenities that make life easier and more pleasant. As it grew, the city became crowded and dirty, snarled in traffic, and hamstrung by civic mismanagement. This gave Taipei a lingering, bad reputation, a sorry situation that did not change until the 1990s, when the elected government finally turned its attention to the capital city's infrastructure and made much-needed improvements.

Eventually, it became clear that the Nationalists had no chance of retaking mainland China, and Taiwan turned its full attention to the economy, where it had great success.

Building a road in the early days of Chiang Kai-shek's Republic of China.

A worker at a flower farm; Taiwan is one of the leading exporters of orchids.

Building a model economy

In the 1950s, the government promoted agriculture through land reforms. Because Chiang had no power base in Taiwan, he had no entanglements to overcome or special interests to protect, and was able to introduce sweeping changes. Sharecroppers were given sharp rent reductions, public lands were sold to tenant farmers at 2.5 times the value of one year's main crop, and a land-to-tiller program forced landlords to sell land they did not farm themselves. By leveling the playing field and sowing the seeds of equal economic opportunity, the land reform launched Taiwan on the road to prosperity.

In the 1960s, using its prosperous agriculture as an export base – especially of sugar and pineapples – Taiwan shifted to light industry, the government emphasizing the manufacture of labor-intensive exports such as textiles, paper, and electrical goods. With its low labor costs and hardworking people, Taiwan soon became a successful exporting country.

In the 1970s, to fuel the transition to more advanced industry, the focus was on infrastructure, and several projects were initiated, including the North-South Freeway and the Chiang Kai-shek (now Taiwan Taoyuan) International Airport, plus railways, roads, harbors, and a nuclear power plant. Then, as land and labor costs rose, Taiwan moved into high-tech manufacturing and shifted labor offshore, much of it to China.

In 1980, in a stroke of far-sighted genius, and long before other countries in Asia caught on, Taiwan realized the importance of electronics, and government planners launched the Hsinchu Science-based Industrial Park (today the Hsinchu Science Park), which would become the epicenter of Taiwan's electronics industry and a global leader in semiconductor manufacturing. As the capital of a rising economic power, and home to many corporate head offices and regional headquarters, Taipei found its niche as a services center and became the administrative hub of the country.

Taiwan's smooth transition from rural backwater to powerhouse high-tech exporter makes it, in many ways, a model economy.

Chiang Ching-kuo (left) and Lee Teng-hui (right).

Today, Taipei is a high-tech, modern city.

Losing political clout

Politically, however, things were not going as well. In the 1970s, several critical changes altered Taiwan's relationship with the world. The government-in-exile had long been considered the legitimate administration of China, and was supported by the world's anti-communist powers. Taipei hosted a succession of world leaders, and considered itself a capital city of global stature.

All that changed in 1971, when the UN admitted China and expelled Taiwan. A year later, President Richard Nixon made his landmark visit to China, paving the way for formal US recognition of the People's Republic. Following this watershed 1979 announcement, Taipei was gripped for days by anti-American riots that engulfed the US embassy. Uneasily, Taiwan was forced into playing second fiddle to China, a huge and unpredictable country of growing political and military influence.

Long road to democracy

At the time of Chiang Kai-shek's death in 1975, the country was prospering, but the Taiwanese, whose ancestors arrived more than three centuries ago, still considered the China-born Nationalists as outsiders. Despite the persecutions of martial law, dissent percolated throughout the island, finally boiling over with the Kaohsiung Incident, a landmark event in the development of Taiwan's democracy.

It occurred in December 1979, when a pro-democracy journal called *Meilidao*, "Formosa

---

SPARKLING MRT

Used by over two million passengers every day, the Taipei MRT, or metro, is the epitome of the country's modern miracle. Opened only in 1996 with the 10.5km-long (6.5 mile) Muzha line and just 12 stations, it has experienced rapid development. Every few years a service on a new line begins operations, and as of the end of 2018, the network is 136.6km-long (84.9 miles), has five lines and 117 stations. This doesn't include the newest Airport MRT line, which opened in early 2017 – it is run by a different company and is not part of the Taipei Metro. Several new routes are under construction and the long-term vision is that the MRT system will be extended to more than 290 kilometers (180.2 miles).

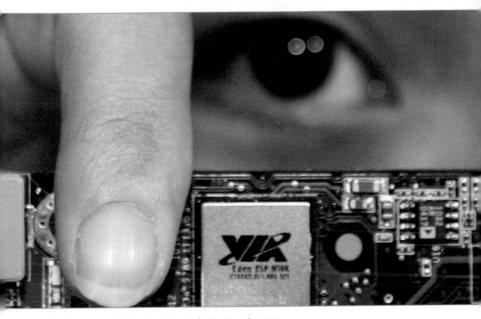

Electronics has been one of Taiwan's mainstay industries since the 1980s.

Magazine," organized a rally in Kaohsiung. The rally was repeatedly interrupted by riot police and tear gas, and it soon became a violent confrontation. The rally organizers, including famous dissident Shih Ming-teh and Annette Lu, who later became vice-president, were charged with sedition. They were defended by a team of lawyers that included Chen Shui-bian, who later became president, and Frank Hsieh, who later became premier. The riots and subsequent trial galvanized the people of Taiwan against martial law. It was the crucible in which the opposition Democratic Progressive Party (DPP) was forged, and a turning point in modern Taiwan's history.

After the Kaohsiung Incident, the situation had to change. Chiang Kai-shek's son, Chiang Ching-kuo, had become president in 1978. Unlike his father, the younger Chiang was

ELEGY OF SWEET POTATOES

In Taipei, as elsewhere, political repression spawned a generation of heroes. Among them were well-known dissidents like Peng Ming-min and Bo Yang, men who were imprisoned for their beliefs and later became outspoken advocates of freedom. But the tyranny also created quieter heroes, including the remarkable Tsai Tehpen, author of an extraordinary work of prison literature called *Elegy of Sweet Potatoes: Stories of Taiwan's White Terror*.

Tsai spent 13 months in the Nationalist gulag, beginning in October 1954, and he recounts his nightmare in a straightforward style that is as much of a pleasure to read as possible. Accused of owning a book about Mao Zedong,

Tsai's ordeal began with five days of fatigue investigation, without sleep or water, and ended in a re-education camp, where he was forced to recite propaganda about the greatness of Chiang Kai-shek. In the end he was acquitted, but not before spending many terrifying months in prison.

The book is filled with gripping and tragic stories from fellow inmates, combined with acute observations about prison conditions, guards, and lifestyles. The horror of the White Terror was carefully chronicled by Tsai, for which students of Taiwanese history have a profound gratitude. The Chinese edition of the book has garnered three major literature awards.

friendly and personable. He also clearly saw the need for reform. Across Asia, the tide was turning in favor of democracy; martial law under autocrat Ferdinand Marcos was lifted in the Philippines, and pro-democracy protests were under way in Korea and China. International pressure to end martial law in Taiwan was increasing, particularly from the US. In 1987, Chiang announced the lifting of martial law, and the people were allowed to travel to China for the first time since 1949. Chiang died in 1988, and the ban on political parties was formally ended the following year.

Lee Teng-hui became the island's first Taiwan-born president in 1988, and, in 1996, its first president ever elected by popular vote. His triumphant march through the streets of Taipei, to a rising chorus of heartfelt cheers, was a momentous event for the people.

Coming of age

Taiwan's 2000 presidential election saw DPP candidate Chen Shui-bian claim victory, ending 55 years of Nationalist rule on the island. This was a milestone in Taiwan's long journey from dictatorship to democracy. Chen served two terms, but an ever-widening whirlpool of scandals

The city's iconic Taipei 101 tower.

brought the DPP low in the 2008 elections, with middle-of-the-road voters turning to the KMT en masse and bringing Ma Ying-jeou to power. Despite growing concerns that Taiwan's sovereignty was eroding under Ying-jeou's rule, he was re-elected president in 2012. However, tens of thousands took to the streets in 2014 in what became known as the Sunflower Movement, protesting Ma's plans to sign a Cross Strait Service Trade Agreement with China. The proposed deal was seen as pushing Taiwan too close to China and doing nothing for the local economy.

This growing dissatisfaction brought the DPP back into power in the 2016 elections, winning both the presidential election and the Legislative Yuan elections, and making President Tsai Ing-wen Taiwan's first female head of state. Her election angered Beijing, which subsequently began squeezing the island on the international stage by blocking Taiwan's access to international organizations, luring its diplomatic allies to switch sides (breaking the diplomatic truce of Ma's era), and limiting the number of mainland tourists and students allowed to go to the island. Tsai, struggling with many local issues such as pension reform, stagnating wages, and pushing through legalizing same-sex marriage, has vowed to wean Taiwan off the mainland by seeking more economic partners in the Southeast and South Asian region.

Taiwan remains a major goods exporter with busy ports.

Cross-strait tensions

The ongoing tension between Taiwan and China is one of the world's biggest headaches – a hotspot that could potentially ignite a global conflict.

The two countries have an emotional relationship: mainland China has a deep desire to retake Taiwan, which it considers a breakaway province, and has repeatedly threatened to take it by force. But polls show that the majority of people in Taiwan prefer the status quo – that is, de facto independence from China. That stance has toughened since the 1990s, as China-born "mainlander" immigrants have lost influence, and a Taiwanese identity has strengthened. Many Taiwanese see no compelling reason to join China, which they view as a poorly governed country where laws and courts are suspect, personal freedom is limited, and quality of life is not as good.

The two states are far apart politically, but economically they are comfortable bedfellows. Taiwanese investments in China have surged since 1990, with a slight dip in recent years in part because of the US-China trade war. In 2018, Taiwanese investment in China came in at just under US$85 billion. About one million Taiwanese, businesspeople and dependants, now live in China and importantly, China is Taiwan's largest trading partner.

With the Kuomintang's return to national power in 2008, the economic doors to China were thrown open. The business sector was pleased with events, but pro-independence advocates were aghast, seeing all efforts at rapprochement as appeasement and setting the stage for an eventual attempt at reunification. Nevertheless, there are now direct flights between the two countries, and Chinese tourists are allowed to enter Taiwan territory – although Beijing cut back on the number of tourists allowed to visit, especially those going with group tours, following the DPP's election win in 2016.

Throughout the 1990s, the Taiwan-China dialogue was shaped by politician Lee Teng-hui, who did a lot to further pro-independence sentiments; China had little success with him. In 1996, as Taiwan prepared to hold its first popular presidential election, China tried to derail Lee's campaign by launching missiles near the island, but the move backfired, and Lee won the majority.

The third major player in the conflict, the US, does not support Taiwan's independence. But the Taiwan Relations Act, an agreement signed between the US and Taiwan in 1979, implies that America will defend Taiwan against attack. As the stalemate drags on, Taiwan continues to act like an independent country, electing its own leaders and pursuing its own foreign policy, though the current administra-

Taiwanese military maneuvers in 1996.

tion tries hard not to antagonize Beijing. It maintains a strong military, although it is phasing out conscription; currently males born after 1994 need only attend a four-month training. There are approximately 215,000 active personnel.

Meanwhile, on the streets of Taipei, the existence of a distant threat does not dampen the spirit of overall prosperity.

In Dalongdong Baoan Temple.

RELIGION

Taipei is one of the most religiously tolerant cities on Earth; every god is welcome and represented here. Buddhism, Taoism, and Confucianism are the main formal religions, but the old folk customs, beliefs, and superstitions guide daily life and permeate all levels of society.

Religious freedom in Taipei has lent the city a colorful atmosphere that can be found in few other places, and certainly not in China, where many temples were destroyed and religions almost hounded out of existence during the Cultural Revolution. Indeed, Falun Gong (a religious group that practices breathing exercises and meditation and has been banned in China since the late 1990s) is very active in Taiwan. Many ancient Chinese rituals and ceremonies are still performed with great pomp and pageantry in Taiwan, though they have all but disappeared in China and been reduced in scale elsewhere. The city is filled with an astonishing variety of temples and monasteries that welcome visitors and provide vivid local color. Exuberant festivals, such as a deity's birthday celebrations, take place year round.

Buddhism and Taoism are Taipei's main religions, while Confucianism provides a daily code of ethics for many of its citizens. At the same time, Christian missionaries walk the streets, and churches and – to a lesser extent – mosques dot the neighborhoods.

According to Ministry of the Interior statistics, in 2017 there were just under 15,300 places of worship in the country (708 in Taipei), including over 12,000 temples and about 3,000 churches. A total of 27 different religions are

In the hills around Taipei, Buddhist groups have built huge monasteries, which on weekends are filled with city dwellers seeking peace through meditation.

Paper money to be burnt for the gods.

recognized by the government, no mean feat considering that religious groups must meet certain requirements – such as having a minimum number of local believers and sufficient funds – to achieve official recognition.

Traditional customs, beliefs, icons, and old superstitions permeate all levels of society in Taipei. Most adults – even those who may not profess a particular religion – routinely worship at a church or temple, and engage in spiritual activity. It is common to see homes and shops with an illuminated shrine, or people burning incense to honor a deity, hero, or ancestor. Most families perform ancestor worship, and at important times – such as when a son or daughter takes a university entrance exam – parents will visit a temple to burn incense, light candles, and solicit divine help. Many drivers in Taiwan adorn their cars with charms, statuettes, and religious invocations for protection against accidents.

The role of folk religion

In his book *Private Prayers and Public Parades: Exploring the Religious Life of Taipei*, Mark Caltonhill observes: The "Han-Chinese, who form the vast majority of Taipei's population, tend to say they are people of 'Three Religions' *(San Jiao)*... Confucianism *(Ru Jiao)*, Daoism *(Dao Jiao)*, and Buddhism *(Fo Jiao)*... [It is not] that these religions are not important in the lives of many Taipei citizens, but rather, that the day-to-day religious practices seen around the city really belong to a 'folk' or 'popular' tradition that runs alongside, beneath, or above these Three Religions."

Most people in Taipei subscribe to a kind of folk religion that has its roots in Buddhism, Confucianism, and Taoism, but also includes a broad mixture of other mystical and

Preparing offerings for the Baosheng Festival.

superstitious beliefs, and a vast pantheon of deities, beings, and spirits, both fearsome and benevolent. An important component is ancestor worship. Many Taiwanese believe that upon death a person becomes a spirit, and that the spirit has the same needs as a person on Earth: food, shelter, money, and a place to live. So when a loved one passes away, members of his or her family will burn "hell money" and miniature paper houses, and offer food and other items of use in the afterlife.

A pragmatic approach to prayer

The approach to prayer in Taipei is essentially pragmatic: What has this god done for me lately? If a god fails to deliver – usually money, marriage, or a promotion – the petitioner may turn to another deity. But it works both ways.

A supplicant at Longshan Temple.

Taiwan folk traditions are opportunistic. Whereas faiths like Christianity require believers to adhere exclusively to their doctrines, most Taiwanese embrace a deity or practice that brings them succor.

A worshipper lights incense.

filled with atmosphere – and thick incense smoke – and are the focal point of the city's religious life. Most temples in Taipei are mixtures of different deities, practices, and rituals. Buddhist, Taoist, and folk icons reside together. The key gods will always be located in the main hall, which will be fronted by a courtyard, and most lesser folk gods, who have origins in Chinese antiquity, are located in the rear of the temple complex.

Buddhist temples are quieter than their Taoist counterparts, and are geared more toward reflection than worship. Many are located in hillside monasteries, and these have a more hushed and reverent tone. Visit Shandao Temple for an example within the city. By Western standards, they may not be that quiet, yet they are not the hives of activity that Taoist temples are. Guanyin, the Goddess of Mercy, is featured in many Buddhist temples.

Buddhism is expanding rapidly overseas, and the epicenter of this global Buddhist renaissance is Taiwan. The island may seem like an unlikely place for a religious revival, but it makes sense: Taiwan is rich, and it has religious freedom. As elsewhere, many people in Taiwan are finding

Worshippers can ask gods for divine assistance, but they usually must express gratitude by burning paper money, lighting incense and candles, offering fruit or drinks or food, or even performing penitential rites during a festival. If a petitioner fails to return a favor, bad fortune may follow.

To witness the role of religion in the daily life of the city, a visitor should head straight for one of the temples. These intoxicating places are

The icon of Mazu at Baoan Temple.

FAMILY ALTARS

A family altar sits in the main room of many Taiwanese homes. This is where household gods and ancestors are worshipped in an ancient tradition that has changed little over the centuries. On the altar are small statues of the household god(s), and to the left are the ancestral tablets that contain family records, including the names of ancestors dating back many generations. Incense is offered daily, and on special days, offerings of food are placed on the altar. The set-ups take many forms: in some homes a simple shelf hangs on the wall, while others boast large, intricately carved shrines that take up a great deal of space.

Catholic worshippers at St Christopher's Church.

The Guandu Temple's ornate roof.

that material wealth does not satisfy their spiritual needs and are going in search of enlightenment.

A new brand of Buddhism

Taiwan's Buddhism is not the gentle philosophy of self-denial and meditation that Westerners may associate with Buddhism; its powerful groups have come down from the mountains and into the world, so to speak, with the mission of practicing a compassionate religion suited for modernity. Powered by Taiwan's economic prosperity, they have extended their vision of "Buddhism in the human realm" far beyond the island's shores. They are rebranding this ancient religion, and transforming it into a dynamic force that can compete with other faiths for the hearts and minds of the world's religious believers.

There are five main Buddhist organizations in Taiwan, each led by a charismatic nun or monk. All five groups are wealthy and have

MAZU, PATRON OF SEAFARERS

Mazu, the patron saint of seafarers, is perhaps the most popular folk deity in Taiwan. According to legend, Mazu was born in the Song dynasty (960–1279) as Lin Mo, the daughter of a fisherman, on an island off the coast of China's Fujian Province. One day, her father and brothers were caught in a typhoon while at sea, and their ship sank. The young Lin Mo saw them in a dream, and tried to save them using mystical powers. Upon waking, she learned that her brothers, but not her father, had been miraculously saved. She died at 28, but continued to save other seafarers, often through miraculous means, and she soon became known as Mazu, or "maternal ancestor."

Because the Taiwan Strait is a treacherous body of water, early immigrants from the mainland carried with them statues of Mazu, or incense ash from one of her temples. Upon arrival in Taipei, or elsewhere, they erected temples in her honor. The icon of Mazu is usually immediately recognizable by her dark blue visage. She is flanked by a pair of dramatic statues with huge, exaggerated eyes and ears, called Eyes that See a Thousand Miles, and Ears that Hear upon the Wind, who help the goddess locate sailors in distress. Her birthday celebration, observed on the 23rd day of the 3rd lunar month, is one of Taiwan's most important religious festivals.

built extravagant temples, but also founded schools, hospitals, and charities. They are Fo Guang Shan, Chung Tai Chan, Tzu Chi, Ling Jiou Mountain Buddhist Society, and Dharma Drum Mountain. Fo Guang Shan is the biggest, with over 200 branches in 30 countries. Chung Tai Chan (*chan* is Mandarin for Zen) is maybe the least traditional: its unusual young monastery in central Taiwan boasts giant TV screens to broadcast its mission to the spiritually and physically needy. It has more than 90 meditation centers all over the world, including eight in the United States.

The third is Hualien-based Tzu Chi Foundation, mostly a charity organization that runs one of the world's largest registries of bone-marrow donors, plus a string of hospitals and an international relief organization that has rendered aid everywhere from Afghanistan to tsunami-struck Indonesia. Ling Jiou Mountain, the fourth, opened the Museum of World Religions in 2001 in suburban Taipei, while its large and still expanding "sacred mountain" complex is on the northeast coast. The fifth is Dharma Drum Mountain, which opened the massive Dharma Drum Mountain Nung Chan Monastery complex just north of Taipei in 2005, and in 2012, added the Water-Moon Dharma Center. The focal feature of the center's scenery is a mirror-like pool in front of the main hall. The mission of Dharma Drum Mountain – embodied by its ecological seminars, social-welfare programs, and meditation retreats – remains to "build a pure land on Earth."

The growth of Christianity

Aside from these essentially Asian beliefs, a large number of people in Taipei are practicing Protestants (as was Chiang Kai-shek himself) and Catholics. Christianity was first brought to Taiwan by the Dutch and Spanish, who occupied the island in the 1600s. With the traders came the missionaries, who learned the native languages and converted the indigenous peoples. Mark Caltonhill writes: "Missionaries were particularly successful among the indigenous population, perhaps because of the egalitarian nature of their approach compared with the discriminatory policies of the Japanese administration and the entrenched prejudices of the Han-Chinese majority." Even today, many Christians are descended from the native peoples of Taiwan. Today, more than 95 percent of Taiwan's 537,000 indigenous people belong to a Christian denomination. Sadly, in recent years, anti-gay conservative Christian groups have been behind the move to block same-sex unions and sex education in schools.

Buddhist nuns in Jinguashi.

A newly married couple pose at the Museum of Drinking Water.

FESTIVALS AND CELEBRATIONS

The capital hosts a calendar of celebrations that shed light on Chinese culture and provide a dramatic spectacle for visitors.

Most religious festivals adhere to the Chinese lunar calendar, so dates vary from the Gregorian calendar (see page 245). The first annual event – and most important – is the Chinese Lunar New Year, greeted with firecracker blasts to scare away ghosts. The traditional 15 days of feasting, reunion, and visiting are largely conducted among family and friends, and the city becomes quiet during the holiday from work, which may last the entire first week. But the festival run-up, when shops sell traditional *nianhuo* (New Year goods), is interesting for tourists. In summer, the Dragon Boat Festival is celebrated (see pages 78 and). Equally interesting is the Mid-Autumn Festival, dedicated to the harvest moon. Among the grand celebrations are more solemn observances. During Ghost Month, after Hell's Gates open on the 1st day of the 7th lunar month, the city is filled with incense smoke from offerings and the superstitious tread lightly. Throughout the year, the various gods' birthday festivals are significant for religious Taipeiers.

Giant puppets (shenou) such as this, representing various supernatural beings, are often seen at religious processions. Another eerie practice sometimes seen is the self-flagellation of temple mediums who enter a trance.

The birthday of Confucius is observed on Teacher's Day at Taipei's Confucius Temple. During this highly ritualized event, the main celebrants of the ceremony – often high-ranking government officials – welcome the spirit of the great sage with rites, incense, and offerings.

During the ritual fire-walking, those fulfilling penitential vows race across burning coals carrying a deity's palanquin.

NON-RELIGIOUS AND THEMED FESTIVALS

Taipei plays host to many secular festivals. The best known is National Day, or Double Tenth Day, a country-wide event on October 10 that honors the founding of the Republic of China in 1912 by Dr Sun Yat-sen. The event starts with a public parade through Taipei, the president of Taiwan gives a policy speech, and firework displays light up the city.

Experience Chinese culture at a local event.

One of the most anticipated annual events is the Taiwan Culinary Exhibition, held at the Taipei World Trade Center every July or August. With dramatic chef contests, food for sale, cooking classes, and pavilions featuring Taiwanese and regional Chinese cuisines, this fair is one of the island's exhibition highlights. Two major movie events are the Taipei Film Festival held every summer and the Taipei Golden Horse Film Festival, Taiwan's answer to the Oscars, arriving in November. Both showcase talent from Taiwan and the region as well as independent movies from across the world. Book tickets online in advance because they sell out quickly. Taipei also boasts smaller festivals, such as the Yangmingshan Flower Festival in spring and the Yingge Ceramics Festival in summer. At the ceramics festival, visitors can tour working kilns and watch artisans at work.

Performers wear papier maché masks at Baosheng Festival.

Intricate and precisely choreographed mass displays are a highlight of the National Day celebrations, which take place in front of the Presidential Office Building in west-side Taipei.

The Lantern Festival is the cheeriest annual celebration in the city, as downtown Taipei turns into a swirling sea of colorful lanterns. It marks the final night (Yuan Xiao) of the Chinese New Year celebrations, and is traditionally a night for singles looking for love.

A performance of the Taipei Dance Circle.

THE ARTS

Taipei's lively arts scene, while respecting the antiquity of Chinese tradition, is distinguished by its New Wave cinema and modern dance, and enlivened by its minority-language literature, experimental theater, and a vibrant gallery scene.

When most people think of the arts in Taiwan, they call to mind the National Palace Museum, the world's premier collection of imperial Chinese art and antiquities. Indeed, the museum remains a must-see for visitors to the country, but bear in mind that the treasure trove of artifacts on display there forms just the tip of Taipei's artistic iceberg.

Today, the arts have become a medium for the Taiwanese to explore the issues of identity so often fought over in Taipei's rambunctious legislature. Many of the arts that speak of the greatness and antiquity of Chinese heritage are nowadays joined by arts that revel in the emergence of a local Taiwanese culture, adding dynamism to the city's cultural mix.

Preserving traditions

For much of the second half of the 20th century, the Chinese Communist Party on mainland China directed waves of social movements aimed at obliterating tradition and modernizing the country, dealing crippling blows to the arts there. As such, Taiwan became something of a custodian of traditional Chinese culture, and its capital is in

> The Taipei International Book Exhibition (TIBE) is held every February at the Taipei World Trade Center. The size of the crowds is testament to how much the Taiwanese love to read.

Traditional hand-puppet show at the Taiyuan Asia Puppet Theatre Museum.

some ways a better place to get a glimpse of traditional Chinese art and performances.

Beijing opera in its original form lives on, with almost nightly performances alternating among Taiwan's pre-eminent troupes, of which the leading one is the Fu Hsing Academy. Taipei's National Theater and National Concert Hall regularly schedule full-length operas and dance performances. The Taipei Chinese Orchestra, which performs Chinese instrumental music, plays regularly at Zhongshan Hall.

Traditional Taiwanese puppet theater, a delightful folk art performed in the Taiwanese

TaipeiEYE performance of Chinese opera.

dialect, also survives. Performances can be caught at the Taiyuan Asia Puppet Theatre Museum, where the curator and director of the resident Taiyuan Theatre Puppet Company is Dutchman Robin Ruizendaal, and at the Puppetry Art Center of Taipei.

TAIWANESE LITERATURE

Taiwan has produced no Mishimas or Murakamis – that is, no writers well known internationally. One reason, of course, is that very little Taiwanese literature has been translated into English. Another reason, however, is that for most of the 20th century the island's literature was circumscribed first by the Japanese administration and then by the KMT government, which encouraged writers to work around themes of nostalgia for mainland China and other politically safe issues. One of the few Taiwanese classics available in English, and a chilling indictment of traditional chauvinism and sexual violence, is Li Ang's *The Butcher's Wife*. In 2018, Wu Ming-yi's *The Stolen Bicycle* was longlisted for the Man Booker International Prize.

For a tourist-friendly sampler of these performing arts, the TaipeiEYE holds weekly revues showcasing a bit of everything – Beijing opera, puppetry, Chinese acrobatics, musical ensembles, and even some indigenous Taiwanese dance pieces – with English subtitles where required. This condensed art is well suited to travelers on short visits.

Transitional forms

Taipei is very much a city in transition and is home to a lot of bold experimentation with traditional forms. Prominent examples of the more experimental theater groups that incorporate modern approaches into **traditional Chinese** opera and drama – usually featuring the inclusion of contemporary issues and settings – are Contemporary Legend Theatre and the Green Ray Theater, among a host of others. Ya Yin Ensemble's style is usually labeled "avant-garde" Beijing opera, and while following the performances can be a strain, they are a fascinating example of the ways in which Taiwan is redefining itself culturally.

Yang San-lang's oil painting "Sound of Waves."

Contemporary movements

When martial law was lifted in 1987, Taiwan began to look simultaneously inwards and outwards. Waves of young Taiwanese went abroad to study and work, bringing new ideas back with them when they returned to Taiwan.

Meanwhile, the increasingly pluralistic political environment that eventually led to the defeat of the Nationalists by the pro-independence Democratic Progressive Party in the 2000 presidential elections, and again in 2016, also gave rise to a more lively arts scene. Cinema and dance reached new heights, and minority-language literature, experimental theater, and the gallery scene became enlivened.

By all means take in the traditional arts when in Taipei, but don't miss out on the experience of a modern dance performance, a local film screening, or a tour of some excellent modern Taiwanese art.

Visual arts

Take a stroll along Anhe Road in Taipei's dynamic eastern district, and the many hole-in-the-wall galleries scattered here will attest to the city's thriving contemporary art scene. But for a comprehensive overview of the directions Taiwanese artists have been taking in the visual arts over the past century, there is just one destination: the Taipei Fine Arts Museum. The temporary exhibits here are varied – as likely to feature French Impressionists as the Taiwanese oils of the Japanese colonial era – but the permanent exhibition represents a unique opportunity to see Taiwan's emergence from both colonialism and one-party rule through the eyes of its painters.

For a comprehensive view of what Taiwanese artists have been doing in the contemporary arts over the past few months, past few weeks, or even the past few days, head to the Museum of Contemporary Art Taipei. Few museums in the world are as contemporary (or, for that matter, temporary) as this one. MOCA Taipei presents no permanent exhibitions, only special exhibitions, nor does it purchase works by the artists it exhibits. Going even further, most displayed works are created specially for the exhibitions in which they appear, and many cease to exist except as photographs in the MOCA catalogues when the exhibitions end, which can never capture the experience that the artworks produced in life. The only solution is to make frequent visits whenever the museum changes its galleries.

The Meiji-era Japanese artist Ishikawa Kinichiro (1871–10) is generally credited with being the "father of modern Taiwanese art." His influence gave rise to a first generation of so-called Western-influenced artists, who paid tribute in watercolors to the natural beauty of Taiwan and its then still rustic environment. Chief among these artists are Yang San-lang (1907–95) and Liao Chi-chun (1902–76); the latter's landscape work *Uluanpi Lighthouse* has become emblematic of the era's art.

By the 1920s and 1930s, Japanese experimentation with Expressionism started to take hold in Taiwan, and Taiwanese artists began to apply bold oil colors to their celebrations of the Taiwanese countryside and rural life. The movement was put on hold

Taiwanese director Ang Lee clutches his Academy Award.

Tsai Ming-liang (right) arrives ahead of the Golden Horse Awards, the Chinese-language equivalent of the Oscars, and a still from his 2009 movie "Face."

by the turbulence of World War II, the eventual surrender of Japan and its withdrawal from Taiwan, and the arrival of the Chinese Nationalists. Taiwan's new government put the island under martial law and embarked on a program of fostering only traditional art forms. The inevitable backlash came in 1957, when two art societies were formed with the self-appointed task of modernizing Taiwanese art. The result was avant-garde approaches to traditional forms, such as pen-and-ink landscapes, the most famous exponent of which was Lin Kuo-song (b. 1932).

The 1970s saw yet another backlash, with artists of the "native soil" movement returning to the themes – and to a certain extent even the techniques – of the Japanese era. It is a style that has retained a certain popularity to this day, particularly among the so-called "unschooled" rustic artists, who are best and most famously typified by artist Hung Tung (1920–87), who in his day drew enormous critical acclaim. But it is also a style that has been forced to find its niche in a bustling marketplace of artistic ideas that today draws on influences both local and international.

Director Tsai Ming-Liang collects an award at an event in his honour during the Deauville Asian Film Festival, 2014.

Many contemporary Taiwanese artists are more likely to be experimenting with installation art and multimedia than extolling the pastoral splendor of rural Taiwan in oils and canvas. Work by Taiwanese photographers has also received attention lately, as evidenced by the Taipei Fine Arts Museum's recent spending spree over the past decade to amass a collection of such work.

Cinema

In the 1980s, a new generation of directors, notably Hou Hsiao-hsien and Edward Yang, aided by the Central Motion Picture Corporation, began making movies that collectively came to be known as the Taiwanese New Wave. Hou, in particular, between 1985 and 1989, was behind a series of internationally acclaimed and award-winning films, such as *Dust in the Wind*, *A Time to Live and a Time to Die*, and *City of Sadness*, whose evocative neo-realistic depictions of Taiwanese rural life won more fans in overseas art-house cinemas, unfortunately, than

at home. Yang's 1985 effort, *Taipei Story*, on the other hand, was a bleak representation of dislocation and urban ennui among young Taiwanese adults.

With the 1990s came Taiwan's so-called Second New Wave of directors. The most internationally well known of these is the multiple award-winning Tsai Ming-liang. His early trilogy of movies about urban decay filmed between 1992 and 1997 – *Rebels of the Neon God*, *Vive L'Amour* (winner of the Golden Lion at the 1994 Venice Film Festival), and *The River* – are formally beautiful and very sparing with dialogue.

Hou Hsiao-hsien continued to be a major force in the 1990s and beyond, with *Puppet Master*, which won the Jury Prize at Cannes in 1993, and *Flowers of Shanghai* (1998), cumulatively garnering him the accolade of "Director of the Decade" in a 1999 poll of movie critics by the New York weekly *The Village Voice*. His prestige stretches to the modern day, and in 2015 he won Best Director at Cannes for *The Assassin*.

Meanwhile, the Second New Wave saw the emergence of a young director who was to take his work decidedly into the mainstream. Ang Lee launched his career with *Pushing Hands* (1991), *The Wedding Banquet* (1993), and *Eat Drink Man Woman* (1994). *The Wedding Banquet* raised eyebrows in then conservative Taiwan with its depiction of a gay couple, one of whom is forced into a heterosexual marriage of convenience. But the movie was a hit overseas, winning the Golden Bear at the 1993 Berlin Film Festival. Lee has gone on to further international success, directing *Crouching Tiger, Hidden Dragon*, *Brokeback Mountain*, and *Life of Pi*, as well as the Chinese-language *Lust, Caution*. In contrast to Ang Lee's mainstream successes, both Hou and Tsai have continued to make movies in the styles that have made them darlings of the art-house circuit. Tsai's

Taipei is host to Asia's version of the Oscars – the Taipei Golden Horse Film Festival, which is held every November screening some of Asia's best as well as an international selection. Films are shown at cinemas in the capital.

Yun-Fat Chow in the box-office smash, "Crouching Tiger, Hidden Dragon."

Wayward Cloud (2005), a movie that combines the musical, dance, and pornographic genres, created a sensation at the Berlin Film Awards, where it premiered. It raised so many questions that it earned itself the distinction

BOX-OFFICE TIGER

Ang Lee's 2000 film *Crouching Tiger, Hidden Dragon*, which was produced with about US$15 million, was the first non-English movie to make more than US$100 million in the US, and the first ever A-list kung fu movie, starring Michelle Yeoh and Yun-Fat Chow. Lee has continued to break down boundaries in his work, following *Crouching Tiger* up with *Brokeback Mountain* in 2005, which won the Golden Lion at Venice, four Golden Globes, and three Oscars, including for Best Director. Lee garnered the Academy Award for Best Director the second time for the 2012 film, *Life of Pi*, which received 11 nominations in total and collected four Oscars.

of having the longest press conference in the awards' 55-year history. It went away with the FIPRESCI Prize and the Silver Bear.

Hou's *Café Lumière* (2003) was nominated for a Golden Lion at the 2004 Venice Film Festival, while his ode to love, *Three Times* (2005), was nominated for the Palme d'Or at the 2005 Cannes Film Festival.

In 2008 and 2009, Wei Te-Sheng's music-drama *Cape No. 7* was an unprecedented box office success in Taiwan, surpassing such Hollywood blockbusters as *Jurassic Park* and *The Lord of the Rings*. It won 15 awards in total and led to the revival of Taiwanese cinema. Subsequent huge hits with the Taiwanese audience have included Giddens Ko's romance *You are the Apple of My Eye* and Fung Kai's *Din Tao: Leader of the Parade* (both 2012).

However, it's Tsai Ming-liang that continues to be one of the most acclaimed Taiwanese filmmakers in the world. His 2013 drama *Stray Dogs*,

Dance is one area of the arts in which Taiwan has drawn international acclaim. The island's most famous troupe is Cloud Gate Dance Theatre, directed by Lin Hwai-min (who is due to step down at the end of 2019).

shot in Taipei, was another success, winning a Grand Jury Prize at the Venice Film Festival. In recent years, the capital of Taiwan also served as a backdrop for the Hollywood science-fiction movie *Lucy* (2014), directed by Luc Besson and starring Scarlett Johansson.

Dance

The "matriarch of Taiwanese dance" is perhaps the legendary Tsai Jui-yueh, who learned modern dance in Japan and brought it back to Taiwan, founding the China Dance Arts Institute in 1953. Her talents were neglected in the early days of Nationalist rule, when traditional Chinese dance was promoted over all other forms. But as the island inched towards liberalization in the 1960s and artists began to look to foreign influences again, Tsai began to train a new generation of Taiwanese dancers in a modern idiom. She retired to Australia in the early 1980s. Tsai passed away in 2006. Her lovely Japanese courtyard-style former Taipei studio complex, which was gutted by fire in 1999, has been refurbished and renamed the Tsai Jui-yueh Dance Studio – Rose Historic Site and declared a national heritage spot.

Tsai's influence is rivaled by Liu Feng-hsueh, who established a studio in 1967 and then went on to set up the Neo-Classic Dance Company in 1976, which continues to perform today. Meanwhile, as Liu was emerging as a major influence on modern dance in Taiwan, Lin Hwai-min was in the US, studying under Martha Graham – a woman whose influence on dance has been compared to Picasso's on painting and Stravinsky's on music. The result was the Cloud Gate Dance Theatre (www.cloudgate.org.tw), which Lin formed after he returned to Taiwan in 1973. His early themes were taken from Chinese legend, but he was quick to turn to the subject that has concerned so many other Taiwanese artists – the question of identity. His first

major work on this subject was the 1978 production Legacy, an epic which told the story of Taiwan's early pioneers.

Lin's work, while continuing to evolve, has dodged back and forth between intimate local subjects – such as his 1997 show *Portrait of Families*, a sweeping story of life in Taiwan under Japanese rule – and themes that draw on a diverse range of sources in India, Southeast Asia and China, such as the eclectic *Songs of the Wanderers* (1997), which has been performed to great acclaim in Europe. These remain key works in the Cloud Gate repertoire.

Lin, who is due to retire at the end of 2019, has been a formidable influence in Taiwan, and many former members of his troupe have broken away to form schools of their own. Notable among these are Lin Hsiu-wei, whose Taigu Tales Dance Theatre (www.taigu-tales.com) performs stark meditative acts that are redolent of Japan's *butoh* tradition. Another Cloud Gate breakaway was Liou Shaw-lu, who formed the Taipei Dance Circle in the 1980s. Following his death in 2014, the troupe was taken over by his wife, Yang Wan-rung.

A performance at the annual Tsai Jui-yueh Dance Festival.

CUISINE

Like much else in Taipei, dining has undergone a renaissance since the 1990s. The old-school restaurants serving authentic regional specialties are increasingly joined by a new wave of stylish outlets that excel in pan-Chinese fusion. Meanwhile, the humble street snack still satisfies late-night cravings.

Not so long ago, a dinner in the capital meant a visit to a Chinese restaurant with red and gold decor, Spartan tables and chairs, but wonderful food and friendly old waiters. These are the old favorites that secured Taipei's culinary reputation as one of the best in Asia. Word of mouth is the best way to find one of these small and nondescript places tucked in the neighborhoods. People in Taipei are not fixated on the "great restaurant" concept, and they do not give out stars and awards. The food at these traditional establishments is regionally "pure": East never meets West, and fusion cuisine is not an option. Shanghainese is heavy and stewed, Sichuanese is hot and spicy, Cantonese is fast-cooked and fresh, and Taiwanese is mild and tends toward seafood – exactly the way they were meant to be.

But eventually, visitors may want to forgo the Formica tables and fading decor, and head uptown for the next generation of restaurants, whose excellent fare and elegant interiors have raised the bar for the city's eateries.

The new wave of dining

The 20- and 30-somethings who have led the latest dining trends may have abandoned their

What's that smell? It must be stinky tofu: every nightmarket is suffused with its pungent odor. But those who love this unusual food swear that getting past the odor rewards one with a great flavor.

Fine dining at the Grand Hotel.

parents' restaurants, but they have not abandoned their parents' food. Why would they? Chinese food is still king, but the new restaurants have lost the strict ethnic divisions, and serve a pan-Chinese fusion cuisine that is heavy on flavor but light on oil. Waitstaff are uniformly young and the ambience sophisticated. The newest trend is for Western-style service, with one dish served at a time rather than the all-at-once approach of the typical Chinese culinary experience (literally 20 minutes of flying chopsticks and it's all over).

Today Taipei is awash with new and buzzing venues, filled with eye-catching designs

Tucking into dumplings, a feature of Shanghainese cuisine.

and clientele. The food is typified by superb, judiciously used ingredients. The menus are often small, featuring expertly cooked dishes. But don't·be fooled by the upscale settings: even at the most chic places diners can let the chopsticks fly and drip sauce on the tablecloths.

If that is one too many bowls of *bai fan* (white rice) for you, Taipei also offers an array of non-Chinese cuisines. Of course, top of the

list is Japanese fare, thanks to its one-time status as a colony of Tokyo. Some claim that Taiwan has the best Japanese food outside Japan. It's certainly less expensive. The city also boasts numerous excellent French restaurants, all serving the fattest goose liver this side of the Seine and exhibiting extensive wine lists.

Taipei also has simple, alfresco Italian bistros, Western sandwich shops, burger joints,

THREE CUP CHICKEN

San bei ji or "Three Cup Chicken," an island specialty most often experienced by foreigners in local beerhouses, is perhaps Taiwan's most representative dish. It was perfect for farming folk in pioneer days because it allowed them to be away in the field.

The ingredients are simmered in an earthenware pot for hours, meaning no need for constant attention to a hot fire, in a "three cup" sauce, one of soy sauce, one of rice wine, one of sesame oil. Simple. Some substitute cane sugar for the sesame oil. The traditional recipe also calls for ginger and basil leaves, perhaps a more surprising ingredient. The dish is served in the pot when the sauce is

almost fully absorbed into the meat, the chicken sizzling – almost popping with the heat – just the right side of burning. This original slow-cook dish is then eaten with rice or congee.

Locals say that a place that can't prepare *san bei ji* properly is not a true Taiwanese eatery. They also like to try such variations on the chicken as pork and dried beancurd, as well as more exotic options, such as frog, squid, and so on. Local men – each a self-confident Chinese-food expert – will also tell you that eating their favorite *san bei ji* without cold Taiwan beer is not a true three-cup experience.

Stinky tofu is a classic nightmarket dish.

Cooking sizzling eggs in bulk.

excellent Indian restaurants, and all the other culinary virtues that accompany wealth and a cosmopolitan populace. Most recently, upscale vegan and organic eateries have joined the party. Visitors are spoiled for choice.

Taiwanese cooking

Among the various Chinese regional cuisines, Taiwanese cuisine, or *Taicai*, is less well known and more difficult to find beyond the island's shores, so visitors may not even know it exists. This may be due to Taiwan's long political isolation, or perhaps to the simpler, more rustic character of this style of cooking.

Descended from the culinary traditions of southern Fujian Province, Taiwanese cooking evolved in response to the geographical, economic, and agricultural conditions the island's early immigrants faced. Abundant seas and mountainous terrain gave rise to a reliance on fish and seafood. Squid is routinely grilled or stir-fried, oysters added to vermicelli soup or omelets, clams are eaten raw, and dried anchovies are fried with peanuts. Hardship and scarcity in the early days gave rise to humble fare. Watery rice congee was filled out with sweet potatoes and accompanied by salted radish omelets and braised pig's trotters. An interesting local innovation is the use of basil to flavor dishes, as exemplified by the famous *san bei ji*, or "Three Cup Chicken".

Street snacks

Some of the best known and most loved local foods, however, are the *xiaochi*, or "small eats." Throughout town, many of the city's devoted foodies will be found in neighborhood nightmarkets, perched on plastic stools and eating hot snacks from temporary tables. Unlike in Singapore and Hong Kong, these street stalls have not been herded indoors into sterile malls and oil-stained parking lots. Vendors ply their trades outdoors, under strings of bright lights,

Tianbula is a local nightmarket standard, a unique Taiwan version of Japanese tempura. The art of batter-frying meats was taught to the Japanese by early Spanish and Portuguese missionaries.

The fast and flaming wok of Cantonese cooking.

with flames a-leaping and wafts of smoke ascending skyward.

The food is invariably freshly cooked because the turnover is high. Many stands concentrate on a single dish, and the variety is remarkable. A Taipei nightmarket is a movable feast of congee, oyster omelets, stinky tofu, scallion pancakes, soup noodles, pork buns (the infamous *gua bao*), roasted corn, dumplings, and piles of soy-braised tongues, innards, and other more exotic offerings. The grilled squid, brushed in sesame oil, hoisin and chili sauce, and dusted in cayenne pepper, is especially delicious.

But the real street classic of Taipei, sold from mobile carts all over town, and the local equivalent of the New York hot dog, is the humble barbecued sausage. Many a late-night drinker has emerged from a pub and walked straight to one of the town's ubiquitous sausage vendors. The sausages are cooked over the hot coals until the fat sputters and smokes; the smell of these salty-sweet sausages is as much a feature of Taipei as the motor-scooter exhaust smoke.

Regional cuisines of China

Just about every regional cuisine of China is available in Taipei, including steamed Shanghai dumplings, Northern Chinese wheat-based staples, Mongolian barbecue, Sichuan hot pot, Cantonese dim sum, dried Hunan ham – the list is virtually endless.

Taiwan's turbulent history is largely responsible for this happy culinary miracle. When soldiers and other immigrants poured into Taipei after the civil war in China in the late 1940s, they brought

---

TIME TO EAT

Restaurants that serve breakfast will do so from about 7.30am to 9.30am. Kitchens will be open for lunch from noon until 2pm, and most people will eat dinner between 5pm and 7pm, though restaurant kitchens will be open from about 5pm to 9–9.30pm. The Taiwanese do not have a brunch tradition, and most eateries following a Western-style schedule, closing in between the main mealtimes, will not be open at this time. Several restaurants, especially those in international hotels, now offer afternoon tea. Food courts in the basements of most shopping malls will serve food all day, as will most streetside cafés.

Fragrant soup.

chicken is stuffed full of ham, dried shrimp, mushrooms, scallions, soy sauce, Shaoxing rice wine, and a hint of black pepper; the juice from these fillings marinates the bird. Another favorite is sautéed beef with ginkgo nuts; the chunks of beef are marinated, then stir-fried with ginger and black pepper.

Don't miss the *dong po rou*, that famous marbled pork that warms body and soul on a winter day. The artery-clogging layers of meat and fat are salty, sweet, and tender, and literally melt in the mouth. It's not health food for sure, but it does taste good.

Deservedly or not, Shanghai also gets credit for one of the most delicious of Chinese foods, the *xiao long bao*. The slightly chewy skins of these mouth-watering "little dragon" dumplings contain a juicy filling of succulent minced pork and a delightfully warm and fragrant burst of gingery soup.

Related to Shanghainese cuisine is the fine, light food of Hangzhou, considered the most refined regional food in China. Hangzhou cookery stresses fresh ingredients and mild spices, plus the hallmark flavors of red vinegar and rice wine. A beautiful introduction to this delicate cuisine is freshwater shrimp with Longjing tea. The shrimps have a tight, crisp texture and a mild sweet flavor, while the tea leaves add a slightly bitter note.

with them their favorite foods from all over the mainland. Many of the best restaurants in Taipei were first opened by newly arrived expert chefs who had previously worked in private households.

Sichuan cuisine

The star of this popular cuisine is undoubtedly the Sichuan pepper, or *hua jiao*, a spice infamous for imparting a "numbing" sensation to the tongue. Together with black pepper and chili pepper, it has given Sichuan cooking its reputation for spiciness. But the chili oils and hot sauces used by Sichuan cooks to season their foods are not always strong, and the dishes usually have a sweet or sour flavor as well to provide balance. *Gongbao jiding*, known in the West as "Kung Pao Chicken," is a classic dish of chicken cubes stir-fried with chili and peanuts. Also famous is *mapo* tofu (spicy bean curd with minced pork), and *yin si juan*, a fried bread roll that sometimes serves as a substitute for rice.

Shanghainese cuisine

Taipei's version of this cuisine is lighter, less oily, and not nearly as sugary sweet. A perennial favorite is Beggar's Chicken. A tender spring

A vendor grills corn at a street stall.

Northern cuisine

The salty, mild, and lightly seasoned Northern Chinese stews and braised foods use vinegar and garlic as key flavorings. In Northern cooking, wheat flour largely replaces rice, and many of the dishes are served with pancakes or sesame seed-coated buns.

The signature dish is, of course, Peking duck. Slices of crispy roasted duck skin, light and crunchy as wafers, are served with mild spring onion and sweet sauce on a pancake. Another good choice is stewed preserved cabbage with sliced pork, made in a rich soup stock with tender streaky pork, aged chicken, and sour preserved cabbage.

Jiang rou, a stewed meat served cold with a *wasabi*-like mustard, and *la pi*, a cold noodle dish, are worth trying, as are the chicken strips dipped in egg white and cooked with sweet peas – mild but full of subtle flavor.

Cantonese cuisine

Because so many immigrants from Guangdong Province in Southern China settled in the West and opened restaurants, Cantonese food is the one

The pineapple cake is a central Taiwan concoction that is today a top local courtesy gift choice. Available at traditional-style bakeries, it is a bite-sized pastry with a chewy filling of fragrant pineapple paste.

most often associated with China. In Cantonese cooking, the freshness of the ingredients is of paramount importance. Fish, for instance, should ideally still be swimming just before it is cooked. Seasoning tends to be light, and preparation quick. A classic dish is steamed fish with a mild garnish of cilantro, ginger, pepper, sesame oil, and soy sauce. For stir-fried dishes, the "breath of the wok" is all-important, and the mark of a master chef.

For some reason, Cantonese food is not as popular in Taipei, although all of the classic dishes can be found here. These include beef and broccoli with oyster sauce, diced chicken with cashew nuts, barbecued pork, steamed lobster, shark's fin soup (not recommended for ethical reasons), abalone and bok choy, and the numerous kinds of dim sum.

Delicate dim sum.

Delectable fresh fruits for sale.

Taiwan is home to some of the best teas in the world.

Tea

With its sun-drenched mountain slopes – the island has dozens of peaks over 3,000 metres (10,000ft) high – Taiwan is perfect for tea growing, and it produces some of the world's finest teas. Taipei itself is filled with teahouses and tea drinkers.

Taiwan's most famous tea is Dongding Oolong, which comes from the rolling foothills of Taiwan's Central Mountain Range. These humid peaks are often covered in cloud and mist. Tea needs this cool climate; if the weather is hot, the tea leaves grow too fast, and become tough and bitter. Mountain teas are famous for their mildness, and Dongding Oolong is no exception. It is gentle and refreshing, with a hint of springtime.

A more unique variety of tea is Baihao Oolong, also known as "Oriental Beauty" (*Dongfang Meiren*). This tea has a robust, perfumed flavor, like an Earl Grey but earthier and more natural.

Also notable are the lightly fermented Baozhong, and the more heavily fermented Tie Guanyin (Iron Goddess), which has a caramel color, a full, mature flavor, and a sweet aftertaste. These are just a few of the varieties available in the capital, and the tea one drinks can depend upon the time of day, the time of year, and which part of Taiwan one is currently visiting.

Sipping tea at a Chinese teahouse involves more than just a beverage. The methodical brewing of a pot of tea is a soothing practice and a cultural experience in its own right.

As Taipei prospers, the locals continue to refine their palates and sharpen their desire for fine food. As a result, modern Taipei boasts the sort of uniform dining excellence found only in the world's great culinary cities, and you will find that eating out is indeed the city's top form of recreation.

KAOLIANG WINE

Visitors to Taipei may encounter a wickedly strong drink called Kaoliang wine. This fiery distillate is a banquet favorite. Many older Taiwanese men have a soft spot for it, which they associate with their youthful days of military service on Kinmen Island, where the most famous brand is brewed.

Kaoliang wine is made from sorghum steamed in vats for two hours, then fermented in bins for 10 days. The sour mash is then squeezed, and the resulting liquid distilled into raw liquor. Like olive oil, the first press is the best. Kaoliang-drinking etiquette forbids sipping – the entire shot glass must be tossed back in one big gulp. *Gan bei!* – literally, "dry glass"!

SHOPPING

As in many other Asian cities, similar businesses tended to cluster together in the Taipei of old. While specialist shopping areas still exist, modern Taipei offers consumers an alluring array of destinations at which to spend their cash.

Upmarket designers can be found in the Xinyi shopping district.

Shopping in Taipei used to be a simple affair. If you wanted the best selection of shoes, you went to the shoe street, which was literally lined with shoe shops and nothing else. Another area might specialize in furniture, say, or cameras.

Air-conditioned shopping malls dominate the Taipei shopping experience and they are especially welcome in the sweltering summer months. In some malls, you will find very similar businesses side by side – recalling the old days of Taipei shopping.

In fact, the free-spending Taiwanese have come to love shopping malls and department stores so much that Japanese company Mitsukoshi has built four of them in eastern Taipei's modern Xinyi District, a short walk south of the Taipei City Hall MRT station, forming the popular Xinyi New Life Square complex. Overkill, perhaps, but heaven for mall fans. There are at least six more malls within walking distance, including one at the base of the Taipei 101 tower.

The Xinyi malls are not all identical though; each is aimed at a different clientele. An upmarket outlet operated by Mitsukoshi is packed with luxury chains like Chanel and Louis Vuitton, while the Breeze and Eslite Centers (both chains of malls) mix more high-street names in with the luxury brands, and are therefore more popular with 20-somethings and hip teens (you will find them all over the city). Even though clothing – particularly women's fashion – dominates sales floors in the area, you

VAT REFUND

Foreign travelers who make purchases of NT$2,000 or more on the same day from the same Tax Refund Shopping (TRS) store are eligible for a refund of the 5 percent VAT paid.

To claim the refund, an application must be made – within 30 days of the date of purchase – at the port of departure. The goods must be shown to be taken out of the country. Visit the "Foreign Passenger VAT Refund Service Counter" at the airport or seaport.

For more details and information, including a useful list of TRS retail outlets, visit the Tourism Bureau website at www.taxrefund.net.tw/ttr.

Dedicated followers of fashion shopping on into the evening.

The best clothing bargains are found at markets rather than malls.

will find a wide range of other goods, including books, consumer electronics, audiovisual equipment, and appliances. Most malls have a wide selection of eateries in their basement food courts.

Couture connection

The Xinyi malls are ideal if you are in a hurry and want to shop in air-conditioned comfort, but much of what you see will be the same familiar brands you might find in New York, Singapore, or London – and the prices will seem familiar too. For more variety and better bargains, you will have to venture further.

Clothes are sold all over Taipei – from nightmarkets, where you can outfit yourself in polyester brand-name knockoffs for little more than spare change, to Asian chain stores like Giordano and Hang Ten, which are full of reasonably priced apparel. But the more statuesque foreign visitor might have trouble finding sizes that fit. A Taiwanese "L" is more like a US or European "M."

Expatriate residents head for the export shops in the Tianmu area in north Taipei. On Zhongshan North Road Section 7, just north of Tianmu East Road, are a number of shops selling clothing originally manufactured for export to the US and Europe.

Not only will you find larger sizes, but some real bargains too. Many of these shops sell factory seconds and out-of-season items at tremendous discounts. You may even see noted brands like Calvin Klein and Donna Karan – usually with the labels partly snipped out to indicate they are not for export. While most are indistinguishable from garments selling for 10 times more overseas, you should check these carefully, because you will occasionally spot flaws like missing buttons, torn seams, or minor variations in the cloth color.

Those with a penchant for the pop star-inspired, youth-oriented street fashions of the moment will be amply rewarded in the side streets of Ximending (see page 106) or the wholesale haven of Wufenpu (see page 154).

High-tech haul

Taiwan is one of the world's largest manufacturers of high-tech electronics, so many visitors to the island expect to find personal computers and other gadgets cheaper than they are

> Small stores are the best places to buy cutting-edge electronics. Department stores and a few specialist chains offer them, but prices are higher, selection is limited, and staff not as well informed.

at home. Whether or not you go home with a bargain, however, depends very much on what you are looking for. Generally, products that are cheap in other developed nations will be even cheaper in Taiwan, but high-end items are actually more expensive in Taiwan. This is because there is not much demand locally for top-of-the-line products (due to slightly lower average incomes than in the West), so they retail in smaller quantities and at higher prices.

At the corner of Xinsheng North Road and Civil Boulevard is the Guang Hua Digital Plaza (see page 142), a six-story building packed with literally hundreds of shops selling computers, computer parts, digital cameras, music players, and other electronic gadgets. The vendors from the famous old Guanghua Market, a labyrinth under a nearby expressway flyover that has been demolished because of safety concerns after a major earthquake, are located on the second and third levels. The fourth and fifth floors house vendors from another now defunct electronics market, and the sixth floor is home to a number of specialist repair shops.

Another electronics mall, the Syntrend Creative Park, opened in mid-2015 right next to the Guang Hua Digital Plaza and linked to it by a sky bridge. The city government's intent is to make the district the world's number one location to shop for cutting-edge electronics.

Thriving markets

Oddly juxtaposed with the modern offerings of Guang Hua Digital Plaza are smaller markets selling jade and antiques. Most can be found on the east side of Xinsheng South Road. The casual antiques buyer might prefer the antiques shops on Yongkang Street (close to the corner of Jinhua Street), which is also a delightfully bustling neighborhood area. Antiques buyers should keep a sharp eye out for the high-quality fakes and over-restored items that abound.

The area around Yongkang Street is also home to a few stores selling local and foreign handicrafts. Unlike, say, Thailand, Taiwan does not produce large amounts of attractive, low-cost handicrafts aimed at foreign tourists. But recently there has been a surge of interest in traditional arts and crafts combined with more contemporary styles. The large

The section of Boai Road where there is a high concentration of camera shops.

Treasures at Bai Win Antiques.

A piece of liuli glass art.

government-sponsored Taiwan Cultural and Creative Gift Center and the newer National Taiwan Craft Research and Development Institute are very useful for travelers, although they are a little pricier than private shops, because they house the many types of representative Taiwan handicrafts under one roof and ship overseas (see page 130).

Glass and porcelain art

Opinion is divided as to whether it is true art or expensive kitsch, but the often colorful glass art known as *liuli* certainly has a distinctive esthetic, and remains a unique product of Taiwan.

Artist Loretta Yang, owner of Newworkshop (Liuli Gongfang), is a former actress of great regional fame who stunned fans in 1987 by turning to an art form where, as she has explained, aging brings respect rather than rejection. Her works are true to Chinese classical and Buddhist themes, with functionality of minor importance.

Artist Heinrich Wang, of Tittot, is a former movie director and actor who dropped celluloid for glass in 1987, and more recently, dropped glass for porcelain. His works, which are attractive while being functional around the home and office, have won prizes and acclaim around the world.

Exotic teas

Plenty of high mountain slopes and a local market where almost everyone is a connoisseur have combined to make Taiwan home to some of the finest-quality Chinese teas in the world. In fact, certain prized Oolong varieties are only produced and sold in Taiwan, such as Baozhong, Dongding,

RECEIPTS AND WARRANTIES

Many small stores will not give you an official receipt as they operate under small business laws that allow them to avoid paying sales tax. This even applies to big-ticket items like personal computers. On request, they will usually write out a bill of goods, listing the items you have bought and the purchase date.

Products are rarely sold with an international guarantee. Local guarantee terms are usually as follows: free replacement with an identical item if you encounter problems within the first week, and full parts and service guarantee for the first year – but check the details if possible, as terms can vary considerably.

A selection of Taiwanese teas for sale, presented in elegant tins.

and Baihao (Oriental Beauty). The best way to shop for tea is to visit one of the many teahouses, such as Wang De Chuan Fine Chinese Tea (95 Zhongshan N. Rd, Sec. 1; daily 10am–9pm; tel: 02-2561 8738, www.facebook.com/dechuanTEA), cha FOR TEA (152 Fuxing N. Rd; daily 9am–10pm; tel: 02-2719 9900, www.chafortea.com.tw), or one of the establishments on Hengyang Road off Chongqing South Road Section 1. Here you can sample different varieties before deciding which to buy, and owners are steeped in tea expertise.

The best tea is sold loose, not pre-packaged. Any local expert will recommend the spring crop, which is handpicked from the finest young tea leaves grown at elevations above 1,500 meters (5,000ft). Most of this tea is organically grown. Spring tea is always in short supply and can easily cost more than NT$3,000 for a *catty* (about 600g or 21oz). Indeed, the famous and costly Oriental Beauty will set you back no less than NT$3,000 for a *catty*. Tea of "ordinary" quality generally costs upwards of NT$1,000 for the same amount, good enough for the tea neophyte and still far better than the tea dust that finds its way into Western tea bags. Most teahouses also sell the full set of equipage for brewing, but the town of Yingge (see page 230) is renowned for its ceramic tea sets.

PAY THE NAMED PRICE

A word of advice about bargaining in Taipei: don't. This is not China or India, and inflated "tourist prices" are almost unheard of. There are very few exceptions to this rule, and haggling is often only necessary for unique items like antiques. Sellers may be offended by hard bargaining, especially over small sums of money, since this implies they are being both inhospitable to a guest (you), and impecunious enough to be concerned about a dollar or two. Where prices are not marked, a polite request for a discount is acceptable. Shopkeepers will occasionally even reduce the price for you if you forget to ask.

Nightmarkets

If you find the glass and marble malls too sterile for your tastes, then Taipei's bustling and sweaty nightmarkets (see page 86) offer a dizzying variety of products, as well as bizarre – but useful – local favourites such as hand-held battery-powered fans or ones that strap to a pushchair to keep your toddler cool. However, the quality of nightmarket products tends to be as low as the prices. Visitors will enjoy the nightmarkets more if they go to look and savor the atmosphere rather than buy.

Jade Market

Jade has traditionally been valued in Chinese societies as highly as gold has been in the West. This gemstone offers a combination of toughness and physical beauty.

What's more, jade is believed by the Chinese to protect against evil spirits and misfortune, which is why you will often see a jade pendant dangling from the rearview mirror of one of Taipei's speeding taxis (as it races through a red light).

Whether you get there by taxi, or at the more sedate pace of the MRT (the market is located a few minutes' walk from Daan Park Station), you will find a whole world of jade (see page 142) at Taipei's Jianguo Weekend Jade Market, in the cool shade of the Jianguo Expressway flyover.

Stallholders squint at veined stones of lustrous green, pearly white, and blood red. Rickety tables hold an assortment of bracelets, earrings, pendants, figurines, and just about anything else imaginable – even delicate carved jade flowers and oddities like popular cartoon characters.

Contrary to popular belief, jade occurs in a wide variety of colors, and not just green. Its coloring also tends to become more vivid with age, particularly when warmed and polished by wearing close to the skin. Traditionally this phenomenon is explained as the jade absorbing the bad luck that would otherwise have afflicted the bearer.

Good-natured arguments break out over an item's value. It is generally seen as acceptable to improve the color of cheaper jade pieces by bleaching, and to firm up the structure by impregnating it with wax or resin, but these techniques considerably reduce the value; it is tricky for the inexperienced shopper to spot the difference.

Jade shopping for beginners

The pace of business is relaxed and stall-holders offer cups of tea to customers. With the most prized jade pieces fetching tens of thousands of US dollars, they can afford to bide their time. But do not be discouraged; there is something for everyone here. You can easily pick up a simple but attractive jade pendant for just a few hundred Taiwanese dollars.

Bargaining is advisable for the most expensive items, but less effective with the cheapest pieces. The Jianguo Weekend Jade Market Council has a desk at one end of the market, and it is worth consulting them if you are considering an expensive item. They speak little English, but will try to help.

Some of the Jade Market's wares.

The weekend market is fun for the visitor, but it is not the only place to buy jade in Taipei. Another much smaller market is open every day a short walk north, at the corner of Xinsheng South Road and Bade Road. Jewelry shops also offer a selection, generally of higher quality and price than found in the markets; many will provide certificates of authenticity on request.

SPORTS, FITNESS AND PASTIMES

Taipei may not be the biggest sporting town, but it does have one very popular spectator sport – baseball – and a number of interesting participant sports, ranging from solemn early morning tai chi gatherings to quirky late-night ballroom dancing.

Of Taipei's spectator sports, baseball is the most popular. The Chinese Professional Baseball League (CPBL, www.cpbl.com. tw) games are loud, energetic contests, played with enthusiasm and gusto.

The city also has an on-again, off-again professional basketball league. Basketball games were popular in the mid-1990s, but attendance declined, and the league folded in 1997. However, in 2004, the league was revived as the Super Basketball League (SBL), and is thriving today.

Taipei also has its favorite participant sports. Among these, nothing can touch the martial arts for popularity.

Baseball

Visitors seeking an enjoyable Taipei cultural experience, but with a touch of the familiar, should attend a professional baseball game. The rules are the same as elsewhere – nine-inning games, four bases, three strikes and you're out – but the spectacle is quite different.

There are no true "home" teams in the CPBL. The four teams have a regional base, but wander the island playing many "home" games in many different stadiums. This

Basketball remains popular with locals.

curious set-up guarantees that fans of both teams show up at every game. They carry whistles, trumpets, and drums, and greet every play with a crescendo of raucous noise. The cheering is organized and synchronized, and is led by hyperactive, self-appointed cheerleaders.

The food is different as well: replacing the famous hot dog is the local lunch box, with meat, rice, and cold vegetables. Another choice is grilled sausage, which comes not in a bun, but with a clove of raw garlic. The beer and soft drinks are the same, though, and so is the relaxed and happy atmosphere.

> Taoism is a key element of the martial arts. "The best soldier is not soldierly," wrote Taoist philosopher Lao Tzu. "The best fighter is not ferocious; the best conqueror does not take part in war."

Dragon boat teams race for the finish.

A venerable history

More than 100 years ago, the Japanese taught the Taiwanese to play baseball, and the locals later beat their colonial masters in a landmark game in 1930. The sport surged in popularity in the 1960s and 1970s, when Taiwan's little league team began to dominate the world, eventually winning 17 world titles.

In the 1990s, baseball really took off. The CPBL played its first season in 1990, and then, in 1992, Taiwan's national team won a silver medal in the Summer Olympics in Barcelona. The CPBL quickly grew in popularity, and in 2001, Taiwan hosted the World Cup of Baseball. The home team took third place, beating Japan in the bronze medal game. That victory ignited a joyful celebration, as thousands of fans took to the streets and staged a spontaneous parade.

That dramatic moment was followed by another key national victory, this time against

DRAGON BOATING

For one day each May/June, Taipei's Keelung River becomes a hive of activity, filled with brightly colored boats, pounding drums, and splashing paddles. This is the Dragon Boat Festival. The festival has its origins in Chinese antiquity, but today's races are ultra-modern, and attract teams of local and international competitors. Many of the boats are paddled by highly fit racers who train for months prior to the event. Most boats have 18 paddlers, plus a drummer – the heartbeat of the dragon – and a helmsman. In Taiwan, a 21st person rides on the prow to snatch the victory flag at the end of the course. The distance of a standard dragon boat race is 500 meters (1,640ft).

The Dragon Boat Festival is traditionally held on the 5th day of the 5th lunar month, on or near the summer solstice. It was originally believed that this season of oppressive heat was prone to pestilence and drought. Water-borne festivities thus evolved to counteract this.

With time, the festival has become more associated with the tragic story of Warring States patriot Qu Yuan, who drowned himself in a river in despair over being discredited by rivals for the emperor's favor. It is said that concerned citizens threw zongzi, rice dumplings, into the river to prevent the fish from eating Qu Yuan's body. The festival is thus also celebrated with the eating of zongzi.

In summer 2017, Taipei hosted the XXIX Summer Universiade, or the World Student Games, an international sports event for university athletes from more than 160 countries.

arch-rival Korea in 2003, which catapulted Taiwan's baseball team – playing under the moniker of Chinese Taipei – into the 2004 Summer Olympics. During the fraught game against Korea, groups of people huddled around their radios throughout Taipei, and erupted into loud cheers when the 5-4 victory was finally secure.

In recent years the league has been reduced to just four teams and around 2009 regular-season attendance dropped to about 3,000 per game as a result of two games-fixing scandals. In recent years, it has bounced back thanks to higher wages for players and the CPBL investing in a more entertaining experience, such as the addition of cheerleaders and photos offered with mascots. By 2017, the opening game for

the CPBL's 28th season sold out with a record 12,500 seats. The many fans who cannot watch from within the modern 10,000-seat venue catch broadcasts outside the ballpark, on a giant screen set up by the city government.

Martial arts

Percolating through Taipei life, everybody seems to have some connection to the martial arts – a mother-in-law who is a devotee of tai chi, perhaps, or a colleague who competes in wushu. In fact, many of China's most accomplished martial artists sought refuge here following persecution on the mainland.

Martial arts is a broad term that includes many disciplines. In the "hard arts" like Long Fist and Wing Chun, force is opposed by force, concentrating on points of attack, and focusing energy into punches and kicks. In tai chi, Xingyiquan, and other "soft arts," force is turned against the attacker. These focus on movement principles, relaxing one's body, and circulation of *qi*, or vital energy.

Each one has various schools, with its stylized rituals and fighting applications. And

Martial arts retain many devotees here; young people can get in some practice at the Youth Activity Center.

A morning tai chi session in the park.

Enjoying some alfresco ballroom dancing.

all have health benefits. According to a study done in Taipei, seniors who perform tai chi regularly have less than half the decrease in oxygen uptake, compared to a control group. In other words, tai chi practitioners tend to be more limber and fit. Tai chi also performs a social function, as the practitioners often go to the same places every morning to practice, where they talk and socialize. Early rising visitors to Taipei will see evidence of this in many local parks.

The steady popularity of martial arts in Taiwan is partly explained by its spiritual dimension; more than a sport, these self-defense disciplines are both a lifestyle and a philosophy. Western forms of unarmed combat, such as boxing and wrestling, are effective as fighting techniques, but lack the philosophical core.

Dancing

Occasionally you may spot seniors engaging in ballroom dancing, not in dancehalls or ballrooms, but in outdoor parks, on summer evenings – and sometimes during the day-time too – under the shade of the trees. Couples whirl and waltz in the semi-darkness into the night, making for an unusual and memorable sight. Younger fans now flock to small dance clubs and studios dotted all over the city – some hidden high up in apartment buildings – to learn and practice international styles including tango, salsa and swing dancing.

Climbing and hiking

Rock climbing is another sport that has surged in popularity in the last few years. Unlike some other sports, climbing does not require a large body size. On weekends, many climbers head for Longdong, on the Northeast Coast about 90 minutes from Taipei, to climb the sheer rock walls that soar above the ocean.

Hiking is also popular, and on weekends, people head to Yangmingshan National Park (see page 188). It is not as wild or spectacular as other mountain getaways, but Yangmingshan has one great advantage: it is right on Taipei's door-step. That means a day hike in Yangmingshan can end with a hot dinner in the city, rather than in a windswept tent at 3,000 meters (10,000ft).

Traditional remedies

In Taipei, a city that celebrates its heritage, traditional Chinese medicine is alive and well, and highly regarded by people, who use it to enhance their well-being.

The city's many strange-smelling apothecaries are filled with row after row of drawers containing exotic animal, mineral, or plant extracts. Among the ingredients are cinnabar and amber to calm the nerves, antelope horn to relieve pain, peach pits and safflower to promote circulation, and ginseng to fortify the lungs.

Indeed, the use of herbal mixtures is one of the key treatment strategies of Chinese medicine. The prescriptions often feature four or more ingredients – some are agents, others help counteract side effects, and others promote general good health – that a patient takes home and boils for hours to get a potent and usually bitter brew. The herbal remedies are extensive, with more than 2,000 in the literature, and about 150 commonly used.

Concepts

Chinese medicine is rooted, like the martial arts, in the theory of yin and yang, the concept of *qi*, or vital energy, and the Five Elements, said to classify the properties of all things. Traditional Chinese doctors aim to maintain the smooth passage of *qi*, and the proper equilibrium of yin and yang and the Five Elements, by using acupuncture, herbs, massage, and other methods. Unlike Western medicine, which concentrates on alleviating symptoms, Chinese medicine aims to keep a patient in good health by targeting any underlying imbalances. The physician performs an external diagnosis by observing a patient's complexion, taking the pulse, and peering at his or her tongue. This stems from a belief that one's internal systems can be observed from the exterior.

Besides herbal therapy, another popular treatment is massage, or *tuina*, which unclogs meridians of *qi*, relieving problems like joint injuries and muscle sprains. More dramatic is baguan, or the technique of using suction cups to stimulate circulation. The cups are heated inside with a wad of flaming cotton to create a vacuum, then placed upon a few vital points of the body. The flesh swells into the cup, causing superficial bruising. This treatment is said to be effective for respiratory problems.

Chinese medicine is gaining acceptance worldwide, and it has shown promise in treating chronic conditions like diabetes and heart disease. Acupuncture is becoming more common in the West, and

Preparing a Chinese herbal prescription.

its use as an anesthetic is no longer news. Chinese physicians also do not dispute the superiority of Western medicine in the treatment of acute pathology such as traumatic injuries. Like the many Taiwanese who visit both Chinese and Western-trained doctors, they see traditional remedies as a complement to Western medicine, not a substitute.

NIGHTLIFE

With none of Bangkok's restrictive closing hours or the expatriate exclusiveness often seen in Hong Kong, Taiwan's capital has developed a winning diversity of evening entertainment in recent years.

Happy punters.

Old-timers complain Taipei's nightlife heyday is but a memory. Certainly the city has matured and lost edginess, but to say it is past its prime is to fail to be attuned to all that Taipei has going for it after dark.

Nightmarkets

When Taiwanese abroad get nostalgic for home, they miss the *renao* – heat and noise – of the nightmarket. After all, before there were bars, pubs, and hip-hop clubs – dancing was outlawed under martial law 30 years ago – there was the local nightmarket (see page 86). But

if you're hankering for more raucous late-night action, read on.

Beerhouses

For many foreigners, beerhouses, or *pijiuwu*, are Taipei's after-hours highlight. Rowdy and come-as-you-are, the quintessential Taiwan beerhouse has cavernous halls, big picnic tables, greasy nightmarket foods, watery draft beer in kegs of many sizes, and low, low prices.

Let's go singing

When the Taiwanese want to loosen up with colleagues or friends, they're more likely to say "let's go singing" than "let's have a drink" – though the singing is usually accompanied by lots of rapid-fire toasting and quaffing of alcohol. Karaoke is a Japanese import, of course, but the Taiwanese have taken to it as if it was their own, and Taipei is studded with palatial karaoke chains that do booming business. One of the most popular, Partyworld, has outlets with lobbies so opulent that some newcomers mistake them for five-star hotels. Even if you're nervous singing in public, when you get an invitation from Taiwanese friends to go out singing, accept – all the big KTVs have a selection of English-language hits.

Bars and clubs

In times past, the "Combat Zone," centered on Shuangcheng Street behind the Imperial Hotel, was Taipei's prime cluster of expatriate watering holes. Sometimes called "Sugar Daddy Row," this stretch had its heyday before 1979, when the US military had a

Beerhouses are a quirky Taiwan feature.

Partying at loud and lively Carnegies, which is renowned for its lengthy shooter menu.

base nearby. The formula was Western pub food, imported beer, canned retro-rock, and friendly female bar staff. Today, the area looks more than a little tired, and much of the action has moved to alternative locations and alternative, more sophisticated and gender-neutral styles of drinking.

A long-standing alternative to the Combat Zone has been the Shida university district. Popular with foreigners studying Chinese or teaching English in Taipei, this area has enjoyed a minor renaissance in recent years, after a period of decline. On weekend nights you'll see crowds of foreigners gathering in the Shida Nightmarket area for a quick bite before heading off to their chosen music venues.

The main players are Blue Note, a cozy jazz-venue icon at the corner of Shida and Roosevelt roads, 45 Pub on Heping East Road, and Revolver, upstairs for live bands, around the corner from the Chiang Kai-shek Memorial Hall.

The long section of Anhe Road that runs between Heping East Road and Xinyi Road, along with the alleys running off it, is the area that is upstaging Taipei's traditional nightlife districts. In the early 2000s, in what seemed

the blink of an eye, it became home to countless drinking venues, ranging from the big and brash Carnegies – renowned for its bar-top grooving patrons – to hole-in-the-wall lounges featuring ambient beats and some impressive selections of wine and spirits. Some of the choicest lounge-bars are down the alleys, so be a little adventurous. Note that they tend to be better for couples than for single drinkers looking to strike up conversation with like-minded people.

The shift to Anhe Road in recent years has been accompanied by increasing sophistication. Cocktail speakeasies and fashionable DJ

OUTDOOR BARS

If you fancy some al-fresco drinking, there are a few choice spots in the capital. The gay bar street behind The Red House is fabulously open air; the gardens at the Spot Café Lumiere are leafy and elegant; but if you want a more down and dirty vibe, head to the riverside behind the Museum of Drinking Water in Gongguan, where half a dozen huts serve beer, spirits, and snacks (closed if too cold or wet in winter).

clubs are more and more the kind of places that Taipei's fashionistas like to flaunt their stuff. Another very welcome addition to the bar scene is the popularity of craft beer and specialist bars with some delicious local brews on tap. You will find them all over town.

As for the club scene, it has evolved from one of marginal interest, having gone through a phase of frequent police crackdowns, to finally becoming mainstream. Do note that clubs tend to shut down or change name frequently. Try the upmarket Wave Club in the ATT4FUN mall or the more down-to-earth Triangle, which also holds gay dance parties one or two nights a month.

Pop and rock

Taiwan is arguably the pop music capital of the Mandarin-speaking world, churning out a steady stream of hits that are warbled by fans in KTV parlors throughout the Chinese diaspora. Such is the music's popularity, it is often necessary to hold concerts in stadium venues to accommodate the crowds. Check local newspapers for information.

There is no shortage of drinks on offer at this trendy Taipei lounge bar.

Girls on the town.

A more recent development has been the explosion of Taiwan's band culture. The independent music scene was kick-started by the Spring Scream music festival in 1995 in Kending, in southern Taiwan. Today this ongoing festival is complemented by the Ho-Hai-Yan Music Festival, with three to five days of live music held annually in July at Fulong Beach on Taiwan's northeast coast.

CRAFT BEER

The best thing that's happened to the Taipei drinking scene in recent years is the craft-beer craze. And that's both in terms of locally brewed names and in establishments where you can enjoy a full-bodied micro-brewed lager or ale. There are now well over two dozen independent brewers on the island. Names to look out for are Redpoint (often on tap), Zhang Men, and Taiwan Head Brewers, who dedicate their beer to their "beautiful country, Taiwan". Many brews are tinged with local fruit flavours – or tea – and taprooms where you can taste before buying can be found all over downtown.

Taiwan's pop culture

To many ordinary Chinese, Taiwan is a breeding ground for new talents waiting to be discovered and a place to fulfil superstar aspirations.

The territory has produced numerous pop icons in the Chinese entertainment industry, from evergreen singer Teresa Teng to screen goddess Brigitte Lin Ching-hsia and Taiwanese tourism ambassador, singer Zhang Huimei (affectionately known as "a MEI").

Of course, this inevitably makes for a love-hate relationship between the stars and entertainment journalists. Taiwan has become a hunting ground for the juiciest gossip and fodder for hundreds of Asian tabloids. As in Hong Kong, Taiwanese paparazzi spare no effort to get the best headline for the front page. Celebrities know the rules of the game and craft the symbiotic relationship skilfully. Those not in the know have disparaged these reporters as "vile pigs." Robbie Williams unwittingly pushed up the tabloid circulation numbers when he pointed at journalists at Taiwan Taoyuan International Airport and said, "I didn't insult your country, I will insult you."

An all-important element of Chinese television has always been the drama serial. In recent years, however, it has undergone a transformation. Insipid melodramas are no longer the norm; instead, youth-obsessed "idol dramas" have become de rigueur on channels. Only the good-looking need apply. JVKV (formerly F4), Taiwan's answer to boyband One Direction, has driven thousands of pre- and post-pubescent teens to high-octave screaming in airports and hotel lobbies, and elevated "groupism" into an art form. This group of four attractive men with their long hair and fairy-tale princely personas has created a multimillion-dollar industry, spawning a wave of copy-cat boy (and girl) bands, with groups like 5566, Fahrenheit, Ice Man, JPM, Lollipop F, and S.H.E. competing for a slice of the burgeoning teen market. When it comes to solo acts, Jay Chou and Jolin Tsai have long occupied the thrones of pop royalty.

Teen culture

Taiwan teens, who once manically embraced Japanese pop culture, are now more obsessed by South Korean music and fashions – as is the rest of Asia. In the ultra-funky district of Ximending, "coolness" and "in-your-face" attitudes are defined with bold use of colors in hair, tattoos, and exaggerated accessories. American musical genres like R&B and hip hop have been eagerly accepted as well: youngsters decked out in baseball caps and oversized jeans are a common sight.

A Mei at a press conference in Taipei, 2014.

While the Taiwanese are still traditional in other aspects of life, Western pop influences have created a more liberal attitude in the local media. Steamy bedroom talk, poking fun at politicians, and humiliating celebrities are almost obligatory in the highly popular variety and talk shows televised by satellite across Asia.

NAVIGATING THE NIGHTMARKETS

These nightly bazaars – unique, unplanned, and colorful – offer traditional snack foods, shopping, and an authentic taste of crowded local street life.

Nightmarkets are one of the most popular attractions on the island, rivaling even the National Palace Museum. And it seems like every neighborhood in Taipei has one. Admittedly, one has to put up with a lot of jostling, clamor, and grease. But with an irresistible combination of bright lights, big crowds, fresh food, carnival games, and hawker stalls, the city's nightmarkets never fail to entertain.

The top attraction is, of course, the local snack foods – often unhealthy, but usually very tasty. Browsing the merchandise on sale is another highlight. But don't overlook the other options – from fortune-tellers to seal-carvers, acupuncturists to blind masseurs.

If you're not sure what to go for, look for the longest queue, which is usually a good indication that whatever is being sold is delicious (or an Instagram sensation!). Stinky tofu, fried chicken, pork buns, and barbecued squid are perennial favourites, but sweet and savoury pancakes, cheesy omelettes, dim sum baskets, sausages, and fish balls do a roaring trade too. If you're vegetarian, there are usually a few carts offering meatless wraps and bowls of vegetarian noodles. These days they will have English signs and sport a green sign.

In recent years, the range of food on offer has become more international, with Southeast and South Asian stallholders livening up the flavors. Most nightmarkets now also offer Vietnamese, Indian, and Thai food. There is also more emphasis on desserts such as cheesecakes, Swiss rolls, and tiramisus. If that all sounds too unhealthy, you can always find chopped fruit and juice sellers.

A colorful and brightly lit Chinese gate serves as the main entrance to Raohe Street Nightmarket, lending a festive ambience. Nightmarkets catering to tourists, both local and foreign, often feature these gates, and have a large number of permanent stalls. Other nightmarkets without permanent outlets only spring up at night.

Shoes on sale at Shilin Nightmarket. Shoppers are often spoiled for choice. Though fashion accessories, clothing, lingerie, and shoes dominate the selection, one can also find watches, tin toys, stuffed animals, carvings, and all manner of trinkets. Prices are low, and bargaining is possible, but all purchases are strictly caveat emptor, for the quality of the products may be low too.

A young couple consulting a traditional Chinese fortune-teller at Raohe Street Nightmarket. With the aid of the Chinese almanac and a person's date and time of birth, the fortune-teller is able to provide astrological forecasts of one's career, romance, health, and other aspects of life. They are also frequently consulted to determine if the astrological signs of two persons planning to marry "clash," or will result in a happy union.

A stall at Miaokou Nightmarket in Keelung selling freshly made runbing, another traditional Taiwanese snack food. Five or six ingredients, mostly vegetables, are rolled in a soft flour skin. Unlike chunjuan or spring rolls, which they resemble, they are not fried.

An alternative to shopping for food or clothes is to pick up a cheerful jade souvenir.

A stall at Shilin Nightmarket selling piping hot shengjian bao. Filled with minced pork or a peppery vegetable filling, these buns are first steamed, then pan-fried to create a crispy bottom crust. Besides this, some of the most popular street foods include yan su ji ("salt crispy chicken"), nuggets of chicken deep fried and seasoned with spices; hujiao bing, a bun filled with minced meat and pepper then baked; herbal pork rib soup; o-a-mi-sua, a congee of vermicelli and oysters; herbal jelly (xiancao) with tapioca pearls; and much more.

The Taipei skyline at sunset.

Boating in Danshui.

Surveying Taipei's most famous landmark.

PLACES

A detailed guide to Taipei and its surroundings, with principal sights numbered and clearly cross-referenced to maps.

Recognizing that most travelers to Taipei come on business, the travel authorities are encouraging longer stays to take in the sights. The city is also improving communications in English; today there is a wealth of information available to those interested in seeing more of the city.

The key to exploring the metropolis is understanding the personalities of its various districts. In the west, by the Danshui River, the old hubs of Wanhua and Dadaocheng are where it all began. Filled with the city's oldest cultural, historical, and religious sites, the cores of these neighborhoods remain much as they were a century ago, but in recent years the buildings have been reno-vated and gentrified into boutiques and bars while keeping their heritage appearance. In

Leisure time in Danshui.

the central districts, the old walls built by the Qing dynasty imperial govern-ment may no longer stand, but the area is graced by architectural monuments in Western styles built by Taiwan's colonial rulers, the Japanese.

In the east, the Xinyi District is Taipei's shining star and the center of economic activity. The most sophisticated department stores, modern theater complexes, and nightlife venues, all built on the grandest of scales, collec-tively swirl around Taipei 101, the city's defining visual icon.

North of the Keelung River are some of Taipei's most popular tourist attractions, including the priceless artifacts at the National Palace Museum, the best traditional Taiwanese snack foods at Shilin Nightmarket, and the healing hot springs of Beitou.

Yangmingshan, just 30 minutes from downtown, is a true rarity – a national park within city limits, with a network of mountain trails and more hot springs. South and east of the city, in Muzha and Nangang, tea planta-tions perfume the hills.

Being surrounded by mountains and hills means that the physical expansion of the vibrant metropolis has been upwards rather than outwards. Today the visitor sees a forest of futuristic structures reaching for the sky, standing side by side with heritage architectural works such as Wanhua's renowned Longshan Temple. Perhaps this best defines the personality of the city – living with the comforts of the old and familiar while enthusiastically embracing the new.

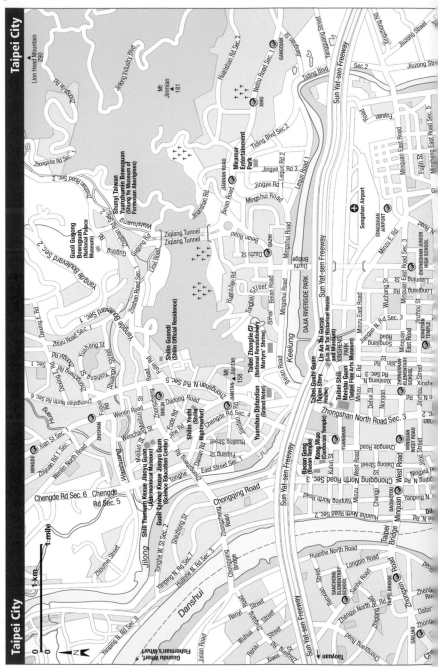

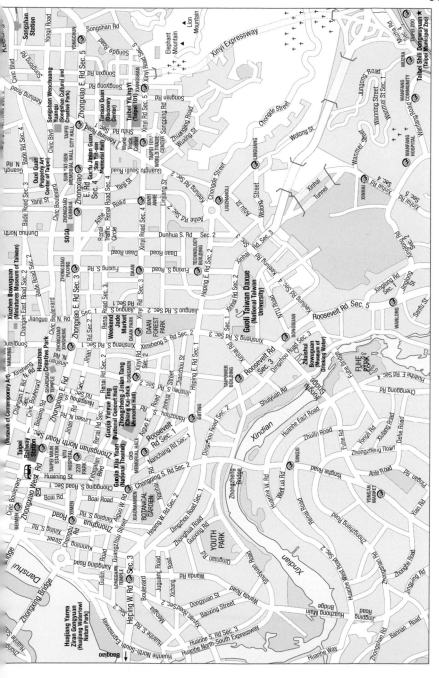

OLD TAIPEI: WANHUA AND XIMENDING

Wanhua is the cradle of Taipei's history and the north's greatest collection of heritage sites, while Ximending, a recreation district set up by the Japanese during the colonial period, is the hub of the city's youth culture.

I n times long gone the Taipei Basin was the site of an inland saltwater lake, formed when tectonic heavings lowered the ground, allowing the sea to rush in. About 400 years ago, the dawn of northern Taiwan's recorded history, the Basin was still a soggy area of marsh, wetland, and swamp. Silting and draining have been extensive since then.

The area that forms present-day Wanhua, situated just downriver from where the Dahan and Xindian rivers meet to form the Danshui, was originally the site of a Ketagalan tribal settlement. This flatland-dwelling people dominated the Taipei Basin before the arrival of the Han Chinese in the early 1700s.

WANHUA

Huajiang Waterfowl Park

The 70-hectare (170-acre) **Huajiang Waterfowl Nature Park ❶** (Huajiang Yanya Ziran Gongyuan), by Huajiang Bridge, is the site of a grand reunion of migratory birds, especially ducks, during the winter season. From September, green-winged teals, northern shovelers, and other feathered beauties are found in abundance in the marshes and on

the mudflats fronting the dedicated 500-meter (1,640ft) long birdwatching path. There are many explanatory signs along the way, though little English.

Taipei's riverside network of bicycle paths, stretching 150km (90 miles) along the Xindian, Danshui, and Keelung rivers, slides by here. The interlinked riverside parks and pathways are a major component of the city's Green Network initiative.

Moving north along the Danshui River to where the marsh ends, one

Main Attractions
Huaxi Street Tourist
  Nightmarket
Longshan Temple
Bopiliao Historic Block
Ximending Pedestrian Mall
Zhongshan Hall
North Gate
Taipei Post Office

Map
Page 100

Making use of Taipei's network of riverside bicycle paths.

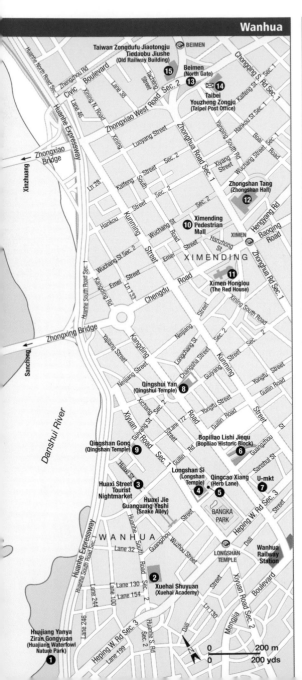

Wanhua

Taiwan Zongdufu Jiaotongju Tiedaobu Jiushe (Old Railway Building) **15**

BEIMEN

Beimen (North Gate) **13**

14

Taibei Youzheng Zongju (Taipei Post Office)

Zhongxiao Bridge

Zhongshan Tang (Zhongshan Hall) **12**

Ximending Pedestrian Mall **10**

XIMEN

XIMENDING

Ximen Honglou (The Red House) **11**

Qingshui Yan (Qingshui Temple) **8**

Bopiliao Lishi Jiequ (Bopiliao Historic Block) **6**

Qingshan Gong (Qingshan Temple) **9**

Longshan Si (Longshan Temple) **4**

Qingcao Xiang (Herb Lane) **5**

U-mkt **7**

Huaxi Street Tourist Nightmarket **3**

Huaxi Jie Guanguang Yeshi (Snake Alley)

BANGKA PARK

Danshui River

LONGSHAN TEMPLE

Wanhua Railway Station

WANHUA

Xuehai Shuyuan (Xuehai Academy) **2**

Huajiang Yanya Ziran Gongyuan (Huajiang Waterfowl Nature Park) **1**

0   200 m
0   200 yds

A snake handler in Snake Alley.

finds the site of Wanhua's original port. Exit into Wanhua through the Guilin Road gate. The ugly cement dikes here were built in the 1960s to protect the city's communities from the typhoon flooding that regularly ravages the Taipei Basin.

From Bangka to Wanhua

In 1709 three pioneers from Fujian established the first legally deeded farm at Dagala, on the banks of the Danshui River, in what is now Taipei. More followed, concentrating their settlements along the banks of the Danshui. One settlement, called "Bangka" in Taiwanese ("Mengjia" in Mandarin), became the Taipei Basin's most important market center, and the seed of today's Wanhua and the city of Taipei.

It served as an entrepôt between local indigenous traders, immigrant Chinese miners and growers, and the mainland Chinese market. The natives gathered here from upriver to sell camphor, sweet potatoes, coal, and other goods to the Chinese. Indeed, the term "Bangka," a bastardization of the Ketagalan word for "canoe," is still more commonly used today by the area's locals than the Japanese-imposed "Wanhua," or "10,000 glories."

This densely populated district did not fully enjoy the benefits of Taiwan's economic miracle in the second half of the 20th century. However, in keeping with the spirit of the "native soil" movement that has surged to prominence since martial law was lifted in 1987, local community leaders and the city administration have taken concerted action to beautify the district. All of the area's well-preserved historic sites are within walking distance of each other, and the majority can be taken in over a leisurely walk of four to five hours.

Xuehai Academy ❷

Located at 93 Huanhe South Road Section 2 is Taipei's only remaining academic building from the Qing dynasty, the **Xuehai Academy** (Xuehai Shuyuan; privately owned, but you can peer at the attractive structure through the railings). The former school building looks like a small temple; its sweeping roof of bamboo-shaped glazed tiles is adorned with carved swallow-tail ridges, writhing dragons, and auspicious figurines. This is unsurprising given the reverence the Chinese have traditionally had for learning. Today it serves as the ancestral shrine for the Gao clan, one of Wanhua's most powerful families in imperial days.

Huaxi Street Tourist Nightmarket ❸

Extending from Guangzhou Street to Guilin Road is the **Huaxi Street Tourist Nightmarket** (Huaxi Jie Guanguang Yeshi; daily 5pm–midnight), better known in English as **Snake Alley**. Once home to a number of snake meat restaurants, the last of these establishments closed its doors in late 2018 – the restaurants falling out of fashion and deemed cruel to animals – though the market remains.

The "Tourist" in its name is something of a misnomer. Even though in the 1990s the many red-light businesses were driven into the shadows, lights were hung up to brighten the place, and a roof was added to protect visitors from bad weather, this nightmarket remains local to the hilt.

Just past Snake Alley on Guangzhou Street and before the intersection with Xiyuan Road is Lane 223, which used to be the site of the **Bangka Fortified Gate**. Several years ago it was demolished and replaced with a wall mural that now marks the spot. The gate was built during imperial times when

Divining or oracle blocks are pairs of kidney-shaped red blocks, each with one convex side and one flat side. The rattle of these wooden blocks hitting the floor is a characteristic sound heard in many a Chinese temple.

Longshan Temple packed with worshippers.

immigrant groups from different districts or provinces of China commonly fought for dominance. This bloody intercommunal conflict did not subside until the latter half of the 1800s, when most of the land was already settled and titled, and there was general prosperity. Every night, and in times of emergency, such fortified gates would be closed and guarded. As was often the case in towns, there were no community walls, but houses were clustered tightly, facing inward, to create effective wall-like perimeters.

Longshan Temple ❹

Address: 211 Guangzhou Street, www. lungshan.org.tw
Opening Hrs: daily 6am–10pm
Entrance Fee: free
Transportation: Longshan Temple
Just east of Xiyuan Road is **Longshan Temple** (Longshan Si), one of Taiwan's most important places of worship and of priceless historical

importance. The temple was first built on a much smaller scale in 1738. The much expanded incarnation seen today is renowned for its

DIVINING BLOCKS

At Longshan Temple and other Chinese temples around Taipei, you'll see people throwing divining blocks to seek advice from the gods. First they stand before the icon and burn three incense sticks. Then while holding the divining blocks, they silently state their name, birthdate, and address, and present their petition in the form of a question. The blocks are then dropped. If one convex side and one flat side show, the answer is positive. Two convex sides are "angry blocks" – the answer is negative. If two flat sides show, no answer has been given, and the supplicant must try again, with the question framed a different way.

exquisite woodcarvings, as well as for its stone sculptures, a noteworthy example of which are the 12 major support columns in the main hall, twined by auspicious dragons hewn from solid stone.

Long ago, a merchant from Quanzhou in Fujian Province stopped here to relieve himself, then forgot his sacred protective incense pouch. Later, locals saw a bright light emanating from the pouch, and found an inscription inside that claimed it came from the renowned Longshan Temple in Quanzhou. This was a clear sign to build a replica, and Taipei's version soon came into being.

Early on, the temples in Wanhua were commonly used as military bases by the market town's rival immigrant groups. Soon, Longshan Temple became the seat of the area's religious, judicial, social, and commercial affairs. In 1885, as French marines stood ready to attack Taipei during the Sino-French War, the local militia rushed to the city's defense. Their banners carried an image of Longshan Temple, their military headquarters.

Huaxi Street Tourist Nightmarket is a world of traditional eateries, antique and curio shops, and foot-massage parlors.

The temple's main deity, Guanyin, the Goddess of Mercy, has over the years proven to be powerful and protective. The area was devastated

One of the stalls on Herb Lane.

by an earthquake in 1815, but it is said that the icon of Guanyin sat through it serene and safe. During World War II, Allied planes hit the temple (Japanese troops were often billeted in places of worship). The bombs and ensuing fire razed the main hall but somehow missed the goddess. Even though the iron railings around Guanyin had melted, nothing more than her toes were singed. This really got the people's attention, and today devotees come to her from morning to night with requests for clarity and assistance.

Herb Lane ⑤

Along the eastern wall of the temple is **Herb Lane** (Qingcao Xiang), a short, covered alley lined with retail and wholesale outlets (daily 8am– 10pm). Piled high in canvas sacks, display boxes, or loosely in heaps, are countless fresh or dried herbs, roots, and medicinal plants. Some are leafy, others knobby or spiny, in shades of green or brown. The aroma of the place is bracing.

The market sprang up beside Longshan Temple in 1738. Food,

Crowds shopping in the bustling district of Ximending.

textiles, and embroidery were originally sold, and later, baked goods and candles for worship. The herbs on sale today are used in traditional food recipes, tonics, and medicines.

Icons at Qingshui Temple.

Bopiliao Historic Block ⑥

Located just to the east, **Bopiliao Historic Block** (Bopiliao Lishi Jiequ) is the alley running both sides of Lane 173 off Kangding Road, just north of its intersection with Guangzhou St (Tue–Sun 9am–5pm). This is one of Taipei's oldest sections, and with Dihua Street in Dadaocheng, among its most intact, stretching back 200 years. The entire block of old buildings, done in the imperial Chinese style and featuring arcades to protect customers from the elements, has been spruced up in recent years to serve as a time portal; it looks like the Taipei of half a century ago and more. Some of the shopfronts have been done up to look exactly as they did in the 1980s, for use as backdrops in the local movie *Monga*, released in early 2010, which tells the story of 1980s Bangka and Wanhua and of the city in general. The name "Bopiliao" literally means "peeling off bark," referring to the main business here in the 1800s when timber would be unloaded at the nearby port and brought here for processing. The block has been developed as an arts and culture zone.

U-mkt ⑦

Just a twist to the left of Exit 3 of Longshan Temple MRT station is this renovated market complex that is noteworthy because of its peculiar U shape. A funky artistic architectural firm, the Jut Foundation, took over the project and have converted the inside into an exhibition space with workshops and studios (free; Tue–Sun 10am-6pm). Several of the original market structures are preserved behind glass or in exhibition spaces, such as the old metal stalls and a chunk of the main door. The building dates back 80 years to the Japanese era but the mood here is definitely modern. The permanent exhibit traces life at the old market, while temporary shows focus on architectural themes.

Qingshui Temple ⑧

Address: 81 Kangding Road
Opening Hrs: daily 6am–9.30pm
Entrance Fee: free
Transportation: Longshan Temple

Further east, Guangzhou Street intersects with Kangding Road. Turn north, and a short distance

WHERE

If you seek advice more specific than the divining blocks can reveal, another type of divination available at Longshan Temple is *qiuqian*, or "drawing lots." After addressing the query to the deity, one draws a bamboo sliver at random from a container. This is exchanged at a counter for a corresponding slip of paper with the oracular advice written on it.

Crowds shopping in the bustling district of Ximending.

The fashion trends embraced by Ximending's peddlers and shoppers may not appeal to the non-teenaged crowd, but the area is still great for people-watching.

Taipei City Wall-North Gate.

away is ornate **Qingshui Temple** (Qingshui Yan), erected in honor of Song dynasty Taoist monk Chen Zhao-ying. Chen is revered for selflessly providing medical care to the poor and for successfully praying for rain when drought threatened. The temple has seven iconic images of Chen, who is also known as the "Divine Progenitor" (Zushi). The most famous statue has its nose in the process of dropping off – a sign of impending disaster. Another shows the nose jumping back on when the crisis has passed. These in no way indicate anything untoward will happen when the visitor is in the building; they are merely didactic devices, believers say, to show what has happened here in the past. Skillfully wrought and extremely detailed depictions of scenes from famous mythological tales concerned with moral guidance enrich the exterior and interior walls and support beams of the temple.

Qingshan Temple ⑨

Address: 218 Guiyang Street Sec. 2
Tel: 02-2382 2296
Opening Hrs: daily 5.30am–9.30pm
Entrance Fee: free
Transportation: Longshan Temple

Just west of Xiyuan Road Section 1 is **Qingshan Temple** (Qingshan Gong). It is known especially for its magnificently carved beams and murals. The small hall at the rear of the temple's courtyard has a shrine to the King of Qingshan. Besides dispelling pestilence, he is believed to dispense justice in the underworld, thus having a direct role in deciding the fate of newly deceased mortals. The temple erupts in plangent birthday celebrations for the King of Qingshan on the 22nd day of the 10th lunar month.

XIMENDING

Ximending is the compact area of narrow streets just north of Wanhua, west of Zhonghua Road, and south of Zhongxiao West Road. *Ximen* means "west gate," and *ding* is the Mandarin pronunciation of the Japanese character for "district." The west wall of the old walled city was where Zhonghua now runs, and the West Gate stood precisely above where Ximen MRT station is today.

The old city walls were torn down by the Japanese, and the area over which Ximending is now spread, once marshy and malarial, was cleared. A well-planned shopping and recreation hub in a precise grid of streets was established. Today the Japanese influence is still evident in several important heritage buildings and, strangely enough, in the fact that the district concentrates on Japanese-inspired youth fashion. The city has accentuated the flavor by adding street decor that evokes Tokyo's Shibuya district.

The core of Ximending is the inter-section outside Ximen MRT station, from which the major streets run at angles outwards, like the rays of the sun on the Japanese naval flag. On weeknights and weekends, Wuchang and Emei streets are closed to vehicles, becoming the **Ximending Pedestrian Mall** ⑩.

A leisurely stroll through the streams of happy, young, and thrill-seeking shoppers brings you past countless downmarket boutiques, shops selling the latest animated movie-character merchandise, and the panoply of pop star-inspired youth fashion musts of the moment. You will also see teens intently devouring comic books in the many small shops that specialize in Japanese-style *manga* (*man-hua* in Mandarin).

The Red House ⑪

Address: 10 Chengdu Road, www. redhouse.org.tw
Tel: 02-2311 9380
Opening Hrs: Sun–Thu 11am–9.30pm, Fri–Sat 11am–10pm, closed Mon
Entrance Fee: free
Transportation: Ximen

The Red House (Ximen Honglou) is a two-story octagonal building with walls of red brick constructed by the Japanese in 1908. It sits directly outside the southwest exit of Ximen

MRT station. It was originally built to house Taiwan's first modern market, specializing in the Japanese foods and goods that the island's colonial masters missed so much. This became the core of the district, attracting other retailers and recreational outlets – including droves of red-light businesses. In its various guises since the Japanese left in 1945, it has served as a movie theater and a venue for traditional folk performances.

Today the main floor houses a small teashop, a display area on the site's history, and a small gift shop. The second level is an attractive 200-seat venue devoted to traditional folk performances, in particular puppetry and children's theater (admission charge). The impressive recessed ceiling is held up by hefty timber support beams original to the building. Attached to the main octagonal building is the **Creative Boutique**, two floors of small stores given over to artists and designers to sell their wares. In the area behind the building is Taipei's gay bar street, a cluster of friendly and lively al fresco pubs that welcome all.

WHERE

Ximending Pedestrian Mall is frequently the venue for celebrity appearances or free outdoor concerts by Taiwanese pop stars such as Jay Chou. To experience the screaming fandom, check local press listings for information.

Inside Zhongshan Hall.

TIP

The street artist-cum-busker phenomenon is relatively new to Taiwan. At weekends favorite performance sites are the Ximending Pedestrian Area and The Red House Area. Styles are both Western and Eastern; the latter includes traditional-style drum groups, martial artists, candy blowers, and makers of dough figurines. Check the city's travel-information counters for details. There is one in Ximen MRT Station.

The Red House.

Zhongshan Hall ⑫

Address: 98 Yanping Road, https://english.zsh.gov.taipei
Tel: 02-2381 3137
Opening Hrs: daily 9.30am–9pm
Entrance Fee: free
Transportation: Ximen

North of Ximen MRT station stands the visually imposing **Zhongshan Hall** (Zhongshan Tang), with its back facing Zhonghua Road and its front on Yanping South Road. The grandiose edifice, built by the Japanese to serve as Taipei City Hall, was started in 1932 and completed in 1936. This was where the Japanese military governor signed the articles of surrender in 1945, turning the island over to the Allies.

There are two large performance halls within and productions are also staged in the large plaza in front of the building, notably during the Taipei Traditional Arts Festival in spring, for which the hall is the main venue. The facility is home to the much-lauded Taipei Chinese Orchestra, Taiwan's first fully professional orchestra dedicated to Chinese music. There are a couple of beautifully furnished cafés inside serving elegant teas and coffees.

North Gate ⑬

Five minutes on foot north of Zhongshan Hall, the **North Gate** (Beimen) sits forlornly in the traffic circle where Zhong-hua, Yanping, and other roads meet, although the removal of the Zhongxiao flyover has opened up the space. This important heritage site is one of the four surviving city gates, and is the only one with its original appearance faithfully maintained. It was renovated and a small garden was planted around it in 2018. Built in 1884 in the Northern Chinese style, this contrasts with almost all other structures from the imperial era built on Southern Chinese designs.

The gate faces the area's highest point, the peak of Mount Qixing on Yangmingshan. By conventional Chinese geomantic principles, the main city gate was supposed to face south. But because Dadaocheng was in its prime in the 1880s and most of the commercial traffic came from

the north, the city's blueprints were flipped. In order to balance the *feng-shui* and block baleful energy from flowing in from the north, the main gate was therefore oriented northeast instead.

Taipei Post Office ⓮

Directly across the street from the North Gate is the old **Taipei Post Office** (Taibei Youzheng Zongju; Mon–Fri 7.30am–9pm, Sat 8.30am–4.30pm, Sun 8.30am–noon). Built in 1929, this old darling is no faded star but a proud and functioning facility.

This edifice manifests the transitional style the Japanese architects experimented with in the 1930s (they "practiced" in their colony before utilising novel concepts in the motherland). Its neoclassical design harmonized with the streamlined simplicity found in the modern buildings of the time. The original structure had three stories. Its front entrance was bracketed by four pairs of symmetrical columns whose Corinthian capitals showed an elegant Egyptian palm design. After Retrocession in 1945, an extra floor was added to accommodate demands for space, and the magnificent first-story terrace was replaced with today's black marble entrance, giving the facade its remarkably unusual two-tone character.

Old Railway Building ⓯

Standing on the northwest corner of Zhong-xiao and Yanping roads is the huge, stately and recently restored **Old Taiwan Railway Administration Building** (Taiwan Zongdufu Jiaotongju Tiedaobu Jiushe; no entry). At the time of writing, further renovations were ongoing in the surrounding area. The Old Railway Building was built by the Japanese in 1919 to serve as the nerve center of a rapidly expanding railway network. Stylistically, it incorporates elements of Tudor and 19th-century Victorian architecture. The first story is covered in the bright red brick that was popular at the time of construction, while the second story is constructed of white limestone.

The Old Taiwan Railway Administration Building.

CHINESE TEMPLE ARCHITECTURE

Beneath its brilliant colors and intricate craftsmanship, temples are built in a strictly formalized layout, without any nails or adhesives.

Look beyond the thick incense smoke and mystic apparatus of a traditional Taiwanese temple, and you will discern an architectural ethos that has been preserved for over 2,000 years.

Temples were traditionally constructed of wood, and, like other important buildings, were raised on platforms. Stylistically, the Taiwanese temple's most noticeable feature is its magnificent roof, and indeed, during imperial times, the different roof forms were codified and their uses regulated.

The spatial planning of a classical building complex revolves around the principles of insularity (the courtyard concept), axiality, symmetry, and geomancy (*fengshui*). The halls of a temple or dwelling face inward onto one or more open courtyards, and the halls and courtyards are arranged along a central longitudinal axis. The left and right sides of the complex are symmetrical along this axis. By conventional geomantic principles, a building faces south (a practice that arose in North China to take advantage of the warmer southeasterly winds and avoid the colder, sand-laden northerly winds), but subtle reorientations in response to the local topography are sanctioned to maximize the unobstructed flow of good qi (vital energy).

An example of a main hall dedicated to Mazu. The icon itself is on an altar in a recessed area. In front of it is a table for ritual offerings, and before that an incense urn. Beside the incense urn are divination implements. A plaque above expresses a benediction for calm seas.

Most temples have a large urn facing the main hall for worshippers to place incense sticks in for the main deity. Another urn, facing the entrance instead, is for the Jade Emperor, who is not represented by any icon. Don't be surprised to see worshippers praying in this direction!

Temple doors are usually painted (sometimes carved) with the images of door gods (men shen), who prevent baleful spirits from entering the temple. Additionally, the doors have raised thresholds as it is believed that ghosts cannot step over them. The central doors of many temples remain shut except during important festivals, as it is believed that these portals are only for the deities' use. Mere mortals enter by the side gates.

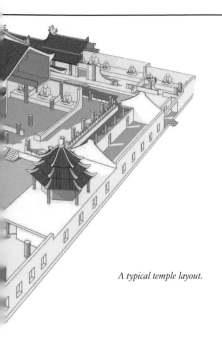

A typical temple layout.

Undoubtedly one of the most impressive features of a classical Chinese building is its raised-beam construction technique, whereby the roof is supported by successive tiers of transverse beams resting on columns. An intricate system of canti-levered brackets and trusses (dougong), fitted together precisely using mortise and tenon joints rather than nails or adhesives, supports the generous overhang of the roof eaves. These wooden members not only provide structural support for the massive roofs, but also afford an avenue for some of the most intricate carvings, intensely colored lacquer, and lustrous gold inlay.

ALTARS AND THE HEAVENLY HIERARCHY

Taiwanese temples almost always play host to more than one deity, and just as the social hierarchy governed the layout of a classical dwelling, the divine hierarchy determines how a temple's various deities are enshrined within. The temple's main deity is invariably given pride of place on the central altar of the main hall. The deity's attendants or guardian spirits flank him/her on the altar. Altars to the left and right of the main deity hold secondary (but important) deities. Lower ranking deities are enshrined in the rear hall, with the most important one(s) in the center and the less so on the left and right. The side halls house the lowest ranking deities or spirits, if any. Often, they are used to enshrine ancestral tablets, or are used as monks' quarters or administrative offices. The roof forms of a temple reflect this hierarchy, with the highest roof reserved for the main hall and the lowest roofs for the side halls. Pay attention to the "circuit" that a devotee makes through a temple, and you will see that the gods are worshipped in order of rank. A point of etiquette to note when visiting a temple: avoid pointing at the icons. It is generally considered impolite and believed to draw the ire of the deity.

In contrast to the more rigid Northern style of such structures as the National Theater (see page 125), Taiwan's oldest temples are built in the floridly decorated Southern Chinese style, the most distinctive feature of which is the gracefully upturned roof ridge ending in "swallow tail" finials. The roof ridges – and indeed most available surfaces – are vehicles for spiritually symbolic ornamentation. The dragon, a symbol of power and bringer of rain, was revered in the traditionally agrarian Chinese society. Also often seen on temple roofs are phoenixes, pagodas, and the gods of Prosperity, Happiness, and Longevity.

OLD TAIPEI: DATONG

Like many aging communities in other modern cities, Datong District's neighborhoods were left behind during Taiwan's modern economic progress. Redolent of the past, these areas have been attracting notice for their living heritage.

A t the core of Datong District are two of Taipei's oldest communities, Dadaocheng and Dalongtong, both long ago absorbed into the expanding city. In many ways, life goes on here as it did 100 years ago. Everywhere one looks, one is staring at history, and the legacies of the hardworking people that brought life to the place.

Dadaocheng

Dadaocheng can be literally translated as "large open space for drying rice in the sun." In the 1850s, the lower sections of the Taipei Basin had been taken over by Han Chinese farming folk. Along the stretch of the Danshui River occupied today by the Taipei metropolis sat two thriving Chinese market settlements, each with over 10,000 inhabitants: Mengjia, today called Wanhua (see page 99), and Dalongtong (see page 120). Dadaocheng, the large undeveloped area between these towns, was where farmers brought their rice to spread out for drying.

In 1853, old tensions between Chinese immigrant groups erupted in Wanhua, this time with more blood spilled than ever before. The

losers – their homes, ancestral halls and places of worship in ruins – straggled to Dadaocheng to begin life anew.

Dihua Street

The settlers' leaders were members of the merchant guilds, the de-facto source of leadership among the Chinese communities in Taiwan at the time, as imperial officials were not present or not trusted. Each guild was made up of immigrants from the same part of China. These

Main Attractions

Dihua Street
Xiahai City God Temple
Chen Tian-lai Residence
Dadaocheng Wharf
Taipei Circle
Musoum of Contemporary Art Taipei
Baoan Temple
Taipei Confucius Temple

Map

Page 114

Shopping at dried-food stores along Dihua Street.

Datong

men set up the standard commercial establishments of those times in shophouses, on what has become today's dynamic **Dihua Street**, the spiritual and commercial center of Dadao-cheng. Exodus leader Lin You-zao's shophouse remains today, at No. 105, on the corner of Minsheng West Road, where the Lin family still lives and runs the shop. Evidence of the bitter 1853 exodus is reflected in its name, **Lin Fu Zhen** ❶ ("Lins Restore Order").

The sections of Dihua Street just north and south of Minsheng are among Taipei's best-preserved streets. This was the core of the original settlement area, and has been the island's most important distribution center for traditional dried foods, herbs, medicines, and other goods since before the turn of the 20th century. Wholesalers still hawk many of the same goods that people have flocked here to buy for over 100 years. Chinese medicine shops cluster around the Xiahai City God Temple (see page 115) and stretch north to Minsheng, while dried-food suppliers predominate north of Minsheng, a one-stop-shopping area for dried mushrooms, tree fungus, dried fish, and shredded squid. The northern end is also home to some fine handicraft stores selling bamboo kitchenware, hand-made lanterns, and leathercraft.

Both in and around the multistory **Yongle Market** ❷ (Yongle Shichang), near the temple, are numerous fabric stores, tailors, curtain makers, and upholsterers (Tue–Sat 10am–6pm).The prices here are reasonable, and old-style textile patterns are available in abundance, including the bright country floral patterns of the Hakka people. Note the upper floors where the **Dadaocheng Theater**, which puts on traditional opera performances and puppet shows.

In recent years, the tourist street has been attracting a younger and more arty crowd, and several of the old shophouses have been renovated and converted to beautiful and atmospheric cafés, design shops, and wine bars.

Dihua's shophouse facades

Among the historic architectural examples along Dihua Street are many shophouses with neo-Baroque facades. These were added to extant structures in the 1880s and 1890s as part of the reforms encouraged by governor Liu Ming-chuan, whose goal was to learn from the West and modernize. The buildings serve as a wonderful metaphor for the reality that such emulation went only skin-deep; beyond the Western facades, the cramped interiors of the buildings are very much that of the traditional shophouse, with a family's multiple generations living in the back and working in the front.

Of particular interest is the single-story shophouse at **No. 154 ❸**, built in the open fields in 1851 by Lin Lan-tian, an entrepreneur. The decrepit structure has had many make-overs through the years, and deserves another, but Lin's descendants still live in the back and rent out the shopfront.

Xiahai City God Temple ❹

Address: 61 Dihua Street Sec. 1
Opening Hrs: daily 6am–7.30pm
Entrance Fee: free
Transportation: Shuanglian

In 1859 things were going well, and Lin You-zao built the **Xiahai City God Temple** (Xiahai Chenghuang Miao). The refugees had brought their resident City God, or Chenghuangye, out of Mengjia. Each urban agglomeration in China had its own City God, who watched over the citizens in the district and decided a person's fate after death.

Today this temple remains the area's religious and social center,

The City God's icon at Xiahai Temple.

and one of Taipei's most important places of worship. It retains much of the same look and trappings as it did in the latter 1800s, for the resident priests believe any change will alter the *fengshui* that has brought so much prosperity to the community. One of its many notable features is the **Martyrs' Memorial Hall**, set up in memory of the 38 young men slain protecting the sacred image during the 1853 clash.

The celebration of the City God's birthday, on the 13th day of the 5th lunar month (usually in June or July), has been called "North Taiwan's No. 1 Festival." The parade of the god's effigy through the streets is, in particular, a boisterous and exuberant pageant of bone-shaking loudness attended by thousands.

Ama Museum ⑤

Address: 256 Dihua Street, www.twrf. org.tw/amamuseum/
Tel: 02- 2553 7133
Opening Hrs: Tue–Sun 10am–5pm
Entrance Fee: free
Transportation: Daqiaotou

At Taiyuan Asian Puppet Theatre Museum you can try out the traditional hand puppets.

Ama Museum.

Opened in December 2016, the **Ama Museum** (A Ma Jia) is Taiwan's first museum devoted to women's rights. The ground floor houses a coffee

shop, while upstairs is an exhibition space and photo exhibit dedicated to the "comfort women" (local sex slaves of Japanese troops during World War II). *Ama* – the Taiwanese word for grandmother – is used respectfully to refer to the victims. The moving museum is privately funded and managed by the Taipei Women's Rescue Foundation, a charity committed to promoting women's rights and ending gender-based violence. The foundation is currently lobbying the Japanese government for an official apology and compensation for the *Amas*.

Taiyuan Asian Puppet Theatre Museum ❻

Address: 79 Xining N. Road, www. taipeipuppet.com
Tel: 02-2556 8909
Opening Hrs: Tue–Sun 10am–5pm
Entrance Fee: charge
Transportation: Beimen

The **Taiyuan Asian Puppet Theatre Museum** (Taiyuan Yazhou Ouxi Bowuguan), formerly the Lin Liu-Hsin Puppet Theatre Museum, serves as workshop, playhouse, and

museum. It is run by a Dutchman, Robin Ruizendaal, whose doctorate is in Chinese marionette theater. This delightful facility is filled with folk art masterpieces – over 6,000 creations from around the globe – and is his contribution to the revival of traditional arts. Lin Liu-Hsin was one of Taiwan's great puppet masters, and the two historical buildings in which the museum and its Nadou

A child plays on the anchors at the wharf.

Bitter tea served with sweet haw pellets.

BITTER TEA

Kucha, or bitter tea, is a "cooling" drink, meaning it has a *yin*, or cool, rather than *yang*, or hot, essence – even when served warm or hot. Locals do not drink *kucha* during cold weather. A single bowl of *kucha* is especially popular in summer, and is said to rid the body of many mild afflictions such as toothache, sore throat, and high blood pressure, all traditionally believed to stem directly from having too much heat in the body. Perhaps Taipei's favorite source is **Kucha Zhi Jia** (House of Bitter Tea), at Changan West Road and Chongqing North Road. Thirty-six herbs are used in its *kucha*, which is boiled for six hours for maximum flavor and effectiveness.

TIP

Bicycles rented at the Dadaocheng Wharf can be pedalled up the river towards Guandu or south towards Xindian and returned at rental stations at each place so you can grab an MRT or taxi home.

Theatre are located were donated by his widow, along with many Taiwan-puppetry treasures.

While the Nantou Theater next door will stay open, the museum itself is closed until summer 2021 so that management can inventory their enormous list of puppets and other stock.

Guide Street

Short **Guide Street** (pronounced "gway-duh") runs south from Minsheng and parallel to Dihua Street. This lane once fronted the river, and was called "Western Houses Street" because it was lined with the factories of rich local and foreign merchants. Generally, warehouses were on the first level, offices and other rooms on the second, and the factory's or owner's residence on the third. Liu Ming-chuan, Taiwan's first governor, convinced rich local families to invest in raising many of the buildings along this street to attract

A reproduction of a Qing dynasty ship is displayed at the Dadaocheng Wharf.

international trading firms, part of his efforts at modernization.

A prime example of the results is the **Chen Tian-lai Residence** ➐ (Chen Tianlai Guju), at No. 73 (private property; no entry). Chen, a tea merchant, was fabulously rich for his time, his wealth deliberately reflected in the architectural motifs and appointments of this edifice. During Japanese rule, visiting members of the imperial family were brought to this "model Taiwanese residence" for a none-too-accurate glimpse of residential life in Taiwan.

Sprouting on the old neo-Baroque buildings are subtle architectural surprises such as elegant water pipes molded in the shape of bamboo. Almost all structures on Guide Street were raised on stone foundations to keep precious goods high and dry when the temperamental Danshui River flooded, common in the typhoon season. Xining North Road, between Guide and Dihua, was

in fact a stream along which small boats plied in days of old. The stream helped with floodwater containment.

Koo Family Salt Hall ❽

One block north of Minsheng is Guisui Street. Down Lane 303 at No. 9 is the **Koo Family Salt Hall** (Gu Jia Yan Guan), an important heritage site both in terms of its architecture and its place in Taiwan's history (private property; no entry). Koo Xian-rong is renowned as the local merchant who met the Japanese forces on their march to Taipei in 1895. Alone, he asked them to hurry, as the leaderless, unpaid, and abandoned mainland Chinese forces had run amok. He almost lost his life, but thereafter he became a local the Japanese trusted, and his fortune was made. He was granted a coveted salt-monopoly license, the guaranteed road to great riches, and for a time this was both the headquarters for the family salt business and the Koo home, and thus a center for power on the island. The Koo family remains one of Taiwan's most powerful today in business and in politics. The Baroque-style residence, restored to its original grandeur at significant family expense with some city help, now houses a kindergarten.

Dadaocheng Wharf ❾

Minsheng West Road ends at an ugly dike built in the 1950s, fronting the Danshui River. On the other side is **Dadao-cheng Wharf** (Dadaocheng Matou). In the days of shipping, dry goods such as tea and rice were trans-shipped from here to ocean-going craft downriver at the port of Danshui. Dadao-cheng's commerce exploded in the 1860s as a result of three factors. First, rival Wanhua's harbor became drowned in silt, a fate Dadaocheng would only suffer in the 1890s. Second, the river was opened to Western firms by the 1858 Treaty of Tianjin after the Second Opium

A deity icon at the Baoan Temple.

War. Third, British trader John Dodd saw the potential of the nearby hills for growing Oolong tea for export, initiating the growing and processing that soon made tea the Taipei Basin's major export, followed by camphor. In 2017, the wharf was livened up by the addition of a cluster of stalls, some with rooftop seating for top views of the river, selling pizza, fast food and beer. Pier 5, as its known, is open from late afternoon until 10 or 11pm.

Blue Highway (Lansi Gonglu) river cruises launch from Dadao-cheng Wharf and head north for Guandu Wharf or Danshui's Fisherman's Wharf. The cruises offer a good way to get a clear sense of the mass and beauty of the mountains that surround the Taipei Basin. A bicycle path passes by the wharf, part of the city's larger network of bike paths that runs almost right around the city and on to the north coast at Danshui, along the Jingmei, Xindian, Danshui, and Keelong rivers.

Fazhugong Temple ❿

East of Dihua Street, down Lane 344 on Nanjing West Road, stands the unusual, multistory **Fazhugong Temple** (Fazhugong Gong; daily 8am–10pm; www.facebook.com/FaChuKungTemple), whose main altar is on the second story. The powerful icon housed within, Fazhu – a slayer of snakes and demons not widely worshipped in Taiwan – was brought from Fujian Province in imperial times by a tea merchant. With time, the god's ability to help devotees prosper in business and recover from illness became apparent, leading to the temple's role as a center of worship for Dadao-cheng's tea merchants.

On the 22nd day of the 9th lunar month (October or November), the raucous "Big Turtles Festival" is held to celebrate the deity's birthday. Supplicants ask Fazhu for red "turtle" cakes – made of glutinous rice or flour – representing a godly favor. If their request is granted, they are expected to "pay interest" by bestowing the temple with two such turtles at the next festival.

Museum of Contemporary Art Taipei ⓫

Address: 39 Changan Road, www.mocataipei.org.tw
Tel: 02-2552 3720
Opening Hrs: Tue–Sun 10am–6pm
Entrance Fee: charge
Transportation: Zhongshan

On the eastern end of Changan West Road is the **Museum of Contemporary Art Taipei** (Taibei Dangdai Yishu Guan), which once served as the city hall. This heritage site was built in 1919 by the Japanese in a red-brick hybrid of Victorian and Edwardian styles. With 11 galleries spread over two floors and no permanent exhibits, MOCA Taipei regularly juxtaposes works by foreign and local artists, concentrating on the themes of art, design, and architecture.

Dalongtong

The community of Dalongtong, at Datong District's north end, once rivaled Wanhua as a river port. The Danshui River used to flow close by (where Yanping North Road Section 4 now runs), but silting in the late 1800s caused by rapid opening up of land upstream changed its course and cut off the community's economic lifeline. Save for visits to two magnificent cultural sites, this area is relatively quiet, largely bypassed by locals and visitors alike on their way to other districts.

Baoan Temple ⓬

Address: 61 Hami Street, www.baoan.org.tw
Opening Hrs: daily 7am–11pm
Entrance Fee: free
Transportation: Yuanshan

Baoan Temple (Baoan Gong) formed and still forms the core of the old settlement; in early days the Danshui and Keelung rivers met immediately northwest of here. Begun in 1805, it took 25 years to complete. All the materials were brought over from mainland China, along with the artisans to work them. This architectural masterpiece is recognized as among Taiwan's most elaborate, and an overhaul brought an honorable mention in the 2003 Unesco Asia-Pacific Heritage Awards.

The temple's main deity is Baosheng Dadi, the God of Medicine, a real-life figure and legendary physician from the Song dynasty, born in Fujian Province's Tongan County, where the settlers in Dalongtong came from. Other important deities are Shennong, the God of Agriculture, and Mazu, Goddess of the Sea. It is believed that in the late 19th century, prayers to Shennong brought heavy rains, ending a drought lasting months. Grateful believers thereafter enshrined the icon, now in the hindmost court, honoring their otherworldly rescuer.

The temple's birthday celebrations for Baosheng Dadi and Mazu are among the island's most colorful festivals.

Taipei Confucius Temple ⓭

Address: 275 Dalong Street, www. ct.taipei.gov.tw
Tel: 02-2592 3934
Opening Hrs: Tue–Sun and national holidays 8.30am–9pm
Entrance Fee: free
Transportation: Yuanshan

Across from Baoan Temple is the **Taipei Confucius Temple** (Taibei Shi Kong Miao), set amid sculpted gardens in an expansive walled compound. Confucius was a man of simple living, it is said, so temples to the sage are places of dignity and simplicity: no icons, and little of the elaborate carvings and statuary seen on Taoist temples. However, the water dragons on the roof, said to protect the compound from fire, are characteristic of South China and Taiwan. Some believe there are no philosophical inscriptions because none dare compete with one of time's greatest literary masters.

Note the owl images on the main hall's roof. Owls are said to have been unfilial and vicious until educated by the Great Teacher. The grounds are usually quiet, but come to life each Teacher's Day, when solemn, time-honored ceremonies take place. Guided English tours are available.

Don't miss the attached 4D Theater screening two films that help understand both the Confucian system of belief and the Chinese culture (English subtitles, free). The full show takes 35 minutes, during which viewers experience a full range of physical special effects, such as snow and wind. It's a fun way to grasp Confucian thinking.

TIP

A limited number of "first come first served" seats are available for Teacher's Day celebrations at the Taipei Confucius Temple, but you'll have to line up in the wee hours to have a chance. You'll have a much better shot at the full practice run the day before, also first come first served, held in the afternoon from 4–5pm.

Tablets rather than icons represent the Great Teacher at the Confucius Temple.

Morning tai chi in the expansive square in front of the National Theater.

OLD WALLED CITY AND ZHONGZHENG

Formerly the seat of authority for the Qing and Japanese administrations in Taiwan, this area retains its grandeur through its majestic old buildings, dignified monuments, and wide boulevards.

The core of Zhongzheng District is the Old Walled City (Gucheng). Built in the early 1880s during the Qing dynasty, the east wall stretched along today's Zhongshan South Road, the south wall along Aiguo West Road, the west wall along Zhonghua Road, and the north wall along Zhongxiao West Road. In preparation for the naming of Taipei as capital of the newly created province of Taiwan in 1885, the walls were erected to house and protect the administrative seat of power.

The walls are long gone – torn down by the Japanese to facilitate troop movement and improve public sanitation after they took over in 1895 – but the sense of history lives on, as do four of the five original gates. The area is characterized by grand and imposing architectural edifices erected by the Japanese to engender awe and respect – or at least subservience – in their new subjects, and to showcase the model colony, Japan's first.

Today these buildings, all constructed in Western architectural styles, continue to fulfill practical civic functions, and impart an atmosphere of historical gravitas to the area.

To the south of the Old Walled City is a primarily residential area,

with communities centered around parks and gardens, most initiated by the Japanese on a grandiose scale. There is little commercial activity in Zhongzheng, and nights bring a blanket of quiet calm. Residents in need of raucous fun head west to Ximending (see page 106), or east to the malls and department stores of Xinyi District.

The area directly north of the Old Walled City used to be mostly scrubland or farm. The Japanese later decided to build a boulevard from

Main Attractions

Liberty Square
Chiang Kai-shek Memorial Hall
East Gate
Presidential Office Building
Taipei 228 Memorial Museum
National Taiwan Museum
Nanmen Market

Map
Page 125

The grand Presidential Office Building.

WHERE

At Chiang Kai-shek
Memorial Hall, catch the
solemn changing-of-the-
guard ceremony at the
top of each hour
(9am–5pm).

where the east wall stood, straight to the high perch where the Grand Hotel (see page 169) stands today, the location of the great Shinto shrine to which all royal visitors and appointed governors-general from the imperial homeland advanced in grand procession upon arrival. The concourse – today's Zhongshan Road – was aptly called the Imperial Way.

Liberty Square ❶

The best place to begin a tour of Zhongzheng is **Liberty Square** (Ziyou Guangchang; formerly the Chiang Kai-shek Memorial Hall Plaza), located near the Chiang Kai-shek Memorial Hall MRT station at the southernmost point of Zhongshan Road where it intersects with Aiguo Road. Liberty Square – think of the Forbidden City scenes from the movie *The Last Emperor* – is always busy with visitors looking for grand vistas and lots of space to breathe. It serves as a site for public gatherings, as well as being home to some major landmarks and a park featuring lovely sculpted gardens and serene ponds.

Chiang Kai-shek Memorial Hall ❷

Address: 21 Zhongshan S. Road Sec.

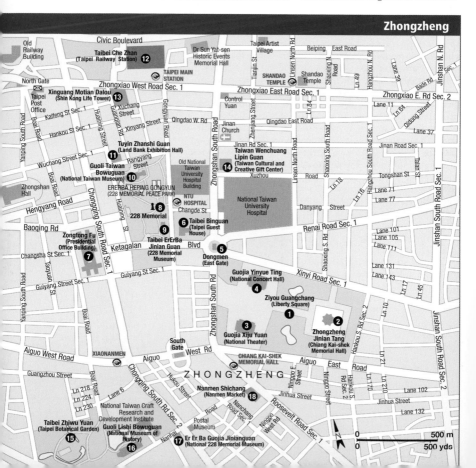

1, www.cksmh.gov.tw
Tel: 02-2343 1100
Opening Hrs: daily 9am–6pm
Entrance Fee: free
Transportation: Chiang Kai-shek Memorial Hall

Start exploring Liberty Square from its most famous landmark, the **Chiang Kai-shek Memorial Hall** (Zhongzheng Jinian Tang). The hall was built in the late 1970s to memorialize the longtime leader of the Republic of China, Chiang Kai-shek.

The magnificent structure, with a marble facade and a twin-eave roof of brilliant blue tiles crowned by a golden spur, is 76 meters (250ft) high. Inside, steps lead up to a dais three stories high, on which sits a massive statue of the Generalissimo. On the ground level are exhibits related to the former President's life, including personal effects, a mock-up of one of his offices, and a bulletproof Cadillac. There are also several exhibition spaces (charge) that host local and international cultural and art shows. English tours of the hall and grounds are available with advance application.

National Theater and Concert Hall

Address: 21 Zhongshan S. Rd Sec. 1, http://npac-ntch.org
Tel: 02-3393 9888
Opening Hrs: open for public performances only
Entrance Fee: charge varies per public performance
Transportation: Chiang Kai-shek Memorial Hall

The massive and ornate **National Theater** ❸ (Guojia Xiju Yuan) and **National Concert Hall** ❹ (Guojia Yinyue Ting) face each other across the square and stage regular traditional and modern productions. Both are built and painted in brilliant Ming-dynasty style. In fact, they are modeled after the Halls of Supreme Harmony and Preserving Harmony in the Forbidden City. The square's tremendous arched entrance, 30 meters (100ft) high and 80 meters (266ft) wide, faces China, the homesick Chiang's beloved birthplace.

One of Taipei's many wedding salons. If you're planning to tie the knot in Taipei, be aware that auspicious dates on the Chinese calendar often result in "peak" periods for nuptials.

Liberty Square gate.

Zhongzheng, which roughly means "central uprightness," is the courtesy name of Chiang Kai-shek, memorialised here; it is also the official name by which he is known in Taiwan.

The East Gate stands in front of the KMT Headquarters.

East Gate **5**

The impressive **East Gate** (Dongmen) stands in the center of the traffic circle off the northwest corner of the square. Especially pretty when lit at night, this was the largest of the five original gates. Today's ornate embellishments are not true to the original, however; renovation work was carried out in 1966 on what was originally a simple structure in Southern Chinese style.

An interesting fact about the East Gate is that this was where the Japanese military first entered the walled city in 1895 on their approach from nearby Keelung port to take possession of Taipei. History books show old photographs of Japanese officers on horseback marching proudly through the North Gate, but in fact, an advance party had slipped in through the East Gate the night before, led by local citizens who were concerned that the city was collapsing under the rampage of the mainland Chinese soldiers whose leaders had already run for home.

Taipei Guest House **6**

West on Ketagalan Boulevard, at the northeast corner of Gongyuan Road, is the exquisite **Taipei Guest House** (Taibei Binguan; www.mofa.gov.tw/tgh), considered the most elegant example of Baroque architecture in Taiwan, augmented with a roof in Mansard style and high Roman pillars. It was built on between 1897 and 1901 to serve as the Japanese Governor-General's residence. Today the site is used by the President's Office for important functions, but it is also open to the public one day a month (8am–4pm, no advance booking is required). Check the website for dates.

Presidential Office Building **7**

Address: 122 Chongqing S. Rd Sec. 2, www.president.gov.tw
Tel: 02-2311 3731
Opening Hrs: Mon–Fri 9am–noon
Entrance Fee: free (passport required)
Transportation: NTU Hospital

Built by Taiwan's Japanese colonial masters in neo-Renaissance style, the **Presidential Office Building**

LIBERTY SQUARE

It was a victory for democracy when the Chiang Kai-shek Memorial Hall Plaza was finally renamed Liberty Square in 2007 under then-President Chen Shui-bian. The imposing square, once named in honor of Chiang – who is now widely regarded as a shameful dictator – was re-dedicated to applaud Taiwan's democratic transition. At the time, however, pro-unification KMT traditionalists, who also dominated the city government, fiercely objected to the change. Statues of and memorials to Chiang Kai-shek are often a focus of controversy around the island, where they are found in parks, schools, and other public buildings. They are now slowly being removed.

(Zongtong Fu) was completed in 1919 and known as the Governor-General's Office. The heavy cost brought intense criticism from the Japanese parliament, but the elaborate red-brick edifice served its purpose, clearly demonstrating Japan's might. The central tower, 66 meters (215ft) high, served as a watchtower against attack. It was long – and by law – Taipei's tallest structure. The building was bombed by the Allies in World War II. Today's huge entrance portico was added during post-war renovations. The building is partially opened and tours given on weekdays, and fully opened for the full day on a series of weekend dates throughout each year, listed on the official website. There is also an art gallery within the complex, featuring new exhibits every few months highlighting Taiwan's fine arts and crafts.

228 Memorial Peace Park

On the north side of Ketagalan Boulevard is the shady and forested 228 Memorial Peace Park (ErErBa Heping Gongyuan). It was created by the Japanese in 1907 and was originally called Taipei New Park. In 1996 the present name was given in honor of those killed in the turmoil surrounding the infamous 2-28 Incident (see page 37) of February 28, 1947.

The park is busiest in the early morning, when it is filled with solemn practitioners of tai chi and other ancient martial arts, and senior citizens sitting under shady trees playing Chinese chess or engaged in songbird competitions. In the park's center, just inside the east entrance, is the towering **228 Memorial** **❽** (ErErBa Jinian Bei), a postmodernist steel spire held up by a base of three gigantic cubes standing on their vertices. The cubes are considered an "unnatural" shape, as opposed to the Chinese concept of the sphere as representing harmony and perfection, and symbolize the disturbance to nature represented by the 2-28 Incident. Remembrance ceremonies are held annually on February 28.

Taipei 228 Memorial Museum

Address: 3 Ketagalan Boulevard
Tel: 02-2389 7228

National Taiwan Museum.

Inside the National Taiwan Museum.

recorded English-language audio tour. There is a simple restaurant next door looking inward into the park, with a quiet, tree-shaded patio.

National Taiwan Museum ⑩

Address: 2 Xiangyang Road, www.ntm.gov.tw
Tel: 02-2382 2566
Opening Hrs: Tue–Sun 9.30am–5pm
Entrance Fee: charge
Transportation: NTU Hospital

Just inside the park's north entrance is the imposing **National Taiwan Museum** (Guoli Taiwan Bowuguan), built by the Japanese in 1915 in Greek Revival style. It was created to house the results of Japanese researchers' work on the natural history of their colony. Inside, the ground floor is reserved for international exhibitions which are usually something to do with wildlife, fossils or geology. The upper floors are reserved for Taiwan specific items, thousands collected over the past 100 years, with unmatched material on the lives of the island's original inhabitants; the indigenous peoples' trove contains more than 7,000

Opening Hrs: Tue–Sun 10am–5pm, closed days after national holiday
Entrance Fee: charge; free Feb 28 & Dec 10 (the latter being Human Rights Day)
Transportation: NTU Hospital

Near the sculpture is the **Taipei 228 Memorial Museum ⑨** (Taibei ErErBa Jinian Guan), in another heritage building built by the Japanese. It housed a radio station that was taken over by protesters in the 2-28 Incident, who broadcast demands for government reform from here. The museum has a number of poignant video presentations, with some English. Among the riveting displays on individual victims of the Incident and later White Terror, visitors can ponder the blood-stained shirt saved by a wife after her husband's execution and writings by survivors detailing the days their family members were either shot or forcibly taken from homes, never to return. There is no English translation in the displays, but the museum provides a good

WEDDING SALONS

One unique entrepreneurial phenomenon found in Taiwan (as well as Hong Kong and other overseas Chinese communities) is the wedding salon. Packages include three or four bridal gowns and the groom's tux for the reception, a pre-wedding photo shoot, wedding-day photo shoot, pre-activity hairstyling sessions, and more. Though pricey – up to US$5,000 and more – they save families a lot of hassle. The two most famous clusters of wedding salons in Taipei are on Zhongshan North Road Section 3, and on Aiguo Street beside the Chiang Kai-shek Memorial Hall grounds, which are always dotted with dressed-up couples posing.

pieces. Among the museum's most prized possessions is the original "Yellow Tiger Flag" created when local notables declared the short-lived Republic of Taiwan in 1895. Just outside the museum entrance is a pair of old steam engines that were two of the first to ply the island's railway network in colonial days, both shipped in from the West.

Land Bank Exhibition Hall ⑪

Address: 25 Xiangyang Rd, www.ntm.gov.tw/
Tel: 02-2314 2699
Opening Hrs: Tue–Sun 9.30am–5pm
Entrance Fee: charge, free 30 mins before closing
Transportation: NTU Hospital

Officially part of the National Taiwan Museum (which is across the road and a ticket for either gets you into both venues), the **Land Bank Exhibition Hall** is much more fun and impressive. Combining elements of classical western architecture and local pavilion-style embellishments, this immense structure was built back in 1923 to house the Taipei office of the Nippon Kangyo Bank. The main hall is packed with dinosaur skeletons, some hanging from the soaring ceiling. At the back you can clamber through reconstructed bank vaults. Best of all you can have a coffee on the second-floor Dino Café overlooking the panoply of prehistoric bones.

Shin Kong Life Tower

Just beyond 228 Memorial Peace Park's north entrance, and across from the mammoth **Taipei Railway Station** ⑫ (Taibei Che Zhan), which resembles the architectural giants the Soviets and Communist Chinese once loved, stands the **Shin Kong Life Tower** ⑬ (Xinguang Morian Dalou; 66 Zhongxiao W. Rd Sec. 1). For several years, the 800ft (245-meter) structure with 51 stories was Taipei's tallest. It was dwarfed by the Taipei 101 tower (see page 150) in late 2004.

At the base of the tower is a very posh and large (14 levels, two underground) **Shin Kong Mitsukoshi Department Store** (Xinguang Sanyue). At weekends, live outdoor concerts are regularly staged on the plaza fronting the tower, or on the grounds of the train station right across the street. Directly behind the tower are the cramped streets of the city's famous 'cram school' area, stuffed with specialist private schools helping students on weeknights and weekends to cram information into their heads in preparation for regular-school and TOEFL exams.

The main station district has been chosen as a construction site for one of the major Taipei projects. In early 2019 the designs for the **Taipei Twin Towers**, a multifunctional space hosting offices, shops, and tourist hotels was released. The taller tower will measure 337 meters in height (1,106ft), while the smaller will be 280 meters (919ft) tall. They have been designed to look like asymmetrical piles of giant blocks that will sit atop the Taoyuan International Airport MRT. The development, which is one of the most expensive

A vase for sale at the Taiwan Cultural and Creative Gift Center.

In the Taipei Botanical Garden.

TIP

Google Street View allows 3D virtual travel through the city's lanes and alleys before you tackle them "live." Especially in the old sections of town, the cramped, narrow-artery neighborhoods can strike the newcomer as labyrinthine.

in the city, is expected to completely overhaul Taipei's old center as the surrounding area is fully revitalized.

Taiwan Cultural and Creative Gift Center ⑭

The **Taiwan Cultural and Creative Gift Center** (Taiwan Wenchuang Lipin Guan; 1 Xuzhou Rd; daily 9am–6pm; tel: 02-2393 3655; www.handicraft.org.tw) has long been the city's most popular one-stop shop for foreign visitors looking to purchase traditional arts and crafts to take home. It is located just off Zhongshan South Road, almost equidistant from the NTU Hospital, Taipei Main Station, and Shandao Temple MRT stations. The large multistory facility stocks more than 40,000 items, everything from porcelain, cloisonné, and oil-paper umbrellas to painted fans, woodcarvings, and crystal. Prices are reasonable as the government-run facility is seen as a public relations vehicle as much as a profit-making one. Overseas shipping services are offered. You will find English-speaking staff on hand to assist you. The center also has an online store offering special discounts.

Taipei Botanical Garden ⑮

Address: 53 Nanhai Road
Tel: 02-2303 9978 ext. 1420
Opening Hrs: daily 5.30am–10pm
Entrance Fee: free
Transportation: Xiaonanmen

South of the Old Walled City are two locations especially worth visiting. From the Presidential Office Building, walk south on Chongqing South Road for about 45 minutes.

Established by the Japanese in 1921, **Taipei Botanical Garden** (Taibei Zhiwu Yuan) is an oasis within the city where all sounds of traffic are shut out. Combined with a visit to the National 228 Memorial Museum (a separate entity from the Taipei 228 Memorial Museum), this will make a fine afternoon outing.

The Botanical Garden is filled with plants and immense trees that were mere saplings when the Japanese started this experimental station and the city's airport still stood right by here, beside the Xindian River. Wide pathways meander through 17 sections of exotic plant life totaling 1,500 species. Most famous are the lotus varieties, which bloom in summer. Oddities include giant Amazonian water lilies big enough to support a man's weight, square bamboo, and two Bo trees (*Ficus religiosa*, or Sacred Fig), the type under which the Buddha achieved enlightenment.

Also found here is the Qing dynasty provincial governor's *yamen*, or headquarters, which was transported here from where Zhongshan Hall now stands.

National Museum of History ⑯

Address: 49 Nanhai Road, www.nmh.gov.tw
Transportation: Chiang Kai-shek Memorial Hall

Beside the Botanical Garden is the **National Museum of History** (Guoli Lishi Bowuguan), which is currently closed for renovation until at least 2021. It is home to about 10,000 one-of-a-kind Chinese artifacts dating from as far back as 2,000 BC. These works, unlike those in the National Palace Museum, were never in the imperial collection. The permanent exhibits on Tang dynasty tri-color pottery and Shang bronzes are especially noteworthy.

National 228 Memorial Museum ⑰

Address: 54 Nanhai Rd, http://www.228.org.tw
Tel: 02-2332 6228
Opening Hrs: Tue–Sun 10am–5pm
Entrance Fee: free
Transportation: Chiang Kai-shek Memorial Hall

A five-minute walk from Chiang Kai-shek Memorial Hall MRT station, this, the second museum dedicated to the memory of the victims of the 228 Incident in Taipei, has an excellent English audio guide of all exhibits, which lay out in detail the transgressions of justice under the early decades of KMT rule. The museum calls for a national commitment to restorative justice, and is housed in a stately corner colonial mansion that dates back to 1931.

Nanmen Market ⑱

Just south of the CKS Memorial, **Nanmen Market** (Nanmen Shichang) is Taipei's biggest and best-known day market, held on this spot for over a century (8 Roosevelt Rd Sec. 1; Tue–Sun 7am–8pm; tel: 02-2321 8069; www.nanmenmarket.org.tw). "Nanmen" means "south gate," a reference to the nearby old walled city gate. It opened in the Japanese colonial era as a vegetable distribution center, called Qiansui (Thousand Year) Market. Originally

a single-story structure, it was completely overhauled in 1983 and emerged multi-storied. In 2012, it was thoroughly refurbished yet again, and now it is bright, stylish, and air-conditioned in all areas.

Goods are brought in from all around Taiwan, and for many years the market has been a key Taipei source for Jiangzhe (China's Jiangsu and Zhejiang provinces) produce. Before Chinese New Year, the place is really hopping, for here you'll find some of the most popular holiday foods, such as sausages, traditional preserved hams, cooked foods, snacks, cookies, steamed mincemeat-stuffed buns, and steamed breads. If any one booth can be recommended it should be Yi-chang Yufang (Yi-chang's Imperial Workshop), which has won the Top Cooked-Food Vendor award during the Taipei Traditional Market Festival several times. It specializes in Jiangzhe cuisine and has more than 100 cold and hot-prepared-food choices.

A display at the National Museum of History. English signage is sporadic; invaluable English-language tours are given at 10.30am and 3pm daily.

The Taipei Fine Arts Museum.

CENTRAL TAIPEI

Much of this area, while in a central part of the city, is not exactly "downtown." In fact, visitors looking to experience a sampling of heritage, culture, or just some green open spaces, will be amply rewarded.

Taipei residents tend to think of the Zhongshan District as the primarily open, green area of parkland on the southern bank of the Keelung River. In fact, this central district, bounded in the south by Civic Boulevard, covers a larger area.

From the 1950s until the late 1980s, tree-lined Zhongshan North Road was the epicenter of Taiwan's fashion scene, where the big clothing brands set up shop. The city's international hotels were also located here. But the temples of fashion have since migrated to the boutique areas east, and the newest big-brand hotels are also mostly located in the eastern business district. A stroll along Zhongshan Road from south to north reveals an area with a slightly more genteel flair – perhaps giving a better feel of the city's pulse than its more frantic environs.

Shandao Temple ❶

Address: 23 Zhongxiao E. Road Sec. 1, www.shandaotemple.org.tw
Tel: 02-2341 5758
Opening Hrs: Tue–Sun 8am–5pm
Entrance Fee: free
Transportation: Shandao Temple
Shandao Temple (Shandao Si) was opened in 1935; one of seven major temple sites constructed by Japanese

Buddhists during the colonial period. Today it is the largest of the city's most important Buddhist temples. The nine-story structure is architecturally quite unlike other Taiwan temples, faintly resembling a giant funerary tower in its stark austerity. Inside, it also lacks much of the clamor and jostle typical of other temples.

Taipei Artist Village ❷

Address: 7 Beiping E. Road, www.artistvillage.org
Tel: 02-3393 7377

The meditative Shandao Temple hall.

Central Taipei

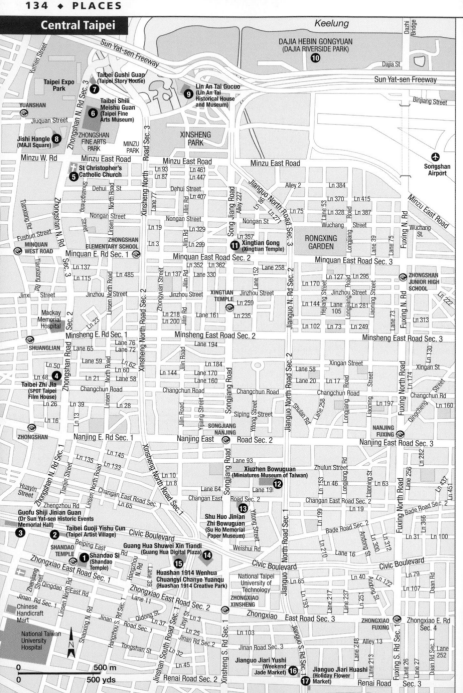

Keelung

Dazhi Bridge

Sun Yat-sen Freeway

Yumin Street

Taipei Expo Park

Taibei Gushi Guan (Taipei Story House) **7**

Lin An Tai Gucuo (Lin An Tai Historical House and Museum) **9**

DAJIA HEBIN GONGYUAN (DAJIA RIVERSIDE PARK) **10**

Dajia St

Sun Yat-sen Freeway

Binjiang Street

YUANSHAN

Jiquan Street

Taibei Shili Meishu Guan (Taipei Fine Arts Museum) **6**

ZHONGSHAN FINE ARTS PARK

MINZU PARK

XINSHENG PARK

Songshan Airport

Jishi Hangle (MAJI Square) **8**

Minzu W. Rd

Minzu East Road

Minzu East Road

Minzu East Road

Minzu East Road

St Christopher's Catholic Church **5**

Ln 352 Ln 87 Ln 461 Ln 447

Xinsheng North Road

Jianguo North Road

Alley 2 Ln 384

Ln 370 Ln 415

Tianxiang Rd

Zhongshan N. Rd Sec. 3

Linsen North Road St

Shuangcheng Street

Dehui Street

Dehui St Ln 407

Alley 227

Song Jiang Road

Ln 271

Ln 75 Lane 53

Ln 328 Ln 387

Fushun Street

Nongan Street

Ln 19

Nongan Street

Nongan St

Wuchang

Lane 49

Fuxing N. Rd

Wuchang St.

MINQUAN WEST ROAD

Zhongshan N. Rd Sec. 3

ZHONGSHAN ELEMENTARY SCHOOL

Ln 3

Jilin Rd Ln 329

Jilin Rd Ln 299

Ln 357

Xingtian Gong (Xingtian Temple) **11**

RONGXING GARDEN

Longjiang

Liaoning

Ln 39 Ln 75

ZHONGSHAN JUNIOR HIGH SCHOOL

Ln 222

Minquan E. Rd Sec. 1

Minquan East Road Sec. 2

Minquan East Road Sec. 3

Ln 137

Ln 485

Ln 137 Rd

Ln 352 Lane 330

Jinzhou Street

Lane 152

Lane 258

Ln 170

Ln 127 Ln 295

Heijiang St

Ln 313

Ln 115

Zhongshan Road

Zhongshan N. Rd Sec. 2

Jinxi Street

Jinzhou Street

XINGTIAN TEMPLE

Ln 259

Jinzhou Street

Lane 105

Ln 144

Lane 281

Fuxing North Road

Ln 73

Mackay Memorial Hospital

Ln 23

Linsen North Street

Ln 218 Ln 200 Rd

Lane 161

Ln 235

Ln 102 Ln 73 Ln 249

SHUANGLIAN

Minsheng E. Rd Sec. 1

Minsheng East Road Sec. 2

Minsheng East Road Sec. 3

Lane 76 Lane 72

Lane 194

Lane 65

Ln 62

Jilin Road

Ln 144 Lane 170 Lane 160

Lane 184

Lane 58

Jianguo North Rd Sec. 2

Xingan Street

Lane 130

Xingan St

Ln 50 Ln 48 **4**

Ln 60 Ln 21 Lane 58

Lane 20 Ln 17

Ln 174

Taibei Zhi Jia (SPOT Taipei Film House)

Changchun Road

Changchun Road

Changchun Road

Lane 258

Changchun Rd

Ln 197

Ln 160

Ln 26 Ln 39

Ln 13

Ln 28

Yijiang Street

Jilin Road

Siping Street

Yitong Street

Shulan Rd

Lane 19

Qingcheng Street

Ln 16

ZHONGSHAN

Nanjing E. Rd Sec. 1

SONGJIANG NANJING

Nanjing East **Road Sec. 2**

Jianguo North Rd Sec. 2

NANJING FUXING

Nanjing East Road Sec. 3

Ln 135 Ln 133

Ln 145

Xinsheng North Road Sec. 1

Lane 93

Ln 282

Zhongshan N. Rd Sec. 1

Tianjin Street

Linsen North Street

Ln 10 Ln 8

Changan East

Xiuzhen Bowuguan (Miniatures Museum of Taiwan) **12**

Zhulun Street

Lane 256

Ln 437 Ln 451

Huayin Street

Zhengzhou Rd

Changan East Road Sec. 1

Ln 65

Lane 64

Road Sec. 2

Ln 153 Ln 46

Ln 63

Ln 19

Bade Road Sec. 2

Ln 366

Guofu Shiji Jinian Guan (Dr Sun Yat-sen Historic Events Memorial Hall) **3**

Taibei Guoji Yishu Cun (Taipei Artist Village) **2**

Civic Boulevard

Shu Huo Jinian Zhi Bowuguan (Su Ho Memorial Paper Museum) **13**

Songjiang Road

Bade Road Sec. 2

Ln 210

Lane 16

Ln 31 Ln 100

SHANDAO TEMPLE

Shandao Si (Shandao Temple) **1**

Guang Hua Shuwei Xin Tiandi (Guang Hua Digital Plaza) **14**

Weishui St

Civic Boulevard

Andong St

Ln 312

Ln 79

Civic Boulevard

Zhenjiang Street

Zhongxiao East Rd

Beiping East Rd

Hangzhou N. Rd

Huashan 1914 Wenhua Chuangyi Chanye Yuanqu (Huashan 1914 Creative Park) **15**

National Taipei University of Technology

ZHONGXIAO XINSHENG

Ln 65

Ln 277 Ln 237

Ln 251

Ln 40

Ln 122

Ln 107

Zhongxiao East Road Sec. 1

Qingdao Rd

Hangzhou S. Rd

Lane 11

Zhongxiao East Road Sec. 2

Lane 1 Ln 3

Zhongxiao East Road Sec. 3

Ln 193

ZHONGXIAO FUXING

Fuxing S. Rd Sec. 1

Zhongxiao E. Rd Sec. 4

Jinan Rd Sec. 1

Linsen North Road

Jinan Rd Sec. 1

Qidong St

Ln 25

Jinan Road Sec. 2

Ln 37 Ln 3

Ln 32

Ln 103

Jinan Road Sec. 3

Ln 213 Ln 248

Daan Rd

Lane 27

Lane 252

Chinese Handicraft Mart

Shaoxing N. Rd

Tongshan St

Ln 45

Renai Road Sec. 2

Jianguo Jiari Yushi (Weekend Jade Market) **16**

Jianguo Jiari Huashi (Holiday Flower Market) **17**

Xinsheng S. Rd Sec. 1

Jianguo S. Rd Sec. 2

Renai Road Sec. 3

Ln 26

National Taiwan University Hospital

N

0 — 500 m

0 — 500 yds

Opening Hrs: Tue–Sun 11am–9pm
Entrance Fee: free
Transportation: Shandao Temple

Located just 5 minutes on foot west of Shandao Temple is the **Taipei Artist Village** (Taibei Guoji Yishu Cun). It is housed in a heritage building that was constructed by the city's Public Works Bureau in 1953 and rescued and restored in 2001. At the Taipei Artist Village the focus is on experimental cross-cultural creation; local artists and overseas talents are brought together in an artist-in-residence program to stimulate and share their creative juices. These artistic practitioners are drawn from all disciplines: visual, literary, musical, moving image, photographic, performance. The facility has 10 live-in studios serving as artists' accommodations and work spaces. There is also an exhibition space, a lovely small garden and a small café/bar. In 2010, a twin artist village in the Treasure Hill was opened, which – because it is located far from urban residential areas and has lots of space – is able to hold much more vibrant cultural activities than the TAV (see page 164).

Dr Sun Yat-sen Historic Events Memorial Hall ❸

Address: 46 Zhongshan N. Road Sec. 1
Tel: 02-2381 3359
Opening Hrs: Tue–Sun 9am–5pm
Entrance Fee: free
Transportation: Taipei Main Station

West of the Taipei Artist Village is **Dr Sun Yat-sen Historic Events Memorial Hall** (Guofu Shiji Jinian Guan), a little oasis transplanted from old Japan into the middle of the modern metropolis whizzing by on all sides. Sun Yat-sen stayed here in 1913 when in Taiwan to drum up support to retake power in China from the usurping warlord Yuan Shikai. This was then the Umeyashiki Inn, one of Taiwan's few high-class accommodations. The walled compound features a small sculpted park in Japanese style, lined with footpaths, gurgling pools, and miniature bridges (open daily). Inside the wood-frame inn, paraphernalia on Sun's life and times are displayed. Incidentally, the inn was once about 50 meters (165ft) northeast, where Civic Boulevard now runs; it was shifted here decades ago when the railway line was moved underground

Dr Sun Yat-sen Historic Events Memorial Hall.

SPOT Taipei Film House ❹

Address: 18 Zhongshan N. Road Sec. 2, www.spot.org.tw
Tel: 02-2551 7786
Opening Hrs: daily 10am–midnight, café closes at 9pm
Entrance Fee: charge (SPOT Cinema)
Transportation: Zhongshan

About 15 minutes north is the white stucco **SPOT Taipei Film House** (Taibei Zhi Jia). This heritage building was constructed around 1925 in a loose American-antebellum style. It was first used as the US consulate, then served as the ambassador's residence for the US when Taiwan and the US still maintained formal diplomatic relations. Today the facility is dedicated to non-mainstream movies, notably independent and arthouse works. The former garage has been converted into the cozy 98-seat SPOT Cinema.

In the main structure is a small bookstore with books and products related to film. SPOT Le Ballon Rouge, a wine lounge, is on the airy second level, and a café, SPOT Café Lumière, on the ground level. The courtyard is a wonderful place for leisurely reading and people-watching.

Little Manila

Most days of the week, the area around Zhongshan Road and Dehui Street, about 20 minutes north of SPOT Taipei Film House, is quiet. But on Sunday, the weekly day off for the many Filipino workers, the area is transformed into their social turf, colloquially known as **Little Manila** (Xiao Manila) and centered on the modest looking **St Christopher's Catholic Church** ❺ (51 Zhongshan N. Rd Sec. 3; Sun 8am–dusk; tel: 02-2594 7914). The church offers services in English and is packed from mid-morning into the early afternoon with Filipino worshippers. There are also a number of Filipino-owned grocery stores and eateries in the area. English and Tagalog fill the air for the day, as does music from the home islands, often accompanied by impromptu dancing. Best of all, however, is the sheer sense of joyful revelry that prevails. Little Manila is just a 10-minute walk east of Minquan West Road MRT station.

Taipei SPOT Film House.

Taipei Expo Park

Created as the site for the Taipei International Flora Exposition in 2010, the Taipei Expo Park is a multifunctional performance and exhibition venue (www.taipei-expopark.tw; opening hours vary across venue; tel: 02-2596 1546). Apart from hosting the Taipei Fine Arts Museum, the Taipei Story House and Lin An Tai Historical House and Museum, this enormous three-sectioned park is also home to a number of sights, including the Expo Dome (whose architecture resembles a bamboo basket); the Expo Hall; the Pavilion of Angel Life, which has an art gallery and serves afternoon tea; the EcoARK, a massive boat-building made from 1.52 million recycled bottles; and fun MAJI Square, an outdoor food court that shows movies at night, with a small merry-go-round and pub-style bars at the rear.

Taipei Fine Arts Museum ❻

Address: 181 Zhongshan N. Road Sec. 3, www.tfam.museum
Tel: 02 2595 7696
Opening Hrs: Tue–Sun 9.30am–– 5.30pm, Sat until 8.30pm
Entrance Fee: charge, free on Sat after 5pm
Transportation: Yuanshan

Situated directly across Zhongshan North Road on the eastern side of the complex is the **Taipei Fine Arts Museum** (Taibei Shili Meishu Guan). The entry fee of just NT$30 is one of the city's best deals. It has over 4,500 pieces in its permanent collection of works by local and overseas artists. Most of them are contemporary and are paintings. The second-level galleries reflect Taiwan's history through contemporary art – primarily oil paintings – in exhibits rotated every six months. Guided tours in foreign languages can be provided with advance notice, and there are also audio tours.

Taipei Story House ❼

Address: 181-1 Zhongshan N. Road Sec. 3, www.storyhouse.com.tw
Tel: 02- 2586 3677
Opening Hrs: Tue–Sun 10am–5.30pm
Entrance Fee: charge
Transportation: Yuanshan

One of the Filipino grocery stores in Little Manila. Workers from the Philippines account for the second-largest group of foreign laborers in Taiwan.

Taipei Fine Arts Museum.

The view from the riverside is even better at night.

Right beside the museum is the charming **Taipei Story House** (Taibei Gushi Guan), colloquially known as Yuanshan Villa after the hill just north of the river, on which today's Grand Hotel is perched. A mock Tudor mansion built in 1914 by a Dadaocheng tea merchant, it was used during the colonial period by the Japanese police to incarcerate and interrogate political activists. The building currently houses an art showroom and exhibits on the history of Taipei, focusing on the importance of the common working folk and the tea industry – but at the time of writing was closed for restoration (check the website for updates).

MAJI Square ❽

Address: 1 Yumen Street, http://www.majisquare.com
Tel: 02-2597 7112
Opening Hrs: daily 11am–10pm
Entrance Fee: free
Transportation: Yuanshan
MAJI Square (Jishi Hangle), near the MRT station, is an outdoor foodcourt that has a wide selection of international fare, healthy options, and

fried goodies. It's particularly lively at night when they switch the big screen on for movies. MAJI Square is under the flight path of planes landing at the nearby Songshan Airport, so it can be quite dramatic. Live music and beer complete the picture.

Lin An Tai Historical House and Museum ❾

Address: 5 Binjiang Street, http://english.linantai.taipei
Tel: 02- 2599 6026
Opening Hrs: Tue–Sun 9am–5pm
Entrance Fee: free
Transportation: Yuanshan
About 15 minutes on foot east of the Fine Arts Museum is the **Lin An Tai Historical House and Museum** (Lin An Tai Gucuo). This is one of the few traditional courtyard complexes still extant in north Taiwan, and the best-preserved in Taipei. The Lins were a powerful merchant family from Fujian Province and their wealth is evident. They flouted imperial rules when they used swallow-tail roofs, then the exclusive privilege of high-level mandarins. In fact, many merchant families in north Taiwan

scorned these restrictions and the representatives of the Qing court sent to keep an eye on things. Such families had private militias for protection since the officials were inadequate at keeping law and order. Building of the complex started in 1820, and the stone used was brought by ship from Fujian, as were the artworks and craftsmen. The flagstones of the wide forecourt before the main entrance were ballast from the Lin ships.

The large pool before the forecourt is a *fengshui* device; its shining surface deflects negative *qi* from sweeping in through the main portal. It also had practical functions, such as to raise fish, as a water source to quell fires, to cool incoming breezes, and as a defense line if under attack. Be sure to pick up the brochure at the ticket office, the only information in English at the complex.

Dajia Riverside Park ⑩

Dajia Riverside Park (Dajia Hebin Gongyuan) is a 12km-long (7-mile) green belt on the south bank of the Keelung River, starting from just east of the Taipei Fine Arts

Museum and running all the way to Nangang Software Park. The section of the river nearest the museum was "straightened" in the mid-1990s to ease water flow and alleviate constant flooding. It is the venue for the city's annual Taipei International Dragon Boat Race Championships, which attracts teams from around the globe.

The city's bicycle-path network runs along both sides of the river, and bike rentals are available. Bikes can be dropped off at other kiosks along the network. The dike walls that shut off the park from the city proper are

Bicycles can be rented for rides in Dajia Riverside Park.

The fairytale facade of the Taipei Story House.

lined with attractive city-sanctioned graffiti art; the authorities paint over the walls every four months and the artists start again. There is food and drink available, from licensed vendors who drive in little catering-type trucks and set up temporary open-air eateries and cafés.

Xingtian Temple ⑪

Address: 109 Minquan E. Road Sec. 2, www.ht.org.tw
Tel: 02-2502 7924
Opening Hrs: daily 4am–10pm
Entrance Fee: free
Transportation: Xingtian Temple

At the corner of Songjiang Road and Minquan East Road is the thriving **Xingtian Temple** (Xingtian Gong), a large complex built in the 1960s dedicated to Guan Gong, the God of War. Guan Gong was originally a mortal, a renowned general during the Three Kingdoms Period (184–280). His gift for strategy and tactics has also made him the patron deity of businessmen – hence the

Praying in Xingtian Temple.

sleek cars often found parked in front of the temple. Black-bearded Guan Gong is easy to identify from among the Chinese pantheon of deities because of his red face, said to have been given to him in his youth by an immortal as a disguise after he killed a local bully. Known from folktales as a defender of the weak, and revered for his righteousness and loyalty, he is a key figure in the Chinese classic *Romance of the Three Kingdoms*.

In 2014, the temple began restricting food offerings and the burning of incense and paper, so you can no longer see the incense urn with two golden-winged dragons clinging to each side. Instead, people clap their hands and bow their head to pray. Some of the temple workers are allowed to light special joss sticks that emit less smoke. In the evenings the temple transforms into an ethereal world, as delicate small lanterns are lit and believers walk about with candles.

Just outside the temple, the underground pedestrian passages under the Songjiang-Minquan intersection are filled with fortune-tellers, who do a brisk trade. Within each stall, the faithful sit wide-eyed, intently listening to the prognostications of the oracles on matters such as the right time to open a business or sign contracts, when to hold a wedding or whether to hold one at all, how a child will do in an exam, and other pivotal moments in life.

Miniatures Museum ⓬

Address: B1, 96 Jianguo N. Road Sec. 1, www.mmot.com.tw
Tel: 02-2515 0583
Opening Hrs: Tue–Sun 10am–6pm
Entrance Fee: charge
Transportation: Songjiang Nanjing

The **Miniatures Museum of Taiwan** (Xiuzhen Bowuguan) houses a superb collection of miniatures from around the world, brought together by the husband-and-wife owners. Instantly bringing out the inner child in adult visitors are the many wonderful works such as the tiny Roman ruins, a Lilliputian world, the inside of Buckingham Palace, and Thunder River, an old Colorado pioneer town regularly and convincingly hit by a particularly violent thunderstorm. But the museum's signature piece is the mini Rose Mansion by renowned miniatures artist Reginald Twigg, which took him four years and has been judged one of the most important miniature artworks in modern times. The original mansion, now demolished, was for a long time a Los Angeles landmark.

Su Ho Memorial Paper Museum ⓭

Address: 68 Changan E. Road Sec. 2, www.suhopaper.org.tw
Tel: 02-2507 5535
Opening Hrs: Mon–Sat 9.30am–4.30pm
Entrance Fee: charge
Transportation: Songjiang Nanjing

WHERE

Less well known than the jade and flower markets, but certainly worth a look, is the long gallery of stalls under the Jianguo flyover on the south side of Xinyi Road. Various handicrafts made by people with mental and physical impairments are sold here.

Making paper at the Su Ho Paper Museum.

A park food vendor.

The Chinese have a love affair with the written word and the paper it is written on. Indeed, paper was considered one of the "Four Treasures of the Study" *(Wenfang Si Bao)* by classical Chinese scholars.

The **Su Ho Memorial Paper Museum** (Shu Huo Jinian Zhi Bowuguan) was founded by the Chen family in loving memory of Chen Shu-huo, one of Taiwan's last few masters of papermaking, who was killed in 1990 in a plane crash. There are exhibits here on the materials and processes of papermaking, its history in Taiwan, and the handmade papers of different periods and cultures. There is a fine mock-up of a traditional handmade paper workshop, and guests can even try their hand at creating their own paper mementos, as well as making the paper itself, and engage in science games to understand paper better. There is also a great paper-themed gift shop.

Guang Hua Digital Plaza  ⓮

Housed in a six-level building featuring state-of-the-art amenities, **Guang Hua Digital Plaza** (Guanghua Shuwei Xin Tiandi) is located on Civic Boulevard between Jinshan and Xinsheng roads (www.gh3c.com.tw; daily 10am–9pm; tel: 02-2391 7105). This is the city's best place to scout for computers and related gadgets and peripherals, pulsing with a steady stream of technology lovers fervently shopping for the latest electronics. There are hundreds of outlets, all stuffed to the rafters, and both buyers and sellers know their stuff. Many of the goods are Taiwan-made, and while prices don't match, say, Hong Kong, they are certainly lower than in Western countries. Many vendors can speak a little English – or rather, techno-speak. Just next door, another tech-mall, the futuristic-looking **Syntrend Creative Park**, was opened in 2015. The intent is to make the district one of the world's most important sites for shopping for the newest high-tech electronic goods, superior to Tokyo's Akihabara Electric Town.

Huashan Creative Park ⓯

Address: 1, Bade Rd Sec. 1, www.huashan1914.com
Tel: 02-2358-1914
Opening Hrs: varies with venue, park open 24 hrs
Entrance Fee: free except for exhibitions or events
Transportation: Zhongxiao Xinsheng

This sprawling park is built around a renovated wine factory dating from the Japanese colonial era. The ivy-clad brick buildings and their spooky corridors house a number of decent restaurants and cafés, pop-up shops selling the work of young designers, SPOT Huashan (sister arthouse cinema to the SPOT cinema in Zhongshan), performance spaces, and huge warehouses where temporary, and often international exhibitions, are held. Previous events include the Upside Down House and the animated magic of Japan's Studio Ghibli (of *Spirited Away* fame). To the rear of the complex is an actual green leafy park with a lily-padded pond and a rock garden.

Weekend Jade Market ⓰

Further south, on the north side of Renai Road under the Jianguo flyover, is the **Jianguo Weekend Jade Market** (Jianguo Jiari Yushi), which springs to life on weekends (Sat–Sun 9am–6pm; see page 75). It is north Taiwan's mecca for lovers of this shiny stone, and with about 850 vendors, it is one of Asia's largest jade markets. On sale are crafted pieces both antique and contemporary, plus cut stones au naturel.

The myriad small pieces make good gifts. Prices are quite reasonable, and haggling is accepted for anything about NT$1000 or higher. The gift-buying possibilities are augmented by such handicrafts as woodcarvings, bambooware, and ceramic tea sets. Be prepared to brave the crowds, as some 20,000 to 30,000 throng the jade and flower markets each weekend.

Holiday Flower Market ⓱

On the south side of Renai Road, also under the Jianguo flyover, is the **Jianguo Holiday Flower Market** (Jianguo Jiari Huashi; www.fafa.org.tw; Sat–Sun 9am–6pm), to which growers come from Neihu, Yangmingshan, or as far away as central Taiwan to sell their blooms. The scores of small stalls sell both common and exotic flowers and much more, such as pot-holders, vases, seeds, seedlings, garden tools, and many types of plants, including bonsai *(penzai)*. Prices are far lower here than at local florists. Some stalls have prices posted, but many don't to allow sellers to gauge buyer interest. Haggling is possible, and experienced buyers often wait until shortly before closing time to make a purchase, knowing sellers will be eager.

Bangles at the Jianguo Weekend Jade Market.

The Taipei 101 tower, the city's principal icon and formerly the tallest building in the world.

TAIPEI EAST

The city's east end is about money; this white-collar world pulses with the exuberance of those who know how to make it and those who have the insatiable desire to spend it. Further east, the skyscrapers give way to hillside tea plantations.

U p to the early 1970s, Taipei's eastern district was largely an area of sugar-cane fields and rice paddies. Then there was an upsurge of new construction on the east side of Fuxing Road. Residents from the west flocked to the new facilities in search of fun. Pacific SOGO Department Store went up in the early 1980s, attracting myriad other entertainment and retail enterprises and establishing the area as the city's financial, commercial, shopping, and entertainment core. In the mid-1990s, the remaining open area between Keelung Road and the mountains was developed, and it is this, the Xinyi District, that is the city's new heart and the island's definer of chic upscale fashion.

DINGHAO

The **Dinghao** shopping and entertainment area is concentrated along the main thoroughfares and back-alley mazes spreading out from the Dunhua North Road and Zhongxiao East Road intersection. *Dinghao* translates as "top best." The area grew eastward from SOGO, and that department store remains its fulcrum. Accessed via key bus routes and two MRT lines, this is the city's prime area for people to link up after

work and on weekends. Here the visitor finds cocktail and craft beer bars, fashion boutiques serving upscale customers, more youth-oriented outlets, quality restaurants and inexpensive eateries, cinemas showing Western films, jewelry shops, art galleries, and more.

SOGO Department Store ❶

The original **Pacific SOGO Department Store** (Taipingyang SOGO Bai-huo Gongsi; Sun–Thu 11am–9.30pm, Fri–Sat and the day

Main Attractions
National Dr Sun Yat-sen
  Memorial Hall
Discovery Center of Taipei
Taipei 101
Four Beasts Mountains
Raohe Street Nightmarket
Ciyou Temple
Museum of the Institute of
  History and Philology

Map
Page 146

Staff of the Pacific SOGO Department Store.

The light-filled and airy central atrium of the Breeze Center, with its modern glass interpretation of the classical dome, imparts a touch of class intended to appeal to the mall's well-heeled clientele.

before holidays 11am–10pm; tel: 02-2776 5555; www.sogo.com.tw) is located just outside the Zhongxiao Fuxing MRT station at 45 Zhongxiao E. Road Sec. 4. The station is fed by two major lines and sees a tremendous flow of commuter traffic. SOGO launched the department store craze in the 1980s, leading to the super-mall craze that has gripped the nation since the late 1990s. Through the years, what locals simply call "SOGO," though there are now other outlets, has continued to be a popular department store.

Its basement connects directly to the underground East Metro Mall (10am–10pm), which is lined with retail outlets, eateries, and tasteful artworks, and runs from Zhongxiao Fuxing past Zhongxiao Dunhua MRT station.

Breeze Center ❷

The massive **Breeze Center** (Weifeng Guangchang; Sun–Wed 11am–9.30pm, Thu–Sat 11am–10pm; tel: 0809-008888; www.breeze-center.com), just north of SOGO at 39 Fuxing South Road, is a competitor in the super-mall stakes, providing a mix of upmarket facilities targeted at white-collar workers. Shopping, dining, and entertainment options are all under one roof. There is a six-screen cineplex of international caliber. There are now Breeze Centers all over the city.

Just south of Dinghao, where the wide, tree-lined Dunhua South Road and Renai Road cross paths, is **Renai Traffic Circle** (Renai Yuanhuan), on and around which a number of big-name international designer boutiques have a presence.

Eslite Bookstore ❸

Immediately north of Renai Traffic Circle is perhaps the most popular bookstore in the city, the former flagship outlet of **Eslite Bookstore** (Chengpin Shudian) at the corner

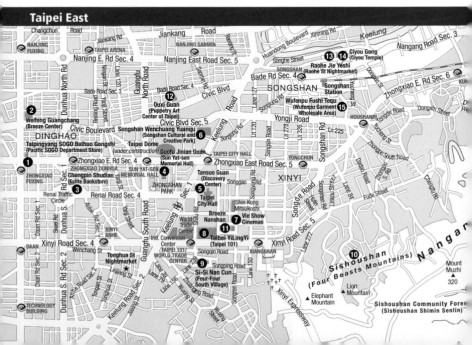

Taipei East

of Dunhua and Anhe roads (daily 24 hours; tel: 02-2775 5977; www.eslite.com). It is home to the city's best selection of English titles. Opened in the early 1990s, this venue transformed the island's book-buying scene. It was the first bookstore in Taiwan to give browsers wide aisles, a well-lit and smart-looking interior (with hardwood floors), and places to sit for more comfortable perusing. Other big outlets have been forced to follow suit to survive. This was also the world's first bookstore-chain outlet to open 24 hours. People-watching is raised to an art form in the adjoining café, which looks into the always-busy store, and on the basement levels are boutique outlets and a good food court.

Sun Yat-sen Memorial Hall ➍

Address: 505 Renai Road Sec. 4, https://en.yatsen.gov.tw
Tel: 02-2758 8008

Opening Hrs: daily 9am–6pm
Entrance Fee: free except for stage performances
Transportation: Sun Yat-sen Memorial Hall

East of Dinghao is the **National Dr Sun Yat-sen Memorial Hall** (Guofu Jinian Guan), dedicated to the man called the "father of modern China" in both China and Taiwan. The memorial sits in the expansive, beautifully sculpted **Zhongshan Park** (Zhongshan Gongyuan), which is full of colorful flowers and shady groves of lushly foliaged trees. The grounds are filled at all times with people of all ages, giving it a real community feel. In the morning come to see the organized legions of tai chi practitioners, and at night and on weekends this is a popular spot for kids to fly kites. Another glimpse into local ways awaits on the north side of the building, where you'll see a long, straight pathway of

Patrons of the Eslite Bookstore on Dunhua Road are welcome to browse as long as they wish; the store is open 24 hours daily.

Café at the Songshan Cultural and Creative Park.

Taipei East

ANG
Nangang Rd Sec. 1
ec.2
Zhongxiao East ⊘ Road Sec.7
er NANGANG
ruction) Hengke Rd
Hongdao St

Lishi Wenwu Chenlie Guan
(Museum of the Institute of History and Philology) ⑰

Academia Sinica ⑱

n t a i n
Hu Shi Jinian Guan
HU SHI GONGYUAN (Hu Shih Memorial
(HU SHIH PARK) Hall) ⑯

Academia Road Sec. 3

ang
Second Northern Freeway
ge

0   800 m
0   800 yds

N

At the Discovery Center of Taipei, a free audio and text guide is available by depositing your ID. Free English tours are available for groups of 30 or more (advance notice is required).

In the Sun Yat-sen Memorial Hall.

cobblestones set in cement with their ends up rather than laid flat. Using the same principles on which acupuncture is based, locals take their shoes off and walk the path, massaging their feet and improving the metabolism.

Just inside the hall's main entrance is an imposing six-meter-tall (19ft) bronze statue of the iconic "national father." In the exhibition area, visitors can watch a 30-minute multimedia presentation on his life and times, and take in historical photos and other physical documents from his day, many of which were his personal items. Cultural performances are regularly staged at the hall.

Discovery Center of Taipei ❺

Address: 1F, 1 Shifu Road, http://discovery.gov.taipei/en/museum
Tel: 1999
Opening Hrs: Tue–Sun 9am–5pm
Entrance Fee: free
Transportation: Taipei City Hall

The multilevel **Discovery Center of Taipei** (Taibei Tansuo Guan), in Taipei City Hall, takes visitors through the history of the city, with an emphasis on hands-on displays. The Taipei Impressions Hall on the first floor is a visual introduction to the city, featuring five screens that showcase various facets of Taipei. The second level features special exhibitions related to the city's seasons, festivals, and current issues. The third floor has displays on the city's ever-changing skyline and major thoroughfares, and its efforts to make itself a cultural capital, bring a renaissance to its old west side, and make itself a true eco-friendly living space. The fourth level is the pearl, full of educational displays such as mock-ups of the old walled city gates and cutaway models of the city's wetlands and imperial and colonial buildings. Scale models show the Taipei Basin's waterway-reservoir system, the city's old sections in imperial days, and a ship's hold

carrying pioneers from China in the mid-1600s.

There is an abundance of vintage photographs and old film footage, including a video clip showing Chiang Kai-shek's daily open-limo ride down Zhongshan Road from his residence in Shilin District.

The 200-seat **Discovery Theater** (Faxian Juchang) is on the fourth level of the center. It features a 360-degree wraparound screen, with a quartet of short movies shown in sequence at regular times, exploring Taipei's past, present, and projected future. A virtual tour of the Discovery Center of Taipei is available free at http://vr.taipeitravel.net.

Songshan Cultural and Creative Park ⑥

Address: 133 Guangfu South Road, www.songshanculturalpark.org
Tel: 02-2765 1388
Opening Hrs: daily 9am–6pm
Entrance Fee: free
Transportation: Taipei City Hall

Set in sculptured gardens and built out of a renovated Japanese tobacco factory complex, the **Songshan Cultural and Creative Park** (Songshan Wenchuang Yuanqu) is a tranquil space filled with arty cafés, design shops, deliriously overgrown courtyard gardens, exhibition spaces, and workshops. Just to the north is the glass monster Eslite shopping mall and hotel that also houses an arthouse cinema and concert performance hall in the basement.

Xinyi

While the Dinghao area has some retail outlets catering to families or the middle-class shopper, the **Xinyi** shopping and entertainment area (Xinyi Qu) has as its primary target the 30-somethings with ample disposable incomes. All-in-one malls and department stores abound, filled with international brands, designer boutiques, music stores, cineplexes, performance venues, bookstores, and other amenities, all built on the largest

An interactive exhibit at the Discovery Center of Taipei that allows you to consult your "fortune."

Taipeiers stream in and out of a busy MRT station.

The circular motif is not only the "zero" in "Taipei 101," but also the shape of a traditional Chinese coin, a potent symbol of wealth.

Xinyi area's Shin Kong Mitsukoshi department store.

possible scale. Since the MRT Xinyi Line opened at the end of 2013, Xinyi has become one of the fastest developing and trendiest districts of Taipei.

Vie Show Cinemas ❼

The Xinyi outlet of **Vie Show Cinemas** (Weixiu Yingcheng) was the first true cineplex to open in Taiwan, then going by the name of Warner Village Cinemas. It complements its 17 movie screens with lots of glitzy, flashy neon and leisure facilities such as eateries, an arcade, coffee shops, and retail outlets (online booking: www.vscinemas.com. tw). Many Western movies are shown here (undubbed, with Chinese subtitles), making this a favorite haunt for Western expat movie lovers.

Taipei 101 ❽

Address: 89F, 7 Xinyi Road Sec. 5, www.taipei-101.com.tw
Tel: 02-8101 8899
Opening Hrs: Observatory daily 9am–10pm
Entrance Fee: charge
Transportation: Taipei 101/World Trade Center

The official name of the sky-high **Taipei 101** (Taibei YiLingYi) tower is the Taipei Financial Center (Taibei Jinrong Dalou). It is located south of City Hall.

After its opening in 2004 it was for years the world's tallest building, measuring 508 meters (1,667ft) in height. It is now dwarfed by many other constructions, with the Burj Khalifa in Dubai at the forefront. The tower has 101 floors above ground, and is designed with sections like a giant bamboo stalk, symbolizing the unbreakable strength-in-pliability of Taiwan's people. Pedestrian skybridges lead to the adjacent Grand Hyatt Taipei and the super popular ATT4FUN shopping mall.

Opened in early 2005, the **Taipei 101 Observatory** (Taipei YiLingYi Guanjing Tai) is located on the 89th story of the tower. The world's fastest elevators whiz visitors up at 1,010 meters (3,315ft) per minute, reaching the top in 39 seconds flat; but you won't feel a thing in the high-tech pressure-controlled shuttles. The ticket booth and elevator entrance

are located on the 5th floor. Once there, be sure to take in the short documentary movie on the history of the tower. Free audio equipment is also provided for self-guided tours in English and many other languages, detailing sights and the history of the Taipei Basin from 30,000 years ago to the present. Four powerful sets of mounted binoculars extend the range of your view.

The 89th floor has an observation deck from where visitors can enjoy commanding views of the city and the Taipei Basin, from 382 metres above the ground. There is also an interior viewing platform for the tower's massive **Tuned Mass Damper**, hanging from cables stretching between the 92nd and 87th floors. The 730-ton steel sphere holds the record for the planet's largest, heaviest, and only publicly visible damper.

The outdoor deck on the 91st floor offers an utterly different viewing experience, but it's accessible only on certain occasions and if the weather permits.

The **Taipei 101 Mall** (Taipei Yi-LingYi Gouwu Zhongxin; tel: 02-8101 8800), a building linked to the tower, houses five massive floors with more than 100 retail and food outlets offering pretty much everything one might desire. In the basement, along with a massive foodcourt, is **Jasons Market Place**, which stocks items from the globe's four corners that are very hard to find anywhere else on the island: truffles, foie gras, caviar, cheeses, Indian delicacies, kimchi, Hokkaido catch, and about 600 types of imported health foods.

Four-Four South Village ❾

Just opposite Taipei 101 and across Xinyi Road is the Four-Four South Village (Si-Si Nan Cun), a little patch of history in this modern slice of the capital. It is made up of several small streets of renovated housing that was used by Kuomintang soldiers and their families when they first fled the mainland in 1949. There's a small museum, several cafés, and design gift shops. It is most lively on the weekends.

Four Beasts Mountains

The Nangang Mountain Range is the line of low peaks, southeast of Taipei 101 and Four-Four South Village, which runs all the way to the city's eastern reaches in Nangang District. The four westernmost peaks are collectively called the **Four Beasts Mountains** ❿ (Sishoushan), said to resemble the elephant, tiger, panther, and lion. Their peaks do not top 200 meters (600ft), making for easy hiking options.

Covering much of the hills is **Sishoushan Community Forest** (Sishoushan Shimin Senlin), so named because local residents have taken the initiative, with city assistance, to maintain the trails and other facilities. The intricate network of pathways here takes one past small temples, pagodas, and pavilions.

Inside the Vie Show Cinemas.

Evening crowds out in Xinyi.

WHERE

Ciyou Temple and Raohe
Street Nightmarket are
a few minutes' walk
from Songshan MRT
station (at the end of the
green line).

Unlike at Yangmingshan (see page 188), which is harder to access on weekends and tends to have steeper trails, here you'll see many middle-aged folk and senior citizens from the neighborhoods immediately below out on their daily constitutionals or doing tai chi in strategically located spots with the best views of the city sprawled below. The trailheads that are easiest to find are near the end of Zhuangjing Road, which runs south from the Taipei World Trade Center toward Elephant Mountain, the westernmost peak.

Songshan District

North of Xinyi District and south of the Keelung River is the primarily residential **Songshan District** (Songshan Qu). In imperial days, the section along the river was a riverport and small market town based around Ciyou Temple. The Japanese made this a suburban enclave in the colonial days, renaming the area "Songshan," meaning "pine mountain," even though nary

Admiring the tower from the vantage point of Four Beasts Mountains.

a pine grew here. They were just looking north at Yangmingshan and pining for their beloved homeland Japan.

Breeze Nanshan ⓫

Address: 17 Songzhi Road, www.breezecenter.com/branches/001
Tel: 0809 008888
Opening Hrs: Sun–Wed 11am–9.30pm, Thu–Sat 11am–10pm
Transportation: Taipei 101 MRT station

As if reaching for Taipei 101's heights, the sleek black Taipei Nanshan Plaza stands 272 meters (892ft) tall, towering over everything except for the Taipei landmark that is across the street. Occupying two underground levels and several at its base is **Breeze Nanshan** (Weifeng Nanshan), the city's biggest shopping mall since it opened in January 2019. Because Japanese money went into this project, many of the stores hail from the East Asian country, but come

mealtimes and even in between, most people flock to the basement food courts. More pricey but fancier are the restaurants and bars on the 46th and 47th floors that offer gasp-worthy views of Taipei 101 as if you are mid-air.

Puppetry Art Center ⑫

Address: 99 Civil Boulevard, www.pact. org.tw
Tel: 02-2528 9553
Opening Hrs: Tue–Sat 10am–5pm
Entrance Fee: charge
Transportation: Nanjing Sanmin

About a 10-minute walk from Nanjing Sanmin MRT station, the **Puppetry Art Center of Taipei** (Taibei Ouxi Guan) has at its core a private collection of almost 5,000 string puppets, shadow puppets, glove puppets, and related objects. The first level of the large four-story center is dedicated to DIY workshops and seminars. The second houses the permanent collection that is always open to the public. The history and different forms of puppetry are explained, and demonstrations of puppet-making and manipulation are sometimes scheduled. The many puppet characters seen in the vast Chinese storytelling repertoire are also introduced. The third level is for special exhibits.

Raohe Street Nightmarket ⑬

The **Raohe Street Nightmarket** (Raohe Jie Yeshi) is Taipei's newest nightmarket (daily 5pm–midnight), blossoming into its present form in the 1980s around the old vendors beside Ciyou Temple. It stretches the length of Raohe Street between the temple and Keelung Road. There are about 400 vendors in all, permanent outlets on either side and movable stalls in two rows down the center. You will find all manner of things for sale including clothing, fruits, toys, crafts, and traditional food treats made on site.

Try the oyster vermicelli (*o-a-mi-sua*) by **Dongfa Restaurant** (Dongfa Yinshi Dian) at No. 94; they have served it since the 1930s. At No. 215, **Yuhuaxing Food Company** (Yuhuaxing Shipin Gongsi) has been making traditional pastries

One of the many colorful traditional Chinese puppets on sale at the Puppetry Art Center gift shop.

West of Taipei 101, the Taipei World Trade Center (Shimao Zhongxin) is a regular venue for key trade events, and contains several foreign "trade offices" (euphemism for "embassy" in diplomatically isolated Taiwan).

Worshipping at Ciyou Temple.

and cakes, including Mazu festival treats, since the 1940s. Alternatively, see how sesame oil is traditionally made at **Shandong Xiaomo Sesame Oil Shop** (Shandong Xiaomo Mayou Dian) at No. 84.

The market is best known for its medicinal stewed pork ribs. There are a number of sellers, but perhaps most popular is **Chairman Chen's** (Chen Dong Yaodun Paigu) at No. 160. The smell of the small-size ribs simmering in Chinese herbs in large pots is quite heady, the taste in no way like taking doctor's medicine, however.

Ciyou Temple ⑭

Address: 761 Bade Road Sec. 4
Tel: 02-2766 3012
Opening Hrs: daily 5am–10.30pm
Entrance Fee: free
Transportation: Songshan

Ciyou Temple (Ciyou Gong) is located just across from Songshan Railway Station and MRT stop. Elderly commuters hauling their sacrificial offerings are a familiar, comforting sight at the station; many

come from outside the city. This Mazu temple dates from 1757, and was the core of the small Xikou river-port, which was long ago absorbed into the city. Today, though the Keelung River runs just north, it is out of sight behind the urban build-up. But the area still has a small-town rural feel about it; in fact, until the early 1990s, the land between here and Keelung Road was mostly open rice paddy.

This temple is the venue for what are among Taipei's loudest Mazu birthday celebrations in terms of color and cacophony. The temple roof is richly ornamented; note the flying dragon, a common motif on temples because dragons are the source of rain, always hidden behind clouds, and thus protect the wood-built complexes from fire.

Wufenpu Garment Wholesale Area ⑮

The **Wufenpu Garment Wholesale Area** (Wufenpu Fushi Tequ) is a god-send for budget shoppers seeking

non-branded clothing and fashion accessories at low prices (daily 11am–10pm). This bustling, concentrated area of over 1,000 small wholesalers is located between Zhongxiao East Road and Songshan Railway Station, a 5-minute walk west of Houshanpi MRT station (exit 4). You'll find the full range in tastes here, from items that rival those of brand-name designers to the kitsch. Testament to the "quality at low prices" of Wufenpu is the fact that the majority of Taipei's street and nightmarket vendors selling clothing and accessories come here for stock. The items are sourced in Taiwan, Hong Kong, Korea, Japan, and other countries, and in terms of style run the gamut from demure items for 30-somethings to street fashion, grandma clothes, pop-idol Korean and Japanese fashions, hip-hop, punk, and athletic wear, and more.

Nangang

East of Songshan is **Nangang**, which means "south port." In imperial times, this was the southernmost navigable location on the Keelung River. It is primarily a residential area whose business activity centers on family-run shops and small-scale factory workshops.

The area's claim to fame is the prestigious **Academia Sinica**, Taiwan's leading academic institution, the Nangang Tea Plantations, and two new facilities that have sprung up since the mid-1990s as a result of a concerted city government economic-stimulus blueprint, Nangang Software Park and the sleek new Taipei World Trade Center Nangang Exhibition Hall, a massive complex with its own station on the blue Neihu MRT line. Academia Sinica sits in a valley in Nangang's south. On its grounds are two sites of interest to tourists: Hu Shih Memorial Hall, and the Museum of the Institute of History and Philology. The district is also busy building a new landmark – the **Taipei Music Center**, which is set to be the country's most professional

WHERE

The Small No. 5 bus, which can be caught outside Nangang Exhibition Center MRT station, travels past Academia Sinica's front door and through the local tea-plantation area. Riders can hop on and off at any point in the latter area.

A variety of street fashion for sale in the Wufenpu Garment Wholesale Area.

music performance venue. Slated for completion by the end of 2018, it is currently still under construction.

Hu Shih Memorial Hall

Address: 130 Yanjiuyuan (Academia) Road Sec. 2, www.mh.sinica.edu.tw/koteki
Tel: 02-2782 1147
Opening Hrs: Tue–Sat 9am–5pm
Entrance Fee: free
Transportation: Taipei Nangang Exhibition Center and taxi

Hu Shih (1891–1962), philosopher, writer, academic, and statesman, was one of the foremost public figures in China in the 20th century. He served as head of Academia Sinica in his later years, and passed away in his residence, now the **Hu Shih Memorial Hall** (Hu Shi Jinian Guan). His democratic leanings and outspokenness repeatedly got him in hot water with Chiang Kai-shek; he was recalled from his post

The grounds of Hu Shih Memorial Hall.

as ambassador to the US (1938–42) and had troubles thereafter. On the first level is an exhibit hall featuring his many works, various personal effects, and explanations of his life and times. Elsewhere, his study, bedroom, and living room remain precisely as they were on the day he departed. The quiet **Hu Shih Park** (Hu Shi Gongyuan), the site of Hu's tomb, is on the slope across the street from the Institute.

Museum of the Institute of History and Philology

Address: 130 Yanjiuyuan (Academia) Road Sec. 2, http://museum.sinica.edu.tw
Tel: 02-2652 3180
Opening Hrs: Wed, Sat and Sun 9.30am–4.30pm
Entrance Fee: free
Transportation: Taipei Nangang Exhibition Center and bus 205, 620 or taxi

The **Museum of the Institute of History and Philology** (Lishi Wenwu Chenlie Guan), though not well known, showcases superb finds in archeology and ethnology made by researchers from Academia Sinica.

The first story concentrates on archeology, with artifacts of ancient Chinese civilizations from Neolithic times to the Zhou dynasty. The second story offers a cornucopia of historical records in six themes: wooden slips from the Han dynasty, rare books, imperial court archives, ethnic groups from southwest China, stele ink rubbings and historical documents from Taiwan, and special exhibits. All the artifacts have explanations on how they made their way into the collection and their academic importance.

The use of glass for the floor of the second level and connecting pathway is an impressive design concept. It gives the feeling of going below ground when descending to the main level, as if entering an archeological dig. On the main level is a virtual time corridor, again of glass, physically and chronologically linking the separate displays.

To get here, take bus No. 205 or 620 from Nangang Exhibition Center MRT station.

Nangang Tea Plantations ⑱

Right by the Institute and Hu Shih Park, Jiuzhuang Road branches off from Academia Road and soon leads to the **Nangang Tourist Tea Plantations** (Nangang Guanguang Chayuan), most of which are on Section 2. Not as well known or as developed for tourism as the Muzha plantations (see page 162) directly to the south beyond the peaks of the Nangang range, these rustic locales and the numerous small teahouses are nevertheless well worth a visit. Nangang is the birthplace of Baozhong tea, one of the island's most famous varieties; its bushes were brought here by a Fujianese immigrant cultivator in 1885. The local farmer's association has put up signs outside farms that welcome tourists, so during picking season (spring and fall) visitors can watch the picking and processing.

"Jiuzhuang" means "old village," and among the terraced fields and scarecrows are a number of old-style three-sided red-brick farmhouses with a central courtyard. See the **Yu Family Historical Residence** (Yujia Gucuo) at Lane 316, Jiuzhuang Street Section 2, the largest complex of earth-and-stone buildings still extant in Taipei (private, not open to public). Beside the now abandoned old hamlet of this tea-growing clan is a large old camphor tree said to be over 200 years old, also said to be the most painted tree in Taipei.

A view from the Taipei 101 Observatory.

TAIPEI SOUTH

Centered around two of the island's best colleges, this area has a slower, more bohemian, "university town" feel, despite sitting in the busy city. Further south are Muzha's popular tourist tea plantations.

The presence here of National Taiwan University and National Taiwan Normal University – two of the island's top post-secondary institutions – means that many students and faculty members reside in this area. There are also many foreigners, teaching or studying at various language institutes. The presence of this educated crowd means an unusual number of bookstores and shops that cater to the literati, selling paintings, calligraphy sets, antiques, and such. A stroll along Heping East Road Section 1, by National Taiwan Normal University, brings one past many such establishments, the proprietors of which can most often speak at least some English.

In the area's two big nightmarkets and in the neighborhood across Xinsheng South Road from National Taiwan University, countless small eateries, pubs, cafés, and teahouses have sprung up, catering to the limited-budget student crowd.

In the hills of Muzha in the far south of the city, tranquility and a slower pace take center stage – at least once you have escaped the traffic in the city below and squeezed your way into a parking spot near one of the many teahouses in the plantations. On weekends and late nights, visitors stream uphill to enjoy a little tea and scenery.

Daan

Daan Forest Park ❶ (Daan Senlin Gongyuan; daily 24 hours; free), with its own MRT station, is one of Taipei's newest parks, created after the homes of a long-standing squatter community of scrap-collecting families were razed in the mid-1990s after repeated warnings and much

Strolling in Daan Forest Park, which provides a great escape from the heat of the surrounding streets.

protest. It offers a welcome respite from the baking cement and asphalt of the surrounding city. At its core is an amphitheater where free concerts are frequently staged on holidays, often featuring well-known pop stars. Many exotic tree species have been planted here, most labeled, providing botanical variety and many shady spots. Like everywhere in Taipei, the place is very crowded on weekends and holidays, so come early. The Jianguo Weekend Jade and Flower markets (see page 143) are on its immediate northeast side, making for a nice weekend outing.

Yongkang Street ❷

Running south from Xinyi Road is the narrow but bustling **Yongkang Street** (Yongkang Jie), located in an otherwise very quiet residential neighborhood centered around tiny Yongkang Park. Often crowded on weekends and evenings, the street and surrounding lanes are bursting with eateries selling local food, restaurants serving cuisines from around the globe, non-chain fashion boutiques, and shops selling

traditional Chinese clothing and items such as calligraphy and tea sets. There are about 400 outlets on the street and down side alleys.

During the Japanese colonial era, this area was mostly paddy field. It had a notorious Japanese prison in the middle and the homes of personnel surrounding it. After World War II, civilians who came with the KMT moved in. Commercial development exploded in the 1970s and the paddy fields were soon gone.

Taipei Grand Mosque ❸

Address: 62 Xinsheng S. Road Sec. 2, www.taipeimosque.org.tw
Tel: 02 2321 9445
Opening Hours: daily 9am–6pm
Entrance Fee: free
Transportation: Daan Park

The large and distinctive **Taipei Grand Mosque** (Taibei Qingzhen Si) is across Xinsheng South Road from Daan Forest Park. It serves the 10,000-plus-strong Muslim community in Taipei. Most of the island's Muslims came to Taiwan with the KMT exodus from China in the late 1940s. Family names such as Jin,

The Taipei Grand Mosque is open to non-Muslims during the week in non-prayer hours. Call for confirmation.

If visiting Wistaria Teahouse in a group, request a private room with tatami mats.

Guo, Bai, and Ma – as in well-known Taiwan politician Ma Ying-jeou – are said to indicate likely Muslim ancestry. The Taipei Grand Mosque was built in the Islamic architectural style, with two minarets that are over 20 meters (65ft) tall. Many Islamic countries, including Saudi Arabia, contributed to its building, when the ROC still had formal relations with them in the 1950s.

It is said that during the 1970s oil crisis, the mosque's special relationship with King Faisal ensured continued oil supply to Taiwan, and at preferential rates. Friday prayers are held just after noon. The city declared this a heritage site in 1999 to protect it from demolition resulting from a decades-old land dispute and today the mosque is as busy as ever. Non-Muslims are invited to visit Monday to Friday outside prayer times.

Wistaria Teahouse ❹

Address: 1, Lane 16, Xinsheng S. Road Sec. 3, www.wistariateahouse.com
Tel: 02-2363 7375
Opening Hrs: daily 10am–10pm
Transportation: Taipower Building

Southwest of Daan Forest Park is the **Wistaria Teahouse** (Ziteng Lu), one

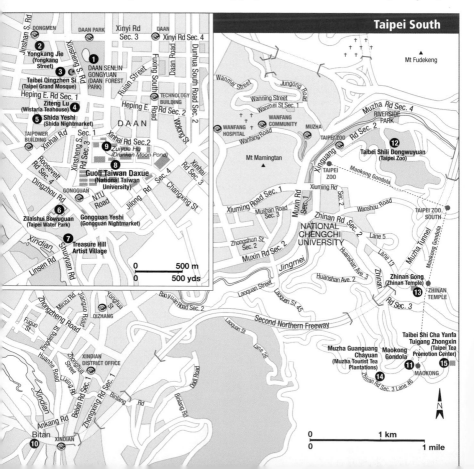

Staff pouring tea at Wistaria Teahouse.

of Taipei's most popular teahouses and an important historic landmark. This heritage building draped with wisteria vines was a dormitory for mid-level Japanese officials during the colonial period. The *tatami* mats and screen doors are a legacy of this period. Later, it became a favorite meeting place for dissidents during the long terror of the martial law period. Today it is a haven for quiet conversation and contemplation. The intellectual conversation is calmer; poetry readings and other arts and literary events are often held.

All of the island's most famous teas are available here, especially Puerh teas. A decades-long dispute over ownership has finally been settled, with the government the official owner of the heritage site but the family that has put so much money into the place allowed to run it "forever."

Shida Nightmarket ❺

The **Shida Nightmarket** (Shida Yeshi; daily 4pm–midnight) is located west of Wistaria Teahouse on Longquan Street. Vendors here excel in the specialty dish of *gongwan tang* (pork meatballs in soup), among other foods. On parallel Shida Road, south of National Taiwan Normal

Shida Nightmarket and pub area has a markedly younger and hipper feel than some of the more traditional markets elsewhere in the city.

In the genteel Wisteria Teahouse.

Muzha tea plantations

The Muzha hillsides have long been given over to tea bushes, and since the 1980s most of the plantations have opened teahouses that are very popular with day-trippers.

The hills of south Taipei come alive each night with sparkling, dancing pinpoints of light as the scores of teahouses dotting the high slopes of Muzha fill up with lovers of the golden brew. Several are open 24 hours or until the early hours of the morning, and the revelry reaches its fullest pitch only after midnight. Visitors come seeking a cool escape from the often steamy Taipei Basin below. The view of the big city laid out beyond like a scintillating carpet at the sippers' feet is a visual complement to the flavor of the local Oolong tea specialties: Tieguanyin (Iron Goddess) and Baozhong.

Taiwan's former president Lee Teng-hui started the tourism renaissance here in the early 1980s when, as mayor of Taipei, he re-zoned the district to allow commercial establishments (the teahouses) to be built on what had previously been land restricted to farms. The growth in revenue and number of tea bushes has since been explosive.

The teahouses are perched on the higher slopes of a narrow 3km-long (2-mile)

View from a teahouse at Muzha.

valley called Maokong, or "cat's hollows" – a reference to the hollowed erosions like pawprints found in the rocks along the Zhinan Stream. Hikers come for refreshing walks during the day; students and night owls come in flocks at night to socialize.

Tea has been grown in Taiwan for more than 300 years, but it was British trader John Dodd who put Muzha on the map in the 1860s (see page 119). Arriving after the Second Opium War, he saw that the area's conditions were perfect for Oolong tea. New bushes were brought from China and Dodd & Co. encouraged new cultivation by guaranteeing purchase of the entire crop.

Where to taste tea

A visit to the plantations must begin at the **Taipei Tea Promotion Center** (see page 167), where visitors can see displays and live demonstrations on processing and brewing, and enjoy free tastings. English group tours can be arranged with three days' notice (per person fee). Be sure to visit the experimental plantation grounds behind the complex too for riveting views of the city.

Two of Taiwan's best teahouses are located just east of the center and it is no coincidence that they are also on the highest points of the loop road that heads up from Chengchi University at the valley's mouth. *Yaoyue Teahouse* ("Inviting the Moon") is at eye level just outside the restaurant and its open-air pavilions, which sit right at the edge of a promontory (6, Lane 40, Zhinan Rd Sec. 3; www.yytea.com.tw; tel: 02-2939 2025; open 24 hours, meals served daily 11am–2am, weekends until 3am; charge). This is a favorite late-night haunt for the island's pop stars. The *Big Teapot Teahouse* is known for "tea cuisine" (37-1, Lane 38, Zhinan Rd Sec. 3; www.bigteapot.idv.tw; tel: 02-2939 5615; Tue–Sun 10.30am–10pm). These dishes feature locally bred free-range chicken, and are considered especially suited to being enjoyed with tea.

In general, choose teahouses on the highest slopes for the best views and quality. Further downslope, the quality tends to slide; some of the places are a bit ramshackle.

University (colloquially known by the shortened "Shida"), is an area chock-a-block with pubs, bars, eateries, and restaurants, all moderately priced because this is a student area. Many Western language students and teachers live in the area or frequent it.

In recent years, complaints from nearby residents of excessive noise and pollution from the market have forced many vendors to close. However, the smaller version is still fun and well worth a visit.

Taipei Water Park ⑥

Address: 1 Siyuan Street, https://waterparken.water.gov.taipci
Tel: 02-8733 5678
Opening Hrs: Tue–Sun July–Aug 9am–8pm, Sept–June 9am–5pm
Entrance Fee: charge
Transportation: Gongguan

It all started with the **Museum of Drinking Water** (Zilaishui Bowuguan) housed in Taipei's first pumping station and filtration plant. In 1896 the Japanese consulted Scottish engineer William K. Burton, who suggested that water be pumped from the Xindian River and

treated at this site, then stored at the facility atop the hill so that gravity would bring the water to residents. The facilities, completed in 1908, no longer provide the city with water.

A museum is now housed in the original Renaissance-style waterworks building. Exhibits show how the piping and delivery systems work, and explain the history of Taipei's water-purification activities.

The museum first opened as a stand-alone attraction in 1998, but the city soon realized it had a good thing going. The **Taipei Water Park** (Taibei Zilaishui Yuanqu), targeted at children, has since sprung up around the museum and adjoining Gongguan Purification Plant (Taipei Water Park ticket includes entry to museum). The top draw is the Aqua-Friendly Experience and Education Area (separate admission fee, separate entry on Lane 160, Tingzhou Road Sec. 3), also called Road Castle, where tots get to frolic in water-based amusements. Swimsuits are a must. Next in popularity is the **Pipe Sculpture Area**, where slides and tunnels have been built to mimic

WHERE

To get to Muzha tea plantations by public transport, you have two choices. Alight at Taipei Zoo station and take the brown No. 15 minibus up the windy hillside or ride the cable car up on the Maokong Gondala (http://english.gondola.taipei/) – the gondola entrance is a 5-minute walk from the Taipei Zoo station.

View of the Xindian River at Bitan.

The Museum of Drinking Water, with its grand rows of classical columns, is a favorite location for wedding shoots.

the waterworks piping. There are also short trails and flower gardens around and on the hill originally used to store treated water. It is very, very crowded here on hot summer days – especially weekends and during school vacation.

Treasure Hill Artist Village ❼

Address: 2 Alley 14, Ln. 230 Tingzhou Rd Sec. 3, www.artistvillage.org
Tel: 02-2364 5313
Opening Hrs: daily 24 hours (indoor exhibitions until 6pm, closed Mon)
Entrance Fee: free
Transportation: Gongguan

This is one of Taipei's most eccentric communities. Situated on the slope of a hill overlooking the Xindian River, southwest of National Taiwan University, **Treasure Hill Artist Village** (Baozang Yan) is a community of German-built homes raised by Kuomintang soldiers after World War II, when they were posted at an anti-aircraft battery here to defend against Communist attack. Residents were evicted from the illegal site in 2007. The city refurbished the structures, put in sewage pipes and other amenities, and the residents have moved back in. Artists have moved in too, with a thriving artist-in-residence program, and the city is using this as a showcase for environmentally sustainable urban communities. It has become an "artivist" compound. It is a most unusual place, an ugly duckling with true quirky beauty, declared by the New York Times to be one of Taiwan's "must-see" spots. The Treasure Hill Artist Village opened in 2010 and is home to over a dozen artist's studios and exhibitions spaces, which regularly host contemporary art shows. It's a parallel project to Taipei Artist Village (see page 133). Two or three times a year an "Open Studio" is held, an event allowing guests to visit all studios in both villages and meet Taiwanese and international artists in residence.

The hillside complex of the Zhinan Temple.

National Taiwan University

Often referred to colloquially by the abbreviation "Taida," the **National Taiwan University ❽** (Guoli Taiwan Daxue; www.ntu.edu. tw) is the island's premier educational institution. Established by the Japanese as Taihoku (Taipei) Imperial University in 1928, the institution was renamed after World War II. The sprawling 110-hectare (270-acre) main campus is dotted with historic buildings in Western architectural styles, filled with tree-lined boulevards and laced by footpaths, attracting those in search of quiet and a cool, comfortable stroll. The walkways converge on a park surrounding the placid **Drunken Moon Pond ❾** (Zuiyue Hu), where loved-up couples are serenaded by birds. The main gate of the campus is near the corner of Xinsheng South and Roosevelt roads.

Bitan

A few stops south of Gongguan on the Xindian MRT Line is the recreation area of **Bitan** (daily 24 hours; free). It is centered on a wide, slow-moving, and picturesque section of the Xindian River that has the feel of a lake. The jade-green waters (*bi* means "jade green," *tan* means "lake") are nicely framed by high foliage-covered bluffs on the south and a wobbly pedestrian suspension bridge on the west. A teahouse with an open-air patio and great views, very popular with locals, sits at the foot of the bridge on the south bank. A food market selling regional snacks as well as dozens of seafood eateries and restaurants line the north bank of the river. Paddleboats in the shape of birds are available for a fee at the water's edge.

Muzha

The **Muzha** area is situated in a narrow valley formed by the lazy Jingmei River on its mid-reaches. Because of its relative isolation, this was one of the last areas in the Taipei Basin to be settled by the Chinese.

Despite prohibitions and formal agreements with the indigenous inhabitants, the settlers kept moving upriver, which caused a lot of friction. So, in the first half of the 1800s, the isolated settlers set up row after row of *muzha*, or wooden palisades, to protect themselves. The descriptive colloquial name for the settlement soon stuck. Today the area is easily reached via the Muzha MRT Line.

Maokong Gondola

Maokong Gondola (Tue–Thu 9am–9pm, Fri until 10pm, Sat 8.30am–10pm, Sun until 9pm; tel: 02-2720 8889, https://english.gondola.taipei) is immensely popularity with visitors. The cable-car line operating between Taipei Zoo and Maokong is 4.3km (2.7 miles) long and has four stations, which also include Taipei Zoo South and Zhinan Temple, and it is worth taking a ride just for the beautiful scenery and commanding views of the city. For a truly breathtaking sensation of gliding through the sky, go for a Crystal Cabin, which has a special glass bottom. Note that in the event of bad weather, such as storms

A ceramic teapot for sale at the Taipei Tea Promotion Center.

The old waterworks at the Museum of Drinking Water.

or high winds, the Maokong Gondala is closed for safety reasons.

Taipei Zoo ⑫

Address: 30 Xinguang Road Sec. 2, www.zoo.gov.tw
Tel: 02-2938 2300
Opening Hrs: daily 9am–5pm
Entrance Fee: charge
Transportation: Taipei Zoo

Located just outside the Muzha Line terminus, the **Taipei Zoo** (Taibei Shili Dongwuyuan) has undergone much upgrading since the 1990s to bring some of the animal habitats up to international standards, although several of the enclosures are still pretty depressing, such as those housing the bears and the apes. An unusual feature is the **Formosan Animals Area**, home to over 20 endemic species not likely to be spotted elsewhere. These include the Formosan giant flying squirrel and the Formosan clouded leopard. A number of species are endangered. Kids, especially, flock

to the **Insectarium**, which features a two-level educational center and a 10-hectare (25-acre) valley behind with more than 125 butterfly species and where educational hikes are conducted. The zoo's biggest attraction is the **Panda House** (separate admission fee; closed first Mon each month; visitor numbers strictly controlled), home to two giant pandas given to Taiwan by China in what was described as a goodwill gesture.

Zhinan Temple ⑬

Address: 115 Wanshou Road, www. chih-nan-temple.org
Tel: 02-2939 9922
Opening Hrs: daily 4am–8.30pm
Entrance Fee: free
Transportation: Taipei Zoo and taxi

Zhinan Temple (Zhinan Gong), perched atop the mountain spur behind the zoo, is one of Taipei's most important places of worship. It is also known as the Temple of 1,000 Steps, for the 1,275 steps that were long the only way up to the temple

The Maokong Gondola offers great views.

– talk about dedicated followers! Popular belief suggests that conquering each step brings you 20 extra seconds of life.

The temple is dedicated to Lü Dongbin, one of the Eight Immortals who are at the core of the Chinese pantheon. Since the temple's establishment in 1891, the complex has grown in size and importance. For tourists, its unusual multistory design is an interesting variation on the traditional.

In popular lore, the Eight Immortals and other deities lead lives much like mortals. It is said that long ago, lusty Lü Dongbin chased Guanyin (the virtuous Goddess of Mercy) through the skies to Taiwan. Exasperated, she settled into the shape of the eponymous **Guanyin Mountain** and created the Danshui River to keep Lü at bay. He settled on the Zhinan Temple spur and is said to still be looking forlornly at her.

The park area surrounding the Zhinan Temple is also home to the golden-hued **Auspicious Dragon**. Legend has it that the dragon is the steed of the Jade Emperor. The mythical animal has traditionally been revered as a deity, and it epitomizes nobility, honor and success. The dragon has 3,600 scales and holds the ruler's seal in its left claw.

Muzha Tea Plantations

Muzha Tourist Tea Plantations ⓮ (Muzha Guanguang Chayuan) as well as the **Taipei Tea Promotion Center** ⓯ (Taibei Shi Cha Yanfa Tuigang Zhongxin) at 8-2, Lane 40, Zhinan Road Sec. 3 (Tue–Sun 9am–5pm; free; tel: 02-2234 0568) are perhaps south Taipei's most popular stops for those seeking a brief escape from the city. The plantation's teahouses usually offer entrancing views of the surrounding countryside and city beyond, with the rich smell of tea in the air. The Promotion Center offers demonstrations of the tea production and brewing process.

Lü Dongbin was said to be an amorous fellow, so couples are advised to avoid Zhinan Temple, lest lusty Lü split them up to steal the girl!

Guarding the Martyr's Shrine.

TAIPEI NORTH

North of the Keelung River, Shilin is a land of museums; Tianmu is an expatriate enclave with an international flavor; Beitou has long been known for its hot springs; and Neihu's large open spaces have acquired a variety of shops and attractions.

The districts of Shilin, Neihu, and Beitou are all found north of the Keelung River, and all the main sights are within walking distance of – or a short bus ride away from – an MRT station, making for a pleasant escape from the urban crush of the city center without leaving the amenities of civilization altogether. Note that some of the museums in the area lack detailed information in English, so be sure to take advantage of English-language tours or audio guides where possible.

SHILIN

Grand Hotel ❶

The **Grand Hotel** (Yuanshan Dafandian) is indeed grand (1 Zhongshan N. Rd Sec. 4; tel: 02-2886 8888; www.grand-hotel.org), built in Ming-dynasty palace style and inspired by Beijing's Forbidden City. The facade of this 530-room behemoth is defined by towering red pillars and fronted by a pretty sculpted garden.

The ridge on which the hotel is perched was the location of the main Japanese Shinto shrine in colonial days. The shrine was torn down in anger by the KMT – as were most

things too evidently Japanese – after World War II. The hotel, started in the 1950s, was a pet project of Madame Chiang Kai-shek, who sought to bring the city international stature.

There are few better spots for afternoon tea than the grand lobby. Its recessed ceiling of dragon and phoenix bas-reliefs and its grand staircase flanked by sumptuous artworks will transport you back to imperial days.

Behind the hotel is a staircase that leads to the peak of Yuanshan (Round Mountain). From here,

Main Attractions
Grand Hotel
Shilin Nightmarket
Shilin Official Residence
National Palace Museum
Shung Ye Museum of
    Formosan Aborigines
Beitou Hot Springs
    Museum
Taiwan Folk Arts Museum
Guandu Nature Park
National Revolutionary
    Martyrs' Shrine

Map
Page 170

The Grand Hotel seen from Dajia Riverside Park.

the stirring views of the city below resemble a scale model with tiny toy planes landing at Songshan Airport.

Shilin Nightmarket ②

Regarded by many as Taipei's best, **Shilin Nightmarket** (Shilin Yeshi) is definitely its largest and most popular, and has a history of well over 100 years (daily 5pm–midnight). It is located on the west side of Jiantan MRT station. Unfortunately, many of the stalls have been moved to the basement of an ugly structure in the middle of the market, which has far less atmosphere. However, there are still plenty of places to snack in the lanes.

Long ago, a clash between immigrants from China forced a group of settlers to flee to Yangmingshan. But they periodically came down into present-day Shilin to sell produce, slipping back and forth like ghosts. As such, the market was long called "Ghost Market."

An ice-cold bowl of sweet aiyu is the perfect antidote to a grease-laden supper at Shilin Nightmarket.

Just about every tasty traditional Taiwanese snack that exists is whipped up here for you. Enjoy cholesterol in great quantity and variety: oyster omelets, cuttlefish stew, "coffin boards" (*guancai ban*), deep-fried stinky tofu, potstickers (*guotie*), and much more. The market is popular with both locals and tourists and it can get extremely crowded and claustrophobic. You can find tattoo parlors and massage places at the outer edges of the market.

In the vicinity of the Shilin Nightmarket, close to MRT Jiantan Station, you can see the construction site of the Taipei Performing Arts Center. This state-of-the-art facility is set to house three theaters. The experimental, yet well-thought-out structure of the center rethinks the arrangement of space and removes traditional architectural barriers to the imagination of playwrights and directors, thus allowing it to stage performances that would

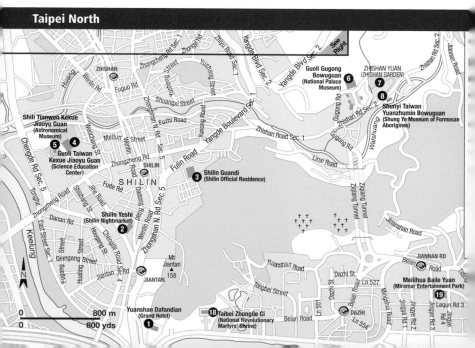

Taipei North

be impossible elsewhere. It will surely be impressive when, and if, it finally opens.

Shilin Official Residence ❸

Address: 60 Fulin Road
Tel: 02- 2883 6340
Opening Hrs: Tue–Sun 9.30am–12pm, 1–5pm
Entrance Fee: charge (gardens are free)
Transportation: Shilin

This expansive estate with the vague name **Shilin Official Residence** (Shilin Guandi) was one of Chiang Kai-shek's abodes during his Taipei years. Tucked at the foot of Yangmingshan's slopes, the sprawling grounds were opened as a park in 1996. The long, tree-shaded driveway opens onto pathways leading to gardens, pagodas, pavilions, and a small chapel where top KMT officials, Christian or otherwise, attended services each Sunday morning – the key to staying within

the inner circle of power. There are also experimental greenhouses here from the Japanese colonial era. The grounds are 10 minutes east on foot from Shilin MRT Station.

It was only in 2011 that the two-story house, where the president lived for 26 years until his death in 1975, opened to visitors, because of objections from those KMT elements of the government loyal to Chiang Kai-shek's memory. The audio guide conveniently makes no mention of the more controversial aspects of Chiang's rule, such as the thousands who were unjustly imprisoned and executed during the White Terror.

Science Education Center ❹

Address: 189 Shishang Road, www.ntsec.gov.tw
Tel: 02-6610 1234
Opening Hrs: Tue–Sun 9am–5pm
Entrance Fee: charge
Transportation: Shilin

During the colonial era, the Japanese brought plants from around the world for synthesis with the Taiwanese soil. The exquisite and exotic results are on display on the grounds of the Shilin Official Residence.

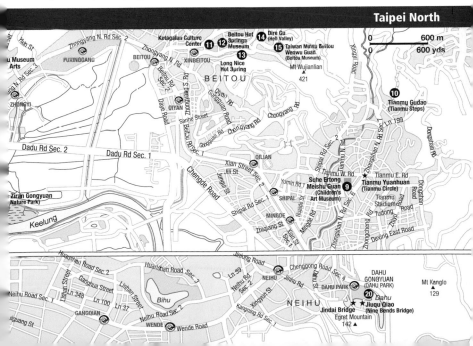

Taipei North

The SkyCycle at the Science Education Center. The center has limited written English, so try to join a free English tour (minimum 20 persons, one-week advance booking). The website has comprehensive information in English.

Taipei Astronomical Museum.

About 15 minutes on foot west of Shilin MRT Station is **National Taiwan Science Education Center**. Kids can run amok in this learning-is-for-fun, hands-on facility. A nine-story-high glass atrium houses permanent exhibits on the physical sciences, earth sciences, and life sciences. Additional tickets must be bought for temporary exhibitions, 3D Theater, Turbo-ride 3D Theater, Earthquake Theater, SkyCycle, and Kid's Learning and Discovery Playground. Be warned that organization at the theaters can be somewhat chaotic. The SkyCycle, erected five stories above ground and exhibiting theories of weight distribution and balance, is also very popular. There is printed info in English, and guided English tours are available for groups of 20 (reservations required).

Astronomical Museum ❺

Address: 363 Jihe Road, https://en.tam.gov.taipei
Tel: 02-2831 4551
Opening Hrs: Tue–Sun 8am–5pm; Sat until 8pm

Entrance Fee: charge
Transportation: Shilin

The **Taipei Astronomical Museum** (Taibei Shili Tianwen Kexue Jiaoyu Guan) stands right beside the Science Education Center. It has three floors of exhibits on such themes as Ancient Astrology, The Earth, Space Technology, The Solar System, and The Stars. But the top attractions are the 3D Theater (polarized 3D glasses used), IMAX Dome Theater, Cosmic Adventure theme-park ride, and the Observatory Dome with telescopes for stargazing (Tue–Sun 10am–noon, 2–4pm; additional session Sat 7–9pm). There is a separate admission fee for the first three.

Reservations are taken three days in advance for the popular Observatory Dome sessions. Most of the theater films are imported and dubbed, so check what English is available. The limited English in the regular exhibits can dampen the fun. You can walk here from Shilin MRT in about 15 minutes; the museum is opposite the Science Education Center.

AIYU JELLY

Aiyu is a cooling yellow-green jelly discovered, so the story goes, in south Taiwan in the early 1900s. A thirsty sojourner came upon a jelly-like substance floating on a stream. The adventurous soul scooped it up and popped it into his mouth, discovering it was both edible and delicious. Learning it came from a local fruit that commonly dropped into the water, he set his daughter to making a summertime dessert using the jelly.

The girl's name, Aiyu, was soon given to both fruit and treat. Since then, aiyu has been a favorite dessert that remains unique to the island. Vendors can be found at Shilin Nightmarket.

National Palace Museum ⑥

The **National Palace Museum** (Guoli Gugong Bowuguan) is one of Taiwan's crowning glories, justly considered the world's greatest repository of Chinese artifacts (see page 184). Once part of the emperors' personal collection, off-limits to the public until after the fall of the empire, the pieces span 5,000 years. At any one time only a small portion of the 650,000 works is on display, the rest tucked away in temperature- and humidity-controlled vaults dug into the mountain behind. Additionally, in an effort to bring culture and tourism to the south of the country, a southern branch of the museum was opened in late 2015 in Chiayi, a 90-minute high-speed rail trip down the island. Exhibits are shared between the two museums. The northern branch of the museum is due for a complete overhaul and will close fully or in part in 2020 for three years.

The museum is far too large to take in on just one trip. English tours at 10am and 3pm daily, led by strenuously trained guides, are invaluable (online reservation needed). In 2008 the museum opened the popular Children's Gallery, helping kids aged 5 to 12 develop an appreciation of the fine arts through fun and games (free; scheduled entry times during museum hours).

Adjacent to the museum is the 1.5-hectare (4-acre) **Zhishan Garden** ⑦ (Zhishan Yuan), an exquisitely landscaped classical Chinese garden (Tue–Sun 8.30am–5.30pm, Apr–Oct until 6.30pm; free with museum ticket or NT$20).

Shung Ye Museum ⑧

Address: 282 Zhishan Road Sec. 2, www.museum.org.tw
Tel: 02-2841 2611
Opening Hrs: Tue–Sun 9am–5pm; closed Chinese New Year's holidays
Entrance Fee: charge
Transportation: Shilin

With its distinctive profile, the **Shung Ye Museum of Formosan Aborigines** (Shunyi Taiwan Yuanzhumin Bowuguan) is located just east of the National Palace Museum. Perhaps Taiwan's best museum for learning about the

WHERE

With one-week advance notice, the National Palace Museum provides wheelchairs as well as tours for those with physical and mental impairments.

The unusual architecture of the Shung Ye Museum.

island's indigenous tribes, unlike other museums there is good English. This facility has played a key role in the movement to generate greater interest in and respect for the tribes' widely varying cultures.

Among the highlights are a large topographical map of Taiwan showing tribal dispersion down to village level, a section on traditional weaponry and one on beliefs and ceremonies, an Ami sea-going craft, and scale models of traditional dwellings. There are multimedia presentations, many with English versions, an English audio guide, and English-language tours can be arranged. The gift shop has many print materials hard to find elsewhere in Taipei, plus cultural products and handicrafts.

Tianmu and Beitou

The suburb of Tianmu lies at the northern end of Zhongshan North Road. Here one finds Taipei's densest concentration of expatriate residents,

The rooftops of hilly Beitou.

The National Revolutionary Martyrs' Shrine.

most business and diplomatic personnel and their dependants. This was an enclave for Japanese officials in colonial times. "Tianmu," or "Heavenly Mother," refers to a revered Japanese goddess. US military officers moved in after World War II, followed by international businessfolk.

The community core is **Tianmu Circle** (Tianmu Yuanhuan), at the intersection of Tianmu Road and Zhongshan North Road Section 7. To serve the foreign community, many Western-style leisure and recreational facilities exist in the area, and more English is spoken and seen here than elsewhere in Taipei.

Children's Art Museum ❾

Address: B1, No. 20, Alley 50, Tianmu W. Road, www.artart.com.tw
Tel: 02-2872 1366 ext. 14
Opening Hrs: Tue–Sun 10am–5.30pm
Entrance Fee: charge

Transportation: Shipai and taxi or bus

West of the circle is the **Children's Art Museum in Taipei** (Suhe Ertong Meishu Guan), a private facility dedicated to children's art education and skills development. In the Magic Room, kids can "inhabit and interact" with paintings, recomposing them to stimulate the visual and tactile senses.

The Art Tunnel is a hall of mirrors that inspires new perspectives. In the Camel Exhibit Area, young masters show off their own creations. Kids must be four years or older and accompanied by an adult; advance registration is required for groups of 15 or more. Take bus Red 12, Red 15, Red 19, or 645 from Shipai MRT station.

Tianmu Steps ⑩

North of Tianmu Circle are the **Tianmu Steps** (Tianmu Gudao), leading east up Yangmingshan from Alley 1, Lane 232, Zhongshan North Road Section 7. The trailhead is clearly marked with a large signboard (with English) showing the route and main sights. The lower section weaves past apartment buildings before opening up and gliding past trees, through tall grasses, by chirping birds and cicadas, and past small temples before winding up at Chinese Culture University (Wenhua Daxue). This was once a side trail on the Pathway of the Fish, and is today one of Taipei's most popular day hike destinations, just under 2 miles (3km) long, teeming with families on non-working days.

Beitou's hot springs

Northwest of Tianmu, along the base of Yangmingshan, is Beitou District. Since the 1890s, the valley has been a favored mineral springs resort. During the 1905 Russo-Japanese War, Taiwan's Japanese governor was ordered to develop the valley on a large scale to treat Japan's wounded,

in the belief that mineral springs have health benefits. Japanese officers and officials came here for R&R and to escape the Taipei Basin heat. The tradition continued in earnest during World War II when the number of military men stationed on the island ballooned. Many *kamikaze* pilots spent their last few days here, "marrying" local Beitou working girls before flying off to glory.

When the American military had a presence in Taiwan, from the early 1950s to 1979, the area developed a reputation as a red-light district. The national sense of shame was so great that at one point the government revoked the licenses of the 600 prostitutes working here. But the *zona rosa* reputation slowly faded as the popularity of hot-spring soaking among locals waned in the 1980s. In its heyday, Beitou had over 70 hotels and inns.

A resurgence of interest since the late 1990s has seen old inns spruced up and new facilities built. The busiest times are in the (relatively) chilly Taiwan winter, when only a good hot soak can warm the bones.

A therapeutic massage of cascading spring water at Spring City Resort.

A hot-spring soak at a spa.

Hot springs

Relaxing in a mineral-rich hot spring is a very popular activity in Taiwan, and three areas within Taipei and Taipei County are particularly well known for it.

Soaking is one of the most pleasurable pastimes on Earth and, happily, is also said to alleviate a host of chronic afflictions, from arthritis to anemia and from skin to liver disease. Even the robustly healthy might benefit from a boost to the blood circulation. (Note, however, that hot springs are not recommended for pregnant women, and in general, should not replace the medical attention of a qualified physician.)

Northern Taiwan has an unusually high concentration of hot springs due to its location above an area of dormant volcanic activity. Water from underground springs is heated geothermally and forced to the surface, laden with minerals. The hot springs epicenter is undoubtedly Beitou. Xinbeitou MRT station is sometimes filled with the

A private hot spring cabin at Wulai.

smell of sulfur, and clouds of white vapor can occasionally be seen wafting through the tree-lined valley. From here, it's a 10-minute walk to the **Millennium Hot Spring** (6 Zhongshan Rd; daily 9am–5pm; charge; tel: 02-2897 2260). The outdoor public baths are divided into men's and women's sections, but swimsuits are required (small fees for soaking and locker).

Choosing a hot spring

Beitou has three kinds of hot springs: green, white, and ferrous sulfur; temperatures range from 38°C (100°F) to 60°C (140°F). The green water is acidic and is said to cure rheumatism and exhaustion. The white water is sulfurous and is said to cure skin problems and liver disease. The ferrous water is clear and, in theory, drinkable. It is good for nerve strain, and clearing stuffed noses.

For a more exclusive experience, try the **Spring City Resort**. Besides its various outdoor baths, it has private indoor baths, some with modern amenities like flat-screen TVs. This luxury comes at a price, of course, and there are dozens of similar resorts.

The hot springs in Yangmingshan National Park are most easily reached by car. These range from outdoor springs to five-star spa resorts. **Lengshuikeng**, or "Cold Water Pit," has free male/female outdoor baths. On the northern slopes of Yangmingshan is **Tien Lai Spring Resort**, reminiscent of a 19th-century European spa resort (1–7 Mingliu Rd, Chonghe Village, Jinshan Township; www.tienlai.com.tw; tel: 02-2408 0000), with fantastic views of the mountain.

Nearer to the city is the **Landis Resort Yangmingshan**. With several dining options in house, you can enjoy tea and a warm meal in addition to a hot soak.

Not to be forgotten is the hot spring haven of Wulai. There are free **Outdoor Hot Springs** here, but for real pampering, visit the **Volando Urai Spring Spa & Resort**. With stunning scenery to uplift the soul and mineral-rich waters to heat the body, hot springs are a perfect antidote to Taipei's chilly winters.

Ketagalan Culture Center ⑪

Address: No. 3-1 Zhongshan Road, www.english.katagalan.gov.taipei
Tel: 02-2898 6500
Opening Hrs: Tue–Sun 9am–5pm
Entrance Fee: free
Transportation: Xinbeitou

The **Ketagalan Culture Center** (Kaidagelan Wenhua Guan) is located just 200 meters (200 yds) east of the Xinbeitou MRT station. It is dedicated to the flatland tribes that once filled the Taipei Basin. The museum building previously housed special military police forces. Today the 10-story facility contains an indigenous culture exhibition, multimedia showroom, indigenous theme library, conference and performance spaces, and a souvenir shop.

In the basement is a display area for arts and crafts by indigenous artists, including embossed leatherwork by accomplished Atayal indigenous talent Mei-mei Mashao.

On the ground level is an exhibit of historical artifacts from Taiwan's various tribes. The second level is dedicated to exhibitions of traditional artifacts and historical information on the plains peoples. Most are now completely absorbed into the Han Chinese community, and the remainder struggle for identity and recognition.

The third level has displays on all of the island's mountain tribes. The center also houses NGO offices and holds classes to help natives improve their work and language skills. Except for video clips among the displays, the exhibits are static, so call ahead to see if performances are scheduled, generally so on weekends.

Beitou Hot Springs Museum ⑫

Address: 2 Zhongshan Road, http://www.beitoumuseum.org.tw
Tel: 02-2893 9981
Opening Hrs: Tue–Sun 9am–5pm

Indigenous dress on display at Ketagalan Cultural Center.

Entrance Fee: free
Transportation: Xinbeitou

East of the cultural center, at the mouth of the valley in which all Beitou's hot-spring inns sit, is the **Beitou Hot Springs Museum** (Beitou Wenquan Bowuguan), built by the Japanese as Taiwan's first public bathhouse in 1913, and the biggest hot-spring facility in East Asia in its day. Abandoned for years, it was refurbished in 1998. The facade is reminiscent of a Tudor mansion.

Inside, the Roman-style male baths on the first level are intact but for display only. On the second level, the wood construction and *tatami*-lined floors are distinctly Japanese in style. The observation deck offers nice views. Exhibits trace the story of Beitou's love affair with soaking and give a virtual tour of Taiwan's hot springs and major mineral springs areas around the globe. Note that visitor numbers are strictly controlled, so there may be a wait on non-working days. Slippers must be worn inside; they are provided free of charge, or new pairs can be bought.

Long Nice Hot Spring

A short walk up the valley from the museum, at 244 Guangming Road, is **Long Nice Hot Spring**, Beitou's oldest operational bathhouse (Thu – Tue 6.30am–9pm, Fri open until 11.30pm; admission charge; tel: 02-2891 2236). Built in 1907, the interiors are predominantly wood and stone, and there are separate male and female pools. This is a purist establishment – patrons cannot stay overnight, nor is food available. The soaking's the thing. The sense of rustic simplicity is heightened by the primitive-looking but comfortably smooth stone pools. A favorite with local old-timers for its sense of aged familiarity. During the Japanese period, this establishment was famed for its low entrance fees, just three cents; it was nicknamed "House of Three Cents."

The roiling hot waters of Hell Valley.

Hell Valley ⑭

About 10 minutes on foot further up the valley, along Zhongshan Road, is Beitou's most famous site, **Hell Valley** (Dire Gu; Tue–Sun 9am–5pm; free), also called Geothermal Valley in English, an ominously bubbling pit in a small cul-de-sac. Steam rises and drifts across the surface of the boiling water, which can reach a temperature of 100°C (212°F). This spot is the likely source of the place name "Beitou." The indigenous people that once lived in the area fearfully called the valley *Patauw*, meaning "sorceress," sure that the other-worldly phenomena seen here were the result of such dangerous, mysterious figures. The Chinese who came here in the late 1600s to extract sulfur for their munitions from one of the 27 sulfur mines in the area then bastardized the indigenous name.

Though the main Hell Valley pool is scalding hot, a runoff channel just inside the entry gate cools the waters just enough to have once allowed the soaking of one's feet, great for athlete's foot (known in fact as "Hong Kong foot" in Taiwan, as Hong Kong was a renowned moist, malarial place before and long after the British landed there). This is no longer allowed, nor is egg boiling, a once-popular activity here. In the mid-1990s, an unfortunate visitor fell in and was scalded to death. Taking no more chances, the city has locked up all the water-access points.

Beitou Museum ⑮

Address: 32 Youya Road, www.beitoumuseum.org.tw
Tel: 02-2891 2318 ext. 9
Opening Hrs: Tue–Sun 10am–6pm
Entrance Fee: charge
Transportation: Xinbeitou

Housed in a double-story wooden structure is the **Beitou Museum** (formerly the Taiwan Folk Arts Museum). It is dedicated to all of Taiwan's ethnic groups, indigenous or Chinese, and contains over 5,000

The Guandu Temple complex.

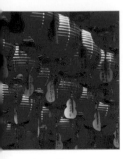

Rows of lanterns hanging at Guandu Temple carry the names of those who receive blessings for making donations to the temple.

At the Nature Center in Guandu Nature Park.

pieces of embroidery, traditional apparel, and arts and crafts. The resplendent Qing dynasty bridal palanquin is a folk treasure of the most intricately carved wood. Most poignant is perhaps the display on foot-binding, a tradition that was suffered by Chinese women at all social levels for centuries except in the Hakka community.

The museum building is a former hot-spring inn built in the 1920s by the Japanese. It was a favorite military officers' club and the most popular spot in Beitou for prepping *kamikaze* pilots. Constructed in Tang-dynasty style – a period during which the Japanese were greatly influenced by Chinese culture – it is set in a traditional garden with a small artificial waterfall in one corner. Socks must be worn inside the museum, lending the place a hushed and reverential ambience.

West of the hot-springs area, in Beitou District's southwest corner where the Keelung River

flows into the Danshui River, are two popular tourist destinations: Guandu Temple and Guandu Nature Park.

Guandu Temple ⑯

Address: 360 Zhixing Road, www. kuantu.org.tw
Tel: 02-2858 1281
Opening Hrs: daily 6am–9pm
Entrance Fee: free
Transportation: Guandu

The **Guandu Temple** (Guandu Gong) complex is tucked under and right up the bluffs beside the Keelung River's north bank. This large, ornate place of worship was originally a small shrine to Mazu, Goddess of the Sea, set up by immigrants from Fujian Province in gratitude for her protection on the dangerous Taiwan Strait crossing. It is said to have first been built in 1661, making it Taiwan's oldest temple, though it has undergone much rebuilding in the intervening years.

The temple is known for having almost perfect *fengshui*: it faces south, with a tall "mountain" bulwark behind it, has good *qi* brought in by a slow-moving body of water moving left to right, and has a wide body of placid water in front – the waters of Guandu Nature Park – acting like a mirror to deflect baleful influences away from the front door.

Behind the temple, a cave leads up through the bluff and onto the crest, where there is a sculpted park with terrific views. Inside the cave, visitors pass many statues of Buddhist *arhats* (saints) and a thousand-armed Guanyin statue, thus seeming to pass through a mystical subterranean world.

Guandu Nature Park ⑰

Address: 55 Guandu Road, http://gd-park.org.tw
Tel: 02-2858 7417
Opening Hrs: Tue–Sun 9am–5pm, Sat–Sun Apr–Sept until 6pm, Oct–Mar until 5.30pm
Entrance Fee: charge
Transportation: Guandu

The low-lying 60-hectare (150-acre) **Guandu Nature Park** (Guandu Ziran Gongyuan) is easily the most accessible large-scale birdwatching site from downtown. Here the Keelung River widens and flows lazily into the Danshui. The tall grasses, mangrove swamp, saltwater marsh, and freshwater ponds present the myriad endemic and migratory birds with nesting and feeding opportunities. Watch for the minuscule version of the fiddler crab native to Taiwan's mudflats. The reserve was created in 2001 after the city bought out the rice farmers here on a large scale – to the tune of NT$430 million. After two years, the wetlands and mudflats had reverted to their natural character.

The **Nature Center** has good exhibits on marshland habitats.

WHERE

The Red No. 2 bus from Yuanshan MRT station goes to all three sites east of the Grand Hotel: Dahu Park, the Martyrs' Shrine, and Miramar Entertainment Park.

Along the Guandu bicycle path.

Boardwalks and three viewing shelters allow easier human access. Numbers are limited, so get there early. There is printed info in English, and English guides can be booked ahead.

The Guandu MRT station is within 10 minutes by foot of both Guandu Temple and the nature park. A bike path zooms by the riverside, and bicycles can be brought on the trains at this station. There are also a number of bike rental shops by the temple.

Blue Highway river tours from Dadaocheng (see page 119) and Danshui (see page 201) also end here, at Guandu Wharf.

National Revolutionary Martyrs' Shrine ⑱

Address: 139 Beian Road, http://afrc.mnd.gov.tw/faith_martyr/index.aspx
Tel: 02-2885 4376
Opening Hrs: daily 9am–5pm

The regal splendor of the Martyr's Shrine.

Entrance Fee: free
Transportation: Jiantan/Dazhi

Just north of the Keelung River, east of the Grand Hotel, three sites of interest beckon. Tucked against the city's northern hills and overlooking the river is the **National Revolutionary Martyrs' Shrine** (Taibei Zhonglie Ci). Completed in 1969, it honors the memory of the more than 300,000 killed in the 1911 revolution that ended imperial rule, the Sino-Japanese War, and the Chinese Civil War. Tablets in Chinese testifying to their deeds are mounted on the four walls of the main building.

The main shrine stands beyond two massive doors lined with oversized brass studs. It is another public edifice in the Ming palace style of Beijing's Forbidden City, specifically the Hall of Supreme Harmony, with bold red pillars, yellow roof tiles, and colorful roof beams. The complex is spread over 3.3 hectares (8 acres) in total.

This was a favorite walking retreat for Generalissimo Chiang Kai-shek, who was portrayed as a Confucian sage of simplicity and austerity. When in the mood for a walk, the entire complex was instantaneously shut down.

Not to be missed is the precision of the 15-minute changing of the guard. It starts at 9am and takes place every hour on the hour, except for the last at 4.40pm. Visitors also love to photograph guards at the main gate, trained to stand as though frozen in time.

Miramar Entertainment Park ⑲

Miramar Entertainment Park (Meilihua Baile Yuan), at 20 Jingye 3rd Road, is another of Taipei's supermalls (daily 11am–10pm; restaurants and entertainment facilities until 11pm; tel: 02-2175 3456; www.miramar.com.tw). Knowing it cannot compete with the scores of brand-name outlets in the eastern district's malls, in part because it lies in an outlying suburb, the complex is positioned as an entertainment-oriented facility targeting young families and youth. Theme-park options complement its mid-range and top-end consumer products. Among the leisure and entertainment facilities here are the mesmerizing neon-lit rooftop **giant Ferris wheel**, a large-screen IMAX theater showing commercial movies, a giant merry-go-round, plus free "water dance" shows and a "seascape avenue" connecting the two main buildings.

Dahu Park ⑳

East of Miramar is **Dahu Park** (Dahu Gongyuan), the scenic core of Neihu, and in contrast to the Entertainment "Park," a bona fide nature area, though human-embellished (31 Chenggong Rd Sec. 5; daily 24 hours; free). Amid wide swathes of soft grass is a natural lake (*Dahu* is, in fact, Mandarin for "big lake"), popular

A dragon detail at the Guandu Temple.

WHERE

In winter the annual Yangmingshan Flower Season is held. The park is "Taipei's back garden," and during Flower Season (Feb–Mar) citizens come en masse to enjoy the lovely flowers in bloom. There are entertainment programs at Yangming Park, Bamboo Lake (with a coordinated Calla-Lily Festival), and other spots, with street performers, music, and exhibits. Special shuttle buses run from Taipei Railway Station and various MRT stations. For more details, ask at one of the Visitor Information Centers (there's one in the train station main hall).

with snow-white egrets, thus explaining the park's other name, "Bailu Park." Other native waterfowl such as Mandarin ducks also flock here. Old fishermen always seem to be present, whiling away their time and landing surprisingly fair-sized catch.

The two bridges over the lake lead to a classical pavilion at the center. The **Nine Bends Bridge** (Jiuqu Qiao), which twists this way and that, calls to mind the Chinese folklore belief that ghosts cannot cross bridges that are not straight, for they can only walk in straight lines. **Jindai Bridge**, which arcs steeply above the waters, imparts a classical Chinese air. Three outdoor swimming pools of good quality are also located here (May–Sept).

On the far side of the lake is **Egret Mountain**, a squat boundary hill 142 meters (465ft) in height with shaded walking trails that pass by small, old temples.

THE NATIONAL PALACE MUSEUM

Not only one of the world's largest collections of Chinese artistic treasures, here is a chronicle of 5,000 years of Chinese history and heritage.

Housed within the museum (see page 173) are over 650,000 artifacts, rare books, and documents, the majority of which were the personal possession of the emperor or part of the imperial archives. The trove has its origins in the Song dynasty (960–1279), but later emperors added to the collection, which reached its zenith in the Qing dynasty, whose Manchu rulers were particularly avid at expanding the trove. When the empire fell and the Republic was established, an Exhibition Office was set up to take charge of the imperial collection.

In 1931, after Japan invaded China, the best of the collection – over 13,000 crates – was hastily hauled away for safety. Shortly before the Nationalists fled the mainland, the top treasures were secretly sent to Taiwan by ship. The collection came to its current home in the 1960s. Hauled over 10,000km (6,000 miles) through 23 towns, over 32 years, it is said not a single piece was damaged. The collection is so vast that only a minor portion can be put on display at any one time. The remainder sits in temperature-controlled tunnels cut into the mountain rock directly behind or is displayed at its newer Southern Branch in Chiayi. The museum will shut or partially close in 2020 for three years to undergo renovation and expansion work. It is expected that during this period many of its treasures will head to the Southern Branch.

Crates of artifacts were stored in Taichung after arriving on the island.

ESSENTIALS

Address: 221 Zhishan Rd Sec.2, www.npm.gov.tw
Tel: 02-6610 3600
Opening Hrs: daily 8.30am–6.30pm; Fri–Sat until 9pm
Entrance Fee: charge, Children's Gallery free
Transport: Shilin MRT and Red 30 bus

The Jadeite Cabbage with Insects is undoubtedly the museum Mona Lisa – its signature piece. It was carved to match the natural colors of the jadeite block used, a response by the artist to nature's own hand. The Chinese cabbage has a white body and green leaves; it is considered to be a symbol of purity and virtue. The katydids on the leaves are a blessing for progeny, and indeed, this Qing dynasty artifact was originally part of the dowry for a concubine.

On the steps at the grand entrance to the National Palace Museum.

This sumptuous work, Four Magpies in Early Spring (only a section is shown here), was created by an anonymous artist of the Yuan dynasty (1279–1368). It is a hanging scroll of silk threads embroidered onto a deep blue base. The fineness of the threads is characteristic of the Yuan dynasty. Depicted are flowers like narcissi, plum blossoms and camellias, decorative rocks, and magpies. Taken together, the piece symbolizes the prosperous and bounteous arrival of spring. The magpies are traditionally believed by the Chinese to symbolize happiness.

The museum is noted for its collection of Song dynasty (960–1279) ceramics, which demonstrate an elegant simplicity very much in contrast to the ornate embellishment that defines Qing dynasty works. The Ru kiln, commissioned exclusively by the court, and a specialist in celadon wares, was the greatest of the major Song dynasty ceramics producers. Today, a mere 50 or so works from this source still exist, and the museum is home to 20 or so, including the delicate Lotus Bowl. Ru ware is known for its warm, opaque glazes, and also known for the fine crackle on the glaze surface, known as "crab claw markings." Ru ware was fired standing on spurs so that the glaze covered the entire vessel.

This globular vase with dragon motif in underglaze blue from the Yongle period (1403–25) of the Ming dynasty is known as a "celestial globe" (tianqiu) due to its large, almost spherical body. The cobalt blue glaze has long been associated with Chinese porcelain outside of China as these were often traded or given as gifts to foreigners during the period.

This Summer Crown is significant not only because it dates from the Qing dynasty, but also because it was worn by the Qianlong Emperor (reigned 1735–96). The study of this and other costume elements in the museum collection has yielded insight into the strict rules governing court regalia at the time.

This meter- (3ft-) long scroll painting (only a small section is shown here) by Qing dynasty (1644–1911) court painters is one of the most dazzlingly detailed paintings in the collection. Entitled Along the River during the Qing Ming Festival, it copies an earlier Song dynasty (960–1279) work, but portrays the lifestyles of the Qing dynasty, such as the lively street entertainment popular at the time. It also shows the influence of Western painting techniques.

This brilliant silk painting by an anonymous artist from the Tang dynasty (618–907) portrays 10 ladies of the inner court at leisure. Entitled A Palace Concert, it shows four ladies playing musical instruments while the others drink tea or wine.

This gilt bronze statue of Shakyamuni Buddha, dating from the Northern Wei dynasty (386–534), is one of the museum's oldest Buddhist artworks. The detail on the gilding is extremely fine. The large halo behind the seated Buddha, for instance, is decorated with flame motifs and the images of seven Buddhas. Behind the halo are scenes from the life of Shakyamuni Buddha. This piece is of Chinese provenance; the majority of the Buddhist artifacts in the museum are Tibetan, including mandalas and other objects.

IN THE ZHISHAN GARDEN

Located on the east side of the museum is the exquisitely landscaped Zhishan Garden. Measuring some 16,000 sq meters (19,000 sq yds), the grounds consciously evoke the great classical gardens of imperial China. Shady pathways meander leisurely among carefully tended trees, shrubs, and flowers. Indeed, the philosophy of classical Chinese gardens has been to create a free-flowing, organic format that invites wandering, unlike the symmetry of buildings.

In the National Museum Palace Garden.

This is a carved red sandalwood curio chest containing 30 items, dating from the Qing dynasty (1644–1911), whose emperors were fond of them. Each chest contained tiny paintings or calligraphic works, porcelain and jade figurines, and even Western miniatures.

Displayed on the wall is a reproduction of the priceless work of calligraphy, Autobiography, by Huai Su, a monk who lived during the Tang dynasty (618–907). When it was written in 777, it captivated the scholarly class with its particularly expressive and unrestrained "cursive" style. It is prized for attaining a spirit of freedom while maintaining a controlled technique. Like other rare works classified as "national treasures," the original piece is only put on display once every three years to prevent rapid deterioration. If it is not on display during your visit, there are other works equally worth admiring. Wang Xizhi of the Jin dynasty (AD 265-420) is considered the "Sage of Calligraphy," and influenced many others. Look out for the Tang dynasty copy of his Clearing After Snowfall.

YANGMINGSHAN

Yangmingshan stands right on Taipei's north doorstep and is Taiwan's crowning national park, a mountain oasis offering an accessible respite from the urban pressures of life in the relentlessly bustling city over which it looks.

The cluster of mountains that forms the westernmost end of the Datun mountain range also forms the northern wall of the Taipei Basin, in which the city sits. Known collectively as Yangmingshan, or Mount Yangming, they were formed in a period of intense volcanic activity about 2 million years ago.

The days of geological excitement are over, but the mountains still give vent to the thermal activity below, creating Yangmingshan's best-loved attractions – fumaroles and hot springs. Hot-spring inns and public pools abound, and in winter the roads are packed into the wee hours with those on their way to and from seeking relief for bones and joints.

Most tourist attractions lie along the Yang-Jin Highway (Yang-Jin Gonglu), which stretches from Shilin District in north Taipei to the fishing port of Jinshan on the North Coast. The highway is also called Yangde Boulevard on the Taipei side. It slides through the saddle between Yangmingshan's two highest peaks, the 1,080-meter (3,543ft) Mount Datun on the west and the 1,120-meter (3,739ft) Mount Qixing on the east. The journey from downtown Taipei to Yangming Park, the starting point for most visits to the national park, takes about 45 minutes by private vehicle.

Yangmingshan National Park

The primary attractions for overseas visitors are the hiking opportunities, which open up green expanses, wide vistas, and a rich variety of resident and migratory fauna. The pristine **Yangmingshan National Park** (Yangmingshan Guojia Gongyuan) takes up the middle and higher

A stunning bird's-eye view from Yangmingshan over the city.

reaches of the mountain. The core of the national park is the lovely, sculpted Yangming Park.

Lin Yutang House ❶

Address: 141 Yangde Boulevard Sec. 2, www.linyutang.org.tw
Tel: 02-2861 3003
Opening Hrs: Tue–Sun 9am–5pm
Entrance Fee: charge
Transportation: Shilin

Right beside the highway, on the lower reaches of Yangmingshan's southern slopes, is the **Lin Yutang House** (Lin Yutang Guju), former home of the renowned linguist, philosopher, poet, and inventor. Educated in the West and a prolific writer in English, Lin (1895–1976) was to the Western world a key voice representing the Chinese in the first half of the 20th century. Swept up in the great Nationalist exodus from China to Taiwan after the Chinese Civil War, he eventually settled in this self-designed villa.

The white stucco residence was built with elements of the Spanish hacienda style. There is a calm inner courtyard with a garden and a fish pond. Inside the house is a memorial library and Lin's personal effects. There is also a backyard café with bird's-eye views, perfect for enjoying fresh mountain air and solitude. Guided tours are available (advance notice).

Yangming Park ❷

Continuing uphill, **Yangming Park** (Yangming Gongyuan) is the first major destination within the national park (daily 8am–6.30pm; free). During the Japanese colonial period, this was an experimental botanical garden, which the KMT government built upon when the national park was established in 1985. The grounds are magnificent – packed with ponds, waterfalls, grottoes, gardens, groves, and brilliant colors. The Feb–Mar bloom of cherry blossoms, azaleas, and camellias is especially delightful, celebrated with the Yangmingshan Flower Season festival. The place gets busy on non-working days; if possible, use public transport. When the crowds lessen, the many resident bird and butterfly species come out of hiding.

WHERE

From Taipei Railway Station, take bus 260 for all sites on the main highway to Yangmingshan Car Park, the bus route's terminus and a 15-minute walk from Yangming Park.

The National Park is a popular place to unwind.

The rooms in Lin Yutang's house, including the bedroom shown here, are displayed basically in the state he left them when he passed away in 1976.

National Park Visitor Center ❸

Address: 1-20 Zhuzihu Road, www.ymsnp.gov.tw (website has information for all the following sights except Bamboo Lake)
Tel: 02-2861 5741
Opening Hrs: daily 9am–4.30pm (closed last Mon of the month)
Entrance Fee: free
Transportation: Shilin

About 400-meters/yds uphill via a connecting trail from Yangming Park is the **Yangmingshan National Park Visitor Center** (Youke Fuwu Zhongxin), which should be the first stop-off point for those wanting to explore the areas outside Yangming Park. Inside is a great mock-up of a volcano and new exhibits on the unique flora, fauna, geology, and trails of the Yangmingshan massif, with a large-scale 3D map invaluable for helping to get your bearings and understand the terrain. The English here and in

the free maps and other print info is good.

This is also the place to book guide services and enquire about the park's few campsites (operated privately).

Yangming Villa ❹

Address: 12 Zhongxing Road
Tel: 02-2861 1444
Opening Hrs: daily 9am–4.30pm (closed last Mon of month)
Entrance Fee: charge
Transportation: Shilin

Off the main highway north of the visitor center is **Yangming Villa** (Yangming Shuwu), a hot-springs inn during the Japanese era that was renovated in 1971 by Chiang Kai-shek, the last of his three Taipei residences. His summer retreat from the city heat, the expansive, heavily wooded grounds have bunkers, barracks, and at least one secret escape tunnel. The buildings are in a dark green hue for camouflage.

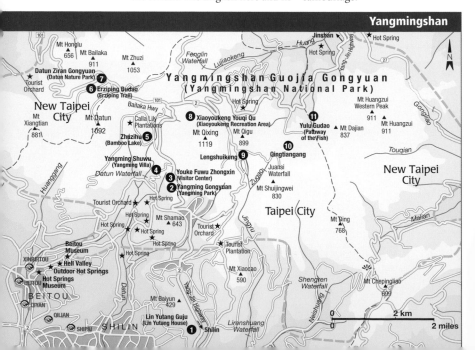

From the second-level balcony of the main residence, one can see the Danshui River snaking all the way to the port of Danshui. Chiang loved the views, which reminded him of China. The interior is as it was in his day. Visitors can sit on the stone bench, amid his plum trees, where he and Madame Chiang sat together feeding the fish.

Caoshan, or "Grass Mountain," was Yangmingshan's original name, referring to the tall silvergrass that covers the highest slopes. Chiang renamed it Mount Yangming after his favorite Ming philosopher Wang Yangming (1472–1529). All visits beyond the Visitor Center are conducted with guides on one-hour tours; tours for individuals are at 9.10am and 1.30pm.

Bamboo Lake ❺

About half a mile (1km) north of the Visitor Center, just before the Yang-Jin Highway passes through the Datun-Qixing saddle, is **Bamboo Lake** (Zhuzihu), situated in a depression created when lava flows from Mount Qixing piled up on its western side.

There is no lake today. The marshy depression was drained by the Japanese to conduct agricultural experiments. This is where the regionally famous Penglai rice was invented, making Taiwan a rice basket for the Japanese empire and China. Today the basin is filled with farms raising crops for sale in the city, and is best known for exotic flowers and, in particular, calla lilies.

Buying flowers and produce is much cheaper here than in the city. Many farms also have dedicated restaurants with courtyard and patio seating, bringing gourmands in great hordes on weekends. Expats in the know like to stroll along the depression's tree-shaded loop road on weekdays, stopping for a light meal and beer at one of the restaurants. In

Yangmingshan is famous for its calla lilies (Zantedeschia aethiopica), and the Calla Lily Festival is a major part of the annual Taipei Flower Festival (Taibei Huaji) organized by the city in the spring.

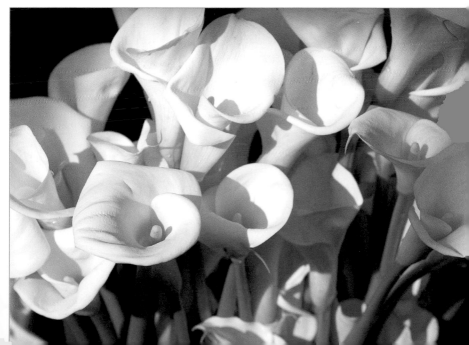

April the area is abloom with white calla lilies.

Erziping Trail ❻

Just north of Bamboo Lake, on the southwestern slope of Mount Datun, the Bailaka Highway (County Highway 101) heads west off the main highway. Follow the path beside the road for about half a mile (1km) to the entrance of **Erziping Trail** (Hudie Hualang). This is a heavily shaded, easy 1.8km (1.1-mile) trail that gives visitors the chance to see some of the area's 151 species of butterfly. Though hot, the period of June–September just after the rainy season (May for higher altitudes) is a good time to visit – it is the peak nectar and pollen season for the butterflies.

Datun Nature Park ❼

The entrance to **Datun Nature Park** (Datun Ziran Gongyuan; daily 9am–4.30pm, closed last Mon of month; tel: 02-2861 7294) is practically across from the entrance to Erziping Trail. This reserve is laced with well-tended raised wooden walkways. One trail snakes through tall swaying silvergrass

The valley of Bamboo Lake.

before nearing the peak of Mount Datun. The vistas from the observation platform are more than worth the walk. There is road access too to this point, as well as to most major spots in the nature park. The peak itself is off-limits, the site of a "secret" military listening post spying on China.

Xiaoyoukeng ❽

Address: 69 Zhuzihu Road
Tel: 02-2861 7024
Opening Hrs: daily 9am–4.30pm (closed last Mon of month)
Entrance Fee: charge
Transportation: Shilin

Back on the Yang-Jin Highway, in the Datun-Qixing saddle, is the **Xiaoyoukeng Recreation Area** (Xiaoyoukeng Youqi Qu), whose star attraction is the fuming Xiaoyoukeng, or "Little Oil Pit." The "oil" is actually acidic water, and the fumarole belches gas and steam. The **Xiaoyoukeng Visitor Center** (Xiaoyoukeng Fuwu Zhongxin) has scale models, a viewing terrace, movie on local nature topics (free), and a parking lot. If possible, avoid this place on weekends. A trail of

medium difficulty leads from here to the top of Mount Qixing. The hike takes about an hour one way. Guided tours are available (booking needed).

Lengshuikeng ❾

Jingshan Road traverses the eastern mid-slopes of Mount Qixing, accessed from the main highway just below Chinese Culture University. The first major tourist spot along here is **Lengshuikeng**, or "Cold Water Pit." Here, waters heated deep beneath the surface mix with cold water gushing from a scar in the earth created by volcanic activity, resulting in a hot spring with lower temperatures than usual. There are public baths (daily 24 hours; free), with separate male/female facilities and a wading pool for foot-soaking. There is also a visitor center with a snack shop and info displays (daily 9am–4.30pm, closed last Mon of month; tel: 02-2861 0036). Guided tours should be booked prior to the visit.

Qingtiangang

Just east of Lengshuikeng is the wide plateau of **Qingtiangang** ❿,

formed by ancient backed-up lava flow from the surrounding extinct volcanoes (daily 9am–4.30pm, closed last Mon of the month; vehicle admission charge; tel: 02-2861 5404). The grass here has been chewed to putting-green consistency by a herd of wild yet generally mellow water buffalo. It is the highest point on the **Pathway of the Fish** ⓫ (Yulu Gudao), an old smuggling route used to get fresh catch from Jinshan port into Taipei Basin past Japanese tax officials. Some who resisted the Japanese military held out for years at Qingtiangang's fortifications. Visit the mock-up of an old gate at the top of the bluffs overlooking Jinshan. The Japanese eventually prevailed, widening the pathway for horse and cannon travel.

The pathway here follows a rushing stream and is dotted with abandoned settlers' huts and picturesque small stone-arch bridges. The rest of the path is today's Jingshan Road and connecting sections of the Yang-Jin Highway. Note that visitor numbers are high on weekends, and vehicle numbers controlled.

Xiaoyoukeng's barren moonscape is covered with bright yellow formations of crystallized sulfur.

Grazing buffalo at Qingtiangang.

Relaxing by Danshui waterfront.

DANSHUI AND BALI

These two river towns – one a former military outpost and port, the other a sleepy fishing village – boast wide waterfront concourses, bike paths, old-style shops and snacks, preserved colonial and historical relics, and the world's northernmost mangrove forest.

Danshui, an old port city about 20km (12 miles) northwest of Taipei, has enjoyed a dramatic revival as a tourist attraction. In the old days, it took an hour to drive from Taipei, and once there, the congested lanes and cluttered waterfront presented formidable obstacles to even the most determined visitors.

Times have changed. The MRT now whisks visitors from downtown Taipei to Danshui (the stop is written Tamsui) in 45 air-conditioned minutes, and Danshui itself has become a tourist-friendly town with wide waterfront concourses, abundant seafood restaurants, boat rides, unique snacks, and carnival games. New attractions aside, it is still home to the colonial-era forts, a former consulate, and other historical sites that first made it famous.

Meanwhile, across the river, an equally remarkable renaissance has taken place in Bali, a once-sleepy town that now boasts its own tourist attractions, including a waterfront bicycle path, a well-preserved mangrove swamp, and the astounding Shihsanhang Museum of Archaeology. Ferries ply the placid Danshui River, carrying day-trippers back and forth between these two

tourist hubs, now one of Taipei's most popular weekend getaways.

Danshui

Located at the mouth of the Danshui, this spot and the nearby city of Keelung are where Taiwan's early Western colonists – the Spanish and the Dutch – made their landings. Danshui's high bluffs provided strategic views of river and ocean, and began to be fortified in 1629. Under this protective umbrella, seaborne trade thrived, and Chinese and other

Main Attractions
Old Street
Fuyou Temple
Fort San Domingo
Former British Consulate
Waziwei Nature Conservation Area
Shihsanhang Museum of Archaeology
Fisherman's Wharf

Map
Page 196

Colonial Fort San Domingo.

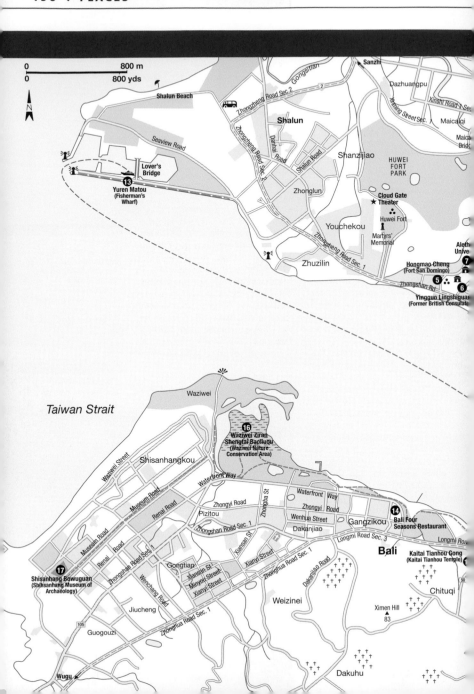

0 | 800 m
0 | 800 yds

N

Shalun Beach

Zhongzheng Road Sec. 2

Gongzithan

2

Sanzhi

Dazhuangpu

Xinshi Road Sec.

Minning Street Sec.

Maicaqi

Maica
Bridg

Shalun

Seaview Road

Zhongzheng Road Sec. 2

Danhai Road

Shalun Road

Shanzijiao

HUWEI
FORT
PARK

Lover's
Bridge

13
Yuren Matou
(Fisherman's
Wharf)

Zhonglun

Cloud Gate
★ Theater

Huwei Fort

Youchekou

Martyrs'
Memorial

Aleth
Unive

7

Zhongzheng Road Sec. 1

Zhuzilin

Hongmao Cheng
(Fort San Domingo)

5

6

Zhongshan Rd

Yingguo Lingshiguan
(Former British Consulate)

Taiwan Strait

Waziwei

16
Waziwei Ziran
Shengtai Baoliuqu
(Waziwei Nature
Conservation Area)

Waziwei Street

Shisanhangkou

Waterfront Way

Museum Road

Renai Road

Waterfront Way

Zhongyi Road

Zhongshan St

Zhongyi Road

Wenhua Street

Gangzikou

14
Bali Four
Seasons Restaurant

Pizitou

Zhongshan Road Sec. 1

Xianyi Street

Dakanjiao

Longmi Road Sec. 3

Longmi

Renai
Road

Museum Road

Zhongshan Road Sec. 1

Gongtian

Xianshi St.

Minyou Street

Xianyi Street

Xianzi St

Zhonghua Road Sec. 1

Dakanjiao Road

Bali

Kaitai Tianhou Gong
(Kaitai Tianhou Temple)

17
Shisanhang Bowuguan
(Shihsanhang Museum of
Archaeology)

Wenchang Road

Zhonghua Road Sec. 1

Jiucheng

Weizinei

Ximen Hill
▲
83

Chituqi

105

Guogouzi

Wugu

Dakuhu

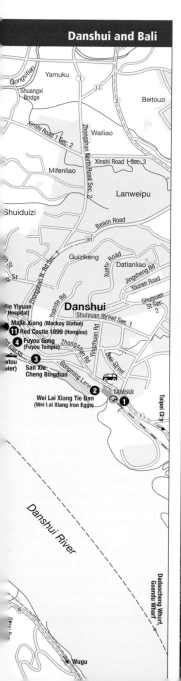

Danshui and Bali

seafarers made regular visits. It was also a vital watering stop (*Danshui* means "fresh water") on the trade routes that connected Hong Kong and Southeast Asia to Japan and the US. Additionally, its location on a fertile stretch of seacoast supported a thriving fishing industry.

Today, Danshui's location and history attract tourists in abundance. But instead of scouring the seas for enemy ships, visitors to old Fort San Domingo now gather to admire the sunsets. The nearby sea still supports a viable industry, but the commercial fisheries now supply the local seafood restaurants. Even the traditional snacks have historical origins. The trading companies long ago left for Taipei, but their descendants are still here, plying the tourist trade. The area surrounding **Tamsui MRT station ❶** is abuzz with street musicians and artists, giving it a lively, vacation atmosphere rarely found in Taipei city.

Danshui's giant ice-cream cones.

Vacuum-packed iron eggs make for a great edible souvenir to take home.

Shopping for beach footwear and treats on Old Street.

Gongming Lane

Walking west from the MRT station along the waterfront, you reach bustling, pedestrianized **Gongming Lane**, a typically Taiwanese night-market street chock-a-block with grilled seafood, hot battered fishballs, fried tofu, cheap clothes, souvenirs, and more.

Right at the entrance is **Wei Lai Xiang Iron Eggs ❷** (Wei Lai Xiang Tie Dan; tel: 02-8631 0171). Since 1946, this shop has been making *tie dan*, or iron eggs, a famous Danshui snack invented to preserve eggs for local fishermen. These are chicken or quail eggs cooked for many hours in a pot filled with fermented bean paste, soy sauce, sugar, and various spices, until the eggs turn jet black. They taste better than the name sounds – the outside of the egg is rubbery but flavorful, while the inside is a crumbly, tasty yolk. They come in five flavors, from sweet to very spicy.

Old Street

Gongming Lane eventually merges into Zhongzheng Road, often called

Old Street (Lao Jie), home to wonderful renovated old trading houses. These thin and elegant buildings are five or six stories tall, and hark back to the days when Danshui was a key trading port. Also of interest are the many little shops selling folk crafts and other items and snacks reminiscent of yesteryear.

Definitely worth a stop is **San Xie Cheng Bingdian ❸**, which has been serving dozens of traditional Taiwanese confections since 1935 (81 Zhongzheng Rd; daily 9am–8pm; tel: 02-2621 2177; www.sanxiecheng.com.tw). There are free samples of their sesame crisp (*zima su*), green tea biscuit (*lücha gao*), pineapple cake (*fengli su*), and other goodies. But be warned: try one, and you might get hooked.

The pumpkin pastry (*jinguarou bing*) is superb. When here, take the time to go to the basement to view the informal but impressive display of traditional Chinese confectionery molds, many of which are used to make the turtle-shaped cakes that serve as prayer offerings (turtles symbolize long life). There are no signs

leading to this unofficial museum of sorts; just go down the stairs in the rear of the shop.

Further up Zhongzheng Road, at No. 200, is **Fuyou Temple** ❹ (Fuyou Gong). This venerable Taoist temple is dedicated to the goddess Mazu, patron saint of fishermen and seafarers. The temple is thick with the smell of candles and incense, and the beams are blackened with the smoke of long years. The place has an eerie, unearthly feel, especially on a rainy afternoon.

From here, a good strategy for a one-day visit to Danshui is to take a 10-minute taxi ride up to Fort San Domingo, before strolling back down to the waterfront and taking a ferry to Bali.

Fort San Domingo ❺

Address: 1, Lane 28, Zhongzheng Road, Danshui

Tel: 02-2623 1001
Opening Hrs: daily 9.30am–5pm, Sat and Sun until 6pm, closed first Mon of the month
Entrance Fee: charge
Transportation: Danshui

Fort San Domingo (Hongmao Cheng) is perhaps the most famous attraction in Danshui. From the entrance, a short walk up a garden path leads to the red stone buttresses of the ancient fort, which overlooks the mouth of the Danshui River. This sturdy building neatly timelines much of Taipei's colonial history. The Spanish built it in 1629 and the Dutch occupied it in 1642. Twenty years later it was rebuilt by Chinese invaders, after Qing-dynasty forces seized control of Taiwan. Its name in Chinese roughly means "fort of the red-haired ones," referring, of course, to the Western colonizers.

WHERE

Fort San Domingo can be reached by taking bus Red 26 from Tamsui MRT station. This bus continues onward to Fisherman's Wharf.

The bust of George Leslie Mackay.

In 1867, the British leased the fort, painted it red, and turned the entire compound into a consulate. A footpath runs from the fort to the **Former British Consulate** ❻ (Yingguo Lingshiguan), a Victorian structure completed in 1891. It is a fine example of colonial architecture, and its graceful verandas and vaulting bay windows evoke impressions of a distant era, when Taipei was considered an exotic posting on the remote side of the world. Because it commands such lofty views of the Danshui River and the Pacific Ocean, this was once a good place from which to fire cannons. Now it is a good place to view the famous Danshui sunsets. Even though Britain was one of the first countries to recognize mainland China over Taiwan, it kept the consulate open here until 1972.

Sweet treats.

Aletheia University

After leaving Fort San Domingo, a left turn up a steep road leads to the entrance of what is known today as **Aletheia University** ❼, at No. 32 Zhenli Street. Founded by Canadian missionary Rev. Dr George Leslie Mackay (see page 198), it was Taiwan's first Western-style educational institution, with a broad-based curriculum. Across a garden and pond is the original Oxford College building, completed in 1882; designed by Mackay, the building blends Eastern and Western elements in unique ways. The bricks and roof tiles were imported from Xiamen, China, and the symmetrical structure is laid out in the traditional Chinese format. But the doors and windows are decidedly Western, and on the roof, pagoda and cross stand side by side in perfect harmony. The Presbyterian Church, built in the gothic style, may fool some – it was actually built in 1997. Inside is one of Taiwan's largest pipe organs at 10 meters (32 feet).

Zhenli Street's A-Gei

Further down narrow Zhenli Street are hole-in-the-wall eateries, home of a famous Danshui snack called *A-Gei*. This Japanese-inspired dish consists of vermicelli crystal noodles stuffed inside a tofu skin, sealed shut with fish meat, and drenched in a savory red sauce. Try **Wenhua A-Gei** ❽ at No. 6-1 (daily 6.30am–6pm; tel: 02-2621 3004). One portion makes for a nice, light lunch.

Mackay memorials

At the end of Zhenli Street, cross Xinsheng Street and go down Jianshe Street until you reach a tiny, triangular park. Here is the **Mackay statue** ❾ (Majie Xiang), a large, black granite bust of the elegantly bearded man. West of the statue, narrow Mackay Street leads to **Mackay**

Hospital ⑩ (Huwei Jie Yiyuan), which was Taiwan's first Western hospital (no entry). It was built by Mackay, and is another example of Western colonial architecture combined with Chinese touches.

East of the Mackay statue, atop a hill reached by 106 stone steps, sits the **Red Castle 1899** ⑪ (Honglou) restaurant, a wonderfully remodeled colonial building. Built in 1899, the British structure was reopened as a restaurant in 2000. The red brick colonnades and green balustrades are punctuated by a sweeping banyan tree in the courtyard. Red Castle commands a magnificent view of the Danshui River and waterfront, although these days the vista is interrupted by a few ugly multistory buildings.

Danshui waterfront

At dusk, visitors gather to watch the sun set behind Guanyinshan across the river. The waterfront becomes a swirl of activity, with carnival games, blasts of smoke from grilled sausage and squid vendors, the shouts of happy children, and the lure of hawkers urging visitors to try their seafood.

Visitors may notice people carrying enormous ice-cream cones. These are another Danshui specialty: you can buy a 20cm (8-inch) swirl of soft-serve atop a cone, while those with better balance and bigger appetites can buy a 50cm (20-inch) swirl.

The Danshui **ferry pier** ⑫ (Duchuan Matou) connects Danshui to Bali and to Fisherman's Wharf. Two ferry companies serve Bali from the Danshui pier.

Fisherman's Wharf ⑬

From Danshui ferry pier, one service heads towards the river mouth to **Fisherman's Wharf** (Yuren Matou), a long pier and harbor that has mostly forsaken its fishing past and become another tourist attraction.

Danshui's waterfront is a magnet for Taipeiers of all ages.

FACT

The Shihsanhang archeological site was discovered in 1955 by an air force pilot, whose compass went crazy when he flew over the iron-rich site. The Shihsanhang people practiced the first native iron-smelting technology in Taiwan.

The highlight of the wharf is its signature pedestrian bridge, Lover's Bridge (Qingren Qiao), an elegant suspended structure in the style of a sailing ship's mast and rigging, which spans the harbor and makes a dramatic addition to the visual esthetics of the area. This pier is a favorite with starry-eyed romantics and sunset photographers.

Bali

Bali is the quiet *yin* to the lively *yang* of Danshui. Instead of a buzzing funfair atmosphere, once you are free of the ferry pier, Bali offers a gentle riverside path that extends the 5km (3-mile) length of the waterfront, sometimes called the Bali Left Bank, and beyond into Taipei Basin. It passes the Waziwei Nature Conservation Area on the way to the Shihsanhang Museum of Archaeology. Bicycles and tandems can be rented, and the ride to the museum is flat and peaceful.

Shihsanhang Museum of Archaeology.

Quality of bikes vary, so check them closely.

As a tourist attraction, Bali is young, and it shows in the boardwalks and young buildings and parks that dot the waterfront. From the comfortable alfresco perch of the **Bali Four Seasons Restaurant ⓮**, Danshui looks like a small strip of lights lying at the foot of the brooding Datun peak.

A short distance away from Bali's ferry pier is the main road, Longmi Road, from where visitors can catch a bus to the Shihsanhang Museum. Across the road is **Kaitai Tianhou Temple ⓯** (Kaitai Tianhou Gong), originally built in 1786, dedicated to the goddess Mazu, a cherished figure in a town that once made its living by fishing and trading. Even by Taiwanese standards, this temple bristles with dragons and other Taoist icons. Mazu is most commonly seen with a dark blue visage, but here has the rarer golden complexion.

About 1.5km (1 mile) west of the ferry pier, reached via Waterfront Way or bike path, is the **Waziwei Nature Conservation Area ⑯** (Waziwei Ziran Shengtai Baoliuqu), the northernmost mangrove forest in the world. Nature-lovers flock to the area to watch the tiny fiddler crabs pop out of their holes and then scuttle back to the safety of the sand, among other ecological wonders. In Chinese, these claw-waving crustaceans are known as "the crabs who call the tide."

Shihsanhang Museum ⑰

Address: 200 Bowuguan Road, Bali Township, https://en.sshm.ntpc.gov.tw
Tel: 02-2619 1313
Opening Hrs: Apr–Oct Mon–Fri 9.30am–6pm, Sat–Sun 9.30am–7pm, Nov–Mar daily 9.30am–5pm, closed first Mon of the month
Entrance Fee: charge
Transportation: Danshui

The US$13 million **Shihsanhang Museum of Archaeology** (Shisanhang Bowuguan) is a remarkable achievement. The building is a modern architectural masterpiece that has won widespread recognition – and the coveted Far East Architecture Award in 2003 – for its dramatic, angular design and user-friendly layouts. The exhibits boast detailed English – a rarity in Taiwan – and the museum is staffed by knowledgeable and friendly guides who can speak good English or Japanese.

But the main attractions are the exhibits, which present a rich and moving cultural experience that illustrates Taiwan's prehistory. The museum is built atop an archeological site rich in relics from the Shisanhang people, who occupied this fertile land some 500 to 1,800 years ago, and who were the first in Taiwan to have iron-smelting technology. They practiced agriculture and harvested clams and other seafood from the rich Danshui delta. Among the displays are cross sections of pits filled with clam shells, shark bones, and deer teeth – evidence of their diet. They were also open to barter and trade and coexisted peacefully with the Dutch, Portuguese, and Chinese traders who frequented Danshui. But they were eventually overwhelmed by the flood of Chinese immigrants who settled in the Taipei area beginning in the 1600s. *Shisanhang* means "13 Companies," referring to the original 13 trading *hang* that operated here during the Qing dynasty.

The museum's most remarkable feature is the Timeline, an elegant suspended bridge that hovers four stories high, providing a bird's-eye view of the exhibits and a unique historical perspective.

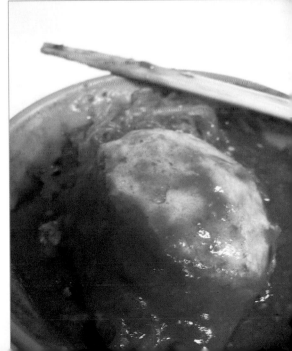

Gung ho gourmands can try the extra spicy A-Gei, which delivers a blast of peppery spice that will have you crying for a cold drink.

Local treats on Jishan Street.

Shopping for goodies at Jishan Street's food stalls.

TAIPEI'S SURROUNDINGS

Just outside Taipei, New Taipei City and Keelung offer many quick and easy day-trip options, featuring rugged coastal and mountain scenery, rejuvenating hot springs, and a glimpse of old-time, small-town life.

On the city's doorstep, and easily accessed via the efficient road and rail networks, are several day-trip options that will satisfy the demands of all visitors. Whether you are interested in exploring the island's history or delving into its religious institutions, there is plenty to see. Alternatively, those seeking to embrace nature, some time away from the crowded city, or simply a soothing soak in a mineral spring, will be spoiled for choice. All of the excursions presented in the following chapters can be reached in just an hour or so.

On the north and northeast coasts, there are sporting options in the surf, tanning and volleyball on the sands, hang-gliding opportunities, camping facilities, and explorations of coastal geology. For the history buff, some of the island's oldest ports in and off the coastal

Rocky Heping Island.

towns will provide the key to understanding the interest exhibited in Taiwan's northern region over the past 400 years by pirates and traders, Spanish, Dutch,

Enjoying the beach at Baishawan.

and Japanese colonists, Chinese settlers, and Canadian missionaries, among others. In the small hill towns of Jiufen and Jinguashi on the northeast coast, one can dig deep into Taiwan's mining history and also discover the harsher legacies of Japan's colonization of the island through the remains of a notorious World War II prisoner-of-war camp.

Directly to the city's south, the town of Wulai enables contact with the island's northernmost indigenous peoples and immersion in its hot-springs soaking culture. Sanxia and Yingge are two towns southwest of the city. Aside from its preserved 19th-century Old Street, Sanxia is host to one of the finest extant examples of temple architecture in Taiwan. Yingge is a center of artistic creativity and has been the heart of the island's ceramics production for the past 200 years.

It is no coincidence that full-day and half-day outings to all of these locations, which are located in a tight ring around the city, are run on a regular basis by Taipei's experienced tour agencies. This is your best option if you are not familiar with the island and local dialects. In general, they provide superb value.

THE NORTH COAST AND KEELUNG

This region is host to the sublime and the surreal, and a synthesis of the two: a giant stone gateway formed by millennia of lapping waves, a temple whose main deity is a dog, a hilltop tomb that sings for visitors, and miles and miles of coastline.

Encompassing the northernmost tip of Taiwan, this area is demarked by the Danshui River in the west and Keelung Harbor in the east. It is washed by the Pacific Ocean and the East China Sea. A line of extinct volcanoes still simmering down under, the Datun Range, forms its back. This is the north coast, with its crashing surf, blue waves, fresh ocean catches, and the most bizarre and beautiful stone sculptures crafted by Mother Nature.

NORTH COAST

Most of the North coast is incorporated into the **North Coast and Guanyinshan National Scenic Area** (Beihaian Ji Guanyinshan Guojia Fengjing Qu), an easily accessible place of calm as well as natural ruggedness.

Baishawan ❶

Provincial Highway No. 2 is the only road that runs along the north coast between the breakers and the mountainside. Commonly referred to as the North Coast Highway, its first few kilometers east of Danshui negotiate undulating hills. The sea appears abruptly at **Baishawan**, or "White Sand Bay," a beach tremendously popular with locals on non-working

days. The soft white sand found here is a rarity along the mainly rocky coastline, and there are shower facilities and eateries. Those not keen on basting themselves in the hot sun can rent equipment for surfing and windsurfing. The lifeguards on the beach are quite bossy and will herd everyone back who strays into the roped off area. The winds are best when the cool northeasterlies blow from November to March. Locals avoid the place during this period, resulting in thinner crowds.

Main Attractions
Shimen
Temple of the 18 Kings
Jinbaoshan
Ju Ming Museum
Yeliu Geological Park
Miaokou Nightmarket
Zhongzheng Park
Ershawan Fort
Heping Island Park

Map
Page 210

Jinbaoshan's neat rows of tombs.

NSA headquarters

The **National Scenic Area headquarters** (Bei-Guan Guojia Fengjing Qu Guanli Chu; daily 9am–5pm; tel: 02-8635 5100; www.northguan-nsa. gov.tw) is located right by the beach at the Baishawan Visitor Center. This large facility has some good exhibits with usable English, plus useful maps.

Shimen ②

Sitting right by the highway a few kilometers east of Baishawan is the most unusual natural landmark on the coastal route, **Shimen**, or "Stone Gate." Shimen is a huge coral formation that was gradually pushed high above the waterline by heaving tectonic activity over the recent eons. As it rose, pounding wave action ate away its center, leaving a hole large enough to drive a truck through. A narrow and steep flagstoned path leads to the low summit and panoramic views.

Temple of the 18 Kings ③

Tucked under a bluff beside the highway is the **Temple of the 18 Kings** (Shibawang Gong), surely one of Taiwan's most unaffected cultural experiences (daily 24 hours). Of the 18 gods celebrated here, 17 are human and one is a dog.

The story goes (there are variations galore) that a ship went down offshore here on a rough crossing from China in the Qing dynasty. Seventeen merchants drowned, and after failing to save its master, a dog came ashore, sat down here, and starved while steadfastly waiting for its master to appear. A temple was built by locals inspired by its loyalty.

As the gods were businessmen when mortals, those who worship wealth come here in droves. Members of the underworld frequent the place late at night, making for a raucous festival atmosphere. Snack vendors, trinket sellers, and old-style games stands abound, as do families

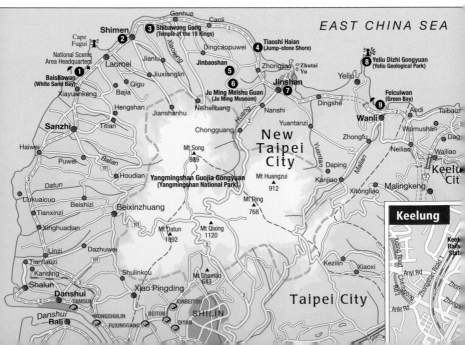

and young couples, making for a one-of-a-kind cultural scene that is great fun and entirely safe.

Tiaoshi Haian ❹

The highway heads southeast to Jinshan District along a section colloquially known as **Tiaoshi Haian**, or "Jump-stone Shore," on some Chinese-language tourist maps. The origin of this moniker is evident from the massive boulders – some bigger than houses – that have fallen onto the beaches from the bluffs towering above the highway.

Jinbaoshan ❺

At the 34.8km or 39.7km mark on the highway, turn inland and uphill to **Jinbaoshan** (daily 24 hours; free; tel: 02-2498 5900).

This is not your average tourist site. It is a graveyard that is the nearest thing Taiwan has to Graceland. The highlight is the tomb of Teresa Teng, a Taiwanese songstress who died of asthma in 1995 at age 43. She sang in many languages, and is revered by the Japanese, Hong Kongers, and other Asian tourists you'll see at the tomb. A special jukebox of sorts has been set up by the tomb to allow public enjoyment of Teng's musical legacy.

Others come here for the solitude, magnificent tomb architecture, and thrilling views. The entire upper slope is neatly lined with the tombs of Taiwan's esteemed and famous. Buried here is master puppeteer Li Tian-lu. The gardens are evocatively sculpted in mystical Buddhist style, complete with a tunnel of macabre sculptures under a pagoda, depicting man's passage from chubby new life to decrepitude and death, signifying life's impermanence.

Ju Ming Museum ❻

The roads to Jinbaoshan also lead to the **Ju Ming Museum** (Ju Ming Meishu Guan; Tue–Sun May–Oct 10am–6pm, Nov–Apr 10am–5pm; charge; tel: 02-2498 9940; www.juming.org.tw), on a nearby plateau with sweeping views. The 10-hectare (26-acre) museum, with Taiwan's

WHERE

Dedicated shuttle buses leave for the Ju Ming Museum from beside the Jinshan Township Office in Jinshan. Get there via the Jinshan line bus from Tamsui MRT station. Times for the shuttle vary; check the museum website.

Teresa Teng's tomb at Jinbaoshan.

North Coast

0   3 km
0   3 miles

Liandong

Mt Jilong
2   587
g Dao   Badouzi
uah   Shenao   Ruibin   Jinguashi
g Island Park)   Jiufen
nqiao
rshawan Paotai
aimen Tianxian)   **Ruifang**

New Taipei City   Sandiao
Peak
ung   Linyukeng   523   102
Houdong
Mt Sanguazikeng
536
Sijiaoting   Mt Wufen
757
uannuan

❶
Xinlu
Xinwu Rd   ZHONGZHENG GONGYUAN
(ZHONGZHENG PARK)
Shorshan Road

Guanyin
Statue

300 m
❿ Miaokou Yeshi   300 yds
(Miaokou Nightmarket)

Lee Hu Pastry Shop (est. 1882), at No. 90 Rensan Street, is considered by many to be Taiwan's best purveyor of sweet pineapple cake (fengli su), a bite-size cube-shaped pastry shell filled with chewy pineapple paste (daily 9am–9.30pm; tel: 02-2422 3007; www. lee-hu.com.tw).

Street vendor in Jinshan town.

largest outdoor sculpture garden, is filled with some 500 of the thickly sliced rock figures by Ju Ming, one of Taiwan's best-known artists. It is home to an equal number of his paintings.

Jinshan ⑦

There isn't very much to see in the little fishing town of **Jinshan**, but do make a quick stop at **Jinbaoli Street** (Jinbaoli Jie) in the town's overflowing old center. It is one of the last streets in Taiwan to retain the look of its Qing-dynasty origins.

There is a high viewing platform on the edge of town with views of the aptly named **Candlestick Islets** (Zhutai Yu) offshore.

Yeliu Geological Park ⑧

East of Jinshan is the **Yeliu** ("Wild Willows") **Geological Park** (Yeliu Dizhi Gongyuan; daily 8am–5pm; charge; tel: 02-2492 2016; www.ylgeopark.org.tw), where there are no willows but instead a rich grove of bizarre sandstone, lava, and coral sculptures eroded by wind and waves. Its most famous rock is one

that resembles a bust of Egyptian Queen Nefertiti.

A footpath climbs steeply up toward the tip of the long, narrow promontory. The views from the lighthouse here are worth the ascent.

Green Bay ⑨

Feicuiwan, or **Green Bay** (24 hours; free; tel: 02-2492 6565) is another popular beach resort. Equipment for hang-gliding, parasailing, jet-skiing, and windsurfing is available. This is also one of the few spots in northern Taiwan where surfing is possible.

On weekends you'll see paragliders floating down from the bluffs behind. Riders are willing to ride tandem with thrill-seekers for a small fee. But note that these are not accredited instructors, and have no connection with the nearby resort. A popular company is **Mustang Paragliding Club** (tel: 0932 926 289; https://mustangparagliding.com). One thing that heightens the soaring fun is the presence of a camouflaged hilltop Patriot missile battery and hillbottom ammo dump; errant gliders are constantly irritating the soldiers.

KEELUNG

Keelung is Taiwan's second-busiest seaport, and the maritime gateway for the island's north. Sandwiched between high hills and saltwater, there are a number of interesting cultural and historical sites here.

Miaokou Nightmarket ⑩

Just east of the harbor's inner end is **Miaokou Nightmarket** (Miaokou Yeshi; daily dusk–midnight; www.miaokow.org), one of Taiwan's most renowned. It runs for 300 meters/yds along Rener Street in front of old **Dianji Temple** (Dianji Gong). There are hundreds of delicious traditional Taiwanese snacks to try. Fresh seafood figures prominently. Sample the *tianbula*, a Taiwanese adaptation of Japanese tempura served with a slightly sweet and spicy red sauce.

Zhongzheng Park ⑪

From the harbor you can see the white statue of Guanyin, the Goddess of Mercy, standing atop a hill to the east, watching over ships, sailors, and residents. This is peaceful **Zhongzheng Park** (Zhongzheng Gongyuan; daily 6am–10pm; free) on Shoushan Road. Climb up into the 25-meter-tall (75ft) statue for the best views. Behind is a tranquil Buddhist temple.

Haimen Tianxian ⑫

Higher up the hill are the remains of **Haimen Tianxian**, better known as Ershawan Fort (Ershawan Paotai; daily 9am–5pm; free), built by the Qing government in 1840. Entry is through an impressively refurbished classical fortress gate. Quiet pathways lead through the grounds, and reproduction cannons in the original gun emplacements overlook the harbor and sea. *Haimen Tianxian* translates literally as "Sea Gate Heaven Danger," implying that those who trespassed below would call down the wrath of the heavens. The fort saw action in the 1884–85 Sino-French War, but its effectiveness was diminished because its cannons were locked in position. This is an official "First Rank" Taiwan heritage site.

Heping Island Park ⑬

Heping (Peace) Island, reached via a short bridge near the harbor mouth, is where the Spanish built their main fort in 1626. No ruins remain today, but this hilly rock is the location of **Ho Ping Island Hi Park** (Heping Dao Gongyuan), full of bizarre rock formations and wind-swept paths – rather like a smaller and less touristy version of Yeliu (daily 8am–6pm; charge; tel: 02-2463 5452; www.hpipark.org). Included in the fun are a small beach, a half-hour round the island mountain hiking trail, a marina, a cave and the Radar Station Café (9.30am-9.30pm daily) with dreamy views of the ocean.

WHERE

From Tamsui MRT station, travelers can catch a bus that plies Provincial Highway No. 2, along which are most of the tourist sights. The bus route terminates at the commuter railway station in front of Keelung Harbor.

At the Temple of the 18 Kings, a faux gold-plated icon of the canine deity is installed. Oddly enough, worshippers stick burning cigarettes in the incense urns rather than joss sticks. Rubbing the dog is also said to bring good luck.

A dramatic evening view of the coast from Jiufen.

JIUFEN, JINGUASHI, AND THE NORTHEAST COAST

Offering some of the most rugged and spectacular scenery found in north Taiwan, this area is defined by lofty mountains and surging sea. The long-isolated mining towns of Jiufen and Jinguashi, on Mount Jilong, are drenched in history and nostalgia.

Much of this region falls within the official boundaries of the **Northeast and Yilan Coast National Scenic Area** (Dongbeijiao Yilan Haian Guojia Fengjingqu).

Jiufen is reached via County Highway No. 102, the Ruijin Highway, which winds east from Keelung. Just east of Jiufen, Jinguashi sits in a steep, narrow valley on the southeast side of Mount Jilong.

JIUFEN

A town of steep lanes and steps, Jiufen has become a prime tourist destination for locals since the release of Taiwanese director Hou Hsiao-hsien's acclaimed movie *City of Sadness*, partially filmed here. The film depicts the sufferings of Taiwan's people when Chiang Kai-shek's KMT party set up its exile government in the 1940s. The town's narrow streets are lined with old red-brick, wood-frame buildings left over from the gold-rush days of the late 19th and early 20th centuries. Many have since been converted into teahouses with stunning views.

Jiufen was dubbed "Little Shanghai" at the height of the gold rush in the 1920s and 1930s, when it was jammed with theaters, seedy teahouses, wine houses, and brothels,

Jiufen's steep Shuqi Road.

its glittering lights clearly visible from far out at sea. The town's only through road, called Qiche ("Car") Road, is one of the few traffic arteries wide enough for four-wheeled vehicles. Walking tours generally start at the junction of Qiche Road and Jishan Street, going downhill via Shuqi Road back to the highway.

Along Jishan Street

Along **Jishan Street ❶** (Jishan Jie), a narrow pedestrian lane with only the occasional scooter, the sky is for long

Main Attractions

Jishan Street
Shuqi Road
Jiufen Folk Art Gallery
Gold Ecological Park
Nanya
Fulong Beach
Cape Sandiao Lighthouse
Maoao Fishing Village
Beiguan Tidal Park
Caoling Historic Trail

Maps

Pages 216, 220

The design of the City of Sadness Restaurant evokes the Japanese colonial era; best of all is the open-air rooftop teahouse-cum-dining area, with the town looming above and the sea crashing below.

stretches almost blocked from view by the awnings of the densely packed eateries, galleries, jewelry shops, and souvenir stands.

Each tourist destination in Taiwan has its *mingchan*, or local "famous products," and fish stew is one of Jiufen's. Visit **Grandma's Fish Stew ②** (A-Po Yugeng; daily 8.30am–5pm; tel: 02-2497 6678), at No. 9 Jishan Street, for a taste. Other local specialties are fried taro and sweet-potato balls, and spicy beef noodle soup. Drop in at **Jiufen Old Noodle House ③** (Jiufen Lao Miandian), at No. 45, where the secret house ingredients add a unique twist to the beef broth in which the thick beef slices and noodles are boiled (daily 10.30am–7.30pm, Sat–Sun until 8.30pm; tel: 02-2497 6316).

Shuqi Road ④

Near the end of Jishan Street is the junction with the renowned **Shuqi Road** (Shuqi Lu), a steep and

exceedingly narrow stone stairway that fairly plummets downhill (362 steps!), home to most of the picturesque shooting locations for *City of Sadness*. The lane is lined with teahouses, a number in heritage buildings, all with great views of the hills, coast, and ocean.

City of Sadness Restaurant ⑤

The wood-framed, three-story **City of Sadness Restaurant** (Beiqing Chengshi Chalou), on the corner of Shuqi and Qingbian roads, was one of the main locations for the film's local shoots (35 Shuqi Rd; daily 24 hours; tel: 02-2496 0852).

Gold Mining Museum ⑥

The small but interesting **Jiufen Gold Mining Museum** (Jiufen Jinkuang Bowuguan; daily 10am–6pm; charge; tel: 02-2496 6379) is off Qingbian Road and down short Shibei Lane, at No. 66. If you want to

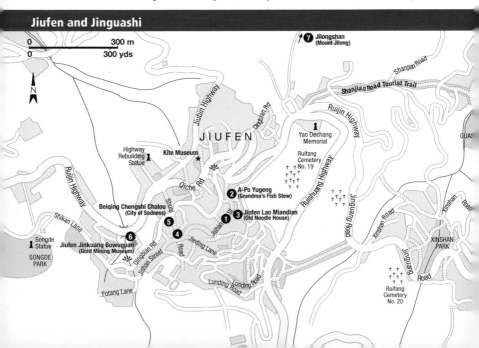

learn all that is needed to get your-self launched in gold mining and processing, there is no better place; the friendly curator teaches the art of panning and smelting, and often lets visitors try it out.

Mount Jilong ❼

At the north end of town, take the long grass-swept path that climbs up to the crest of **Mount Jilong** (Jilongshan), an extinct volcano that stands between Jiufen and the sea. The flagstoned walk ends at a few pagodas with an awe-inspiring 360-degree vista. On weekdays the area is very quiet.

JINGUASHI

A marked footpath, **Shanjian Road Tourist Trail**, guides visitors from Jiufen to Jinguashi. This valley was the site of a notorious Japanese POW mining camp during World War II. The abandoned mining and smelt-ing facilities, the old guesthouse

originally built for a visit by Emperor Hirohito, and other facilities from the bygone era of mining prosperity are now being developed for tour-ism, and offer stimulating walks that evoke the turbulent past.

Gold Ecological Park

Though Jinguashi's most important historical relics are all spread out through the valley, they are under the common administration of the **Gold Ecological Park** (Huangjin Bowu Yuanqu; Mon–Fri 9.30am–5pm, Sat–Sun 9.30am–6pm, closed first Mon of the month). Access to the "park" – the valley, in other words – is free, but admission is charged for the main attractions – all those intro-duced below and a few others.

Information centers

The place to start is the **Tourist Information Center ❽** (Youke Fuwu Zhongxin; 51-1 Jinguang Road; tel: 02-2496 2800; www.gep-en.ntpc.gov.

The curator of the Jiufen Gold Mining Museum happily demonstrates the art of panning for gold to visitors.

The old refinery ruins near Jiufen.

Jiufen and Jinguashi

Jinshui Highway
Qitang Road
Guashan Sports Center
Wuhao Road
Qitang Road
Qitang Road
JINGUASHI
Jinguang Road
Fuwu Zhongxin (Tourist Information Center) ❽ ❶
❾ Huanjing Jiaoyu Guan (Environment Education Center)
❿ Taizi Binguan (Crown Prince Chalet)
Benshan Wukeng (Benshan Fifth Tunnel)
Huangjin Bowu Yuanqu (Gold Ecological Park)
⓫
⓬ Huangjin Bowuguan (Museum of Gold)

Jinguashi literally means "gold melon rocks," in reference to the yellow sulfur-coated boulders strewn along the stream that hurtles down the gorge.

tw/). Free parking is provided here – almost impossible to find elsewhere in the valley. There are introductory displays with some English and tickets are on sale. It is located in the old Taiwan Motor Transport bus station.

East of the Information Center is the **Environmental Education Center ❾** (Huanjing Jiaoyu Guan), an old mining company administrative building offering fixed exhibits and multimedia presentations on Jinguashi's natural ecology and the history and culture of mining. There is also a good introductory movie shown on the park.

Crown Prince Chalet ❿

Just south of the Environmental Education Center is the **Crown Prince Chalet** (Taizi Binguan), a villa in traditional Japanese style with a landscaped garden, archery field, and, incongruously, a mini-putt. It was built in 1922 in preparation for a grand tour of the colony by the future Emperor Hirohito of Japan, then Crown Prince. In the end, the tour did not take place. The chalet itself is not open for public visits.

Benshan Fifth Tunnel ⓫

Just before the top of the valley is **Benshan Fifth Tunnel** (Benshan Wukeng), a long shaft in which visitors can get a decidedly gloomy glimpse of life in the mines, an experience heightened by piped-in sounds of drilling, miners talking, and explosions (additional admission charge). The nine tunnels in the valley stretch 600km (370 miles) and go as deep as 132 meters (433ft) below sea level. The Japanese wanted gold to finance their war activities, and both sulfur and copper for the armaments they required. They set up the infamously brutal Kinkaseki mining camp here.

Museum of Gold ⓬

Right by the Benshan tunnel, the **Museum of Gold** (Huangjin Bowuguan), devoted to the precious metal and its extraction, is housed in a glass-and-steel retrofit of an old Taiwan Metal Mining Co. building. In the **Gold Panning Experience**, you can try your luck and can take home anything your Midas touch reveals.

NORTHEAST COAST

Along the northeast coast, the majestic Xueshan (Snow Mountain) range spills into the Pacific, making for lovely vistas with blue waters in front, narrow slivers of flatland on the coast, and towering bluffs pressing in behind. Weekends and holidays see every coastal nook and cranny crowded with day-trippers from the Taipei Basin.

Fishing is the primary industry here, and all along the coast you will come across brightly painted craft packed like sardines in little harbors. A single road – Provincial Highway No. 2, commonly called the Coastal Highway – is etched into the base of the high bluffs along the shore.

If you are driving on the heavily used Coastal Highway, to get to the most southerly points and back in

Tableaux at the Benshan Fifth Tunnel.

one day requires an early morning start. An alternative is the Taipei-Yilan expressway for one leg of the journey. Though tunneled and not offering a lot in terms of view, it allows you to reach Yilan County in just 40 minutes instead of two and a half hours or more, leaving more time for each coastal scenic spot.

Avoid using Provincial Highway No. 9 to Yilan, which starts from Xindian, south of Taipei. It is a windy, dangerous, and extremely unpleasant mountain traverse – though quite pretty.

Nanya ⓭

Traveling southward, **Nanya** is the first site within the National Scenic Area (NSA), at the 89km mark on the Coastal Highway (roadside markers indicate distances, calculated using the city of Keelung as the base). Strange rock formations abound here, the result of wind and water erosion of the area's sandstone. The stone, which used to be underwater long ago, has been pushed up by tectonic activity. It is laden with veins of iron, making for efflorescent

striations that are quite dazzling when exposed.

Boardwalks here make walking between and atop boulders very pleasant. Be sure to leave time to head away from the crashing surf and line fishermen in order to sally under the highway and into the deep, narrow valley behind, where you will see farmers in traditional conical bamboo leaf hats tending stamp-size plots on steep slopes.

Cape Bitou

Cape Bitou (Bitoujiao) juts out into the ocean at the highway's 93km mark. It covers an area of almost 500 hectares (1,235 acres). Caves, plateaux, and other landforms can be found at the base of its craggy cliffs, eroded by surf and wind.

Atop the cape, watching over the crashing waves, is the gleaming white **Bitou Lighthouse** ⓮ (Bitou Dengta). It was built by the Japanese in 1896, and was given its present form after being bombed by the Allies in World War II. You can reach it along a trail that snakes up from beside the highway; the highway passes under the

At the Museum of Gold in Jinguashi you can caress for luck the gold bar that holds the Guinness Record, weighing in at 220kg (485lbs).

A striated rock formation at Nanya.

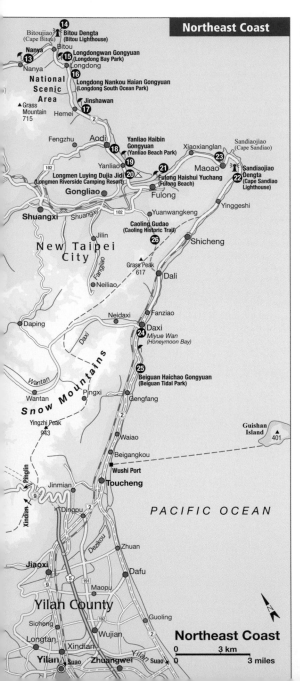

Northeast Coast

cape through a tunnel. Atop the bluffs you'll be rewarded with spectacular views of mountains falling into the sea, as far as the eye can see.

Longdong

One of the most popular swimming spots on the northeast coast and also one of Taiwan's premier diving locations – certainly the best in the north – is **Longdong Bay Park 15** (Longdongwan Gongyuan; daily 8am–5pm weather permitting; charge; tel: 02-2490 9445) at the 95.5km mark. It contains a great variety of marine life in its cool, clear waters. The recreational facilities within the park include a good range of equipment for water activities. There are also vertical cliffs good for rock climbing at the tip of the cape.

The bay was named *Longdong*, or "dragon cave," either because it seems like the entrance to a dragon's lair, or because the Mandarin name stems from a similar-sounding indigenous word.

At the south end of Longdong Bay is **Longdong South Ocean Park 16** (Longdong Nankou Haian Gongyuan; daily 8am–6pm; charge), its entrance at the 96km mark. The naturally formed pools, once abalone ponds, are just knee-deep at low tide, but surge to 9 meters (30ft) in depth at high tide, making for good snorkeling and scuba-diving, with sightings of shrimp, crab, starfish, sea urchins, mollusks, and sea anemones. The visitor center houses an exhibition on geology and different forms of land and marine life found on the northeast coast. There is also a marina here. Starting at the north end of Longdong South Coast Park is a meandering, coast-hugging pathway of majestic viewpoints leading back to Cape Bitou. Note there is also a vehicle parking charge at both Longdong locations, with limited free opportunity along the highway, especially on weekends.

Jinshawan ⑰

At about the 100km mark on the highway is **Jinshawan**, the aptly named "golden sand bay." The fine 200-meter (660ft) stretch of sand is constantly packed with sun-seeking beach lovers. Facilities include a children's recreation area and beach volleyball courts.

Aodi ⑱

The fishing village of **Aodi**, at the 103km mark, is renowned for the still-flapping, still-crawling freshness of its seafood. Like the fish that pose expectantly in the tanks lined up at their entrances, the restaurants here jostle together right along the highway, which is also the town's main thoroughfare.

Yanliao

South of Aodi is **Yanliao Beach Park** ⑲ (Yanliao Haibin Gongyuan), the largest developed recreational site on the northeast coast, with golden beaches that stretch south all the way to Fulong. The waterfront pond and

garden here are well designed and a pleasure to walk through.

In 1976 the **Yanliao Colonial Resistance Historical Site** (Yanliao Kangri Jinian Bei) was set up to honor the fighters from Taiwan and China who tried to repel the Japanese troops who landed here in 1895 after China ceded the island upon losing the Sino-Japanese War.

Longmen Riverside Camping Resort ⑳

The **Longmen Riverside Camping Resort** (Longmen Luying Dujia Jidi) is at the highway's 107.8km mark (daily 8am–7pm; charge; tel: 02-2499 1791). *Longmen*, which means "dragon's gate," refers to the debouchment of the Shuangxi River, the largest waterway in the northeast. The 37-hectare (91-acre) resort offers a superb range of facilities. The campsite includes three log cabins and roofed wooden platforms. Watersports facilities are in abundance. From here Yanliao beach can be accessed by foot or bike (rentals

Taipeiers flock to Aodi on weekends and holidays for the winning combination of fresh seafood and a seaside drive.

The rocky cliffs of Cape Bitou.

The Ho-Hai-Yan Music Festival, Taiwan's biggest rock festival, is held over three days at Fulong Beach each summer. Some 20,000 revelers attend at any one time. Admission is free. Trains run hourly between Taipei and Fulong, and shuttle buses to and from Fulong station.

Surfing at Honeymoon Bay.

available) along trails which bring you across a postcard-perfect suspension bridge spanning 200 meters (660ft) over the Shuangxi River. There is also a parking fee here.

Fulong Beach

Fulong Beach (Fulong Haishui Yuchang; daily 8am–6pm; charge), at the 108.8km mark on the Coastal Highway, is undoubtedly the northeast coast's most popular beach. It boasts a complete range of watersports facilities. The waters are comparatively sheltered here, making it suitable for non-powered boating activities such as windsurfing, rowing, and kayaking. The **Fulong Visitor Center** (Fulong Youke Fuwu Zhongxin; 36 Xinglong St, Fulong Village; daily June–Sept 8am–6pm, Oct–May 9am–5pm; tel: 02-2499 1210; www.necoast-nsa.gov.tw), located beside the National Scenic Area administration headquarters, has exhibits, print materials, video briefings, and other information on the area's natural and cultural treasures. Note the smaller stretch of sand just south and next to the temple is free.

A carved rock on Caoling Historic Trail.

Cape Sandiao

The tip of **Cape Sandiao** (Sandiaojiao) is Taiwan's easternmost point. The **Cape Sandiao Lighthouse** (Sandiaojiao Dengta; Tue–Sun 9am–4pm; free; tel: 02-2499 1300), gleaming white on a pristine green lawn, was built in 1935. The lane to the lighthouse is at the 116.5km mark on the Coastal Highway. "Sandiao" is a rendering of "San Diego," a name bestowed in the 1620s by the Spanish on their first trip to scout for sites to build the forts needed in order to contest the Dutch.

Maoao Fishing Village

Just north, tucked seemingly right under the eroding cliffs of the cape, is perhaps Taiwan's loveliest little harbor, **Maoao Fishing Village** (Maoao Yucun). The *ao* means "fishing harbor" in Taiwanese. The bright fishing boats float shoulder to shoulder and

there are numerous quaint old stone houses built by early settlers. Under the cliffs boardwalks have been built, and at low tide you can walk out to the breakers.

Daxi (Honeymoon Bay) ㉔

Nestled in a horseshoe-shaped cove given the popular moniker "Honeymoon Bay" (Miyue Wan), **Daxi** (131.5km mark) offers the north's best surfing. The waves are generally 2–3 meters (6–10ft) high. On weekends and holidays you'll find many aficionados who have risen before dawn to get in a full day's surfing. Non-surfers also abound, lured by the black sand, ghost crabs, and vivid sunrises.

Beiguan Tidal Park ㉕

At the 136km mark is **Beiguan Tidal Park** (Beiguan Haichao Gongyuan; daily 8am–midnight; free; parking fee), where twisting pathways sculpted out of coral and heaved high by tectonic activity lead to the top of a rugged, massive oceanside outcrop with stunning views of sea and mountain. Below,

cuesta formations and rock jostle for space. Beiguan was fortified in the late Qing dynasty to watch for enemy ships. A cannon emplacement is on display. The crowded line of small eateries, though now a bit ragged, features some very tasty and fresh seafood.

Caoling Historic Trail ㉖

The northeast coast also offers pleasant walks in the hills away from the surf. The **Caoling Historic Trail** (Caoling Gudao) was part of a key pathway connecting northwest and east Taiwan in the past. It was an indigenous trail expanded by Han Chinese pioneers in the early 1800s. Today most of the original trail has returned to nature, but the Caoling section has been rescued and spruced up. The trail takes about four hours to complete, one way; there are some challenging grades.

The views along the pathway are quite inspiring, and there are also a number of protected historical relics. The southern trailhead can be accessed from Dali train station, at the 127km mark of the coastal highway.

EAT

Hikers on the Caoling Historic Trail are advised to bring along their own food and drink, for there are no vendors or other refreshment facilities along the way.

An old stone house at Maoao.

KINKASEKI

More than 1,000 Allied prisoners were brought to Kinkaseki during World War II. More than one-third died. They performed slave labor in the deep mines where paid, local miners refused to go – 250 meters (800ft) below sea level, on hands and knees, in temperatures up to 55°C (130°F). Their Spartan diet consisted of rice and watery vegetable soup. The POWs were subjected to regular beatings, especially if the heavy daily quotas were missed. Incarceration in the wooden coffin-like "Ice Box" was dreaded.

A memorial that marks the remnants of "Hell Camp" was erected in 1997. An annual commemorative ceremony is held here.

The Wulai Cable Car affords a great view of the valley.

WULAI, SANXIA, AND YINGGE

At the base of the foothills just south of the
city are three towns of distinctive character,
offering insight into local indigenous and
hot-springs culture, age-old religious
tradition, and artistic expression in ceramics.

Day trips to these three towns
are a breeze via the island's
modern, convenient highway
system, whether one is driving one-
self or with a tour group. The trio lie
in valleys through which two large
rivers flow north into Taipei.

Wulai nestles in a narrow valley
along one of the upper tributaries of
the Xindian River. Sanxia and Yingge
sit close to each other in a broad valley in the mid-reaches of the Dahan
River. Their differing topographies
meant that while Han Chinese pioneers moved up the Dahan, displac-
ing the resident indigenous people,
Wulai's isolation slowed the ingress
of settlers and provided protection,
preserving it as the northernmost
settlement of the island's Atayal tribe.

WULAI

Wulai is 40 minutes south of Taipei
city along Provincial Highway No.
9A. Buses to Wulai can be found
outside Xindian MRT station.
Alternatively, most tour companies
in Taipei offer package tours that
include entry to several attractions.

Though most of Wulai's permanent residents are Atayal, most of
the businesses in Wulai Village are
owned and run by Han Chinese.
The town is divided into two main

areas, one focused on hot-springs
soaking, the other on indigenous
people-themed recreation and entertainment. "Wulai" is the Chinese
rendering of the Atayal term *ulai*,
meaning "poisonous." The first settlers thought the rising steam from
the hot springs made the air and
water here unsafe.

Traffic into the town is restricted.
Visitors park (for a fee) in the large
lot situated just north of the bridge-
cum-entrance to the town. The bus
station and police station are also

Main Attractions
Wulai Atayal Museum
Outdoor Hot Springs
Wulai Falls
Cable Car
Temple of the Divine
  Progenitor
Old Street
Yingge Ceramics Museum
Old Pottery Street

Maps
Pages 226, 228, 230

Sanxia Old Street.

Rice cooked in bamboo tubes, one of the local foods on sale at Wulai Village.

The dramatic Wulai Falls.

here. The busy hot-springs resort area sits between the Tonghou and Nanshi rivers, which meet here. Steam rises from the waters and sand in certain spots, and one may see individuals soaking up the minerals in self-dug pits by the riverside – an age-old local practice – especially in the early mornings.

Wulai was badly hit by two typhoons in 2015 that caused huge landslides and washed out roads. The mountain town has been slowly rebuilding itself since then.

Wulai Atayal Museum ❶

One of Wulai's cultural attractions is the attractive multi-story **Wulai Atayal Museum** (Wulai Taiya Bowuguan; 12 Wulai St, Wulai Village; Mon–Fri 9.30am–5pm, Sat–Sun 9.30am–6pm, closed first Mon of the month; free; tel: 02-2661 8162; www.atayal.ntpc.gov.tw), telling the story of Taiwan's northernmost tribe, a mountain-dwelling people.

The complex sits just before the Old Street section of eateries as you enter Wulai Village. The many displays are clearly laid out, with good English. Highlights include models of the Atayal's traditional bamboo structures, which no longer exist, exhibits on weaving complex patterns from simple looms, for which the women are famed, and traditional facial tattooing, indicating status.

Wulai Village ❷

The hot-spring area, called **Wulai Village** (Wulai Xiang), is filled with hot-spring inns, eateries, and gift outlets along Wulai Old Street (Wulai Laojie) selling indigenous trinkets and packaged traditional snack foods. New money has come into the area, and many of the newer hot-spring resort hotels are first-rate. But they are expensive – the demand for soaking facilities far outstrips the supply in Taiwan, no matter how much concrete developers pour into the game.

Outdoor Hot Springs ❸

A walk straight through the village takes just a few minutes and leads to a bridge spanning the Nanshi River. At the far end, follow the signs on the right to get to the local **Outdoor Hot Springs** (Lutian Gonggong Yuchi; daily 24 hours; free) by the river. Rocks have been used to construct walls that regulate the flow of cool river water into the natural hot-spring pools. Be careful: the water is extremely hot in areas. Do not judge the temperature by watching the locals, who are used to it! If you find yourself overheating, just slip into the main river and get an invigorating dose of cold current.

Wulai Falls ❹

Return to the bridge and continue along the narrow paved road deeper into the Nanshi River valley. The vistas grow ever more dramatic as the gorge deepens and the rock walls climb higher. The spectacular **Wulai Falls** (Wulai Pubu) soon spills into view, surging down a cliff from a height of 80 meters (260ft), ending up largely as spray as the valley's winds buffet the waters about. Rainbows are often the result on sunny days.

Yun Hsien Holiday Resort

The **Cable Car** ❺ (Kongzhong Lanche; daily 7.30am–8pm; charge) runs across the gorge from the culture village to the source of Wulai Falls, high on a plateau. The car provides the only access to **Yun Hsien Holiday Resort** ❻ (Yunxian Leyuan; daily 9am–5pm; entry with cable car ticket; tel: 02-2661 6510; www.yun-hsien.com.tw), an amusement park completely overhauled and updated in recent years. Access to the natural obstacle course and nature trails is free; there is also golf, a swimming pool, paintball, and eco-tours, each with an additional charge. You can stay overnight at the attractive refurbished hotel, which has a good Chinese restaurant, a coffeeshop, pool tables, and karaoke.

SANXIA

Only 20 minutes or so from Taipei via the Second Northern Freeway, the old town of Sanxia is in many

One of the many avian species seen in Taiwan.

WULAI BIRDWATCHING

Wulai is one of Taiwan's 10 best bird-watching areas. Follow the Tonghou River from beside the bus station and head upstream about 7km (4 miles). Even mid-elevation birds can sometimes be seen here in the winter months, making this the perfect choice for birdwatchers with limited time.

Birds are in greatest number from November to February. Common species include riverine birds such as the Formosan Whistling Thrush and River Kingfisher. Rarer types spotted include the Indian Black Eagle, Maroon Oriole, Tawny Fish Owl, and Black Kite.

The only shops are located by the trail entrance, so bring your own food and drink.

FACT

On the outskirts of Sanxia – and just about every town in Taiwan near a highway – you'll see the ubiquitous betel-nut stands. Chewing of betel-nut (binlang) parings is popular in Taiwan, especially with truckers, for its analeptic effects.

ways still living a century ago, most evident in its old core. It sits at the base of several high hills and at the confluence of three rivers that snake out from those hills. The town name literally means "three gorges." It was long the market center for farmers hauling their produce out of the river valleys and for miners hauling coal down from the nearby mountains. But the age of truck transport meant the town could be bypassed. This was not necessarily beneficial to the town's economy, but it was a boon to tourists, as local heritage sites have lived on without threat from developers, as if the second half of the 20th century never occurred.

Qingshui Zushi Temple ❼

The physical and spiritual heart of this historic town is the **Temple of the Divine Progenitor** (Qingshui Zushi Miao; daily 4am–10pm; tel: 02-2671 1031; www.longfuyan.org.tw), which stands at 1 Changfu Street. The temple

is dedicated to a patriot from the Song dynasty, Chen Chao-ying, who fought bravely against the Mongols when they swept down from the north. This inspired his people, and his descendants eventually helped overthrow the invaders. He is also said to have been a master of medicine and a sorcerer, unselfishly using his powers to help his countrymen.

An icon of Chen was brought here in 1769, it is thought, and the temple first raised. There have been numerous renovations since, leading to what is one of the most profusely adorned of all Chinese temples. It is well known for its carvings in high relief. A terrible earthquake almost destroyed it in 1834, the Japanese burned it in 1895 when they found out that the temple was the headquarters for the local resistance, and it was virtually razed again in World War II by Allied bombers because the Japanese were using it as the local military barracks and headquarters.

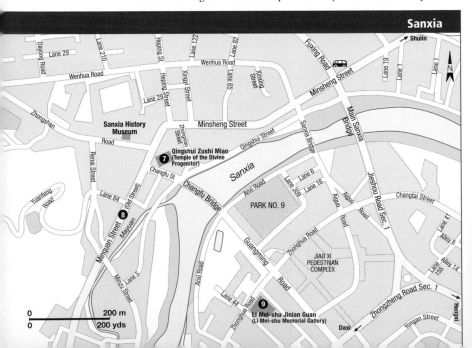

Sanxia

The complex is always at its noisiest and most colorful just after the Chinese New Year. On the sixth day of the first lunar month, worshippers come flooding in by the hundreds bearing offerings and lighting incense to celebrate the birthday of the Divine Progenitor. Amid the smoke and firecracker blasts, elaborate decorated floats are paraded into the spacious front courtyard. A competition is held each year to grow the heaviest sacrificial pig, called a *shenzhu* (literally, "divine pig"). These monstrously proportioned beauty contestants are displayed, slain, and offered to the god as tribute. The winning family is guaranteed good fortune for a year. After the ceremonies, a huge feast is held, to which all visitors are welcome.

Old Street ❽

Sanxia's other great draw is **Old Street** (Laojie), a section of Minquan Street next to the temple. The two rows of double-story red-brick shophouses have been refurbished, creating the longest and best-preserved of the over 170 "old streets" in Taiwan. The imaginative can walk back a century and form a solid picture of what a town in northern Taiwan looked like in the years after the Japanese marched in. This was long the town's main commercial artery. In 1916 the Japanese straightened out the twisting thoroughfare to allow better troop movement, easier access for the Japanese-instituted fire brigade, and better sanitation. This was made easier by the fact that many buildings had been destroyed in the fierce resistance fighting.

As elsewhere, the Japanese incorporated diverse architectural elements into the structures, all of which are fronted by arcades. Facades carry symbols traditionally used by old samurai families, who had turned their energies to business once their traditional martial role in society

WHERE

Deeper in the lovely gorge in Wulai is *Doll Valley* (Wawa Gu). Here one leaves the day-trippers behind, entering a valley of pristine streams with sparkling small waterfalls and cool pools that has the feel of a hidden-away Shangri-La. Genuine Atayal residences dot the area, and hikers like to camp out under the stars. This is one of the best day-hiking spots in north Taiwan. Any travel beyond the valley requires a mountain-hiking permit.

Sanxia's Qingshui Zushi Temple.

WHERE

On a hill northeast of Yingge train station is *Parrot Rock* (Yingge Shi), a huge boulder with a foliage crown giving it the vague likeness of a parrot's bill and body. Hence the town's name; *yingge* means "parrot." The story goes that after liberating Taiwan from the Dutch in 1662 to set up his own regime, Ming patriot Koxinga led his army north. At Yingge they were attacked by a giant parrot, which the fearless leader killed with his magic cannon. Where it crashed, it became the boulder seen today.

had been suppressed as part of the Meiji Restoration. The mortar used is made of glutinous rice and crushed seashells, a trick learned from the Dutch, whose engineers found themselves without mortar supplies from Batavia when they occupied Taiwan in the 1600s.

Li Mei-shu Memorial Gallery ⑨

Across the Sanxia River is the **Li Mei-shu Memorial Gallery** (Li mei-shu Jinian Guan; Sat–Sun 10am–5.30pm; charge; tel: 02-2673 2333; https://limeishu.org.tw/) at 10, Lane 43, Zhonghua Rd. A native son of Sanxia, Li Mei-shu (1902–83) is perhaps best-known outside Taiwan as one of its most accomplished artists, a master of Western-style naturalist painting who depicted the spirit of Taiwan's countryside.

Less well-known is that he spent 36 years of his life leading master craftsmen in renovating the town's

great temple after World War II, remaining faithful to the Tang and Song dynasty motifs that dominate the important heritage site and shrine. His son carries on the intricate work – go to the rear of the temple to see the artists.

The gallery is a tribute to Li Mei-shu's talent and devotion to his culture. In one area are his favorite personal memorabilia, providing insight into Taiwanese life in the early 20th century, and in a second area are his works of art.

YINGGE

In Taiwan, the words "Yingge" and "ceramics" are close to synonymous. The town has been the island's center for pottery making for over 200 years, since it was found that the local water and clay were particularly suited to the art. This pottery town has scores of kilns, large and small, and numerous retail outlets, many fronting the factories. Locals and

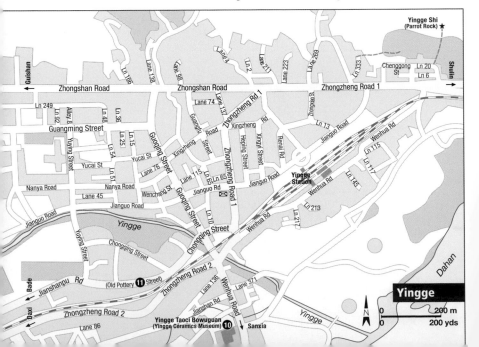

tourists come from far and wide to purchase items that range from the practical, such as pots and cups, to the masterfully artistic.

Yingge Ceramics Museum ❿

With bold exterior lines and curves, the structure that houses the **Yingge Ceramics Museum** (Yingge Taoci Bowuguan; 200 Wenhua Rd; Mon–Fri 9.30am–5pm, Sat–Sun until 6pm, closed first Mon of the month; tel: 02-8677 2727; charge; www.ceramics. ntpc.gov.tw) is itself a striking architectural work of art.

Inside the sunlight-filled glass, concrete, and steel facility are exhibits on both historical and contemporary works and techniques, including Prehistoric, Indigenous, and Taiwanese Works of Ceramics, and Development and Techniques of Ceramics in Taiwan. Free English audio tours are available.

The art-filled outdoor plaza is popular with families, and inside there are always kid-friendly hands-on exhibits. A visit here before strolling among the local shops is strongly suggested to enable more informed buying. Of special note is the brightly colored *koji* or *jiaozhi* ceramics, Taiwan's own unique contribution to the art form.

Temple-roof figures were traditionally made of broken tile pieces as the island's people were very poor. Items are fired at a low temperature, about 900°C (1,652°F), making them comparatively brittle. The results were so attractive that decorative pieces for the home were soon in demand. The Japanese in particular liked the style, hence the greater currency of the term "*koji*."

Old Pottery Street ⓫

The 300-meter/yd-long cobblestoned **Old Pottery Street** (Taoci Laojie) has long been the town's core production area, and is heavily imbued with an idyllic sense of history. It is lined with over 100 shops, and stuffed with tourists. The street is one section of Jianshanpu Road. The shops overflow with ceramic pieces of all sorts, including reproductions of art treasures from the Taipei National Palace Museum.

TIP

Many of Yingge's larger pottery outlets allow visits to their kilns, and also handle overseas shipping. On Old Street, a good number have open workshops and stage DIY sessions.

Traditional pottery on Old Street.

Local taxis.

TRANSPORTATION

TRAVEL TIPS
TAIPEI

TRANSPORTATION

A – Z

LANGUAGE

TRANSPORTATION

GETTING THERE AND GETTING AROUND

By air

Taiwan's pivotal location means it is part of or sits below Asia's most important air routes. Thus, every major airline operating in Asia provides regular service to the island. With air travel over the Pacific growing steadily, advance reservations are advised; this is especially true around the week-long Chinese New Year holiday period, which generally falls in late January or early February.

All major US international airlines fly into Taoyuan Airport, and as of December 2017, China Airlines has begun Taiwan's only non-stop connection between Taipei and London (Gatwick). Other popular connections are through Hong Kong with Cathay Pacific or Dubai on Emirates. US flights through West Coast hubs and UK flights through Hong Kong take about 12–14 hours. Qantas and other airlines fly to and from Taiwan; Air New Zealand works with cooperation partners.

Taiwan Taoyuan International Airport

Formerly known as Chiang Kai-shek International Airport, this facility serves the island's northern and central areas. The original terminal,

now Terminal 1, was given a makeover in the early 2000s. But most international airlines seek space at Terminal 2, which has more upscale restaurants, duty-free shopping, and dedicated lounge facilities. A shuttle links the two terminals. The construction of Terminal 3, which has been delayed multiple times, is now due to be finished by 2022. For more info on the airport, tel: 03-273 3728 or visit www.taoyuan-airport.com. Since 2017, the airport has been linked to Taipei by an express MRT line.

The **Tourism Bureau** operates info counters in both Terminal 1 (baggage claim area; tel: 03-398 2194) and Terminal 2 (arrival hall

exit; tel: 03-398 3341). Transit passengers with a layover of over 7 hours within a 24-hour period before their connection can enjoy a free half-day tour of Taipei by presenting their passport and ticket. Participants must have a valid ROC visa or come from a country eligible for visa-exempt entry. Visit their website for details (www.taiwan.net.tw).

Songshan Airport

This is Taipei's domestic airport, located in Songshan District at 340-9 Dunhua N. Rd (tel: 02-8770 3460; www.tsa.gov.tw). Flights go to other major cities in Taiwan and to the offshore islands of Kinmen

KEY AIRLINE INFORMATION

Air New Zealand
11F, 25 Chang An E. Rd, Sec.1
Tel: 02-2537 0146
www.airnewzealand.com
American Airlines
11F, 25 Chang An E. Rd, Sec.1
Tel: 02-2563 1200
www.aa.com
Cathay Pacific Airways
Tel: 02-8793 3388
www.cathaypacific.com.tw
China Airlines
131 Nanking E. Rd Sec. 3
Tel: 02-412 9000
www.china-airlines.com
Delta Air Lines

Tel: 0080-665-1982
www.delta.com
EVA Airways Corporation
1F, 117 Changan E. Rd Sec. 2
Tel: 02-2501 1999
www.evaair.com
KLM (Royal Dutch Airlines)
Tel: 02-7707 4701
www.klm.com
Qantas
11F-1, 111 Songjiang Rd
Tel: 02-2509 2000
www.qantas.com.au
United Airlines
Tel: 02-2325 8868
www.tw.united.com

(Quemoy), Matsu, and Penghu as well as to mainland China, Japan, and South Korea. The advent of the Taiwan High Speed Rail system has had a big impact on the domestic air carriers: a number have ceased operations, and the others have severely cut services. Check the airport website to be sure what routes are being offered. Save for holiday periods, bookings are easily made right at airport counters. Return ticket prices for domestic destinations average about NT$2,500, and no flight takes more than an hour.

There is limited English used on domestic flights. Note that flights to offshore islands are frequently canceled because of fog and other inclement weather. Direct bus services connect Songshan and Taoyuan International Airport. Flights to and from **Kaohsiung International Airport**, that city's domestic hub, enable connections to regional flights from there, including regular service to and from mainland China.

By train

There are two types of service available, the regular system run by the **Taiwan Railway Administration (TRA)** and the super speedy **Taiwan High Speed Rail (THSR)**. The THSR runs on its own set of tracks, elevated in dramatic fashion high above the plains.

From Taipei, the regular system has two lines running along the west and east coasts to the far south, connecting all major cities and towns. Trains are cheap and often full during holidays and long weekends, so book ahead. Those who do not mind the physical strain can opt for standing-room tickets. Trains are efficient and inexpensive.

There are three regular train types – all are air-conditioned. *Ziqiang* services are faster than *Juguang*. The *Qujian Che* are short-to medium-distance commuter trains with no assigned seating. The fastest trains are a tilting version of the Ziqiang that run along the east

ONLINE PURCHASE OF TRAIN TICKETS

The TRA allows online purchase of tickets 14 days ahead for trains, with collection of tickets within three days of booking at the train station itself, or within 24 hours if booked online (pick up at station or convenience store) and bring your passport. Visit www.railway.gov.tw/en.

coast to Taitung. You must have a reserved seat for this service.

For more information, call the service hotline (tel: 0800-765 888), the main ticketing office at **Taipei Railway Station** (tel: 02-2371 3558), where English is spoken, or visit the TRA website, which is useful, relatively clear, and in English (www.railway.gov.tw/en).

THSR (tel: 4066 3000; www. thsrc.com.tw) offers a high-speed link between Taipei Railway Station and Zuoying in Kaohsiung. Express trains complete the journey in 96 minutes, while regular THSR trains making all ten stops along the way take two hours. There are standard and business carriages on each train; the system runs 6am to midnight.

By bus/coach

Long-distance bus travel is popular with locals because of the low cost – a bus ticket from Taichung, in central Taiwan, to Taipei is only about NT$300. In addition, since most bus terminals are right around Taipei Railway Station, connection to the MRT and city bus systems is easy. Many companies operate 24 hour-services.

A bus trip from Kaohsiung in the south normally takes about 5 hours, and costs NT$500–800, depending on the time of day. During holidays, however, it may take much longer. At these times, planes or trains are the way to go. Bus travel down the cliff-hugging east coast is not possible from Taipei.

Many private companies run inter-city services to Taipei. Ask your hotel concierge for advice on which service to use and for help in getting to the terminal. By departure time almost all buses are fully booked; it is best to buy

reserved-seat tickets at the station one or two days prior to departure. Services range from standard to deluxe, with sofa chairs and large TVs in the coach. Videos are always played, often at full volume, save late at night; earplugs are advised.

GETTING AROUND

From Taoyuan Airport

Located in Taoyuan County, 45km (28 miles) south-west of Taipei city, Taiwan Taoyuan International Airport is linked to Taipei's north area and downtown by the Sun Yat-sen Freeway, and to the city's south and east via a link expressway and the Second Northern Freeway. Travel time to Taipei on both routes is about 45 minutes.

By taxi

Only registered airport service taxis can pick up passengers at the two terminals. A 50 percent surcharge is added to the fare displayed on the meter, and you must also pay highway tolls. A taxi to the city center from the airport will set you back about NT$1,200. By law, taxis must take you anywhere in Taiwan you wish to go.

For trips from the city to the airport, the law says travelers pay only the metered fare, but drivers generally will not agree to a trip (for which they can get no return rider) for less than NT$1,000.

By MRT

Since 2017, a very convenient MRT line connects with downtown Taipei (tel: 03-286 8789; www. tymetro.com.tw). Services run from 6am to 11pm, take just under 40 minutes, stop at both terminals, and cost NT$150 one way (although this fare may rise to NT$160 in October 2019). Downtown there are underground passageways to either Taipei Main MRT or Beimen MRT stations.

By bus

Dedicated airport buses serve both terminals, stopping directly outside the arrival halls. At least four bus companies offer service to and from the airport: **Kuo-Kuang Motor Transport**, **CitiAir Bus**, **Free Go Bus**, and **Evergreen Bus**. Stops are made in the city at many fixed locations indicated by roadside airport-service signs. Kuo-Kuang runs a 24-hour service. One-way fares cost around NT$120 depending on the company and the stop. Ticket counters are in the arrival halls, but if you need further help, approach the airport information counter. The airport website carries information on all forms of transport (see page 234).

From Songshan Airport

As the airport is within the city limits (10–15 min drive to downtown), there is no limo service or shuttle connections to the rail network. Scheduled taxis wait outside the terminal; a surcharge is added. Unscheduled taxis that have just let people off can pick passengers up at the western end of the terminal without surcharge. A taxi ride to/

from about any point in the city should not be more than NT$300. The airport itself has its own MRT station on the brown line; there are also many bus connections. A detailed map showing buses stopping at and around the terminal is given on the airport website (www.tsa.gov.tw). There are buses to Taoyuan International Airport from the station at the western end of the terminal.

Orientation

Taipei City encompasses an area of 270 sq km (104 sq miles), from the district of Wenshan in the south to Yangmingshan National Park in the north, but its urban core is the area of roughly 56 sq km (22 sq miles) bordered by the Danshui and Keelung rivers. Local residents (including taxi drivers) often do not know their city in these terms. The majority know their own immediate neighborhoods only. For many, missing the drop-off point by one or two stops means they get a bit lost.

In general, residents tend to see the city in terms of major arteries and landmarks – large malls, a famous restaurant etc. Luckily, maps with good English are found in all MRT stations (but be careful of the orientation – it is quite rare to see north pointing up). There are also good tourist maps of the city available at all tourist service centers.

EASYCARD

The EasyCard, a stored-value contactless smartcard usable on all local buses, the MRT, parking lots, convenience stores (where it can also be topped up), some shops and cafés, YouBike rentals, the Maokong Gondala, and train travel, is sold for NT$100 – any additional amount is added as stored credit. They are available at MRT stations, bus stations, and convenience stores. You can top them up at EasyCard machines in all stations or at a convenience store. Unused fees

are refundable. For more info, visit www.easycard.com.tw/en. Alternatives to the EasyCard are day passes, which give unlimited trips on the metro or buses within a set time period (1, 2, 3, or 5 days). They are only worth it if you plan on making a lot of trips in a short time. There is also the Taipei Fun Pass which costs a bit more but allows free entry to certain tourist sites. For more info, visit https://funpass. travel.taipei. Both can be bought from any MRT station.

Public transportation

Taipei's public transport system is intricate, efficient, and inexpensive. The ever-expanding MRT system is your key to easy exploration of the city. Bus routes color-coded to the corresponding MRT line launch from each station to almost all points in that station's vicinity.

Metro (MRT)

Widely known as the MRT (*jieyun* in Mandarin), it is easy to reach almost all points of interest using Taipei's Metro and a short bus ride, taxi trip, YouBike cycle, or walk.

In all stations there is a bank of machines from which you may purchase single-trip tokens or top up your EasyCard. The machines provide change if you only have bills. There are instructions and route charts in clear English on the ticket machines. Fares range from NT$20 to NT$65, depending on the distance traveled. The system operates from 6am to midnight daily.

Bicycles are permitted on the end-carriages on weekends and holidays (except for the Wenhu line and a few select stations on other lines), from 6am to end of service; a single-journey ticket for a person with a bike is NT$80 (on weekdays access is limited between 10am-4pm). Bike access to the stations is via the street-level elevators at most stations; these are marked on signboards and the online route map; parking at stations is always in demand.

The MRT system extends to two major points outside the city – north to the port of Danshui and south to the city of Xindian, where buses to Wulai can be caught.

For more details visit the **Taipei Rapid Transit Corporation** website (https://english.metro. taipei) or call the **Metro Taipei Service Hotline** at tel: 1999 (when calling from Taipei) or 02-2181 2345 (24 hours).

Buses

Taipei offers a comprehensive bus network that is cheap and clean

TRANSPORTATION

A – Z

LANGUAGE

DRIVING ADVICE

Locally, the concept of no-fault liability has not taken hold. Each party theoretically pays according to the blame apportioned, though the reality may sometimes be different. Overseas visitors are advised to always call the Foreign Affairs Police (02-2381-8251), whatever the seriousness of an incident. Locals prefer to settle on the spot, avoiding police and insurance companies for less serious incidents, though this sometimes leads to cases of manipulation.

but a bit confusing unless you speak Chinese. The city has implemented a GPS system, with displays showing bus ETAs at some bus stops. On board, upcoming stops are sometimes announced in English and shown on displays above the driver. Google maps can be helpful in finding the right bus number.

Routes extend through the city and often into the surrounding New Taipei City as well. All buses are air-conditioned. The fare is NT$15 (for adults) for each leg of a route (longer routes are broken into separate sections; most journeys that do not cross a river involve just one section). Fares can be paid in cash by dropping the exact amount (no change given) into a glass box by the driver, though most locals use the EasyCard. You should follow other customers in whether to pay (or swipe your EasyCard) in getting on or getting off (or both!) as the driver will change the system depending on where along the route the bus has reached. Last buses leave the terminals at around 11pm. For more detail and route maps, visit www.e-bus.taipei.gov.tw.

Taxis

Taxis are ubiquitous and available any time of day simply by hailing from the street or calling 55688

by cell phone. There are also a number of taxi-hailing apps such as TaxiGo (www.taxigo.com.tw) if you're having trouble finding one. Fares are low, with the average cross-town trip no more than NT$300 or so. Charges are NT$70 for the first 1.25km (0.7 miles) and NT$5 for every additional 200 meters/yds. NT$5 is also charged for every 1 minute and 20 seconds the cab is traveling under 5kph. These rates and fees also apply throughout New Taipei City except in Danshui, Ruifang, and Wulai. For trips further afield the meter will most likely not be used; agree on a fee beforehand to avoid dispute. Starting two days prior to and including the entire Chinese New Year holidays, an extra NT$20 will be added to the total amount for all trips; there is also a standard surcharge of NT$20 added at night.

Most taxi drivers cannot converse in English, so have your destination written down in Chinese. Drivers technically should not refuse an intra-city fare, no matter how short the distance (but some do!). For any complaints, the best resource is the Traffic Division, Taipei City Police Department on tel: 02-2394 9007.

Driving

The city's public transport is very efficient, and few short-term visitors rent vehicles. Traffic is too heavy and parking spaces too difficult to find to make driving in the city worthwhile. Rental companies have branches at Taoyuan Airport and provide service in English. Outside of Taipei, English signage is unreliable except on major highways, and many a newcomer has experienced frustration on driving excursions. Note that roads are also often quite narrow, with many switchbacks and barely enough room for two vehicles, especially on curves.

An international license is required for driving in Taiwan.

Driving is on the right-hand side of the road, and all vehicle occupants are required by law to wear a seatbelt.

Cycling

The city boasts an extensive network of bicycle paths as well as an excellent automated bike-rental system, "YouBike." There are more than 300 rental stations across the whole of Taipei, and bikes can be rented and dropped off at any one of them, which makes the system a comfortable way to shuttle through the city. For a single ride the fee is NT$10 for every 30 minutes within the first four hours, NT$20 per 30 minutes between four and eight hours, and NT$40 per 30 minutes over eight hours; a deposit, which can be paid by a credit card, is required. The EasyCard can also be used to pay for rental (but you will need a local phone number). For detailed rental instructions and a map showing the location of kiosks visit: https://taipei.youbike.com.tw; tel: 02-8978 5511.

Since 2017, the Singaporean share-bike company oBike has been running in Taipei. oBikes can be located by using an app, parked anywhere (legally!), and paid for by credit card. They are not as sturdy as YouBikes and thus only really useful for very short spins.

Taipei Sightseeing Bus

The double-decker iconic red "hop-on, hop-off" bus (service 9.10am–10pm daily, every 40 minutes, NT$500 for a day pass; https://www.taipeisightseeing.com.tw/en) stops at most major tourist sights across the capital. The "blue" route runs north–south between Taipei Main Station and the Palace Museum while the "red" route trundles east-west between the Main Station and City taking in Ximending. It's a good way to see some of city's iconic landmarks but going by MRT is a lot cheaper.

A – Z

AN ALPHABETICAL SUMMARY OF PRACTICAL INFORMATION

A

Accommodations

Upper-end hotels in Taipei are competitive in comparison to North American and European prices. They are renowned for gracious and attentive service, in keeping with the Confucian ethic of striving to be the perfect host.

Taipei being the island's main center for business and one of the globe's most wired cities, the majority of hotels are oriented toward the business traveler. Almost all provide free Wi-Fi access through the property.

Smoking is prohibited in all hotel rooms, as well as in all enclosed public spaces (except where a designated smoking area has specifically been set aside).

Most hotels above two stars provide the option to include breakfast when you book. Rooms will contain kettles along with packets of tea, coffee, creamer, and sugar – and increasingly free top-up soft drinks and snacks in the mini bar.

English is widely spoken except for some lower-level staff and in the cheaper hotels. In any event, whatever your need, an English speaker will be close at hand.

There is a heavy concentration of hotels in the city's core business areas, on and near Zhongshan North Road, the old downtown, and the eastern district, which is the emerging center. Hotels in the Beitou and Yangmingshan areas primarily cater to travelers there for the hot springs. For the most part, there is a dearth of accommodations of international caliber in Taipei South, Zhongzheng, the Old Walled City, and the old districts by the Danshui River, but inexpensive, clean, and pleasant accommodations are generally available there.

While price varies widely according to season and whether there is a big event in the city, top-range hotels will generally cost NT$8,000–15,000. Mid-range hotels with good, clean, basic amenities can be had for NT$2,000–6,000 per night. These establishments cater especially to the businessperson, and managerial staff will be able to speak English. There are few budget hotels; many are located in Ximending but increasingly throughout the city.

While booking online is now normal practice, if you make a booking from the desk at the airport be sure to ask for discounts or special rates. Competition is fierce, and most establishments will grant a discount of up to 30 percent if you book ahead. Major hotels have counters in both terminals of Taiwan Taoyuan International Airport; the Tourism Bureau service counters in the two terminals can also help. Rates are subject to a 10 percent service charge. All Taipei hotels accept major credit cards.

Addresses

Taipei's address system may at first appear a bit complicated, but once you get the knack of it, you'll find it is quite logical and negates the need to memorize countless names in this dense metropolis.

Most addresses have a building number, lane and alley number (if applicable), street name, and section. An example is "No. 15, Lane 25, Zhongxiao East Road Section 3." The city is organized into a grid, with Zhongshan Road and Zhongxiao Road serving as main north-south and east-west axes respectively. All long arteries are divided into sections which are numbered higher the further they are from the central axis. Thus, Section 1 of Zhongxiao East Road is closest to Zhongshan Road, Section 2 further east, and so on. The pattern is mirrored westward for Zhongxiao West Road.

On each section, building numbers start at "1." So there can be a No. 1 on Zhongxiao E. Rd Sec.

1, on Zhongxiao E. Rd Sec. 2, and so on. Lanes branch off from main arteries, and are numbered like buildings. For instance, to find the sample address above, go to Sec. 3 of Zhongxiao E. Rd and find building No. 25; beside it will be a Lane 25. Go down that lane and find building No. 15. Alleys branch off from lanes, so something like "No. 15, Alley 6, Lane 25" means: go down Lane 25 and find building No. 6. Alley 6 will be beside it. Go down the alley to building No. 15.

This efficient system allows one to guess the location of any address quickly.

If you expect to be in Taiwan for any length of time, invaluable orientation is conducted for newcomers by the local expat-run non-profit **Community Services Center** at No. 25, Lane 290, Zhongshan N. Rd Sec. 6, tel: 02-2836 8134, www. communitycenter.org.tw.

Admission charges

All museums, cinemas, and other leisure and recreation facilities will offer discounted admission for children, seniors, students, and people with disabilities. Groups are also offered discounted entry. In Taiwan, museums do not tend to have special free-entry days.

Age restrictions

The legal drinking age in Taiwan is 18, as is the age at which one can obtain a driver's license, even if you hold a valid license from another country. Any person with a valid driver's license from Taiwan or an international driver's license and ID may rent a vehicle. The legal age of consent is 16.

B

Budgeting for your trip

Accommodations of international caliber usually cost NT$5,000 or more per night, though discounts can be had by booking online and well ahead. Taxis are inexpensive, with a cross-city run of about 9km not likely to go over NT$300.

Hotel meals are not cheap, but Western-style restaurants found in them will generally offer set meals at a discount of around 25 percent compared to ordering items à la carte. Good, inexpensive local fare can be had at nightmarkets and local eateries, which serve simple dishes.

Business travelers

Traveling to Taipei on business is a pleasure. All international tourist hotels have full business facilities, and provide in-room Wi-Fi access. Taxis are available any time, day or night; simply stand by the street and raise your hand to hail one. There are now also several taxi-hailing Apps available, for example 55688. The city provides taxi drivers who have passed an official English exam with special stickers for display on windshields. There is also a hotline for foreigners on English-speaking taxi services, tel: 0800-055-850. But be prepared to expect language obstacles, so have your destination and hotel written in Chinese beforehand. If you need a receipt, just say *"shouju"* and draw an imaginary rectangle in the air. A large logo on the outside of a vehicle in the shape of a plum blossom (neon-lit at night) indicates excellent cab drivers who need to meet several requirements set by the Taipei City Transportation department in order to use it.

Traffic can be heavy, especially during the rush hours, so allow extra time for delays when going to meetings. Most locals are used to people showing up as much as 20 minutes late, but phone if you anticipate a longer delay and apologize when you arrive.

Always have your business card ready; it is seen as your badge of identity, and is always exchanged when meeting people formally.

Receive it with both hands, take a real look at it to show respect, do not put it away immediately, and when you do, slide it into a place that demonstrates the new relationship is being taken seriously.

C

Children

Taipei has a fair amount of green space and a number of attractions that will appeal to kids. Bus fares and admission fees to most attractions are discounted for children and are often free for toddlers under six. Some venues declare a height limit of 120cm (4ft) for kids, but this is not vigorously enforced except at locations where safety is an issue, such as at amusement-park rides. Have your child's ID on hand just in case, however.

Traffic is very heavy at rush hour, so avoid moving about with young ones at this time, or leaving them unsupervised at any time. The problem is not crime, but heavy vehicle and foot traffic.

The use of strollers is not very convenient, except in the eastern district of the city, where pedestrian walkways are wider, flatter, and generally unblocked, and many new buildings have wheelchair access. Local parents prefer carrying toddlers in front. The city is working very hard to flatten and straighten out sidewalks throughout all neighborhoods, but this is still hit and miss. Note that down all lanes and alleys there are in fact no sidewalks.

Washrooms in many newer buildings (but certainly not all), and specifically in department stores and international hotels, will have diaper-changing facilities, as do washrooms in all MRT stations. Thanks to a recent campaign hoping to encourage the Taiwanese to have more babies, breast-feeding rooms are also ubiquitous in public buildings. Malls and department stores are good places to bring picky eaters, as all have a good selection of restaurants and a food court with much variety.

Climate

When to visit

Taipei is located in the subtropical region. The average annual temperature is 22°C (71°F), the average annual rainfall is 2,152mm (85ins), and the average number of rainy days is 181.

The hot season stretches from June to early September, and can hit 40°C (104°F) on the baking street. Perhaps "hottest season" is more accurate, as it is over 25°C (77°F) and humid from mid-March to mid-October. This is the period of the southwest monsoon. Being at the northern tip of the island, Taipei is somewhat sheltered from the storms by the island's north-south mountain spine.

Typhoon season stretches from July to October, and Taipei can be deeply impacted by the powerful winds and heavy rains. Flooding is a constant menace, especially in foothill areas of the Taipei Basin. Rigorous prevention measures are taken to minimize damage.

In winter, the weather is often chilly. The air is moisture-laden, and it often rains in late January and early February. Cold fronts move in from the Asian continent, and this is the season of the northeast monsoon.

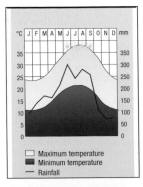

- ☐ Maximum temperature
- ■ Minimum temperature
- — Rainfall

Spring rains fall from March to April, and "plum rains" (*meiyu*) from May to June. During this period, it tends to drizzle rather than rain heavily.

What to wear

In the hot season, bring your lightest and loosest clothing. Most local businessmen go without jacket and tie during the period, opting for short sleeves and open collars. For formal occasions such as meetings, note that hotels, restaurants, and offices are air-conditioned, so tie and jacket can be put on just before arrival and taken off after introductions.

In winter, bring warmer outer clothing that you can quickly take off and carry. Most locals go without raingear, preferring to carry umbrellas to handle the rains, which seem to burst and finish at a moment's notice. Umbrellas are sold everywhere.

Crime and safety

Taipei is an exceedingly safe place. It is fine to walk around even late at night. Violent crime against tourists is almost unheard of, and overseas visitors almost never suffer abuse, physical or verbal.

Stories of snatch theft and pickpocketing are occasionally heard, so take commonsense precautions. The heavy bars often seen on the windows and doors of private homes are to prevent break-ins, but homeowners do not fear violent crime and travelers are in no way affected.

Drivers in Taipei, however, are occasionally a little pushy, notably during periods of heavy congestion, and racing to beat the red light is common. The biggest safety issue concerns scooters as they zip around on sidewalks and narrow alleys – so be alert when crossing the street.

Customs regulations

Individuals aged 20 and over have a duty-free allowance of 1 liter (2

pints) of alcoholic beverages and up to 25 cigars or 200 cigarettes or 450 grams (1lb) of tobacco products only. Foreign currency above US$10,000 will be confiscated if found after not being declared. There is also a restriction concerning the import of Chinese currency. The maximum amount allowed is RMB20,000.

Items which are prohibited and will result in a substantial fine or imprisonment include publications espousing communism, pornography, illicit and narcotic drugs, endangered animals or animal parts, copyright-infringed goods, weapons (including gun-shaped toys), counterfeit currency or forging equipment, gambling apparatus, or foreign lottery tickets. Most recently, heavy fines are being imposed for anyone importing pork products (including processed foods) from swine flu infested areas (China, Mongolia and Vietnam).

An Outbound Declaration Form is required when departing the country if a traveler is taking out the following: over $10,000 in US currency (or equivalent in other currencies), over $60,000 in New Taiwan dollars, gold, antiques, or dutiable items such as laptops and professional photographic equipment that may be brought back into Taiwan for sale.

For more details, contact the **Directorate General of Customs**, Ministry of Finance, at 13 Dacheng St, Taipei, tel: 02-2550 5500 ext. 2116, http://eweb.customs.gov.tw. The Taiwanese Immigration Agency also runs a special website for foreigners who are going to spend lengthier time or come to live in Taiwan (https://ifi.immigration.gov.tw/mp.asp?mp=ifi_en).

E

Electricity

Taiwan uses the same standards as the US. Electrical mains supply 110 volts, 60 Hz AC. Connection is via standard flat two-pin plugs.

EMERGENCIES

Fire/Ambulance: 119
Police: 110
Taipei Foreign Affairs Police:
02-2556 6007
Directory Information in English: 106

International hotels will be able to supply adapters if required. Many newer non-residential buildings have 220 volt sockets.

Embassies and consulates

Taiwan, ie the Republic of China (not to be confused with the People's Republic of China), has formal diplomatic relations with 16 UN member states and the Holy See. Many countries outside this group have set up trade offices, which are quasi-embassies that handle matters such as visa insurance and replacement of lost or stolen passports.

Australia

Australian Office in Taipei
27F, President International Tower, 9-11 Songgao Rd
Tel: 02-8725 4100
www.australia.org.tw

Canada

Canadian Trade Office in Taipei
6F, Hua-Hsin Building, 1 Songzhi Rd
Tel: 02-8723 3000
www.canada.org.tw

New Zealand

New Zealand Commerce and Industry Office
9F, Hua-Hsin Building, 1 Songzhi Rd
Tel: 02-2720 5228
www.nzcio.com

United Kingdom

British Trade and Cultural Office
26F, President International Tower, 9 11 Songgao Rd
Tel: 02-8758 2088
www.ukintaiwan.fco.gov.uk

United States

American Institute in Taiwan
100 Jinhu Rd, Neihu District
Tel: 02-2162 2000
www.ait.org.tw

Etiquette

Long-held traditions are still in force in Taiwan, but if you act courteously, and ask in advance what to do when unsure, you'll do fine. The Taiwanese are very tolerant of non-locals who seek to understand and respect local ways, even if mistaken in particulars.
Dress. Bare feet are generally considered dirty in public places. Nude bathing is illegal.
Eating. When food is served on round tables with a lazy Suzan in the center, pick modest portions when the food reaches you; piling up your favorite is in bad taste. Do not stick your chopsticks straight up in your rice, as this resembles incense sticks in urns at temple funeral rites; it may bring bad luck. Placing chopsticks across the top of your bowl indicates you are full.
Entertaining. In Chinese culture, it is essential for the good host to entertain guests. If in town on business, you'll thus be taken out almost every night. For proper long-term relations, you should reciprocate at least once before departure to express appreciation.

Most entertaining is not done in the home because of cramped quarters, but often at banquet restaurants in hotels. According to tradition, the host sits across the round table from the guest of honor, not beside, though this is not rigorously observed today.

The tradition is to "fight" jovially to pay the bill even if one is the guest, though all know the host will "win" the argument in the end. If you are really intent on paying, get it done on the quiet before the bill is brought to the table. Outside of a business environment, with friends of the younger generation, it is more common to each pay their share.

When offered a formal toast, raise your glass to chest level with both hands.

At the end of formal occasions, the serving of tea indicates the party is over. Though your host may insist the fun continue, the insistence is a polite form only.
Gifts. Always present gifts with both hands, palms facing up. (In ancient China, a palm facing down might conceal a weapon.) Do not give clocks or watches, which suggest the recipient's demise. Handkerchiefs or towels are only given at funerals; at other times, they would be construed as wishing the recipient grief. Do not give knives or scissors, for sharp objects indicate you wish to sever the relationship, as do objects that come in pairs such as chopsticks.
Greetings. The Western handshake has taken hold, so to speak, generally given with a slight nod of respect. Other forms of touch like hugging, backslapping, and so on are not common. A man laying hands on a woman in any way can quickly earn him the unflattering label "se lang," or lecher.
Names. In Chinese, a person's family name comes first, followed by a given name. So the family name of Ma Ying-jeou is "Ma" and the given name is "Ying-jeou." On formal occasions, an honorific like nüshi (Ms), xiansheng (Mr), or a title like jingli (Manager) may be used after a surname, e.g. Li Jingli (Manager Li). But this will usually only occur when Mandarin is the spoken medium. In any case, it is considered overfamiliar to use someone's given name until the person initiates informality.

FESTIVALS

Public holidays are marked with an asterisk (*). For more details on events, see the Taiwan Tourism Bureau website (www.taiwan.net.tw).

January

Pingxi Sky Lantern Festival. One of Taiwan's more unique traditional festivals, and one of ethereal beauty. In the upper Keelung River valley, thousands of glowing "sky lanterns," mini hot-air balloons, are released into the night sky, each carrying personal prayers to the gods. Note that in recent years environmental groups have called for a ban on the release of the lanterns because of the damage they do. Can occur in Feb.

Taipei Lunar New Year Shopping Carnival. Shops in five commercial clusters in Datong District, notably Dihua Street, come together during the two-week run-up to Chinese New Year with myriad special discounts, premium giveaways, snacks for shoppers, and other enticements, making the annual shopping spree something of a party.

February

Taipei Lantern Festival. A 10-day event with thousands of themed lanterns and colorful folk arts closing off the traditional New Year holidays, held around the city.

Taipei Flower Festival. Also called the Yangmingshan Flower Festival, this stretches over almost two months (end of Jan – start of March), when the great army of flowers – including glorious cherry blossom – first planted on Yangmingshan by the Japanese burst in bloom, attracting a flood of admirers to the hills to enjoy special displays, artistic performances, picnicking, and more.

March

Taipei Traditional Arts Festival. Brings in top talent, mostly from Asia, specifically the Chinese world, for a series of about 30 large-scale performances stretching over two-plus months. The main venue is Zhongshan Hall. Tel: 02-2383 2170; https://english.tco.gov.taipei.

April

Tomb Sweeping Day*. Held on April 4 (2020) and April 5 (2021 and 2022); also called Ancestor Worship Day. Cities thin and the countryside fills up as entire clans head to the hills to clean family tombs, pay ceremonial respects with time-honored rituals, and spend a half-day out together.

June

Dragon Boat Festival*. Second of the three big traditional festivals of the Chinese year. It is celebrated around the summer solstice, with city-staged dragon-boat races and traditional-arts performances at Dajia Riverside Park. The boats symbolize the escorting of high-summer pestilence out to sea. Usually takes place in June.

Taipei Film Festival. A platform for the promotion of local movie-makers, with showings from many other countries as well, that spans two to three weeks. Usually runs end-June to July. Most screenings are at Zhongshan Hall. Tel: 02-2308-2966 ext. 220; www.taipeiff.org.tw.

July

Yingge Ceramics Festival. A celebration of Yingge's 200 years as Taiwan's greatest center of ceramics production. The two main venues are Yingge Ceramics Museum and Old Street, with a series of kiln visits, DIY workshops, and entertainment events. Runs into August. Tel: 02-8677 2727; www.ceramics.ntpc.gov.tw.

August

Keelung Ghost Festival. Ghost Month runs the entire seventh lunar month (could start in July or extend into September), with the largest-scale celebrations to appease visiting other-worldly spirits in the coastal city of Keelung, around downtown temples, with a magical floating-lantern ceremony at Badouzi harbor to guide water spirits in. Tel: 02-2422 4170; www.klccab.gov.tw.

Taipei Riverside Music Festival. Music, markets and fireworks along the park centering on the surrounding area over summer weekends.

Taiwan Culinary Exhibition. A hugely popular multi-day food extravaganza in July or August staged at the Taipei World Trade Center. The main focus is on the many styles of Chinese food, with chef competitions, DIY classes, endless sampling, and a bazaar-like food court.

September

Mid-Autumn (Moon) Festival*. Third of the three big annual Chinese festivals, celebrating the harvest moon and bountiful crops. At night, open spaces will be filled with families and groups of friends feasting at hibachi barbecues and admiring the perfect moon, its roundness symbolizing the perfection of reunited families. Scheduled to be held on Oct 1 in 2020, Sept 21 in 2021 and Sept 10 in 2022.

October

Double Tenth National Day*. The October 10 (Double Tenth), 1911 uprising in China that created the Republic is celebrated before the Presidential Office Building with a full-day menu, including the National Day Parade, ceremonial military review, folk performances, and hours of night-sky color with the National Day Fireworks Display.

Taipei Hakka Yimin Festival. Celebrates the unique cultural legacy of the Hakka people with traditional temple processions, shoulder-pole performances, Hakka-style lion dance parade, food bazaars, traditional "tea-picking" opera, and more. Main venues are The Red House, National Concert Hall, and Zhongshan Hall. Sometimes staged in November.

December

Taipei New Year's Eve Countdown Party. Centered on Citizen Plaza at the front of Taipei

City Hall, the entire district pedestrian-only, this is a massive party with pop stars performing non-stop, traditional food and folk-art areas, and a terrific fireworks show over Taipei 101 at midnight.

H

Health and medical care

Taipei has made great strides in ensuring a clean living environment. Rest assured that the food in small eateries and nightmarkets is safe to eat, even though they may be crowded, sometimes greasy, and look somewhat dirty, especially during peak hours. Tap water is treated, but it is recommended that it be boiled before consumption. Bottled water can be found at convenience stores and supermarkets, but it is better to carry your own flask to save on plastic water. You can fill up with hot or cold drinkable water from free dispensers that you can find in banks, train stations and museums. Some MRT stations and parks also have drinking fountains.

The medical treatment available in Taipei hospitals is of a high standard. If you fall ill, have your hotel call a hospital for you. Care is always available on short notice – most hospitals have 24-hour emergency and outpatient service.

It is best to stick with large hospitals and avoid local clinics; the doctors at the former generally speak better English and have access to the hospital's diagnostic services and equipment.

Certificates of cholera inoculation are required for travelers coming from certain countries or who have spent five days or more in infected areas.

The country has emerged virtually unscathed from the epidemic scares of the 2000s such as SARS, bird flu, and swine flu, a testament to its public-health system.

Hospitals with more experience dealing with foreigners are:
Chang Gung Memorial Hospital 199 Dunhua N. Rd, http://www.chang-gung.com/en Tel: 02-2713 5211
Mackay Memorial Hospital 92 Zhongshan N. Rd Sec. 2, www.mmh.org.tw Tel: 02-2543 3535
Taiwan Adventist Hospital 424 Bade Rd Sec. 2, www.tahsda.org.tw Tel: 02-2771 8151
Veterans General Hospital 201 Shipai Rd Sec. 2, http://wd.vghtpe.gov.tw Tel: 02- 2875 7808

I

Internet

All international hotels provide Internet access for guests in business centers and all hotels offer free wireless Internet in rooms and throughout the facility.

The city has a patchy public wireless-access network. Free wireless access can be enjoyed around public buildings, in some commercial districts, in most shopping malls, at major hospitals, on the MRT, including carriages and stations, and in many parts of the city, although speeds are slow and you may find yourself having to keep signing in. If you have a Taiwanese mobile phone number, register an account on the Taipei Free Public Wi-Fi Access website: www.tpe-free.taipei.gov.tw, which has hotspots. Otherwise you should visit one of the Taipei Visitor Information centers where it will be done for you – if you show them your passport.

Almost all cafés, bars and restaurants have free Wi-Fi for customers. You can also buy a local SIM and pay for data to get Internet access. Prices are reasonable.

You can rent a Wi-Fi router at the airport at an affordable daily rate for unlimited 4G access with coverage across the country from Unite Traveler (www.unitetraveler.com).

L

Left luggage

Left-luggage services (self-service) are available at Taoyuan International Airport in the Arrival Hall of Terminal 1 (1F) and in the Arrival Hall (1F) and the Departure Hall (3F) of Terminal 2. There is a charge per piece. Most MRT stations also have lockers.

LGBTQ travelers

The LGBTQ community has traditionally been frowned upon in Chinese society due to the Confucian concern with marriage and progeny. This rarely, if ever, takes the form of physical violence. Open displays of affection will draw looks but nothing more.

Some local gay and lesbian people still hide their orientation from colleagues and relatives, but things are changing, and many are now voicing their concerns publicly in an organized manner. Taipei has an annual gay-pride parade, Taiwan Pride. And, in 2017, Taiwan effectively legalized gay marriage although, thanks to fear-mongering by conservative religious groups, the process is being contested; unions should be able to start in 2019 when Taiwan will be the first country in Asia to allow them. Gay clubs are discreet but now operate openly. Taipei is more tolerant of the LGBTQ community than many other Asian cities. In polls about three-quarters of respondents state they feel homosexual relations are acceptable. More than 100,000 participants attended the annual LGBT pride parade in October 2018 in Taipei (www.twpride.org), the largest in Asia.

The **Taiwan Tongzhi Hotline Association** (tel: 02-2392 1969;

www.hotline.org.tw) provides counseling, support, and a community resource center.

Lost property

Locals will most likely turn found property in at the local police precinct. Your best bet is to contact the Foreign Affairs Police, who speak English, and can attempt to trace the valuables on your behalf.

M

Media

Magazines

With most information now online, the number of English-language magazines has fallen off, but there are still a few of interest to tourists.

Taipei (formerly Discover Taipei) is a City Government bimonthly, available at the city hall bookstore, the city's visitor info centers, MRT stations, and other sites popular with expatriates and foreign tourists. It focuses on sights and events of interest to visitors. Also at www.taipei.gov.tw.

Travel in Taiwan is a Tourism Bureau bi-monthly found at its visitor centers and at hotel counters. It has feature articles and practical info on Taipei specifically and the country in general. Also at www.tit.com.tw.

This Month in Taiwan, available at hotels and online, is also targeted at the tourist. Also at www.thismonthintaiwan.com.

Taiwan Review, a publication of the Ministry of Foreign Affairs, is published every other month, covers cultural and economic issues and is available at major bookstores. Also at http://taiwanreview.nat.gov.tw.

Newspapers

There is now only one local English newspaper, the *Taipei Times* (www.taipeitimes.com). It's

available at convenience stores and hotels. *Taiwan News, online only, is more tabloid-style and has more 'local' stories* (www.etaiwannews.com). Focus Taiwan (http://focustaiwan.tw) is the online English news portal of state media agency CNA; lengthier features that cover regional news too can be read on News Lens International (https://international.thenewslens.com); more youth activism and quirky features are written for *New Bloom magazine* (https://newbloommag.net) and Ketagalan Media (www.ketagalanmedia.com). Daily editions of a good selection of international papers, including the *Asian Wall Street Journal* and *International Herald Tribune*, are available at hotels, major bookstores, and some newsstands.

Radio

The only English-language station in Taiwan is the Taipei-based ICRT – International Community Radio Taipei (www.icrt.com.tw). The FM channel 100.7 is the more popular, with chatty DJ shows, a mix of Western and local pop music, short news broadcasts, the BBC World Report, and so on.

Television

All hotels have cable television, with around 100 channels available. International channels carried as basic service are CNN, Discovery, ESPN, National Geographic, and HBO. Daily schedules are published in the local English papers.

Money

The country's currency is the New Taiwan dollar (NT$). At time of press, US$1 was equal to NT$31. Coins come in denominations of NT$1, NT$5, NT$10, NT$20 (rare), and NT$50; paper notes in NT$100, NT$200, NT$500, NT$1,000, and NT$2,000, though you'll almost never see NT$2,000 bills.

Changing money

Major foreign currencies can be exchanged for Taiwan dollars at large banks. The website of the Tourism Bureau (www.taiwan.net.tw) provides a list of banks (in the Before You Go section). International hotels will exchange currency, but offer the least attractive rates. Travel agencies that cater to overseas visitors may change money, and a few large-scale department stores have exchange counters. Taiwan Taoyuan International Airport has exchange booths in both terminals (24 hours). You will not find licensed private money changers found elsewhere in Asia.

Receipts are given when currency is exchanged, and must be presented in order to exchange unused NT dollars before departure. If possible, wait to exchange at the airport, where the counters carry a wider range of currencies and staff have greater familiarity with the process. It may be difficult to exchange NT dollars overseas, with very unattractive rates given.

Credit cards and ATMs

The major credit cards (American Express, MasterCard, Visa, and Diners Club) are accepted by most merchants except where cash-only transactions are the rule (small eateries, nightmarkets, and such).

Many ATMs allow withdrawals of local currency using major international cards. ATMs have

MAPS

There are plenty of good maps of the city in Chinese, but fewer in English. The free maps available at tourist information centers around the city are, however, more than adequate for sightseeing purposes (and can be downloaded from the website). The App MAPS.ME provides offline maps of Taipei – and the rest of the world.

clear English. Use only those at banks, some MRT stations, convenience stores, and other major institutions. Forgo freestanding units of any kind to avoid periodic scams by organized crime.

Tipping

Tipping is not common or expected in Taiwan. Hotel bellhops generally get NT$30 per piece of luggage. The majority of hotels add 10 percent to food and beverage as well as room charges, as do more upscale restaurants these days. Taxi drivers do not expect tips.

O

Opening hours

Most corporate businesses are open from Monday to Friday, 9am–5pm or 5.30pm. Government offices are open Monday to Friday, 8.30am–5.30pm, with an official lunch hour from 12.30–1.30pm.

Department stores generally open every day at 10–11am and close at 9–10pm. Most open on national holidays except for the first few days of Chinese New Year. Other retail outlets mostly open at 9–10am and close at about 10pm. Outlets of major convenience-store chains, including the ubiquitous 7-Eleven, usually stay open 24/7, and certain large supermarkets will also stay open into the wee hours. Banking hours are 9am–3.30pm, weekdays only.

P

Postal services

Taiwan's postal service is speedy and reliable. Regular airmail will reach North American destinations in about 6–7 days. **Chunghwa Post** (www.post.gov.tw), the national service, also offers express

delivery that costs less than international courier services. Delivery of mail takes about 24 hours within Taipei and 48 hours within Taiwan. Hours for post offices are 8am to 6pm Monday through Friday, with the largest office in each area also open Saturday from 8am to 4pm.

Taipei's **Central Post Office** (tel: 02-2361 5752) is located in front of the old North Gate, on Zhongxiao W. Rd Sec. 1. Staff in the international section speak decent English (staff at other post offices speak Chinese only). Packaging materials can be purchased at most branches.

When using streetside mailboxes, place domestic mail in the green boxes – intra-city items in the right-hand slot and others in the left-hand slot. International airmail goes into the left-hand slot of the red boxes.

Public holidays

The dates of traditional holidays are based on the Chinese lunar calendar, and thus vary each year in the Gregorian calendar. There is a minimum of four days of holiday during Chinese New Year, and depending on where in the week these days fall, up to a full week off work may be granted (but usually staff make up that day by working a Saturday). Taipei is comparatively sleepy at this time, and most shops remain closed.
Foundation Day of the Republic of China: Jan 1
Chinese New Year: Jan/Feb (1st day of the lunar year)
Peace Memorial Day: Feb 28
Children's Day: Apr 4
Tomb-Sweeping Day (Qing Ming Festival): Apr 5
Dragon Boat Festival: May/June (5th day of the 5th lunar month)
Mid-Autumn Festival: Sept/Oct (15th day of the 8th lunar month)
National ("Double Tenth") Day: Oct 10

Regarding dates, note that the Republic (*Minguo*) system of reckoning years is used on

official documents in Taiwan. The founding of the ROC in 1912 is considered year 1, so *Minguo* 109 is 2020 in the Gregorian calendar.

Public toilets

The city provides relatively clean public washrooms in parks, temples, fast-food outlets, shopping malls, MRT stations, and the larger hotels. A few things to remember: only the hotels and the MRT stations always provide toilet paper, so carry some if you're going out for a while. Sometimes paper is provided in one large roll next to the sinks. Unlike some places in Asia, you'll never be charged for washroom use here. Usually western style and squat toilets are offered in public facilities; the door is marked on the outside if you have a preference.

R

Religious services

There are about 10,000 Muslims in Taipei (not including about 4,000 workers from Indonesia), served by **Taipei Grand Mosque** (tel: 02-2321 9445) on Xinsheng S. Rd by Daan Forest Park.

About 6 percent of the Taipei population is Christian, 80 percent of whom are Protestant, mostly Presbyterian. The rest are Roman Catholics, as are the 130,000 or so workers from the Philippines. The following churches conduct services in English:

Anglican/Episcopalian

Church of the Good Shepherd
509 Zhongzheng Rd
Tel. 02-2882 2462
www.
englishchurchtaiwangoodshepherd.
com
Sunday English service at 9.30am. Combined English/ Chinese service at 9.30am, 4th Sunday each month.

Roman Catholic

Tienmu Church
171 Zhongshan N. Rd Sec. 7
Tel: 02-2871 5168
http://www.tienmu-church.org.tw
English services on Sunday at
10am, 12.15 and 7pm, Wed at 7pm.

S

Smoking

Smoking indoors in public places, including bars, is banned throughout Taiwan. Places like restaurants may provide special smoking areas if completely insulated from the non-smoking area. It is also now illegal to smoke in parks and on the street near schools.

T

Tax

Taiwan levies a 5 percent VAT on purchases. Refunds are available to foreign travelers (see page 70). For more details, visit the **Taipei National Tax Administration** (TNTA) website www.ntbt.gov.tw.

Telephones

Taiwan's **international dialing code** is 886. For overseas calls to Taipei, add the prefix 2 before the local number. To make a domestic call to Taipei from outside the city, add 02. No area code is required when dialing within the city.
Dial 002 for **international direct dialing** (IDD)
For **operator assisted international calls**, dial 100
For **international information**, call the toll-free number 0800 080 100
To place **reverse-charge calls**, dial 108
For English-language **directory assistance**, dial 106

Cell/mobile phones

These can be used as long as your phone operates on the GSM network which is common to most countries except the US and Japan. To cut costs, buy a prepaid SIM card, which gives you a local number and an allotted quantity of usage time. They are available at cell-phone retail outlets, where you can also top them up, as well as at convenience stores. Prices for prepaid cards start at NT$300. Mobile network operators in Taiwan include Chungwa Telecom (www.cht.com.tw), which is the largest, FarEasTone (www.fetnet. net), Taiwan Mobile (www. taiwanmobile.com), and the cheapest, Taiwan Star (www. tstartel.com).

Apps

There are a number of handy Apps for any trip to Taipei, especially if you are going to have Internet access on the road. The all-in-one **Travel Taipei App** from the Taipei City Government has updated information on exhibitions, events, and tourist-related city news, as well as a database of hotels, restaurants (including vegetarian and halal), shops, and day tours.
As well as providing a metro map, **Go! Taipei Metro** tells you the nearest MRT station (working in conjunction with your phone's map App) and where the nearest YouBike station is (along with the number of free bikes).
Focus Taiwan is the country's national news agency's English service, with articles on local politics and cultural news.
Pretty much everyone in Taiwan uses the chat App **Line** rather than, say, **WhatsApp**. **Facebook Messenger** is also worth having because almost all businesses, such as hotels, hostels, cafés, bars, and restaurants, as well as some tourist sites, have a Facebook page. The messenger App is often useful for communicating with them to book a table or a room or just to ask if they are open that day.
Finally, **Taiwan Weather** uses Central Weather Bureau data to

TIME ZONE

Taipei and all of Taiwan is +8 GMT, +13 EST (+12 with daylight savings).

give up seven-day forecasts, alerts users when there's a weather warning (storms and typhoons), and even has suggestions for what clothes to wear, whether you need an umbrella, or can hang your laundry outdoors!

Tourist information

The central government's **Tourism Bureau** (www.taiwan.net. tw) has both local and overseas information centers. Locally, the bureau approves and monitors tour agents and works with them to set up appropriate package tours.
The **Taipei City Government** (www.taipei.gov.tw) has information centers with service in English and other languages.

Local tourist offices

Tourism Bureau
Main Office
9F, 290 Zhongxiao E. Rd Sec. 4
Tel: 02-2349 1500
Open: 9am–5pm
Travel Information Service Center
240 Dunhua N. Rd
Tel: 0800-011 765 (24H)
Taipei Railway Station
3 Beiping W. Rd
Tel: 02-2312 3256
Songshan Airport
340-9 Dunhua N. Rd
Tel: 02-2546 4741
Beitou MRT Station
1 Guangming Rd
Tel: 02-2894 6923
Specializes in Beitou's hot springs.
Jiantan MRT station
65 Zhongshan N. Rd Sec. 5
Tel: 02-2883 0313
Ximen MRT station
B1, 32-1 Baoqing Rd
Tel: 02-2375 3096

Tamsui MRT station
1 Zhongzheng Rd
Tel: 02-2626 7613
Taipei 101 MRT station
B1F, 20 Xinyi Rd Sec. 5
Tel: 02-2758 6593

Travelers with disabilities

Taipei is not an easy place to maneuver in for those with physical disabilities. The city has worked hard in the past decade or so to rectify this by smoothening sidewalks, providing ramps, and adding tactile paving surfaces for those with visual impairments to follow. The problem is that there are often no sidewalks, or only very narrow ones.

Most of Taipei's large, modern public buildings (including government buildings and museums) have wheelchair-access ramps. This is only occasionally the case for modern residential buildings. They are not required by law in older buildings. The city's international hotels will have more facilities, but this should be confirmed prior to arrival. Most are good at handling special requests. Many big museums offer wheelchairs and some now have special guided tours for visitors using them.

Each MRT station provides elevator access from street level. There is also a reserved spot for wheelchairs in the first and last car of each train. Avoid using the MRT system during rush hour, when it becomes extremely crowded.

By law, guide dogs are given access to all locations. However, be advised that many citizens are not aware of this and not used to these dogs. The city administration is working hard to advise citizens of the law and promote access.

Pedestrian crossings at major intersections have audio countdown signals to help those with visual impairments. Be aware, however, that drivers are often less than patient with pedestrians.

V

Visas and passports

A stay of 90 days without a visa is available to citizens of 42 countries, including the US, UK, Canada, Japan, New Zealand, and the European Union nations; Australia is currently on a trial 90-day landing visa issuance (up for review in December 2019). Passports must be valid for at least six months. All visitors must have a valid visa for their next destination, if required, and the necessary tickets for onward travel. Citizens from several Southeast Asian nations such as Singapore and the Philippines are now eligible for visa-free entry for 30 or 14 days, while those from most other countries can apply for an eVisa (NT$1,632 for stays of less than 30 days).

For visa extensions, overstays, and all relevant details, contact the **Bureau of Consular Affairs**, Ministry of Foreign Affairs, at 3F, 2-2 Qinan Rd Sec. 1, tel: 02-2343 2888, www.boca.gov.tw.

W

Women travelers

Taipei is much safer for women at night than the average Western city. However, caution is always advisable.

Within the MRT system, there are monitored safety zones at platforms for women, clearly marked in English. Telephone numbers are given at phone terminals for special taxi services (though operators speak little or no English).

Women are on exceedingly rare occasions subjected to surreptitious photo-taking or peeking, with cameras or mirrors hidden in shoes, briefcases, and so on. There have also been instances of secret cameras set up in public washrooms, but this is very rare.

Though a Confucian patriarchy is still dominant in the home, the concept of the independent career woman has gained solid social acceptance; female business travelers can expect full respect.

WEBSITES

www.taiwannews.com.tw: Taiwan News portal, including a directory of Taiwan online (look for the orange button on the home page), the bible for English contact info for organizations, businesses, and other entities.
www.romanization.com: Eclectic info, including guidance on transliteration, street names, and out-of-print books on Taiwan.
www.taiwan.gov.tw: The Government Information Office site, with useful links.
https://english.gov.taipei: The official City Government website, with useful general information.
https://eng.taiwan.net.tw: The official Tourism Bureau website.

www.taipeitravel.net: Run by the city's tourism-related dept., practical info on dining, shopping, shows, etc.
www.tit.com.tw: Issues of *Travel in Taiwan* bimonthly online.
http://hungryintaipei.blogspot.tw: Hungry in Taipei is an excellent blog with hundreds of reviews both positive and negative for eating and drinking spots in Taipei.
https://taiwan-scene.com: An excellent, up-to-date, well-written and free resource with some quirky travel features published by **MyTaiwanTour**, a private tour company. www.nickkembel.com: **Spiritual Travels** is a well-written travel blog with lots of decent articles on Taipei penned by Canadian Nick Kembel, long-time resident of Taiwan.

LANGUAGE

UNDERSTANDING THE LANGUAGE

GENERAL

Most Taiwanese are descendants of immigrants who came in the 1600–1800s from China's southern Fujian Province. Their mother tongue, *Minnanyu*, or Southern Min (sometimes also called "Taiwanese"), is often spoken at home, but somewhat less so in official spheres. This is the result of a century-long history of official suppression by first the Japanese and then the Kuomintang administration. Since the lifting of martial law, restrictions have given way to a lively localization movement (encompassing the Hakka and indigenous languages as well), and today you'll hear announcements on the MRT in four languages.

But **Mandarin Chinese** (called *Guoyu* in the ROC) remains the official language of Taiwan, the native tongue of the large number of "mainlanders" in Taipei and Taiwan generally, and the most useful language to learn for tourists. (Note that the various Chinese "dialects" are mutually unintelligible.)

As for English, despite official initiatives to improve proficiency, many people you walk up to on the street will wilt from the challenge. But there will always be someone around who can speak English, especially among those who are under the age of 30.

WRITTEN CHINESE

Chinese writing uses logograms – symbols to represent each "word" – rather than an alphabetic system. It developed from an ancient practice of using pictographs to write. Though advocates say that this complex system carries the weight of a great Chinese cultural legacy, and that it circumvents the problem of Mandarin's many homophones, it is generally agreed that the system is difficult to learn, requiring the memorization of thousands of separate characters – not practical for short-term visitors. Fortunately, all streets in Taipei have signs with their romanized names.

ROMANIZATION

From the time Westerners first came into contact with the Chinese language, various systems for romanizing the language have been created. Hanyu Pinyin was adopted by the PRC in 1958, and has come to be the international standard. Prior to this, the de facto standard in the West was the Wade-Giles system. Note that these systems are viewed by the Chinese as pronunciation aids, and not replacements of the traditional writing system.

Romanization in Taiwan has been a mess for a long time. The Wade-Giles system had been used since the early 20th century, and the Yale system widely used too, but with the widespread adoption of Hanyu Pinyin worldwide there was pressure to do so here as well. Pro-independence factions were opposed to this because it is associated with China. In the early 2000s the DPP central government adopted Tongyong Pinyin, a Taiwanese innovation, but the city of Taipei went ahead with Hanyu Pinyin under former mayor Ma Ying-jeou. With the return of a KMT national government in the 2008 elections the demise of Tongyong was guaranteed, and in January 2009 Hanyu was declared the official system in Taiwan. Non-Hanyu transliterations persist, however, especially with older individuals more comfortable with the other systems.

SPOKEN MANDARIN

The Chinese consider the basic unit of the language to be the *zhi*, a monosyllable that corresponds to a single written Chinese character. Because there are comparatively few sound combinations in

Mandarin, this leads to many *zhi* having the same pronunciation. A linguistic device that has evolved to distinguish *zhi* is the tonal system. Every *zhi* has one of Mandarin's four pitch contours (listed here in the traditional order): high and level, rising, low (or falling then rising), and falling. For example, the syllable *fa* means "emit" with the first tone, "punish" with the second, "method" with the third, and "hair" with the fourth. These tones are usually the greatest stumbling block for non-native speakers learning the language.

Another common difficulty is the use of aspiration to distinguish certain consonants. Aspiration is the audible exhalation that comes after the "t" in English "top" but not in "stop". This distinction is what differentiates *pai* (to delegate someone) from *bai* (to worship someone). Retroflexion, the curling back of the tongue for certain consonants, is what separates "riches" (*cai*) from "kindling" (*chai*).

The trickier speech sounds of Mandarin are as follows (Hanyu Pinyin, Wade-Giles, Tongyong):
b, p, b "p" in "spot"
p, p', p "p" in "pot"
d, t, d "t" in "stop"
t, t', t "t" in "top"
g, k, g "c" in "score"
k, k',k "c" in "core"
j, ch, j "g" in "Swiss gene" said quickly
q, ch', c "ch" in "mischief"
x, hs, s "ss" in "kiss her" said quickly
zh, ch, jh "j" in "jowl"
ch, ch', ch "ch" in "chore"
r, j, r US English "r"
z, ts/tz, z "ds" in "reds"
c, ts'/tz', c "ts" in "cats"

GRAMMAR

Chinese is relatively straightforward in this respect. One finds no conjugations, declensions, tense changes, or other complicated bits to memorize. The subject-verb-object word order is used (as in English).

a, a, a "a" in "far"
e, e/o, e "ur" in "curse"
i, i, i "i" in "elite"
i, ih/u, ih "i" above but with the tongue further back
o, o, o "o" in "shore"
u, u, u "ue" in "blue"
ü, ü, yu German ü
ye, yeh, ye "ye" in "yes"
ei, ei, ei "ei" in "reign"
ie, ieh, ie "ye" in "yes"
iu, iu, iou "you"
ian, ien, ian "ien" in "Oriental"
ou, ou, ou "ow" in "blow"
ong, ung, ong "owe" with the "ng" of "sing"
ui, ui, uei "way"
uan, üan, yuan German ü with the "an" of "man"

USEFUL TERMS AND PHRASES

Greetings

Hello Ni hao
Goodbye Zai jian
See you tomorrow Mingtian jian
Thank you Xie xie
You're welcome Bu hui
No problem Mei wenti
I; we wo; women
You ni; nin (polite); nimen (plural)
He/she/it; they ta; tamen
My name is... Wo jiao...

Numbers

One yi
Two er (ordinal); liang (cardinal)
Three san
Four si
Five wu
Six liu
Seven qi
Eight ba
Nine jiu
Ten shi
Twenty ershi
One hundred yibai
One thousand yiqian
One million yibaiwan

Time and place

What time? Jidian zhong?
What day? Libai ji?
Yesterday zuotian

Today jintian
Tomorrow mingtian
One o'clock yidian zhong
Two o'clock liangdian zhong
Where is...? ...zai nali?
Very far/near Hen yuan/jin
I want to go to... Wo yao qu...

Transport and lodging

Airport jichang
Airplane feiji
Train huoche
Bus bashi/gonggong qiche
Taxi jichengche
Telephone dianhua
Reservation dingwei
Hotel lüdian/jiudian
Room fangjian
Key yaoshi
Luggage xingli

Basic sentences

I want Wo yao...
Do you have...? Ni you meiyou...?
We don't have... Women meiyou...
I like... Wo xihuan...
I don't like... Wo bu xihuan...

Food and drink

Restaurant canting
Bar jiuba
Alcohol jiu
To eat; let's eat chifan
To drink he
Ice; ice-cubes bing; bingkuai
Water shui
Fruit shuiguo
Tea/coffee cha/kafei
Hot/cold re/leng
Sugar tang
Salt/pepper yan/hujiao
Soy sauce jiangyou
Hot (spicy) la
A little yidian
Bottoms up!/Cheers! Ganbei!
Settle the bill jiezhang

Shopping

Money qian
How much does it cost? Duoshao qian?
Too expensive tai gui
Credit card xinyong ka
Big/Small da/xiao

FURTHER READING

BUSINESS AND PRACTICALITIES

Taipei Living 10th Edition. This handy reference book published by the Community Services Center helps Taipei expats settle in.

CULTURE

An American Teacher in Taiwan by Ken Berglund. A personal account of work, life, and love in Taiwan, written from a perspective of a Southern Californian.

Crystal Boys by Pai Hsien-yung, translated by Howard Goldblatt. An exploration of the difficult lives of gay men in Taipei society in novel form.

Culture Shock! Taiwan: A Guide to Customs and Etiquette by Chris and Ling-li Bates. A concise primer for confused foreigners on the ins and outs of getting on with the locals.

Dos and Don'ts of Taiwan by Steven Crook. A light-hearted guide that gives insight on cultural differences and offers a number of practical hints, ideal for the uninformed first-time visitor.

Formosa Moon by Joshua Samuel Brown and Stephanie Huffman. A couple explore the culture and the people of a place he loves, and a place she is beginning to love. A funny, quirky travelogue.

Formosan Odyssey: Taiwan, Past and Present by John Ross. An entertaining and insightful account of a New Zealander's north-south trek down the island.

Keeping Up with the War God by Steven Crook. A well-written no-holds-barred look into the local culture from a long-time expat resident who loves the island.

Reflections on Taipei: Expat Residents Look at their Second Home by Rick Charette. Taipei's people, culture, and development in modern times through the eyes and experiences of long-term expats.

Taiwan A to Z: The Essential Cultural Guide by Amy C. Liu. Written by a Taiwanese who lived in the US, and fully understands both Western and Eastern cultures, a great primer for anyone wishing to learn more about Taiwan.

Trademarks of the Chinese I and II. These "trademarks" refer to distinctive cultural features, ranging from lion dancing to ancestral spirit tablets, *fengshui* to the Chinese zodiac.

Window on Taiwan by Mark de Fraeye. Beautiful photography by Mark de Fraeye, with essays by experts.

Why Taiwan Matters: Small Island, Global Powerhouse by Shelley Rigger. A comprehensive study and an enjoyable narrative on Taiwan's society, economy, and politics.

Vignettes of Taiwan by Joshua Samuel Brown. A rollicking compilation of articles on local life, often witty and insightful, by a writer who now works in Taiwan's tourist industry.

HISTORY

China's Island Frontier: Studies in the Historical Geography of Taiwan edited by Ronald G. Knapp. Intriguing academic essays on unusual topics such as sugar, walled cities, and pushcar railways.

From Far Formosa: The Island, Its People and Missions by George Leslie Mackay. A look at Formosa by a respected 19th-century missionary well known in Taiwan.

Forbidden Nation: A History of Taiwan by Jonathan Manthorpe. Because of its strategic geographic location Taiwan has always been coveted by others, and is doggedly struggling to free itself.

Taiwan's China Dilemma by Syaru Shirley Lin. A timely (2017) overview of the rocky relations across the Taiwan Strait.

The Island of Formosa: Past and Present by James Davidson. A reprint of a thick and detailed 1903 tome, the first comprehensive study of Taiwan in English.

Statecraft and Political Economy on the Taiwan Frontier, 1600–1800 by John Robert Shepherd. A dense, scholarly dissertation, this is the single best English source available on the period.

Taiwan: Nation-State or Province by John F. Copper. Introduction to the island's geography, economy, history, and more.

Taiwan: A Political History by Denny Roy. A comprehensive, readable account of Taiwan's road to democracy that puts modern developments in historical context.

OTHER INSIGHT GUIDES

More than 180 **Insight Guides** and **Insight City Guides** cover every continent, providing information on culture and all the top sights, as well as superb photography and detailed maps. *Insight Guide Taiwan* explores the country further and is an ideal companion to this book.

TAIPEI STREET ATLAS

The key map shows the area of Area Nameame covered by the atlas section. An index of street names and places of interest shown on the maps can be found on the following pages. For each entry there is a page number and grid reference.

Map Legend

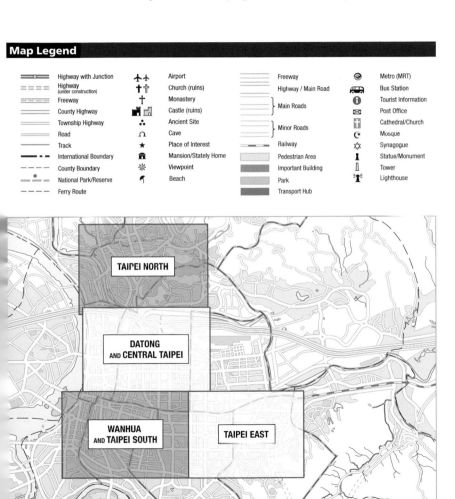

Highway with Junction	✈ ✈ Airport	▬ Freeway	◉ Metro (MRT)
Highway (under construction)	✝ ✝ Church (ruins)	▬ Highway / Main Road	🚌 Bus Station
Freeway	✝ Monastery	} Main Roads	ℹ Tourist Information
County Highway	🏰 🏯 Castle (ruins)		✉ Post Office
Township Highway	⁂ Ancient Site	} Minor Roads	✝ Cathedral/Church
Road	Ω Cave		☾ Mosque
Track	★ Place of Interest	▬ Railway	✡ Synagogue
International Boundary	🏛 Mansion/Stately Home	Pedestrian Area	⚊ Statue/Monument
County Boundary	☀ Viewpoint	Important Building	⛫ Tower
National Park/Reserve	🏁 Beach	Park	🗼 Lighthouse
Ferry Route		Transport Hub	

TAIPEI NORTH

DATONG AND CENTRAL TAIPEI

WANHUA AND TAIPEI SOUTH

TAIPEI EAST

A   B

1

Danshui

Zhengzhou Road

Civic Boulevard

Yanping N. Rd.

Chengde Rd Sec. 1

Huayin St

Museum of Contempo
Art Taipei (M

Ln 19

Old
Railway
Building

BEIMEN

Taiyuan

Civic Boulevar

Xining
Market

S. Rd.

Zhongxiao West Road Sec. 2

Luoyang

Street

Kaifeng

Street

Sec. 2

Xining

Street

Sec. 2

Hankou

Street

North Gate

Taipei
Post Office

Kaifeng St

Hankou St

Zhongxiao North Road Sec. 1

TAIPEI MAIN
STATION

Zhongxiao West Road Sec. 1

Sec. 1

Chongqing North Road Sec. 1

Guanqian Road

Shin Kong
Life Tower

Xuchang St

Taipei
Railway
Station

Caesar Par

Huaning South Road Sec. 1

Xinyang Street

Qingc
Roa

Gongyuan Road

Huanhe Expressway

Huanhe South Road Sec.

Kangding Road

Ln 133

Yatang Street

Riverview

Emer

Street

Wuchang

Street

Kunming Street

Xining

Street

Sec. 2

Hankou

Road

Xiyang
Street

Yanping South Road Sec. 2

Wuchang Street Sec. 1

Zhonghua Road Sec. 2

Zhongshan
Hall

Boai

Road

Lane 16

Jleyang Rd

Yuanting
St

Land Bank
Exhibition Hall

Xiangyang Road

National Taiwan
Museum

Old NTU
Hospital
Building

2

Chengdu Road

The Red
House

XIMEN

Hengyang

Road

Baoqing Road

Hengyang St

228 MEMORIAL
PEACE PARK

NTU HOSPI

Neijiang

Street

Longchang

Changsha St Sec. 2

Changsha

St Sec. 2

Changsha Street Sec. 1

Presidential
Office
Building

Boai Rd

228 Memorial

228 Memorial
Museum

Ketagalan Boulevard

Changde St

Taipei
Guest
House

Qingshui
Temple

Guiyang St

Yongfu

Street

Changsha

Street

Sec. 2

Xining

Street

Sec. 2

Zhonghua Road Sec. 1

Yanping South Road Sec. 2

South

Road

Guiyang Street Sec. 2

Taoyuan

Supreme
Court

Judicial
Yuan

Taiwan
High Court

JIESHOU PARK

Guiyang Street Sec. 1

GUCHENG

East Ga

3

Guilin Road

Longshan
Temple

Herb
Lane

MANKA
PARK

Heping W. Rd Sec. 3

LONGSHAN
TEMPLE

Wanhua
Railway
Station

Bopiliao
Historic
Block

Kangding Road

Sanshui St

Guangzhou

Street

Bangka Boulevard

Kunming

Street

Guilin

Guilin

Road

Nanning

Street

Tuzhou

Road

Ln 48

Ln 81

Ln 188

Heping West Rd Sec. 2

Zhonghua Rd Sec. 2

Guangzhou Street

Ln 91

Ln 95

Ln 258

Aiguo West Road

Ln 36

XIAONANMEN

Dingzhou Rd Sec. 1

Boai Rd

Ln 218

Ln 224

Ln 230

Lane 6

Aiguo W. Rd

South
Gate

Chongqing South Road Sec. 1

Xiyuan Road Sec. 1

Zhongshan South Road Sec. 1

Chongqing South Road Sec. 1

Chongqing South Road Sec. 1

CHIANG KAI-SHEK
MEMORIAL HALL

ZHONGZHENG

Roosevelt Ro

Aiguo

Nat
The

4

Wanda Road

Xizang Rd Lane 125

Zhongzhou Rd Sec. 2

Shuanghe Street

Wanda Rd Lane 237

Juguang

Road

Xizang

Road

Hukou Street

Nanhai

Road

Guoying Road

Dingzhou Road Sec. 1

Heping West Road Sec. 2

Sanyuan Street

Sanyuan Street

Ningbo W. Road

Ln 181

Ln 215

Ln 20

Science Museum to National
Taiwan Craft Research and
Development Institute

TAIPEI BOTANICAL GARDEN

National Museum
of History

National 228
Memorial Museum

Nanhai Road

Duanqiao St

Ningbo West
Road

Hukou St

Chongqing South Rd Sec. 2

Postal
Museum

Nanhai Road

Fuzhou St

Ln 16

Lane 3

Ln 27

Guling Street

Ningbo West

Nanchang Ro

Guling West

Fuzhou

Chongqing South Rd Sec. 3

Heping

A   B

D   E

600 m
600 yds

Lane 147
Lane 119
Lane 107
Lane 85
Lane 83
Linsen North Road
Jilin Road
Lane 90

Changan West Road

North Rd Sec. 1
Tianjin Street
Lane 53
Lane 33
Lane 53
Changan E. Rd Sec. 1
Lane 57
Songjiang Road
Lane 45

Zhengzhou Road

1

Su Ho Memorial
Paper Museum
Lane 23

Taipei Artist Village
Beiping East Road
Tianjin Street
Civic Boulevard
Ln 25
Hong Street
Weishui Road

Beiping East Road
ZHONGYANGIWEN PARK
Syntrend Creative Park
Bade Rd Sec. 1
Civic Boulevard

Jianguo North Road Sec. 1

SHANDAO TEMPLE
Linsen North Road
Shandao Temple
Huashan 1914 Creative Park
Shaoxing N. Rd
Jinshan North Road
Guang Hua Digital Plaza
Lane 40

Zhongxiao East Road Sec. 1
Sheraton Grand Taipei
Lane 54
Bade Road Sec. 2
National Taipei University of Technology

Qingdao East Road
Lane 6
Lane 11
Lane 64
Qidong Street
ZHONGXIAO XINSHENG
Lane 192

Road Sec. 1
Jinan Road Sec. 1
Linsen South Road
Zhongxiao East Road Sec. 2
Zhongxiao East Road Sec. 3

2

raft
Shaoxing South Road
Xuzhou Road
Lane 37
Lane 25
Jinan Road Sec. 2
Lane 197
Lane 103
Xinsheng South Road Sec. 1

d Taiwan y Hospital
Ln 18
Hangzhou South Road
Tongshan Street
Lane 3
Jinshan South Road Sec. 1
Jinan Road Sec. 3
Lane 212

Danyang Street
Lane 71
Lane 72
Lane 45
Lane 119
Lane 5
Lane 51

Renai Road Sec. 1
Renai Road Sec. 2
Lane 57

aipei Youth ty Center (Y17)
Lane 101
Lane 105
Lane 111
Lane 50
Lane 61
Lane 133
Lane 137
Lane 23
Lane 24
Jianguo Elevated Road

Hall
Shaoxing S. Rd
Xinyi Road Sec. 1
Lane 131
Lane 143
Lane 83
Lianyun Street
Jinshan South Road Sec. 1
Lane 139
Lane 145
Lane 304
Lane 111

Square
Ln 117
Lane 45
Jinshan South Street
Ln 71
Ln 48
Lane 157
Lane 318
Lane 99

3

Chiang Kai-shek Memorial Hall
Hangzhou South Road Sec. 2
Ln 75
Lane 160
Lane 161
Lane 165
Ln 31

Xinyi Road Sec. 2
DONGMEN
Xinyi Road Sec. 3
DAAN PARK

Ln 228

Ningpo St.
Ln 59
Ln 21
Aiguo East Road
Lishui Street
Lane 183
YONGKANG PARK
Lane 31
Qingtian Street
Ln 30
Xinsheng South Road Sec. 2

Lane 102
Lane 199
Yongkang Street
Ln 213
DAAN FOREST PARK
Lane 160
Lane 78

Jinhua Street
Lane 132
Ln 13
Jinhua Street
Jinhua Street
Ln 54
Lane 71

Chaozhou Street
Ln 59
Ln 141
Ln 159
Ln 17
Ln 21
Jinshan South Road Sec. 2
Lishui Street
Ln 185
Chaozhou Street
Chaozhou Street
Ln 9
Ln 11
Ln 183
Ln 139
Taipei Grand Mosque
Lane 222
Lane 244
Lane 255

4

Ln 93
Nanchang Rd Sec. 2
GUTING
Ln 14
Lane 12
Qingtian Street
Shida Rd

Heping E. Rd Sec. 1
Heping East Road Sec. 1
National Taiwan Normal University

D   E

A B

Lane 105
Lane 216
Lane 60
Taipei Sports
Office & Gymnasium
Lane 120
Lane 100
Lane 80

Zhutun
Longjiang Road
Street
Lane 55
Lane 4
Taipei
Arena
Taipei
Municipal
Stadium

Lane 45
Lane 45
Lane 256
Lane 51
Cultural
Center

Bade Road Sec. 3

Guangfu North Road

Lane 21
Metropolitan
Hall

1

Changan N. Rd Sec. 2

Fuxing North Road
Bade Road Sec. 2
Ln 33
Ln 358
Lane 31
Lane 45
Lane 80
Lane 100

Dunhua North Road

Lane 12
Yanji Street
Lane 74
Lane 30
Lane 106
Lane 158
Lane 6
Lane 22
Lane 32
Lane 46
Lane 58

Lane 312
Lane 300
Breeze
Center
Alley 70
Alley 57

Civic Boulevard
Civic Boulevard

Lane 40
Lane 79
Lane 131
Lane 180

Lane 217
Lane 237
Andong Street
Daan Road
Lane 107
Lane 160
Lane 62
Lane 181
Lane 205
Lane 233
Yanji Street
Lane 200

SUN YAT-
MEMORIA

2
Lane 52
Lane 187

Zhongxiao East Road Sec. 4
ZHONGXIAO
FUXING
ZHONGXIAO
DUNHUA
Zhongxiao East Road Sec. 4

Pacific SOGO
Department Store
Lane 232
Lane 27
Lane 236
Fuxing South Road Sec. 1
Daan Road Sec. 1
Lane 252
Lane 74
Lane 270
Eslite
Bookstore
Anhe Road Sec. 1
Lane 170
Lane 151
Lane 260
Lane 280
Lane 290
Lane 308
Lane 346

Lane 122
Lane 143
Lane 26
Lane 282

Renai Road Sec. 3
Renai Road Sec. 3
Renai
Traffic
Circle
Renai Road Sec. 4

Lane 147
Lane 151
Lane 253
Lane 169
Lane 175
Lane 22
Anhe Rd Sec. 1
Lane 266
Lane 25
Yanji Street
YANJI
PARK
Guangfu South Road

3
Lane 111
Fuxing South Road Sec. 1
Dongfeng
Street
Swei Road
Daan Road Sec. 1
Lane 295
Lane 90
Lane 127
Lane 135
GUOAN
PARK

Ln 220
Lane 76
Lane 122
Lane 329
Lane 191
Lane 102
Lane 141

Xinyi Road Sec. 3
DAAN
Xinyi Road Sec. 4
Dunhua South Road Sec. 1
Xinyi Road Sec. 4
XINYI ANHE

Wenchang Street
Wenchang Street
Tonghua Street
Guangfu South Road

Lane 78
Daan Road Sec. 2
Lane 154
Swei Road
Dunhua South Road Sec. 2
Lane 39
Anhe Rd Sec. 2
Linjiang Street
Lane 98
Lane 101
Linjiang Street

4
Lane 134
Ruian Street
Lane 120
Lane 123
Lane 143
Ln 144

Lane 71
Lane 151
Lane 160
Fuxing South Road Sec. 2
Lane 160
Lane 106
Lane 170
Lane 178
Lane 5
Tongan Street
Ln 162
Tonghua Street
Ln 186
Keelung Road Sec. 2
Jiaxing Road

Lane 222
Lane 344

Shangri-La's
Far Eastern
Plaza Hotel
Ln 42

0   600 m
0   600 yds

TECHNOLOGY
BUILDING

A B

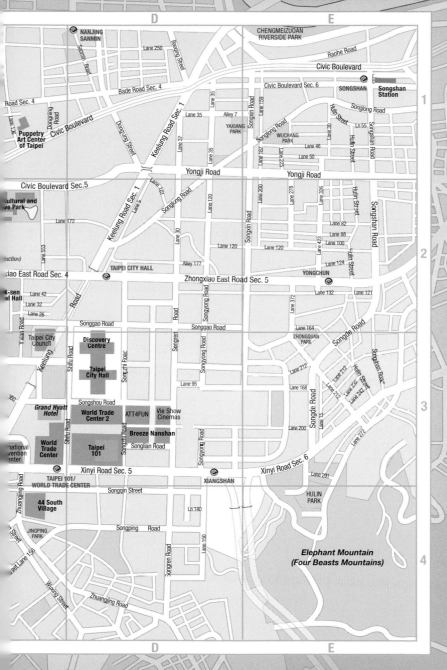

A   B

Huanhe North Road Section 2

Keelung

Sun Yat-sen Freeway

Xinsheng N. R

1

Ln 59
Dunhuang Road
Ln 24
Ln 45
Ln 68
Dihua St
Lane 312
Lane 296
Ln 70
Lane 161
Lane 364
Ln 13
Chongqing North Road Sec. 3
Ln 49
Alley 45
Yanping North Road Sec. 4
Guiling North Road 2

HAMI PARK

Baoan Temple

Hami Street

Confucius Temple

Kulun Street
Ln 24
Chengde Road Sec. 3
Yumen Street

YUANSHAN PARK

Taipei Expo Park

Taipei Story House

YUANSHAN Ⓜ
Taipei Fine Arts Museum

Jiaquan Street
Lane 243
Lane 236
Ln 237

ZHONGSHAN FINE ARTS PARK

2

Lane 223
Ln 215
Ln 208
Ln 223
DALONG PARK
Lane 225
Jiaquan Street
Ln 213
Dalong Street
Ln 187
Ln 176
Ln 205
Ln 22
Lane 314
Minzu West Road
Minzu West Road
Minzu West Road
Minzu East Roa
Ln 146
Lane 152
Lane 159
St Christopher's Catholic Church
Lane 43
Lane 37
Ln 83
Lane 136
Lane 143
Ln 40
Imperial
Lane 120
Ln 113
Lane 129
Ln 181
Ln 91
Lane 113
Dehui Street
Lane 104
Chongqing North Road Sec. 3
Dalong Street
Lane 97
Ln 25
Ln 6
Changji Street
Lane 85
Ln 28
Lane 23
Ln 83
Ln 66
Changji Street
Yumen Street
Ln 18
Lane 19
Ln 61
Jinghua St
Ln 9
Ln 51
Nongan Street
Ln 18
Yining Street
Ln 225
Ln 124
Zhongshan North Road
Ln 6
Ln 133
DAQIAOTOU
Fushun Street
ZHONG
ELEMENTARY SC
Minquan West Road
MINQUAN WEST ROAD
Minquan East Road Sec. 1

3

Lane 272
Lane 247
Lane 48
Lane 128
Ln 137
Ln 70
Ln 485
Yanping North Road Sec. 2
Ln 33
Ln 115
Liangzhou Street
Ningxia Road
Lane 53
Ln 116
Ln 13
Anxi Street
Chengde Road Sec. 2
Jinxi Street
Jinzhou Street
Baoan St
Ganzhou St
Jinxi Street
Yumen Street
Zhongshan North Road Sec. 2
Koo Family Salt Hall
Ln 53
Linsen North Road
Ln 3
Mackay Memorial Hospital
Guisui Street
Guisui Street
Wanquan St
Minsheng East Road Sec
Ln 114
Lane 135
Ln 1
SHUANGLIAN Ⓜ
Ln 72
Lane 65
Lane 80
Ln 109
Ln 71
Ambassador
Alley 2

4

Minsheng West Road
Minsheng West Road
Ln 97
Ln 91
Ln 53
Lane 59
Yongchang N. St
Lane 64
Ln 73
Lane 50
Lane 21
Lane 5
Ln 72
Xiahai Temple
Lane 46
Lane 175
Ln 49
Changchun Street
Ln 46
Yongle Market
Lane 161
Lane 47
Lane 45
Taiyuan Asian Puppet Theater Museum
Pingyang Street
SPOT-Taipei Film House
Lane 26
Lane 39
Lane 2
Nanjing West Road
Taipei Yuanhuan
Lane 33
Lane 20
Royal- Nikko
Dihua Street Sec. 1
Taiyuan Road
Chifeng Street
Lane 17
ZHONGSHAN Ⓜ
Lane 3
Nanjing East Road Sec. 1
Chengde Road Sec. 2
Ningxia Road
Chengde Road Sec. 1
Nanjing West Road
Lane 159
Museum of Contemporary Art Taipei (MOCA)
Zhongshan Metro Shopping Mall (underground)
Lane 147

0   600 m

0   600 yds

A   B

D E

Mingshui Road

Keelung

Dazhi Bridge

DAJIA RIVERSIDE PARK

YINGFENG
RIVERSIDE
PARK

1

Riverside Park Road

Binjiang Street

**Lin An Tai
Homestead**

Binjiang Street

Binjiang Street

XINSHENG
PARK

Songshan Airport

Minzu East Road

Minzu East Road

Ln 461

Ln 447

Ln 443

Street

Jilin Road

Ln 161

Lane 153

Dehui Street

Ln 407

Alley 31

Alley 19

Alley 2

Lane 412

Lane 391

Lane 384

Lane 457

Lane 443

Lane 420

Jianguo North Road Sec. 3

2

Lane 370

Lane 356

Lane 415

Lane 514

Ln 227

Alley 1

Ln 271

Lane 75

Lane 53

Lane 328

Lane 318

Lane 387

Longjiang Road

Ln 161

Ln 488

Fuxing North Road

Minzu East Road

Ln 80

Nongan Street

Nongan Street

Wuchang Street

Jilin Road

Lane 329

Lane 315

Lane 299

Lane 71

Lane 402

Lane 372

Alley 30

Alley 20

Lane 357

**Xingtian
Temple**

RONGXING
GARDEN

Lane 345

Lane 331

Ln 430

Ln 39

Ln 75

Ln 113

Minquan East Road Sec. 2

Minquan East Road Sec. 3

Ln 137

Jilin Road

Ln 175

Ln 352

Ln 330

Ln 362

Songjiang Road

Ln 152

Lane 258

Lane 297

Lane 226

Jianguo North Road Sec. 2

Lane 170

Street

Lane 127

Road

Lane 295

Street

**ZHONGSHAN JUNIOR
HIGH SCHOOL**

3

Jinzhou

Street

Jinzhou Street

Lane 269

Lane 144

Lane 105

Lane 281

Jinzhou Street

Jilin Road

Ln 218

Ln 200

Lane 161

Ln 233

**XINGTIAN
TEMPLE**

Lane 235

Lane 130

Lane 116

Lane 102

Lane 93

Lane 83

Lane 73

Heijang

Longjiang Road

Lane 271

Lane 249

Lane 248

Liaoning

Ln 73

**St John
the Baptist**

Minsheng East Road Sec. 2

Minsheng East Road Sec. 3

Jilin Road

Lane 194

Lane 184

Lane 164

Ln 188

Lane 184

Songjiang Road

Xingan Street

Road

Xingan Street

Street

Fuxing North Road

Qincheng Road

4

Ln 468

Lane 154

Lane 144

Lane 170

Lane 160

Ln 58

Lane 20

Ln 41

Ln 258

Lane 17

Lane 179

Ln 174

Changchun Road

Changchun Road

Changchun Road

Jilin Road

Yijiang Road

Ln 51

Ln 140

Lane 115

Siping

Street

Shulan Rd.

Yitong Street

Longjiang

Street

Liaoning

Lane 197

Ln 141

**SONGJIANG
NANJING**

East Road Sec. 2

Nanjing East Road Sec. 3

**NANJING
FUXING**

Lane 108

Lane 52

Lane 76

Ln 91

D E

A   B

1

Chengde Road Sec. 6

Huang

Wenlin Road

ZHISHAN

Fuhua Road

Fuguo Road

Zhongshan North Road Sec. 6

Zhicheng Rd Sec. 3

Shuangxi Street

Fulin Bridge

Shuang

Waishuang

Waishuang

Wenlin Rd

Wenlin Bridge

Front St

Back St

Fu

Zhongshan North Road Sec. 5

2

National Taiwan Science Education Center

Taipei Astronomical Museum

Jihe Road

Wenchang Street

Meilun Street

Tianrong Street

Haqzhong Street

Macde Street

Wenlin Road

Meilun Street

Furong St

Fustou St.

Jiunsheng St

Huang St

Zhongq

Zhongzheng Road

SHILIN

Chengde Road Sec. 5

Tonghe East Road Sec. 1

SHEZI SPORTS PARK

Zhongzheng Road

Xiashulin St

Fude Road

Jihe Road

Wenlin Road

Dadong Road

Dadi Road

Xiaonu Road

Xiaobei Street

Dabei Road

Danian Road

Zhongshan North Road Sec. 5

3

Shezhong St

Shezeng Road

Yanping Nth Rd Sec. 6

Bailing Bridge

Keelung

Tonghe East Road Sec. 1

BAILING WEST RIVERSIDE PARK

BAILING EAST RIVERSIDE PARK

Danan Road

Fuguang Street

Qiangang Street

JIHE PARK

Shishang Street

Chengde Road Sec. 4

Shilin Nightmarket

Xiaonan Street

Xiaodong St.

Dadong Road

Wenlin Road

JIANTAN

Mt

Huabing Street

Hougang Street

QIANGANG PARK

Qiangang Street

Zhongqing North Road Sec. 4

Yanping North Road Sec. 5

Fuging Street

Huabing Street

Jiantan Road

Chengde Road Sec. 4

Jihe Road

Zhongshan North Road Sec. 4

HUALING PARK

Hougang Street

Tonghe Street

4

Tonghe East Road Sec. 1

Hualing Street

Tonghe Street

Chengde Bridge

Jihe Rd

Grand H

0   600 m

0   600 yds

Sun Yat-sen Freeway (National Freeway 1)

A   B

STONE PARK

ZHISHAN PARK

ZHISHAN GARDEN

heng Road Sec. 1

Yusheng

Street

Yunong Rd

Zhongyong St

Zhiyu Road Sec. 1

Yangde Blvd Sec. 2

Yangde Blvd Sec. 1

Fulin Road

SHUANGXI PARK

SHUANGXI PARK

Lane 254

Zhishan Road Sec. 1

Zhishan Road Sec. 2

National Palace Museum

Gugong Road

Gugong Road

Lixing Street

Waishuang

Linxi Road

g Road

Yunong Rd

Jzheng Rd

Road

Shilin Official Residence

Suchua Street

Ziqiang Tunnel

Ziqiang Tunnel

Ziqiang Tunnel

Huanshan Road

Tongbei Street

Tongbei Street

Tongbei Street

Dazhi Street

Dazhi Street

Lane 527

Lane 501

Beian Road

Dazhi Street

Beian Road

Sihai

National Revolutionary Martyrs' Shrine

ЭU

DAZHI

Beian Road

Mingshui Road

Mingshui Road

Jilong

D

E

STREET INDEX

Yusheng Street 258 C1

Z

Zhengzhou Road 252
   B1, 252 C1
Zhenjiang Street 252
   C2
Zhicheng Road Sec. 1
   258 C1
Zhicheng Road Sec. 2
   258 C1
Zhishan Road Sec. 1
   258 D2
Zhishan Road Sec. 2

258 E1
Zhiyu Road Sec. 1 258
   D1
Zhonghua Road Sec. 1
   252 B2–B1
Zhonghua Road Sec. 2
   252 A4–A3
Zhongqing North Road
   Sec. 4 258 A4
Zhongshan Hall 252
   B2
Zhongshan Metro
   Shopping Mall
   (underground) 256

B4
Zhongshan North Road
   Sec. 1 252 C1
Zhongshan North Road
   Sec. 2 256 B4–B3
Zhongshan North Road
   Sec. 3 256 B1–B2–B3
Zhongshan North Road
   Sec. 4 258 C4
Zhongshan North Road
   Sec. 5 258 C2–C3
Zhongshan North Road
   Sec. 6 258 C1
Zhongshan South Road

252 C3
Zhongshan Stadium
   256 B2
Zhongxiao East Road
   Sec. 1 252 B1–C1,
   C2–D2
Zhongxiao East Road
   Sec. 2 252 D2
Zhongxiao East Road
   Sec. 3 252 E2
Zhongxiao East Road
   Sec. 4 254 A2–B2, C2
Zhongxiao East Road
   Sec. 5 254 D2–E2

Zhongxiao West Road
   Sec. 2 252 B1
Zhongxing St 258 B2
Zhongyong St 258 C1
Zhongyuan Street 256
   C3
Zhongzheng Road 258
   B2–C2
Zhuangjing Road 254
   D4–C4–C3
Zhulun Street 252 E1
Ziqiang Tunnel 258
   E2–E3

ART AND PHOTO CREDITS

Alamy 128
Chris Stowers/Apa Publications
6MR, 6ML, 6MR, 6BL, 7MR, 7M, 7B,
7MR, 8T, 8B, 9ML, 9BR, 9TR, 10T,
10B, 12/13, 20, 21, 22B, 22T, 23,
24, 25R, 25L, 26B, 26T, 27BL, 27T,
30T, 31T, 38, 40R, 42T, 47, 48B,
48T, 49B, 50R, 50L, 51L, 51R,
52/53T, 53B, 54, 55, 56, 62, 63,
64, 65R, 65L, 66, 67B, 67T, 68R,
68L, 68, 69, 70, 71L, 71R, 72, 72,
73L, 73R, 74, 75, 76, 77, 78, 79R,
79L, 80, 81, 82, 83L, 83R, 84B,
84T, 86T, 86B, 87B, 87TR, 86/87T,
87MR, 87M, 88/89, 92/93, 94, 95,
98, 99, 100, 101, 102, 103T, 103B,
104B, 104T, 105, 106T, 107, 108,
110MR, 110MR, 110BL, 111R,
112, 113, 115, 116B, 117B, 117T,
118, 119, 121, 122, 123, 125T,
125B, 126T, 126B, 127, 129B,
129T, 131, 132, 133, 135, 136,
137T, 138, 139B, 139T, 140, 141,
142, 143, 144, 145, 146, 147T,
148T, 148B, 149B, 149T, 150B,
150T, 151B, 151T, 152, 153B,
153T, 154, 155, 156, 157, 158,
159, 160, 161T, 161B, 161TR, 162,
163, 164L, 164R, 165T, 165B, 166,
167, 168, 169, 170, 171, 172T,
172B, 173, 174B, 174T, 175T,
175B, 176, 177, 178, 179, 180T,
180B, 181, 182, 183, 184B,
185TR, 184/185T, 186/187T, 188,
188, 189, 190, 191, 192, 193T,
193B, 194, 197, 198B, 198T, 199,
200, 201, 203, 204/205, 206,
207T, 207B, 208, 209, 211, 212B,
212T, 213, 214, 215, 216, 217T,
217B, 218T, 218B, 219T, 219B,
221B, 221T, 222TR, 222BL, 222TL,
223, 224, 226T, 226B, 229, 230,
231, 232, 234, 238, 248
City Archives 34R, 35
Corbis 37, 38, 39R, 41, 42B, 43
Deni Chung 110/111T

Getty Images 7TR, 7T, 14/15,
16/17, 18, 27BR, 29, 30B, 44/45,
46, 53R, 59, 85, 90/91, 187MR
**Government Information Office,
ROC** 40L
iStock 4/5, 11, 19, 9T, 111L, 195,
227, 250
Jim Smeal/BEI/Rex Features 58T
Kobal 60
National Palace Museum 184T,
185BC, 185M, 186BL, 186TL,
186BL, 187T, 187BR
National Taiwan Museum 28, 32,
33, 34L, 36
Outlookxp 202
Jim Smeal/BEI/Rex Features 58B
Shutterstock 1, 31B, 106B, 109,
137B, 140, 147B, 166, 225
Solomon203 116T
Taipei Tourism 52MR, 52BL
Tsai Jui-yueh Dance Festival 61
Yang San-lang Fine Arts Museum
57

Cover Credits

Front cover and spine: Chiang Kai-
Shek Memorial Hall *iStock*
Back cover: iStock
Front flap: (from top) Ximending at
night *iStock*; Praying in Xingtian
Temple *Shutterstock*; Sanxia Old
Street *Shutterstock*; Nursery in
Songshan Cultural and Creative
Park Shutterstock
Back flap: Wuji Tianyuan Palace
iStock

INDEX

INSIGHT ⊙ GUIDES
TAIPEI

Editor: **Helen Fanthorpe**
Author: **Rick Charette and Dinah Gardner**
Head of DTP and Pre-Press: **Rebeka Davies**
Update Production: **Apa Digital**
Managing Editor: **Carine Tracanelli**
Pictures: **Tom Smyth**
Cartography: **original cartography Wadsworth Graphics and Nelani Jinadasa, updated by Carte. Several source maps were generously provided by the Department of Transportation, Taipei City Government, also updated by Carte.**

Distribution

UK, Ireland and Europe
Apa Publications (UK) Ltd
sales@insightguides.com

United States and Canada
Ingram Publisher Services
ips@ingramcontent.com

Australia and New Zealand
Woodslane
info@woodslane.com.au

Southeast Asia
Apa Publications (SN) Pte
singaporeoffice@insightguides.com

Worldwide
Apa Publications (UK) Ltd
sales@insightguides.com

Special Sales, Content Licensing and CoPublishing

Insight Guides can be purchased in bulk quantities at discounted prices. We can create special editions, personalised jackets and corporate imprints tailored to your needs. sales@insightguides.com; www.insightguides.biz

Printing

Pozkal – Poland

ABOUT THIS BOOK

What makes an Insight Guide different? Since our first book pioneered the use of creative full-colour photography in travel guides in 1970, we have aimed to provide not only reliable information but also the key to a real understanding of a destination and its people.

Now, when the internet can supply inexhaustible (but not always reliable) facts, our books marry text and pictures to provide that more elusive quality: knowledge. To achieve this, they rely on the authority of locally based writers and photographers.

This new edition of *City Guide Taipei* was commissioned and edited by **Helen Fanthorpe**. The entire book was comprehensively updated by **Dinah Gardner**, an experienced travel writer, journalist, and long-time lover of Taiwan.

Her update builds on substantive work by Canadian **Rick Charette**, who has lived in Taipei since 1988 and knows the city intimately. Other original contributors include **Brent Hannon** and **Chris Taylor**.

Taipei-based **Chris Stowers**, a widely published photographer in the region, has contributed most of the images used in this book.

SEND US YOUR THOUGHTS

We do our best to ensure the information in our books is as accurate and up-to-date as possible. The books are updated on a regular basis using local contacts, who painstakingly add, amend, and correct as required. However, some details (such as telephone numbers and opening times) are liable to change, and we are ultimately reliant on our readers to put us in the picture.

We welcome your feedback, especially your experience of using the book "on the road". Maybe we recommended a hotel that you liked (or another that you didn't), or you came across a great bar or new attraction that we missed.

We will acknowledge all contributions, and we'll offer an Insight Guide to the best letters received.

Please write to us at:
Insight Guides
PO Box 7910, London SE1 1WE
Or email us at:
hello@insightguides.com

Taipei Metro Route Map

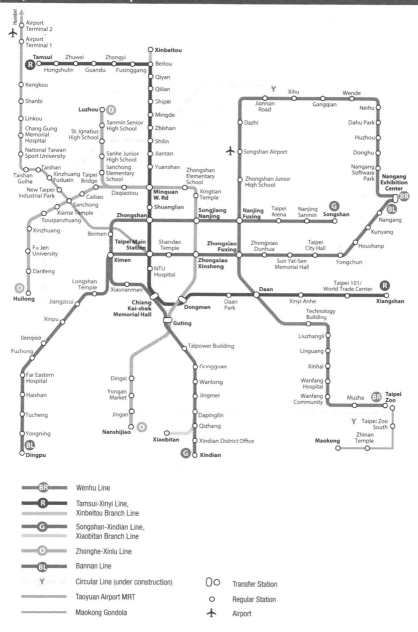

BR	Wenhu Line
R	Tamsui-Xinyi Line, Xinbeitou Branch Line
G	Songshan-Xindian Line, Xiaobitan Branch Line
O	Zhonghe-Xinlu Line
BL	Bannan Line
Y	Circular Line (under construction)
	Taoyuan Airport MRT
	Maokong Gondola
OO	Transfer Station
O	Regular Station
✈	Airport

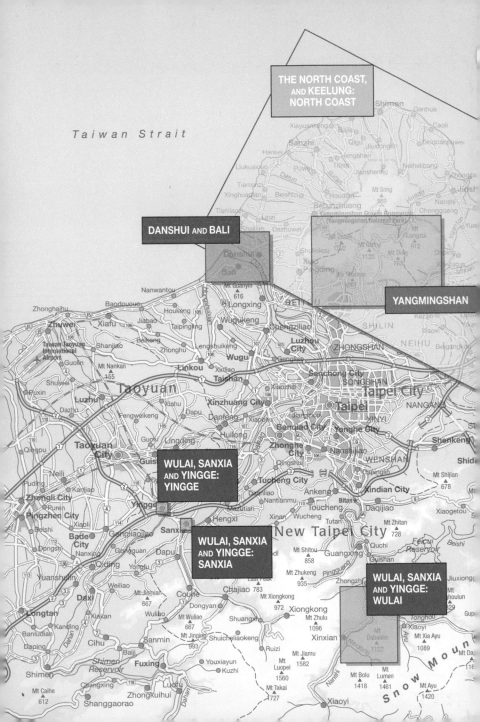